D1527525

In early 1918 the French government adopted the policy of unremitting hostility that characterized its early relations with the Soviet government. That policy brought about political, economic, and military intervention in the Russian Revolution, and the diverse motives behind that intervention emerge in this study.

When a population exasperated by the sufferings of war overthrew the tsarist government in early 1917, French interests – military, diplomatic, business, and financial – hoped that revolution could be turned back. But although the French government viewed with distaste the subsequent Bolshevik seizure of power, it did not reach its decision to intervene without internal debate or dissent. French stakes in Russia were high because of the long-standing Franco-Russian alliance and the heavy French investments there.

As World War I drew to a close in late 1918, the French government planned to send troops freed by the armistice to Russia to begin the task of reversing Soviet power. Events proved this undertaking too difficult for a war-weary French citizenry, who rather admired the government of the Soviets and who had seen more than enough sacrifice. French troops sent to the Ukraine and Crimea were not willing men, and their commanders were unable to rally the local population to fight the Bolsheviks. In April 1919 the last French troops were withdrawn from the Crimea as mutiny swept the French fleet in the Black Sea. Still not prepared to reconcile itself to Soviet Russia, the French developed the policy of a *cordon sanitaire* to contain the revolutionary expansion of Bolshevism until, they hoped, the Russian people would come to their senses and overthrow the Soviet regime.

This book, the first to concentrate on French involvement in the Russian Revolution, is based on an intensive use of French archival sources, closed until recently. It is unique in its examination of the economic motivations behind intervention and provides new insights into France's relations with its allies.

Michael Jabara Carley holds a doctorate from Queen's University and at present works for the Alberta Historic Sites Service.

DK
265.42
.F8
C37

# Revolution and Intervention

## The French Government and the Russian Civil War 1917-1919

MICHAEL JABARA CARLEY

McGill-Queen's University Press
Kingston and Montreal

JUL 2 1 1986

471627

© McGill-Queen's University Press 1983
ISBN 0-7735-0408-7

Legal deposit 3rd quarter 1983
Bibliothèque nationale du Québec

Printed in Canada

---

**Canadian Cataloguing in Publication Data**

Carley, Michael Jabara, 1945–
    Revolution and intervention : the French government
and the Russian Civil War, 1917–1919
    Bibliography: p.
    Includes index.
    ISBN 0-7735-0408-7
    1. Soviet Union – History – Revolution, 1917–1921 –
French participation. 2. France – Foreign economic
relations – Soviet Union. 3. Soviet Union – Foreign
economic relations – France. 4. France – Economic
policy – History – 20th century. I. Title.
DK265.42F73C37      947.08'41      C83-098240-X

---

*To my grandmother*
*Surraya Massad Jabara*

NE PAS SUBIR

# Contents

# *Preface*

This book is an account of the responses of the French government – its various agencies and representatives – to the Russian Revolution. The account covers a period of two years and two months, from March 1917 when the Russian monarchy collapsed until April 1919 when French military intervention in southern Russia ended. The intervention had been provoked by the Bolshevik seizure of power from the Provisional Government of Alexander Kerensky in November 1917. In the capitals of the Entente, and especially in Paris, the Bolshevik revolution pro-voked angry reactions, and before long the French government began to lay plans to intervene in Russia against the new Soviet regime led by V.I. Lenin and L.D. Trotsky.

French interest in Russia was of long standing. In the early 1890s France had concluded an alliance with the Tsar Alexander III, thus breaking the diplomatic isolation imposed after the Franco-Prussian war by the iron chancellor of Germany, Otto von Bismarck. The alliance provided France with a measure of security against Germany and became the centre-piece of French foreign policy before World War I. Indeed, the alliance seemed to prove its worth when war broke out in 1914 and the German high command had to divert troops from its offensive on Paris to meet the threat of a Russian advance into East Prussia.

The war dragged on endlessly, however, and men died by the hundred thousand in bloody trench warfare. Russia, the least economically and technologically advanced of the belligerent great powers, could not sustain this murderous pace, and eventually fell out of the war. In March 1918 the Bolsheviks of Lenin and Trotsky were compelled to sign the peace of Brest-Litovsk with Germany and its allies.

From the outset of the Bolshevik revolution there was debate within the French and other Allied governments concerning how to deal with the new regime. In Paris initial hostility was tempered by reports from French agents in Russia warning against closing all avenues of approach to the Bolsheviks. Indeed, in late January 1918 there began a *rapprochement* of sorts with the Bolshevik government, initiated by the French general staff and based on the principle of mutual hostility toward Germany. Even after the signing of the treaty of Brest-Litovsk the *rapprochement* continued another five weeks. These improved relations were ended, however, by opposition from the Quai d'Orsay, or French foreign ministry, which argued that long-term political and economic interests should take precedence over any limited military advantages to be gained from co-operating with the Bolsheviks against Germany. These views were also put forward in Washington by the U.S. Department of State which also opposed any co-operation with the Bolsheviks – even against the German army.

By mid-summer 1918 the French government and its principal allies were committed to a policy of intervention against the Soviet government. Their most important point of attack was initially in Siberia where the Czechoslovak Legion rose in revolt along the Trans-Siberian Railway. The French government hoped to ride the railway into Moscow, using the Czechs to overthrow Soviet power and re-establish French influence. But the Bolsheviks, although seriously threatened, hung on tenaciously and began to grow stronger, so much so that by October 1918 the Red Army being organized under the leadership of Trotsky seemed capable of threatening Europe. The French government, alarmed by the possibility of Bolshevik revolution spreading westward, intensified its efforts to overthrow the Soviet regime.

Another important factor influenced the actions of the French government. After the conclusion of the Franco-Russian alliance in 1894, French citizens began to make large investments in Russian state securities and later in Russian industry and banking. To solidify the alliance with Russia, the Quai d'Orsay encouraged these investments, first in tsarist bonds sold through the largest French banks, and then in Russian industry. The tsarist government, for its part, was embarking upon a program of rapid industrialization and needed the large amounts of investment capital that the French could then provide. This conjunction of circumstances as well as higher interest rates for tsarist securities led to a vertiginous expansion of French investment in Russia. Important French banks like the Société Générale, the Banque de Paris et des Pays-Bas, and the Banque de l'Union parisienne began to invest in Russian banks and industry. So also did large industrial conglomerates like the Établissements Schneider et Compagnie and later the Société générale d'entreprises. By 1914 French capitalists held an important share of investment capital in Russian banking and a preponderant share in the mining and metallurgical industries, concentrated in the Ukraine. In fact, total French investments in Russia amounted to some 13.25 billion gold francs or approximately 30 per cent of all French foreign investments.[1]

This was no mere bagatelle for the French government. On the contrary, the Quai d'Orsay viewed these investments as vital to its political and economic interests and sought to protect them with all the vigilance of a card-sharper in a high-stakes poker game. The Bolsheviks took a different view. They regarded such investment as a tentacle of western imperialism reaching into Russia to grasp its vital wealth for the profit of a small foreign and Russian capitalist élite. The tsarist bonds, they said, were the debts of the Romanovs and a prop of the autocracy for which the new Soviet government had no responsibility. Moreover, the Bolsheviks believed that state ownership should replace private control of the means of production. Acting according to these convictions, the Soviet government annulled the tsarist debt in February 1918 and began gradually to nationalize the banking and industrial sectors of the economy.

These Soviet actions wiped out French investments in Russia and left outraged French businessmen and bankers in despair. As a result they set up a hue and cry for intervention and tried to organize themselves to lobby the French government. Their efforts were not notably successful, but the government was sympathetic to the demands of business and tried to formulate plans to restore French economic interests in Russia.

Ultimately, for a variety of motives – political, economic, and ideological – the French government sent troops to the Ukraine and the Crimea in December 1918. The expedition, however, was ill-starred. Troop morale was poor, demobilization rapidly thinned the ranks of French forces, and domestic opinion proved unfavourable to intervention. After some four months the French withdrew in none-too-glorious circumstances from their toe-holds on the coast of the Black Sea.

No modern study has ever been made of these events because most of the French state papers concerning the intervention were closed until 1972. Indeed since then the archives of the Service historique de l'armée concerning the revolution and intervention have been reclosed for reasons which are not entirely clear. In any event, France is the only great power about whose intervention in Russia no detailed study has been done.

The present volume attempts to meet this need and seeks to give a somewhat different perspective to the foreign intervention in Russia. Previous studies have characterized the intervention as accidental or inadvertent and as the well-meaning and honourable discharge of an obligation to fallen anti-Bolshevik allies. This book sees the intervention, or at least the French part in it, as a premeditated attempt to overthrow a menacing revolutionary government. There was no appeal to Wilsonian rhetoric or British "fair play" to conceal this objective or the French government's desire to recover its investments and economic influence in Russia. The Quai d'Orsay hoped not only to obtain collateral for defaulted French investments, but also to find markets for French manufactured goods and a guaranteed source of grain and natural resources to help rebuild the war-shattered French economy. The French government saw itself in competition for these prizes with its allies, and sought not to be pushed aside in this race for new markets and resources.

These were certainly not the reactions of a government with any great sense of obligation to former allies. On the contrary, the French harboured a deep-seated and ill-concealed contempt for what they considered to be the weakness and venality of the anti-Bolshevik factions. At the same time, the French intervention was no disinterested campaign to establish the democratic process in Russia. In fact, the Quai d'Orsay hoped for the success of the abortive *coup d'état* of the counterrevolutionary General L.G. Kornilov in September 1917. And the French scarcely blinked an eye when the Bolsheviks dissolved the democratically elected Constituent Assembly in January 1918. As one French general said at the time, he could not see the point in exchanging Trotsky for a "scoundrel" like Viktor Chernov, the Socialist-Revolutionary president of the assembly.[2] Paradoxically, French military personnel even expressed occasional admiration for Bolshevik determination and commitment, and they sometimes posed the question of whether France should not come to terms with Soviet Russia in order to recreate a balance of power against Germany. This sentiment, however, was never strong enough to overcome a visceral aversion within the French government, and particularly the Quai d'Orsay, to any dealings whatever with the Bolshevik regime.

The documentary sources upon which this study is based come principally from the vast holdings of the French ministries of war and foreign affairs. These papers consist of the reports of French diplomatic and military personnel in Russia and the memoranda, notes, and directives drawn up in Paris that lay out French policy toward the Soviet government. I also made use of the smaller archival collection of the ministry of finance and of the *consignes* of the French bureau of the censor located at the Bibliothéque de Documentation internationale contemporaine in Nanterre. Finally, at the ministry of the navy I obtained very limited access to documents concerning the Black Sea mutinies of April 1919.

With regard to private papers I discovered a small but important collection of documents from the Commission générale de protection des intérêts français en Russie, which was the principal defence committee for French investors in Russia. I also consulted the papers of Albert Thomas, the French minister of armaments in 1917, kept at the Archives nationales in Paris. Although I examined the papers of P. de Margerie, C. Barrère, P. Cambon, S. Pichon, and others, they were not of much use in the preparation of this study. I had better luck with private papers in London where I found the personal letters of the British ambassadors in Paris, Sir Francis Bertie and Edward Lord Derby, extremely useful. These letters can be found in the Bertie, Balfour, Curzon, and Lloyd George papers in London. I also made some minor use of the Foreign Office documents at the Public Records Office.

Finally, along the road to the completion of this work I consulted over a dozen French newspapers representing a cross-section of left- and right-wing opinion. Although my MA thesis was devoted entirely to this subject, I did not see the value of introducing large résumés of journalistic opinion into the present work. I discuss such opinion only when it may have played a part in influencing government policy, and this was not very often. Similarly, I made no systematic attempt to describe the development of French domestic politics except where it may have influenced government policy. In any event, Georges Clemenceau, who was premier of France during most of the period covered by this volume, was not one to permit his government to be easily led by the press or by politicians in the Chamber of Deputies.

Not a few individuals contributed to the development of this work. R.H. Davison introduced me to the subject during an undergraduate seminar at George Washington University. Later, I studied under John M. Sherwood, a fine and rigorous dissertation supervisor. Special thanks are also due to Richard K. Debo, Angus D. Gilbert, Mme Marie Gallup-Montlaur, Mlle P. Enjalran, M.J. Laloy, M.P. Schillinger, Mme H. Combe, Mlle Alice Guillemain, M. Pierre Haour, and M. Jean Cabet.

Post-doctoral research was made possible by a grant through the Franco-Canadian exchange program of research scholars in the humanities and social sciences. Chapter III has been adapted from the *Journal of Modern History* 46 (1976): 413–39 and is printed here by permission of The University of Chicago Press; ©1976 by The University of Chicago. This book has been published with the help of a grant from the Social Science Federation of Canada, using funds provided by the Social Sciences and Humanities Research Council of Canada.

Transliteration from Russian is based on the Library of Congress system, but diacritical marks are occasionally omitted. Moreover, some personal names are left in their commonly accepted spellings.

*Revolution and Intervention*

## CHAPTER ONE

# The French Response to the February Revolution

## MARCH-OCTOBER 1917

French intervention in Russia had its beginnings in 1917 as World War I entered its fourth year. Russia was being drawn out of the Allied coalition against the Central Powers by military collapse and a growing public demand for peace. The ponderous Russian war machine, which had inspired so much confidence among the western Allies in 1914, had been shot to pieces by German cannon and wasted by the inept administration of the tsarist government and military high command. In three years of war Russia lost nearly two million men killed, five million wounded, and two and a half million taken prisoner. The terrible casualties and poor leadership of the tsarist government broke the morale óf the Russian army. By the winter of 1916-17 an estimated one million soldiers had deserted their units.[1] Although troops still manned the trenches, they were grumbling, mutinous men, more disposed to shoot their officers than fight the armies of the Central Powers.

While soldiers at the front grew increasingly sullen, the masses in the cities became gradually more discontented because of growing economic hardships. Acute shortages of housing, clothing, fuel, and, more importantly, of food supplies led to galloping inflation and long queues for bread and other necessities. In the countryside, the peasantry was discontented because of conscription and the government's constant demand for more men to fill the broken ranks of the army. The peasantry had borne the brunt of the fighting against the Central Powers and

Until the Bolshevik seizure of power, Russia used the Julian calendar which was thirteen days behind the Gregorian calendar used in the west. Hence, the first revolution which occurred in March by the Gregorian calendar is called the "February Revolution." Similarly, the "October Revolution" culminated on 7 November of the Gregorian calendar.

by the end of 1916 sought to avoid by almost any means a war from which so many had failed to return.[2]

The rapidly growing war-weariness and discontent in the ranks of the army and among the civilian population gradually eroded the authority of the imperial government. In March 1917 the empire erupted in revolution. The tsar abdicated and a Provisional Government was formed to rule the country and to carry on the war against the Central Powers. This collapse of the tsarist regime came as no surprise to the western Allies. Sir George Buchanan, the British ambassador in Petrograd, in an often-cited audience with the tsar in January 1917, had warned that the empire was doomed unless drastic measures of reform were undertaken.[3] Buchanan's warning went unheeded and, in any case, came too late to save the tsar's throne. By then, the regime had lost practically all support in the country. The French ambassador in Petrograd, Maurice Paléologue, reported to Paris early in the year that the tsarist government had against it not only all the "democratic" forces in the country, but even the most ardent defenders of the monarchy.[4] Everyone was dissatisfied, but the tsar remained on his throne: the monarchist and bourgeois political opposition, fearing the discontent of the masses, did not want to loose the whirlwind of revolution.[5]

This fear of popular revolution proved to be entirely justified. Bread riots in Petrograd set off the chain of events which led to the fall of the tsarist government. Indeed, the politicians of the Russian national assembly or Duma who first led the Provisional Government were stupefied, as Paléologue put it, by the force and militancy of the revolution. P.N. Miliukov, the first foreign minister of the Provisional Government, told Paléologue on several occasions that he had not foreseen such a radical political upheaval. "We knew the regime was rotten," Miliukov said at one point, "but we did not understand to what degree."[6] What was even more disconcerting to the men who came to lead the Provisional Government was the "anarchistic" role of the army. Miliukov was thunderstruck by the fact that the best units of the Russian army, the crack Guards regiments, had been the first to go over to the revolution. He and his colleagues had counted on the support of the army and were alarmed by their inability to base the authority of the Provisional Government on this force.[7] Indeed, Paléologue was greatly disturbed by the uneasiness of Miliukov and his friends and feared, rightly as it turned out, that they were not of sufficient mettle to control and direct the force of the revolution.[8]

Real power in the country came to rest in the hands of the Petrograd Soviet of Workers' and Soldiers' Deputies. The Petrograd Soviet was a popular assembly whose members were elected at the outset of the revolution by tumultuous mass meetings of soldiers and workers. Their example was soon followed elsewhere as similar institutions were set up across the country. The Petrograd Soviet was initially controlled by the agrarian-oriented Socialist-Revolutionaries (SRs) and by the moderate wing of the Russian Social-Democratic movement, the Mensheviks. It was with the Soviet that the Provisional Government would have to struggle for control of the revolutionary movement.

The key issue facing both the Soviet and the Provisional Government was the question of the war. Although in agreement with the Provisional Government on the necessity of pursuing the struggle against the Central Powers, the Soviet favoured "democratic" war aims and a peace without annexations and without indemnities. Miliukov, on the other hand, had no intention of sacrificing the traditional Russian objective of gaining control of Constantinople which had been conceded to the tsarist government by the Allies in the secret treaties of 1915 and 1916.

There thus existed a gap between the Provisional Government and the Soviet, a gap widened by the western Allies who wanted to pursue the struggle against the Central Powers and pressed for a renewed Russian war effort. This internal conflict was heightened by the agitation of the left-wing Bolsheviks led by Vladimir Ilich Ulianov Lenin. Lenin, who was in Switzerland at the beginning of the revolution, returned to Russia in April across Germany in a "sealed train," and immediately launched a vociferous campaign against the World War. The Bolsheviks regarded this conflict as a struggle between rival imperialist states in which the working classes of Europe served only as cannon fodder. Lenin excoriated the Provisional Government for failing to make peace and accused it of being a cat's-paw for the imperialist governments of the Entente coalition.

Lenin, however, was no pacifist. War for him was the engine of social change. The war of rival imperialist states, he said, should be transformed into civil wars where the working and peasant classes would overthrow the bourgeoisie and create the socialist revolution. Lenin had no patience with the revolutionary "defencists" who argued that the state had to be defended against aggression. This would only strengthen the power and legitimacy of the ruling classes. Defeat, on the other hand, would have the opposite effect – disorganizing the army, weakening the government, and ultimately making possible a revolutionary seizure of power. Once this had been achieved in Russia, revolution could be spread to Germany and elsewhere. Lenin's government would propose peace to all the belligerent states, but on "democratic conditions" impossible for them to accept. At this point, Lenin hoped that revolutionary war would be set off by the European working classes, outraged by the failure of their governments to disgorge colonies or wartime territorial gains to meet Lenin's conditions for settlement. The working classes which had fought one another across Europe would now join together to overthrow the world capitalist order and bring about a socialist peace.

French diplomatic and military representatives in Russia, who predictably took a dim view of such ideas, noted Lenin's return to Russia and reported that his position on the war was beginning to attract popular attention. Colonel Jean Guillaume Lavergne, the French military attaché, reported at the end of April that Lenin had moved into the mansion of the former dancer Kshesinskaia, and every night spoke to the crowds which gathered there to hear him. More and more soldiers came to these meetings to applaud Lenin's eloquent denunciations of the war. Nevertheless, Lavergne indicated that these views were not widely accepted even among the Social-Democrats, and that there were brawls nearly every day between Lenin's partisans and his opponents.[9]

Generally speaking, French agents in Russia appear not to have had a sophisticated view of the Bolsheviks or to have devoted much attention to them in their reports to Paris. Although Paléologue seems to have more or less understood Lenin and his policies, most French reports characterized the Bolsheviks as "pacifists" and "anarchists," some of whom were certainly in the pay of Germany.[10] As one report put it, their organization was too good to be Russian.[11] Nevertheless, French agents did understand that Bolshevik demands for an immediate peace and immediate expropriation of the great proprietors' estates would not fail to appeal to the war-weary and land-hungry peasant-soldiers of the Russian army.[12]

In March and April 1917, however, the activities of Lenin and the Bolsheviks were of less concern to the French than the weakness of the Provisional Government *vis-à-vis* the Petrograd Soviet, especially because of the latter's impatience for a democratic peace without annexations or indemnities. General Maurice Janin, chief of the French military mission in Russia, warned Paris in the latter part of March that the Provisional Government, despite its good intentions concerning the pursuit of the war, lacked authority because of the influence and strength of the Soviet. As a result, he said, the new Russian government was forced to manœuvre to avoid a direct confrontation with Soviet authorities over war aims.[13] In fact, Miliukov told Paléologue in early April that the government did not dare move against the Soviet for fear of provoking a civil war which it could not win.[14] In view of this situation, both Paléologue and Janin sent off urgent messages to Paris, recommending that the French Socialist party and the Confédération générale du travail, the French federation of trade unions, be asked to appeal to their Russian counterparts, urging them to support the war effort against Germany.[15]

Hence, French agents, almost from the outset of the revolution, began to worry about its repercussions on the Russian commitment to the war. Paléologue informed Paris that Allied support of the Provisional Government would be the best hedge against "the peace movement" in Russia.[16]

The patriotic appeals from French socialists demanded by Paléologue and Janin were not long in coming. Former ministers Jules Guesde and Marcel Sembat, as well as Albert Thomas, then minister of armaments, sent a cable to Alexander Kerensky, the lone socialist cabinet minister in the Provisional Government, encouraging him to press for an energetic prosecution of the war. Pierre Renaudel, the editor of the Socialist newspaper *L'Humanité*, did the same.[17] Shortly thereafter, a mission composed of the Socialist deputies Marcel Cachin, Ernest Lafont, and Marius Moutet went to Russia with the objective of resuscitating Russian enthusiasm for the war.[18] Finally, in April Albert Thomas left for Petrograd on a special mission to relieve Paléologue, who was believed to be too closely associated with the toppled tsarist regime.[19] The French government hoped that the Socialist Thomas would be more influential in Russia than a French diplomat of the old school.

In spite of these efforts, the French government appears to have been pessimistic about further Russian participation in the war and uncertain of the solidity of the Provisional Government. The Quai d'Orsay was slow to recognize the new regime and in fact appears to have acted only after its hand had been forced by the British and Italians who extended recognition on 24 March.[20] Indeed, the mood of the French foreign ministry was well reflected by Pierre de Margerie, the political director of the Quai d'Orsay, who regarded as "nothing but illusions" a view expressed in the American press that the revolution in Russia would revive the country's will to fight.[21]

The problems of the Provisional Government were not made easier by the French high command, which initially did not appear to share the Quai d'Orsay's pessimism. Even before the dust of the revolution had settled in Petrograd, General Robert Nivelle, the commander-in-chief of the French army, ordered Janin to request the Russian high command to launch an offensive to coincide with one planned on the Western Front in April.[22] Janin replied quickly with discouraging news. The revolution in Russia, he said, had thrown the country into political turmoil which had spread to the army and threatened its cohesion. Even assuming that the Provisional Government succeeded in overcoming the pacifist agitation of the left, it would take time before the Russian army could do anything more than hold its present positions. "We should be happy," Janin grimly commented, if the Russian army could do this much.[23]

Paléologue's reports to the Quai d'Orsay were no less pessimistic than Janin's and represent a chronicle of spreading disruption and indiscipline both at the front and in the interior. Officers no longer possessed any authority over their men, industrial production was declining rapidly, and railway services were in a state of growing disorder. By the middle of April Paléologue began to report to Paris that the paralysis of the Russian war effort was becoming irreversible and that consequently the French government should study what measures could be taken to provide against a "more or less complete" Russian collapse. In even blunter language a day later, Paléologue suggested that, in the event of a Russian withdrawal from the war, France should consider the conclusion of a separate peace with Turkey at the expense of Russia.[24]

Janin was of a similar opinion. In a report written in early May he noted that "a tacit truce" already existed in many areas along the front. In fact, to maintain it, said Janin, infantry threatened to bayonet artillerymen who fired on German positions. It was true, he conceded, that the Russian general staff planned to resume offensive operations, but if they failed a serious deterioration of both the military and political situation would result. Consequently, Janin warned Paris that, for the foreseeable future, it should not count on the Russian army. Indeed, he concluded that there was a strong possibility of a Russian withdrawal from the war and that the government should therefore prepare measures which would make it possible to shift the consequences of such a development to Russia.[25] This recommendation was a measure of the alarm both Janin and Paléologue experienced as they witnessed the deepening crisis in Russia. Although the French government does not appear to have replied to these dispatches, they were not the last to propose the conclusion of a separate peace at Russia's expense.

### THE THOMAS MISSION TO RUSSIA

The pessimism of these reports to Paris occasioned a rift between Paléologue and Albert Thomas, who arrived in Petrograd at the end of April with a more positive attitude toward the revolution. Thomas believed that Paris should energetically support the Provisional Government and especially the Trudovik (or unaligned) socialist Kerensky, who was the only member of the cabinet capable of leading the movement to "re-establish order" in Russia and to revive the Russian will to fight.[26] In Thomas's view the French government should put its confidence in the Russian Revolution and support Kerensky to the hilt. Thomas, therefore, pressed for an Allied proclamation of "democratic" and "non-imperialist" war aims to satisfy Russian opinion and to facilitate Kerensky's work of reorganization.[27]

Thomas's views as well as his membership in the French Socialist party seemed to make him an ideal representative of the French government in Russia. But Thomas was more epicurean and bourgeois than uncompromising revolutionary though he tried to play the latter role. Even his appearance betrayed him. Looking rather too well dressed and too well fed, Thomas was viewed suspiciously by the revolutionary crowds to which he addressed himself. Indeed, the Russian socialist press accused him of being a renegade and a shill for western imperialism, a view which Thomas's numerous socialist-patriotic speeches seemed to confirm.[28]

Nevertheless, Thomas arrived in Petrograd full of confidence that he could hold the Russian Revolution loyal to the Allied cause. He also brought with him a letter recalling Paléologue, whose pessimistic views he promptly tried to muzzle by depriving him of the privilege of communication with Paris.[29] Paléologue, however, testily refused to be silenced and complained to the Quai d'Orsay.[30] Thomas was furious, believing that Paléologue was trying to undermine his policies. He warned that if the government chose to follow the ambassador's recommendations, the situation in Russia would only worsen.[31] Alexandre Ribot, the French premier and foreign minister, ostensibly backed Thomas in this quarrel but asked that Paléologue be allowed to communicate his views to Paris.[32] Paléologue stuck to his guns, and again recommended that the government seek a separate peace with Turkey. But Thomas, who had the last word, replied that while the situation in Russia was difficult it was not desperate and that, therefore, Paris should support the Provisional Government.[33]

Thomas held the upper hand and Paléologue soon returned to France. But Thomas had greater difficulties in convincing Paris to adopt his own policies. From the beginning the Quai d'Orsay was opposed to any discussion or revision of Allied war aims which had been determined earlier in the conflict and provided for the acquisition by members of the Entente of various enemy territories. These were scarcely high-minded objectives, and Ribot preferred not to discuss them publicly.[34] For the same reason, the French government opposed a projected meeting at Stockholm of socialists from all the belligerent states to discuss war aims. The French offensive in April had misfired, touching off dangerous and widespread mutinies in the French army. Nivelle, held responsible for the failure, was relieved of command. His successor, General Philippe Pétain, told the government that, if it gave its approval to the Stockholm conference, it would be impossible to restore discipline in the army or hold French troops in the trenches.[35] Ribot agreed, noting that the enemy was much too close to Paris for the government to act as if it had all the great expenses of Russia behind it.[36]

There also seems to have been considerable scepticism in the French government concerning Thomas's relatively optimistic appraisal of conditions in Russia, and hence added reluctance to adopt his policies.[37] Moreover, the Quai d'Orsay had a difficult time finding someone to replace Paléologue as ambassador in Russia. Stephen Pichon, three times foreign minister before the war, who was approached to serve as ambassador (and who would again head the Quai d'Orsay in the government of Georges Clemenceau in November 1917), considered the job hopeless.[38] In May he told a junior official at the Quai d'Orsay that he thought "Russia [had] finished playing a role" in the war. Observing that the Revolution had "passed from the Estates General to Gracchus Babeuf in two months," he deeply regretted that Lenin had not been hanged at the first opportunity. In his view the only option for the Allies was "to hold out" and "wait for America" (which had entered the war in April) because he did not doubt that Russia would abandon the Allied cause.[39]

In spite of this underlying current of scepticism in Paris, the Quai d'Orsay seemed prepared to permit Thomas to do what he could to restore the Russian government's commitment to the war. To this end, Thomas sought to strengthen Kerensky's position in the Provisional Government *vis-à-vis* Miliukov. The latter's insistence on maintaining the old Russian objective of gaining control of the Straits, the Bosporus and the Dardanelles, had provoked a growing hostility on the part of the Petrograd Soviet, and threatened to upset the already precarious position of the Provisional Government. Thomas came to believe that the resignation of Miliukov and a declaration of democratic war aims by the Provisional Government would strengthen its authority and revive Russia's will to fight.

The French government's acquiescence in Thomas's activities in Petrograd was due to instability at home. The mutinies in the French army had seriously alarmed the government, and Ribot feared the repercussions of a rupture of the *union sacrée*, the wartime coalition between the French Socialist and bourgeois political parties.[40] The government, however, was also inclined to go along with Thomas's activities because he seemed initially to be having some success in achieving his objectives.

The conflict between Miliukov and the Soviet which so preoccupied Thomas led to a governmental crisis in early May. Street demonstrations broke out in the capital led by armed soldiers angered by Miliukov's intransigent policy on war aims. These demonstrations eventually brought about the latter's resignation. Kerensky became minister of war and five other Russian socialists entered the Provisional Government with a view to giving it more authority and to ending the oppositionist role of the Petrograd Soviet. Plans were undertaken for a summer offensive and Kerensky, along with Thomas, toured the front and visited local Soviets to drum up support for the war.

Thomas eventually left Russia in the middle of June feeling he had been successful in halting the Russian drift toward peace. In a final dispatch from the capital, he reported that news from the army was encouraging and gave reason to believe that offensive operations would soon be resumed. Even if the projected summer offensive were limited in scope, wrote Thomas, "we will at least have circumvented the danger of a separate peace which I consider more and more as impossible."[41] Unfortunately for the French government, this appraisal of the situation, as events would demonstrate, was hopelessly wrong. Thomas had overestimated his influence on the Provisional Government and on Russian public opinion, which even he admitted was sick of the war and yearned deeply for peace.[42] As one Russian observer in Moscow noted, Thomas's histrionic, pro-war speeches made little impression on Russian soldiers who sneered at his too elegant frockcoat and "scented handkerchief," and whistled down his milk-toast socialist-patriotism.[43]

### THE COLLAPSE OF THE RUSSIAN ARMY

The bubble of Thomas's illusions was soon burst by the Russian summer offensive, which after some early successes, turned into a disastrous rout. The last remnants of Russian morale and fighting effectiveness disappeared. In Petrograd the abortive offensive touched off a spontaneous popular uprising over which the Bolsheviks felt compelled to take control in order not to lose their popularity with the masses. The uprising, however, proved premature and was suppressed by the Provisional Government. Numerous Bolshevik leaders were arrested, and loyal troops sacked Bolshevik offices and print-shops. Nevertheless, this apparent success of the Provisional Government over the Bolsheviks was far overshadowed by the bleak news from the southwestern front where the Russian army was in headlong retreat.

Even before the offensive and in spite of Thomas's optimism, the French military mission continued to send reports to Paris of "deplorable" discipline and morale, of widespread fraternization with enemy troops, and of frequent assassinations of officers. Janin reported that General A.A. Brusilov, then commander-in-chief of the Russian army, had said that "it would be almost impossible [for Russia] to continue the war through another winter campaign."[44] Other reports indicated that the average Russian peasant-soldier was completely indifferent to the war. The prospective division of the lands, advocated by the Bolsheviks, totally absorbed his attention and made him extremely reluctant to risk "his skin" against the Germans.[45] As a result discipline was impossible to maintain and officers had to haggle to get their men to perform the most trivial duties.[46] Moreover, as Brusilov admitted to Janin, there existed an "abyss between officers and men," which often led to ugly acts of violence. In one such incident, a group of soldiers destined for the front, stopped before the quarters of the division commander and asked to speak with him. The general came out but, before finishing the traditional phrase of greeting, was shot through the head. After the shooting the column moved off to the trenches, unmolested, as though it were all just routine.[47] In the view of the French military mission these incidents went unchecked because the Provisional Government was without authority and therefore incapable of repressing mutinous indiscipline in the army.[48] As one French intelligence report observed, even Kerensky's limited influence would not last "because his ideas went against those of the masses," who wanted peace.[49]

The failure of the July offensive only made matters worse, and the French military mission, which had been pessimistic before, now slid into a mood of exasperated despair. Reports accumulated in Paris describing the refusals of Russian soldiers to defend their positions or to go forward into the front lines. Regiments simply abandoned their trenches, leaving other units exposed and thus forcing them to retire as well. Janin forwarded one account describing how a regiment had been seen withdrawing from Tarnopol, rifles hitched over shoulders, followed by German units a few hundred metres behind, who let the Russians retire undisturbed.[50] In another report Janin told how a regiment killed its colonel because he had tried to expel some revolutionary agitators. In the aftermath many of the troops had demanded the execution of all the officers in the regiment but were finally placated with the shooting of "one or two" others.[51]

The cumulative effect of these events was to set off an outcry from the French military mission and the Russian high command for the reinstatement of the death penalty in the army (abolished at the outset of the revolution). One French officer angrily recommended that the Cossacks "be unleashed at full gallop" to put down the mutinies. If energetic measures were not taken, he said, Russia would make peace before winter.[52] Janin agreed. But the problem remained that the Provisional Government was helpless to act. Kerensky, who had no real base of authority, was constantly obliged to manœuvre and to negotiate the most insignificant acts of policy.[53]

In the face of this increasingly desperate situation, Janin turned to Paris and asked that an energetic *démarche* be made to the Provisional Government pressing it to impose the most draconian measures in the army to re-establish discipline and stave off collapse.[54] Although the French government was initially reluctant to take such action, Ribot eventually authorized the new French ambassador, Joseph Noulens, to make a joint *démarche* with his British counterpart, Sir George Buchanan, pressing for action to restore order both in the ranks of the army and in the interior.[55] The government also decided to reorganize and reinforce the French military mission. General Henri Albert Niessel was selected to replace Janin, who, like Paléologue, was considered to be too closely associated with the *ancien régime*.[56]

Niessel was no stranger to army mutiny. In the spring of 1917 he had commanded an army corps on the Western Front when mutiny broke out among French forces. His swift action to suppress disorders among his men may have recommended him for duty in Russia. In any event, Niessel was a cold, arrogant officer who soon was disliked by the Russians because of his self-righteous hectoring about reorganizing the Russian army.[57]

The British and American governments copied the action of the French by sending missions of their own to Russia, neither of which proved any more useful than Niessel's. In June the British sent Arthur Henderson, the Labour member of the war cabinet, to Petrograd on a mission similar to that of Thomas. And at the same time the United States dispatched to Russia the former secretary of state and secretary of war, Elihu Root, with promises of aid in exchange for a more active Russian role in the war.

In spite of such Allied efforts, the French government was by the end of July under no illusions about the likelihood of their success.[58] Thomas had fallen into discredit because of his overly sanguine confidence in the Provisional Government, which, in the hindsight of the abortive summer offensive, seemed ridiculous.[59] Moreover, the gradual accumulation of information from the French military mission in Russia finally had its impact on the general staff which began, in July, to anticipate the possibility of a Russian withdrawal from the war and to consider measures necessary to parry its likely repercussions on the Western Front. Pétain and General Ferdinand Foch, chief of the French general staff, ordered the drawing up of contingency plans to strengthen the Western Front against the transfer of a mass of German divisions freed by the Russian collapse in the east. Anticipating a German offensive in the spring of 1918, Pétain's strategy was to concentrate all available Allied forces in France to hold out until the arrival of new allies, the Americans, could redress the balance.[60] The general staff reckoned that if the Allies could not break German resistance in 1915 and 1916 with a numerical superiority greater than Germany would have in the event of a Russian collapse, then it was to be hoped that the enemy would not be more successful than the Entente in obtaining decisive results.[61]

While these developments were taking place in Paris, the clamour in Russia for the reinstatement of strict military discipline continued and talk of a counter-revolutionary *coup d'état* became more frequent.[62] Toward the end of August reports began to filter into Paris of a dispute between the Provisional Government and the new Russian commander-in-chief, General L.G. Kornilov, over the question of discipline in the army. Conservative elements under the leadership of the liberal Kadet party were said to be organizing against the government and sought to put Kornilov at the head of this movement.[63] In effect, the Kadets had been emboldened by the defeat of the July uprising in Petrograd and began, as L.D. Trotsky put it, to "soap ... the hangman's rope for the revolution."[64]

Other French reports indicated that Kerensky wanted to rid himself of the Soviet and of the unreliable soldiers of the Petrograd garrison, and that he sought to strike a bargain with Kornilov to this end. At the last minute there seemed to be a falling out among thieves, and either Kornilov tried to double-cross Kerensky and take all power into his own hands or Kerensky lost his nerve and attempted to halt the plan. Kornilov refused to agree and attempted to march on the capital to overthrow the Provisional Government.[65] Kerensky, whose influence had been seriously weakened by the disastrous July offensive, was compelled to turn to the left, to the very elements he had hoped to eliminate, to thwart Kornilov's *putsch*. Imprisoned Bolshevik leaders were set free, and the Petrograd population under the direction of the Soviet fortified the city to stop Kornilov's advance. These efforts proved unnecessary, however, because Kornilov's detachments melted away under the influence of revolutionary agitators who moved in among the troops urging them not to be the dupes of the *ancien régime*. The crisis fizzled out when the isolated Kornilov and his entourage were arrested in the middle of September.[66]

The French government, apparently unlike the British, whose military representatives sided with Kornilov, does not appear to have intervened in the struggle except to mediate a settlement between the two sides. In fact, Noulens sent explicit instructions to Janin not to get involved in the conflict.[67] The sympathies of the French government, however, were clearly with Kornilov. Margerie wrote to Jean Doulcet, the French chargé d'affaires in Petrograd, that "French opinion" as well as the Quai d'Orsay had "from the first day, hope[d] ... for General Kornilov's success." Margerie regretted that the generalissimo had acted prematurely and wondered how Russia would ever extricate itself from the chaos of the revolution.[68] Whatever the regrets of the Quai d'Orsay, the significance of the failure of Kornilov's march on Petrograd was not lost on the French government. Noulens reported that Kerensky's popularity had virtually disappeared and that the Bolsheviks were growing in strength and audacity.[69] From such reports grim conclusions began to be drawn in Paris, especially by the French general staff.

## "A PEACE ON THE BACK OF RUSSIA"

In early October the 3$^e$ Bureau of the Groupe de l'Avant prepared a long memorandum on the situation in Russia which postulated that the country was on the brink of both military and economic collapse.[70] Although the 3$^e$ Bureau considered the Provisional Government incapable of controlling the situation, it conceded that, in the present circumstances, no government would be strong enough to lead the country back into the war.[71] As a result, Russia appeared to be on the verge of concluding a separate peace. It was the opinion of the 3$^e$ Bureau that, although the Allies ought to make every effort to delay such an eventuality, they should also consider what measures could be taken to protect against a final Russian collapse. When this collapse occurred, the Entente would have to disrupt enemy plans to take advantage of the Russian withdrawal from the war "and, at the very least, to protect the considerable economic interests of the Allied powers and their nationals in Russia." The ideal solution would be to organize a military intervention strong enough to bolster the Russian army or at least to assure the defence of those areas of Russia most important economically to the Allies. This solution was impractical, however, because the United States and Japan, the only two powers capable of mounting such an operation, were not prepared to intervene. Moreover, the Trans-Siberian Railway, which would have to be the main supply artery of such an intervention, was not efficient enough to fulfil this role.

In view of these problems, the note continued, the Allied would have to be satisfied with a less extensive intervention, the purpose of which would be to take control of Russia's natural resources and means of production as a guarantee of Allied interests. To this end, the Allies should also take over Russian customs, port facilities, communications systems, mining operations, and metallurgical industries. These objectives could be achieved by the action of "a few" American and Japanese divisions supplied by the Trans-Siberian Railway.

The note went on to suggest, however, that a simple Allied seizure of Russia's economic resources would not suffice to protect the Entente against the consequences of a Russian defection from the war. The Central Powers, drawing upon the resources and manpower of a defeated Russia, might be able to hold out indefinitely against the Entente in spite of the American entry into the war. For this reason, the time seemed propitious to consider the possibility of "a peace on the back of

Russia." The Central Powers might be disposed to make a compromise peace in exchange for large concessions in Russia. A settlement would make it possible to control this increase in German power and at the same time guarantee the protection of Allied economic interests in Russia.

Based on this reasoning, the note then laid out the territorial basis for a settlement which entailed the dismemberment of Russia. Germany would be ceded the Baltic region and a sizeable area of White Russia in exchange for the restitution of Alsace-Lorraine, the independence of Belgium, and the payment of reparations for war damages. Moreover, a federation of Poland and the Ukraine would be established under an Austrian protectorate. Finland would be ceded to Sweden and eastern Siberia to Japan. The territorial integrity of Serbia would be restored and Rumania would cede the Dobrudja to Bulgaria in exchange for Russian Bessarabia. Similarly, the Cossack territories of the Kuban and the Don as well as the Caucasus would become independent. Finally, a rump Russian state consisting of western Siberia and the territories of the former Grand Duchy of Moscow would be established under the control of the Entente, thus safeguarding Allied economic interests.[72]

These rather startling proposals were not very practical, among other reasons because Germany was entirely against giving up Alsace and Lorraine, let alone agreeing to the other conditions of the French note.[73] Nevertheless, the plan was taken seriously enough to gain the imprimatur of the French general staff, and in November it was put before the new premier and minister of war, Georges Clemenceau. The note was an extension of Paléologue's initial idea of dividing the German coalition by means of a separate peace with Turkey at the expense of Russia. These drastic solutions signalled dramatically the end of any real hope within the general staff of renewed Russian military resistance.

The 3e Bureau's note also demonstrated just how deeply the idea of peace at the expense of Russia had burrowed in the French general staff. Nor were such ideas limited to the ministry of war. Paléologue, on his return from Russia, continued to press for a separate peace with Turkey and Austria and, to his satisfaction, found a favourable response among the politicians with whom he spoke. He wrote to Jean Doulcet in June that in conversations with Ribot, Paul Deschanel, the president of the Chamber of Deputies, Briand, and Pichon, he had noted "not without some surprise, that they fully approved [his] ideas and were even ready to turn them to account...."[74] In fact, Paléologue told Raymond Poincaré, the president of the republic, that of all the individuals with whom he had spoken only Alexandre Millerand, former minister of war, opposed the idea of a separate peace.[75] Moreover, in the late autumn both Niessel and General Henri Berthelot, the chief of the French military mission in Rumania, took up the by-then familiar refrain, although they, like the general staff, advocated a peace with Germany rather than just with its allies, Turkey and Austria.[76] And France was not the only member of the coalition to consider this idea. Albert I of Belgium told Poincaré in September that he was not opposed to a peace at Russian expense.[77] And in Britain, too, this idea was mooted by a member of the British war cabinet, Alfred Lord Milner.[78]

Hence, on the eve of the Bolshevik revolution, the French government and high command had given up on a revival of Russian military vigour. To be sure, as long as Russia did not sign an armistice, hopes persisted, but no one in the government or high command believed that an Eastern Front could be reconstructed in any real sense.[79] The question then faced was how to respond to this development. Paléologue and others urged the conclusion of a separate or general peace at Russian expense, while the general staff pondered the problem of how to save French and Allied investments in Russia. Pétain, on the other hand, advocated the strengthening of Allied defences on the Western Front while awaiting the arrival of American troops. The Entente coalition would then be in a position to retake the initiative against the Central Powers with or without the support of the Russians. None of these options was without risk for the Allies. But in these circumstances the Bolshevik seizure of power, when it did come, represented for the French the culmination rather than the cause of the military collapse of Russia.

## CHAPTER TWO

# The Bolsheviks Seize Power: Early French Hostility

## NOVEMBER 1917-JANUARY 1918

The Bolshevik seizure of power in early November 1917 was viewed as a calamity by the French government. At first it could scarcely believe that a band of unkempt, wild-eyed radicals and "pacifists" could take and hold power in Russia. Yet, as reports poured into Paris, the worst seemed true and incredulity soon turned to intense hostility. This animosity, however, was initially tempered by counsels of restraint from the French diplomatic and military mission in Russia. French representatives, although they did not like the Bolsheviks, were impressed by their strength and steadfastness of purpose, and thought they might eventually be compelled by circumstances to continue the war against the Central Powers. For the next three months, therefore, the French government, while seeking to encourage and support enemies of the new Soviet regime, did so with a care not to alienate themselves totally from the Bolsheviks.

The main thrust of French policy was to support the anti-Bolshevik Ukrainian independence movement in Kiev. The Quai d'Orsay offered *de facto* recognition to the Ukrainian Rada in exchange for loyalty to the Allied cause. But the Kiev government, menaced with extinction by Bolshevik Red Guards, needed German military support and therefore could not accept the French offer. In February 1918 Kiev made peace with the Central Powers, and the French government was left to re-examine its policy options in Russia.

The strength of the new Soviet regime, which gave pause to the French government and thwarted its efforts in the Ukraine, grew out of the important Bolshevik role in defeating the Kornilov *putsch*. This abortive *coup d'état*, while destroying what remained of Kerensky's credibility, enormously enhanced the prestige of the Bolsheviks. By the end of September the Bolsheviks had won their first majorities in the Petrograd and Moscow Soviets and in early October L.D. Trotsky, the maverick Social-Democrat, recently turned Bolshevik, was elected president of the Soviet in the capital. Lenin sensed that the days of the Provisional Government were numbered, and he began to press the Bolshevik central committee for a decision to seize power from Kerensky's enfeebled regime. In October, after some wavering in the Bolshevik party executive, Lenin's proposal for action was adopted. Preparations began at once, and on 7 November Kerensky was overthrown.

French representatives in Russia do not seem to have been well informed of Bolshevik intentions even though the plans to seize power were not a well-kept secret.[1] The French embassy expected that Kerensky would soon fall, but neither Noulens nor Niessel appear to have anticipated an imminent Bolshevik seizure of power.[2] This perhaps explains why the French government was caught off guard by the news of the revolution in Petrograd. The then French premier, Paul Painlevé, was out of Paris at the Allied conference of Rapallo. General Foch, the chief of staff, was also in Italy, preoccupied with the reorganization of the Italian army in the wake of its defeat at Caparetto in October 1917. In Russia, both Niessel and the recently promoted General Lavergne, the French military attaché, were out of the capital: Niessel on a tour of the front and Lavergne in the Caucasus.[3] Painlevé returned to Paris but was forced to resign on 13 November. Three days later Georges Clemenceau became premier of France and minister of war.

Clemenceau, almost eighty years old, was a short, not unkindly looking man with white overhanging eyebrows and a walrus mustache. The old man's political experience stretched back over almost three generations. In 1871 he had dabbled in revolution during the Paris Commune, but he disliked the brutishness and violence of the revolutionary masses and soon forswore his youthful idealism. Indeed, when he first became premier and minister of the interior between 1906 and 1909, he put down with considerable brutality a wave of strikes mounted by militant French syndicalists. Clemenceau had little patience with his political opponents of whatever party and he treated them all with uncommn scorn and abuse. It was for this reason that Clemenceau had begun to be called "The Tiger," and it was not for nothing that French opinion expected the new premier to be merciless in suppressing both domestic "defeatists" and Russian Bolsheviks alike. Even Lenin and Trotsky were made uneasy by Clemenceau's rise to power.[4]

## THE FIRST REPORTS FROM RUSSIA

The first information received by the government concerning the Bolshevik seizure of power was sketchy and confusing. The French ambassador, Noulens, reported to Paris on 8 November that the Winter

Palace, the last refuge of the Provisional Government, had been besieged and taken by the Bolsheviks and that most of Kerensky's ministers had been arrested. Nevertheless, rumours circulating in Petrograd indicated that Kerensky had joined loyal troops marching on the capital. Although the Bolsheviks controlled the city, they seemed to have only limited support and were said to be disoriented and depressed.[5] The French military mission reported similar information, but warned that the outcome of the conflict would depend on the opinion of the troops. If they went over to the Bolsheviks who offered "immediate peace and partition of the land," Kerensky would be defeated. Events since the first revolution, warned one French agent, gave cause to doubt a satisfactory resolution of the crisis.[6]

French hopes that Kerensky would regain power persisted for several days. The distant sound of artillery fire could be heard in the capital, and encouraged those who opposed the new Soviet regime. Proclamations tossed out over the city by airplane appeared to confirm the approach of troops loyal to Kerensky. However, Noulens observed rather incredulously that life in Petrograd continued at an almost normal pace. Shops remained open, the tramways continued to run, and people went about their business even though the capital was in the midst of a full-blown revolution.[7]

In fact, as the Bolsheviks took power, the streets of Petrograd were full of people strolling or gathering in crowds to discuss the latest political developments. Small groups of Red Guards or soldiers carrying rifles with fixed bayonets carelessly patrolled the streets occasionally suffering the disapproving looks or taunts of passers-by. According to Trotsky, the wealthy pedestrians of the chic Nevsky Prospekt even laughed loudly. "Have you heard? The Bolsheviks have taken power. They won't last more than three days. Ha, ha, ha!"[8]

Even Noulens initially shared this smug optimism. Indeed, so confident was the ambassador of Kerensky's return to power that he cabled Paris recommending the dispatch of eight to ten thousand Allied troops to garrison the Russian capital. Noulens thought that the presence of these forces would afford protection to Allied nationals and more stability to Kerensky's government.[9]

Unfortunately for the French, the optimism that had prompted this request for troops proved to be unfounded. Niessel while still at the front observed in his pocket journal on 13 November that the Bolsheviks were gaining ground against Kerensky. Groups of soldiers armed with machine guns barred crossroads and railroad junctions to prevent Cossack units from joining the deposed leader. Niessel recorded that he saw Kerensky, depressed and unshaven, at Gatchina near the capital on the evening of the 13th. Kerensky told him that he had been able to flee

Petrograd by car. That day, he said, his Cossacks had put some Bolshevik troops to flight, but sailors from the Red Guard had held and reoccupied Tsarskoe Selo near Petrograd. Kerensky complained that no reinforcements had arrived and that the Cossacks who supported him did not want to fight without infantry. General P.N. Krasnov, who was with Kerensky at Gatchina, told Niessel that he saw little hope for anti-Bolshevik forces unless reinforcements arrived immediately. Niessel observed that Krasnov was not confident and that Kerensky was losing time.[10]

In Petrograd Allied observers began to realize that the earlier announcements of Kerensky's imminent arrival in the capital had been premature. Kerensky's troops were said to be melting away under the impact of Bolshevik propaganda. By 16 November it was clear that the Bolshevik *coup de force* had succeeded at least temporarily. Reports reached Paris that Kerensky, after having talked of suicide because of his troops' desertion, had disappeared.[11]

Kerensky's disappearance marked the end of the Bolsheviks' initial efforts to consolidate their power in Petrograd and soon thereafter in most of the rest of the country as well. Their initial struggles had not just been with Kerensky's Cossack detachments, but also with Right SRs and Mensheviks in the All-Russian Congress of Soviets. These delegates who represented a minority in the Soviet, opposed the Bolshevik seizure of power and wanted to establish a broadly constituted socialist government. While the military struggle with Kerensky's small forces remained undecided, the Bolsheviks appeared ready to make concessions on this fundamental question. But after Bolshevik forces prevailed in the battle of the Pulkovo heights on 12 November, Lenin and Trotsky took a harder line, rejecting the idea of a broad coalition government. This is not to say that the Bolsheviks or Left SRs were united on the issue of overthrowing Kerensky. They were not, but Lenin and Trotsky were able to bring their partisans into line. The Bolsheviks and Left SRs, who constituted a clear majority in the Soviet, soon formed a coalition government which lasted until March 1918 when disagreement over the treaty of Brest-Litovsk led to its collapse.

## INITIAL REACTION TO THE
## BOLSHEVIK SEIZURE OF POWER

Once it became clear that Kerensky could not regain power, the Entente embassies in Petrograd began to consider in earnest the problem of what attitude to take towards the new Soviet government. Allied representatives met at the British embassy on several occasions in the middle of November to discuss this and other problems arising from the Bolshevik seizure of power. The ambassadors were unanimous in opposing any official recognition of the new regime on the pretext that its authority was accepted by only a small part of the population. Nevertheless, Noulens advised Paris against breaking off all relations with it since some contact would be necessary over the exit of nationals and "other current affairs."[12]

The first concrete problem with which the Allied embassies had to grapple concerned the refusal of the British government to release two interned Russian Social-Democrats, P. Petrov and G.V. Chicherin, who succeeded Trotsky as commissar for foreign affairs. Noulens, for his part, urged the Quai d'Orsay to advise moderation in London, and eventually the two Bolsheviks were released. The French ambassador reasoned that if differences between the British and Bolshevik governments led to a break, the other Allies would also be obliged to recall their representatives from Russia. This would be regrettable in the event that the Constituent Assembly elected in November and dominated by the Socialist-Revolutionaries should convene. Its meeting might bring unforeseen results in spite of Lenin's numerous measures to destroy its authority. Moreover, the recklessness of Bolshevik propaganda could lead to incidents aborting or dragging out future negotiations for peace between the Soviet and German governments. Noulens therefore recommended stalling for time.[13]

Noulens's moderation toward the Bolsheviks appears to have been due in part to the influence of Captain Jacques Sadoul, a member of the French military mission, and Louis de Robien, an attaché at the French embassy in Petrograd. Sadoul, a French Socialist and lawyer sent to Russia at the behest of Albert Thomas, served in the ensuing months as an important go-between with the Soviet government. As a result of these contacts Sadoul became increasingly sympathetic to the Bolsheviks and in 1918 joined their cause. In the interim, however, he advocated friendly relations with the new Russian government. Robien, a career diplomat, also took a relaxed attitude toward the Bolsheviks and indeed went so far as to advocate the recognition of their government. Although extremely contemptuous of Kerensky, an *ôte-toi de là que je m'y mette*, Robien respected the Bolsheviks as men of conviction, and he debunked accusations then being made in the French press that they were German agents.[14]

Paradoxically, Sadoul was not aware of Noulens's initially cautious attitude concerning the Soviet regime and feared that the ambassador would react with unrestrained antipathy toward the Bolsheviks. He characterized Noulens, a Radical politician and former government minister, as an inflexible bourgeois who was incapable of responding with anything but hostility to the Russian Revolution.[15] As Sadoul put it, everything the French ambassador saw and heard in Russia filled him with stupor and indignation. Worse still, Sadoul regarded Noulens's staff members as unsuited to work in the midst of a revolution and thought they would have been more appropriate fixtures "at receptions of the [old imperial] court."[16] Interestingly enough, Paul Cambon, the long-time French ambassador in London, shared to some extent Sadoul's views. Cambon, who met Noulens *en route* for Russia during the summer of 1917, took a dim view of the "pomp and ostentation" of the new French envoy and his suite. "He travels like a rajah," observed Cambon. "I am astonished that he does not want to make his entry into Petrograd on an elephant."[17] Cambon remarked as well that Noulens and his entourage were not likely to make a good impression on the members of the Petrograd Soviet.[18] The latter observation proved to be to the point. Trotsky, who was president of the Soviet, subsequently described Noulens as a Bourbon, who had "learned nothing and forgotten nothing."[19]

These diverse observations were a fair assessment of Noulens, a short, balding man, who made up for his lack of stature with a prickly arrogance and pretentiousness that only increased as his stay in Russia lengthened. He came to detest the Bolsheviks and, according to one observer, would have had them all lynched.[20] Noulens also had close ties with French industrialists and in particular with the Société générale d'entreprises, a conglomerate with interests in Russia.[21] These connections no doubt heightened Noulens's animosity and later made him a persistent advocate of strong measures to protect French economic interests in Russia.

In view of such associations and attitudes, it is surprising that Noulens was at first able to control his visceral dislike of the Soviet regime. But he explained to Paris that, although the Bolsheviks would not remain in power indefinitely, neither would they be overthrown immediately as some Russian diplomats appeared to believe. After eight months of disorganization, no authority seemed capable of asserting itself. Only General A.M. Kaledin, who was seeking to organize Cossack forces in the Don, had taken any initiative. Unfortunately, his troops were few and unreliable. French agents had also given propaganda support to pro-Allied factions in the Constituent Assembly elections. The Socialist-Revolutionaries had won a majority in the new assembly and were hostile to the Bolsheviks. But on the peace issue, aside from a certain regard for the Entente, they scarcely differed from the Soviet government. The problem was, said Noulens, that everybody in Russia wanted peace. The ambassador, of course, exaggerated the community of views between Bolsheviks and SRs. But his cables to Paris at this time are a measure of the discouragement felt by French representatives in face of broad Russian popular support for an end to the war.

In spite of these reservations, Noulens still favoured action by French agents intended to unite scattered anti-Bolshevik forces. France would thus establish points of support for the future maintenance of its political and economic interests. However, this program could only be pursued by maintaining Allied military and diplomatic representatives in Russia. Their removal would result in the weakening of French influence while Germany was recovering the means to impose its own. France could expect nothing from the Bolsheviks, but they exercised *de facto* power which the French government was incapable of suppressing. French policy, therefore, would have to adapt itself to the circumstances.[22] In Noulens's view this meant modest objectives. Since there was no possibility of organizing a Russian army capable of fighting the Central Powers, the Allies should be satisfied if they could unite forces capable of "re-establishing order."[23]

Noulens's policy recommendations were not accepted at the outset. After Clemenceau's assumption of power, the French government was quick to make known its dislike of the Soviet regime. The first manifestation of this hostility was provoked by Bolshevik efforts to conclude an armistice with the Central Powers. On 21 November Trotsky, as commissar for foreign affairs, sent a note to the Allied embassies formally notifying them of the establishment of the new Soviet government and proposing talks for an immediate armistice and the opening of a peace conference.[24] At the same time the Soviet government ordered General N.N. Dukhonin, who commanded the Russian army in the west, to propose an armistice to his German counterpart.

Clemenceau reacted immediately. On 22 November, apparently without prior Allied agreement, he cabled to Niessel that the French government would not recognize the Bolshevik regime. Niessel was instructed to inform Dukhonin that France counted on him to refuse to engage in any "criminal" peace negotiations and to keep the Russian army in the field against the enemy.[25] Clemenceau's initiative quickly developed into an Allied attempt to encourage the Russian high command to defy the Soviet government. This move, really an attempt to set off a second Kornilov *putsch*, did not succeed. Dukhonin was lynched by his mutinous troops, and the Bolsheviks quickly established their own authority over army general headquarters.[26] The French were thus forced to look elsewhere for indigenous support to oppose the new Soviet government.

On 23 November, without waiting for the results of the *démarche* to Dukhonin, the ministry of war approved a rather vaguely defined policy intended to encourage Ukrainian nationalist disaffection against the Bolsheviks.[27] This potential anti-Bolshevik opposition came from the Ukrainian Central Rada which had been set up during the period of the Provisional Government. The Rada was composed basically of separatist

Ukrainian intellectuals who broke with the Soviet government after the Bolshevik revolution and sought to set up an independent state. From the point of view of the French general staff, this rupture between northern and southern Russia seemed to offer an opportunity to halt the extension of Bolshevik authority and to delay peace in the east. Hence, at the end of November, the ministry of war ordered Niessel to support opposition Ukrainian and Cossack elements, should they break with Petrograd. In this eventuality the Rumanian army, still in the field against the Central Powers, could form a nucleus of resistance around which anti-Bolshevik groups could coalesce.[28] This development in French policy was reinforced by reports from Noulens indicating that the non-Russian nationalities and especially the Ukrainians appeared to offer the single point of support upon which France could base its action in Russia.[29]

As the French government made this first tentative response to the Bolshevik peace initiative, the situation in Russia continued to deteriorate. On 2 December armistice talks began between Bolshevik and German delegates in Brest-Litovsk, and on 15 December a month-long suspension of arms went into effect. In Rumania the situation was no better. On 3 December, with news in hand that Russian peace delegates had arrived at Brest-Litovsk, the Rumanian premier, Ion Brătianu, summoned the chief of the French military mission in Rumania, General Henri Berthelot, and the French ambassador, Auguste de Saint-Aulaire, to inform them that his government was compelled by military necessity to ask for a cessation of hostilities. The next day the Rumanian council of ministers unanimously approved this measure, and on 9 December, in spite of French protests, an armistice on the Russo-Rumanian front was signed at Foscany.[30]

The news of Brest-Litovsk and the Rumanian armistice was not enhanced by the gloomy military intelligence reports coming from Russia. Niessel indicated in December that, although he maintained contact with anti-Bolshevik groups, they did not give the impression of strength or firmness of purpose. Niessel thought that the government should keep open the option of entering into relations with the Bolsheviks should the armistice with Germany collapse. Although Niessel had little confidence in the Soviet government, he indicated that no opposition groups were strong enough to displace it, and that the Bolsheviks were the single party capable of leading further resistance against the Central Powers.[31] As Niessel observed later in December, all the political parties wanted peace with Germany and were quite prepared to allow the Bolsheviks to take responsibility for it in order to be better placed in the civil war which they anticipated would follow. This was especially true in the Ukraine where the government at Kiev was preparing for war with the Bolsheviks, not with Germany. In short, the Germano-Soviet armistice was an accurate reflection of the general popular desire for peace. While the masses followed the Bolsheviks, the upper classes counted on the German army to re-establish the previous social order. Niessel, whose attitude toward the Bolsheviks varied from grudging respect to outright antipathy, posed the then familiar question of whether it might not be wise to negotiate with Germany at Russia's expense, and afterwards overthrow the Soviet government which, he believed, constituted a menace for the entire "civilized" world.[32]

In November General Berthelot had espoused a similar point of view and at the same time General Antoine Gramat, chief of the Groupe de l'Avant, had put before Clemenceau the general staff's October proposals for a "peace on the back of Russia."[33] Although there is no indication of how Clemenceau reacted to the general staff's study, he replied sharply to Niessel, informing him that the suggestion of peace talks with Germany was unthinkable, and that his only concern need be the intensification of the war effort.[34] Clemenceau undoubtedly regarded the idea of a separate peace at the expense of Russia as not only impractical but also unnecessary, since he too espoused the policy of waiting for the American army in order to defeat Germany.[35]

This did not mean, of course, that the French government would do nothing in Russia. Already on 4 December the Quai d'Orsay had informed Saint-Aulaire that unlimited credits were being opened for him and General Berthelot for action in Russia.[36] Although the specific purpose of the credits was not made clear, the Quai d'Orsay was unambiguous regarding the general objective of French policy. As the foreign minister, Pichon, put it later in December, French action aimed at counterbalancing the power usurped by the Bolsheviks in northern and central Russia by the constitution of military resistance in the south intended "to hasten the end of the anarchy in Russia, and to facilitate the re-establishment of order and a legal government."[37]

To improve the management of its policy in Russia, the ministry of war decided to divide authority for French action there between Niessel and Noulens in Petrograd and General Berthelot and Saint-Aulaire at Jassy, the provisional Rumanian capital. The latter were assigned the control of French action in southern Russia with a view to keeping Rumania in the war and establishing support for the Rumanian army in the Ukraine and the Don. To this end, General Berthelot was given complete freedom of initiative to assure the resupply of Rumania and to organize the scattered Cossack and other forces in southern Russia that had not submitted to Bolshevik authority. Niessel and Noulens were to restrict their activities to northern and central Russia.[38] Shortly thereafter, General Berthelot received additional orders to prevent the movement of Ukrainian natural resources to Germany and generally to support centres of resistance "against the Germans and eventually against the Bolsheviks."[39]

The division of authority between French representatives in north and south was intended to avoid compromising the French embassy *vis-à-vis* the Soviet government. In a sense this meant adopting Noulens's less overtly hostile policy toward the Bolsheviks which Clemenceau had initially rejected. Beginning in late December the directives of the ministry of war began to lack the vituperative character of cables from the Quai d'Orsay concerning the Bolsheviks. Whereas Clemenceau's 25 December directive to General Berthelot spoke of "eventual" opposition to the Soviet regime, similar Quai d'Orsay cables made no such qualification and sometimes failed to refer to the Germans at all.[40] As Pichon remarked at the end of December, the government was taking action in southern Russia "intended to ruin Soviet authority and to restore power in Russia to those few elements of order who still survived there."[41] Although the differences in these directives are minor, they represent the first sign of a split of opinion which developed in the new year between the general staff and the Quai d'Orsay concerning the government's attitude toward the Bolsheviks.

While the French government laboured to work out a new policy toward Russia, it also sought to co-ordinate its action with that of the British. On 23 December Lord Milner, a member without portfolio in the British war cabinet, and Lord Robert Cecil, under-secretary of state for foreign affairs, came to Paris to consult with Clemenceau and Pichon. British policy until this point appears to have developed along lines similar to the French. A certain effort was made to conciliate the Bolsheviks in Petrograd while the government authorized British agents in Russia to lend financial support to anti-Bolshevik elements organizing in the south. The war cabinet, concerned by this inconsistency in British policy and by the lack of co-operation between the Allies, took the initiative of sending Cecil and Milner to Paris. They brought with them a memorandum which proposed a division of responsibility for future Allied activities in southern Russia. In the "spheres of action" delineated, France would take responsibility for the Ukraine, Bessarabia, the Crimea, and provisionally the Don area; the British would operate in the Caucasus, Georgia, Armenia, and Kurdistan.[42]

The purpose of the convention, according to the British memorandum, was to facilitate continued resistance to the Central Powers. But the memorandum did not resolve the contradiction in both French and British policy since it called for a continuation of support for the anti-Bolshevik opposition in southern Russia while at the same time avoiding a rupture with the Soviet government.[43] Although Clemenceau and

Pichon quickly approved the terms of the British memorandum, French consent should not be construed as an indication that the Quai d'Orsay had moderated its hostility toward the Bolsheviks. On the contrary, the ambiguities of the British proposal suited the purposes of the Quai d'Orsay since it permitted the maintenance of French agents on Soviet territory, who would then be better able to organize resistance against the Bolsheviks, as Noulens had previously suggested.[44]

The French government had another motive in agreeing to this arrangement. In the pre-war period French nationals had invested heavily in the mining and metallurgical industries of southern Russia, and the French government was interested in protecting these investments, as is illustrated by an exchange of correspondence between General Berthelot and the ministry of war. On 30 December Berthelot, reacting to news of the Anglo-French accord, cabled Paris to draw attention to the importance of keeping the Don region under French control. While stressing the area's military significance, General Berthelot emphasized that the French government should develop its influence in the Donetz basin during the war in order not to abandon to the British an area "so favourable to the future economic development of France."[45] Paris agreed. The ministry of war informed Berthelot that the French interest in the Don region "had not escaped the attention of the government," and that it had sought, by way of the 23 December convention, to maintain his responsibilities for this region until the conclusion of a new agreement. It would be inopportune, the war directive noted, to draw renewed attention to the question since under the circumstances it had been resolved to French advantage.[46] The correspondence between Paris and General Berthelot on this question was thin, but the French government's economic interest in the Ukraine was considerable and would become more evident in the following months.

## THE RECOGNITION OF THE
## UKRAINIAN CENTRAL RADA

The dispositions taken by the French government in December were intended to delay the conclusion of peace and to bring about the destruction of the Soviet regime. Action in northern and central Russia was limited to avoiding a complete rupture with the Soviets while the French government devoted its primary attention to the south where anti-Bolshevik forces were trying to organize.[47] The consolidation of French relations with the anti-Bolshevik Ukrainian Rada at Kiev was a primary aspect of this policy.

During December pressure began to build in Paris for a closer arrangement with the Ukrainian government after it had broken with Soviet central authority in Petrograd. In early December Ukrainian agents approached Noulens for French financial support for a Ukrainian state bank.[48] The Quai d'Orsay was non-commital, but Ukrainian advances continued.[49] Shortly thereafter, the Rada informed General Georges Tabouis, chief of the French military mission in Kiev, that it was prepared to co-operate with the Entente. In return, the Ukrainians requested aid against the Bolsheviks and Germans, and wanted an Allied commitment to defend Ukrainian rights at the future conference of peace. In view of this *démarche*, General Berthelot abruptly recommended the recognition of the Ukraine. He noted that such a step, in spite of breaking up the unity of Russia, would keep enemy influence out of the Ukraine, and would screen at least the southern front from the doctrine of peace at any price.[50]

General Berthelot, however, was scarcely an expert on Ukrainian affairs. During the battle of the Marne he had served as General Joseph Joffre's deputy chief of staff and then in 1916 went to Rumania to supervise the reorganization of the Rumanian army after its defeat against Germany. His proximity to the Ukraine made him the most suitable choice to manage French policy in that area. But Berthelot was one of a breed of French generals assigned to political tasks abroad who became partisans of the governments to which they were accredited.[51] Moreover, Berthelot never liked to be on the wrong side of an issue and so later denounced Ukrainian recognition as though he had never been one of its principal advocates.[52] In short, Berthelot sailed with the wind, and in December 1917 this wind seemed to favour recognition of the Ukrainian Rada.

Nevertheless, the French government initially resisted pressure in this direction. Although not opposed to Ukrainian autonomy, the ministry of war thought that France should retain its freedom of action in regard to the Ukraine's future relationship with Russia.[53] The Ukrainian government, however, was not satisfied and put increasing pressure on French agents in Kiev. Alexander Shulgin, the Ukrainian foreign minister, told Tabouis that, before any agreements could be concluded with the Entente, the question of recognition would have to be resolved. As a result Tabouis, supported by General Berthelot, pressed the French government for recognition out of fear that the Germans would act first and thwart French efforts to keep the Ukraine on the Allied side.[54] Tabouis reported in early January 1918 that a delay in recognition might force the francophile elements out of the Ukrainian government. If this happened, he warned, the enemy would definitely gain the upper hand.[55] Even Noulens, who never approved of unqualified recognition of Ukrainian independence, felt that "at least apparent" satisfaction should be given to the Kiev regime.[56]

Under this mounting pressure Paris moved towards recognition. On 26 December the French government appointed Tabouis French commissioner in the Ukraine. He was given plenipotentiary powers and authorized to enter into relations with the *de facto* government in Kiev.[57] Finally, on 5 January 1918, the Quai d'Orsay notified its representatives in Russia that France had decided "to recognize *de facto*" the Ukraine "as an independent government." Austro-German activities in Kiev made it impossible to delay taking this step any longer.[58] Pichon indicated in an explanatory cable to the French minister in Berne that the government had for several weeks been attempting to encourage "a resistance capable of opposing Bolshevik power at Petrograd" in the Ukraine, Bessarabia, the Caucasus, and the Cossack territories. "Without having any illusion as to the possibility of obtaining a resumption of the struggle against our enemies in this region, which like the rest of Russia, aspired to peace," the government sought to forestall the worst, and, in particular, to prevent the Germans from drawing provisions from the Ukraine, thus breaking the Allied maritime blockade around the Central Powers. The Ukraine could also act as an area of supply for the Rumanian army, and, if need be, a refuge. Pichon added that the government had invested the French embassy and military mission in Rumania with authority over policy in the south to disengage its representatives in Petrograd from a mission which could compromise them *vis-à-vis* the Bolsheviks.[59]

Margerie, the political director of the Quai d'Orsay, put the case more bluntly to the French ambassador in Rome, Camille Barrère. "I do not see," he said, "the possibility in the near future of constituting a Russian bloc capable of escaping German domination. The more Russia remained united under the authority of Petrograd, the more it [would] be dominated now and later by the Germans." Paying no attention whatever to intelligence reports indicating that the Bolsheviks were the only political force capable of mounting further resistance to Germany, Margerie concluded that France had little alternative but to support the constituent nationalities.[60]

Given the impossibility of sending military forces to Russia, the only action the French government could take in the Ukraine was financial. In early December the Ukrainians themselves had asked for French and Allied aid to establish a Ukrainian state bank.[61] Later, in January 1918, Saint-Aulaire recommended the creation of a new Ukrainian currency guaranteed by the Allied powers.[62] Paris initially favoured some kind of large-scale financial support for the Ukraine, and preparations were made to send a French financial mission to Jassy.[63] Nevertheless, this policy of economic aid and diplomatic recognition failed to prevent the Ukraine from drifting closer to an arrangement with Germany. Within days of the French decision to recognize the Ukraine, General Berthelot instructed Tabouis to hold up notification of the Ukrainian government. French agents in Kiev had reported that events were moving in a direction unfavourable to the Entente. They had learned from pro-Allied partisans in the Kiev government that, if the Central Powers offered acceptable terms, the Ukraine would make peace.[64]

Tabouis carried "in his pocket" the notification of "official recognition," but General Berthelot instructed him to turn it over only if justified by the attitude of the Ukrainian government.[65] In addition, Saint-Aulaire informed Ukrainian delegates at Jassy on 17 January that he had authority "to recognize the independence of the Ukraine," and that he was prepared to do so immediately if the Rada would pledge to maintain a pro-Allied policy. The Ukrainians could only respond that they did not have the necessary powers to make such a commitment.[66]

At this point the question of recognition was allowed to lapse because of the continued deterioration of the military and political situation in southern Russia. Under military pressure from the Bolsheviks and on the brink of collapse, the Ukrainian government had no option but to come to terms with Germany. On 9 February, soon after Kiev fell to advancing Red Guards, Ukrainian representatives at Brest-Litovsk concluded peace with the Central Powers. A few weeks later the Rumanians also capitulated after being presented with a German ultimatum. Ukrainian, Cossack, Czech, and Polish forces, which French agents had hoped to organize against the Bolsheviks, either scattered or pulled out of the Ukraine.[67] The French military mission in Rumania was compelled to withdraw. Plans for economic aid to the Ukraine were abandoned, and the Berthelot mission spent approximately 40 million francs in a lost cause.[68]

The collapse of French policy in the Ukraine was due almost entirely to the Allied inability to commit troops in Russia. But with a massive German offensive expected on the Western Front during the spring, the French high command had no manpower to spare. The Ukrainian government, however, was incapable of defending its own sovereignty and needed military support, either Allied or German, to remain in power. Since the Entente could not furnish this support, Kiev turned to the Germans. As the 3e Bureau of the Groupe de l'Avant observed at the end of January, the Central Powers could offer immediate advantages to the Ukrainian government. Since the middle of December the Ukraine had played a skilful double game. While assuring the Allies of its loyalty and condemning the Bolsheviks, it had sent a delegation to Brest-Litovsk allegedly to win time but in reality to examine the possibility of a separate peace with the enemy.[69] When the Bolsheviks threatened, the Ukraine went over to the Germans.

The French government thus tried and failed to barter Ukrainian recognition and financial support for the loyalties of the Kiev regime. This was a high price to pay to keep the Ukraine on the Allied side. The extension of even *de facto* recognition to the Ukrainian government represented a serious dismemberment of the Russian state, and called into question the twenty-five-year-old French principle of maintaining a strong, united Russian ally. French policy was reckless in the extreme since even the limited objectives of Pichon's 8 January directive to Berne were hopelessly beyond the means of France and the other Allies.[70] But the fact that a hostile regime ruled in Petrograd encouraged the French to turn to the governments emerging from the breakdown of Russian central authority.

By the end of January 1918, however, this approach had clearly failed. The anti-Bolshevik parties were in complete disarray or were coming to terms with the Central Powers. The Bolsheviks, on the other hand, had not yet concluded peace with Germany, and a rupture of the talks at Brest-Litovsk appeared more and more likely. The French were thus faced with the alternatives of moderating their attitude toward the Soviet government or abandoning Russia to the Germans. Having failed to sustain their enemies, France turned warily to the Bolsheviks themselves.

## CHAPTER THREE

# "The Decision to Intervene"

## JANUARY–MAY 1918

The new year brought the beginnings of a new French policy toward the Bolsheviks, though in the end it was to be short-lived. The French general staff and indeed Foch himself advocated co-operating in a limited way with the Soviet regime against Germany. This policy, based on wartime expediency, was encouraged by the rupture of the Brest-Litovsk negotiations, but it continued even after the Bolsheviks were forced to truckle under and to sign a draconian settlement of hostilities with Germany. The Bolsheviks suffered this capitulation with great difficulty. Trotsky, who spoiled to fight imperial Germany, was appointed commissar of war, and began, with bumptious energy, to organize a Red Army. He asked for French and Allied assistance in this endeavour and the French government at first agreed to provide its help. But the Quai d'Orsay jibbed at aiding the Bolsheviks in the creation of a revolutionary army which might eventually threaten French interests. Such opposition ended the brief period of Franco-Soviet co-operation and led to the decision to intervene against the Bolshevik regime.

The factors that moved the Quai d'Orsay to press for and win a rejection of the policy of co-operation with the Bolsheviks had little to do with the usual explanations for Allied intervention in Russia. Many western historians, of course, have asserted that the Allies initially wanted to reconstitute an Eastern Front to prevent Germany from concentrating its military forces in France. These historians conclude that the decision to intervene was taken rather haphazardly and was thus neither premeditated, nor the result of an aversion to the revolutionary nature of the Bolshevik regime.[1]

Even some early Soviet scholars conceded that the Allied intervention prior to the Armistice was prompted initially by the desire to rebuild an Eastern Front.[2] To be sure, not all Soviet historians accepted this view. There were those who asserted that Allied intervention was motivated from the beginning by the determination to overthrow the Bolsheviks and to re-establish the *ancien régime*.[3] Later on, the latter interpretation, supported by little evidence but envenomed with Stalinist vitriol, became the standard Soviet version of the origins of the intervention.[4]

All these western and Soviet generalizations concern Allied attitudes toward the Bolsheviks, but how accurate are they when applied to the French alone? For example, did the initiative for intervention develop in military circles or at the Quai d'Orsay? Did French policy evolve "almost imperceptibly" as a result of circumstances over which Paris had no control, or was the decision to intervene deliberate and pre-meditated? And if such a decision was taken, was it motivated by a desire to wage a more effective war against the Central Powers or to overthrow a revolutionary regime which threatened vital French political and economic interests? The answers to these questions emerge from the twisted, often contradictory course of French policy towards the Bolsheviks between February and April 1918.

THE FRANCO-SOVIET RAPPROCHEMENT

With the collapse of French policy in southern Russia, Paris was compelled to reappraise its attitude toward the Bolsheviks, especially in view of the conduct of the Soviet peace delegation at Brest-Litovsk. The negotiations there opened in late December 1917 and from the beginning served the Bolsheviks as a platform for revolutionary propaganda vilifying the German government. Although the Bolsheviks were incapable of continuing the war, Trotsky, the head of the Soviet delegation, behaved as though they could, and played for time in hopes of provoking the German proletariat into a revolution against the war. Richard von Kühlmann, the head of the German delegation, permitted himself to be dragged into irrelevant arguments of principle which stalled the negotiations and made Trotsky appear as if he were successfully fending off the bullying diplomacy of the Germans. Soviet tactics also seemed to generate more tangible results as German troop movements towards France slowed in January and strikes broke out in Berlin and Vienna.[5]

In spite of these circumstances, improvement in relations with the Bolsheviks did not come easily. The Quai d'Orsay initially resisted moving in this direction. On 11 January Pichon informed Cambon in London that the Quai d'Orsay disapproved of the British government's intention to send a special agent, R.H.B. Lockhart, to Russia to establish unofficial relations with the Soviet regime.[6] This view was not shared by the general staff, however. Clemenceau informed Pichon that the presence of Lockhart in Petrograd would prevent the Austro-Germans from gaining a free hand in Russia, and would permit the Entente to profit from any sudden favourable change of policy on the part of the Soviet government.[7] The Quai d'Orsay, however, was not yet persuaded to adopt a less hostile attitude toward the Bolsheviks, and still sought to prevent the complete abandonment of French efforts to organize an anti-Bolshevik coalition in the Ukraine.

Nevertheless, toward the end of January, opposition to government policy in southern Russia began to emerge within the general staff. The 3ᵉ Bureau of the Groupe de l'Avant, in an about-face from the previous October, circulated a memorandum which opposed any dismemberment of Russia by fostering the independence of its constituent nationalities (probably an indirect reference to the government's recognition of the Ukraine). The memorandum argued that a unified Russian state was essential to the maintenance of a European balance of power and suggested that the Bolsheviks, who represented a centralizing force, were the most likely to be capable of holding Russia together. The 3ᵉ Bureau therefore recommended that the government undertake semi-official talks with the Bolsheviks to reach an accommodation and to bring about a rupture of Soviet relations with the Central Powers.[8]

The 3ᵉ Bureau's memorandum appears to have formed the basis of a policy directive intended for Niessel which was sent for final approval to the Quai d'Orsay. This directive contained clauses instructing Niessel to support *Bolshevik* (the ministry of war's emphasis) efforts "aimed at preventing the Ukraine or any other part of Russia from concluding a separate peace." Niessel was also instructed to make it known to the Soviet government that France was prepared to support its attempt to create a unified Russian state. These instructions, had they been approved, would have constituted a clear reversal of previous French policy. However, a marginal note in Pichon's hand states that Foch had consented at his request to remove the clauses concerning better relations with the Bolsheviks.[9]

Pichon did not record his reasons for opposing these policy recommendations, but a few days earlier, on 22 January, the Quai d'Orsay had informed Saint-Aulaire that the government was still not prepared to encourage "a rapprochement between the Bolsheviks and the southern nationalities."[10] At any rate, even though the ministry of war's directive that was sent to Niessel on 27 January did not contain the objectionable clauses concerning a *rapprochement* with the Bolsheviks, it still signalled the beginning of an improvement in Franco-Soviet relations. Government policy did not change in so far as French agents were instructed to continue their efforts to delay a separate peace. But while General Berthelot was ordered to carry on in this sense with anti-Bolshevik groups in the south, Niessel was instructed to exercise his influence on the Bolsheviks in hopes of leading them to adopt a policy more favourable to Allied interests.[11]

In view of the Quai d'Orsay's opposition to an improvement of French relations with the Bolsheviks, the directive of 27 January as finally agreed upon appears to have represented a rough compromise between Pichon and Foch in that it authorized closer ties with the Bolsheviks but allowed for continued relations with anti-Bolshevik groups in the south. The observations of Noulens confirm this impression, for he regarded the directive as an order to set up Generals Berthelot and Niessel in opposing camps.[12] In any case, the exchange of views between the Quai d'Orsay and the ministry of war regarding Russia indicates that the French government was to some degree divided in its attitude toward the Bolshevik regime, and that the general staff took the initiative in calling for an improvement of Franco-Soviet relations.

Shortly thereafter, the ministry of war acted to clear up the ambiguities of its 27 January directive by downgrading the importance of French action in southern Russia. Apparently without further consultation with the Quai d'Orsay, the ministry of war instructed General Berthelot on 3 February to take a reserved attitude toward the Ukraine, and to avoid any action likely to provoke the Bolshevik government.[13] This order, in so far as it reversed French priorities in Russia, signalled the abandonment of efforts to form an anti-Bolshevik coalition in the south. In conformity with this new policy Niessel was ordered on 17 February to assist any groups, whoever they might be, resisting the enemy.[14] The same day the Quai d'Orsay instructed Noulens to make it known to the Bolsheviks that, if they resisted the Germans, France would lend its assistance in money and *matériel*.[15]

As the French government adopted a more friendly attitude toward the Bolsheviks, events in Russia began to unfold with great rapidity. On 10 February the Bolsheviks broke off negotiations with the Central Powers, and six days later the German command announced that the armistice in Russia would be terminated on 18 February. The new German advance went almost unresisted and the Soviet government hastened to come to terms with the Central Powers. This decision was not made easily. Early in the year Lenin had decided that a general settlement of the war would be impossible and that his government would have to seek a separate peace. But his view was not shared by a majority of his colleagues, not even by Trotsky, who preferred to wage a "revolutionary war" against the Germans. Lenin regarded such a policy as absurd without an army prepared to fight. The Bolsheviks, he said, should be careful lest a "revolutionary phrase about revolutionary war ... ruin our revolution."[16] His position, however, did not prevail until the

German army had penetrated deep into Soviet Russia. At the same time Trotsky began to pursue the option of acquiring Allied support for the formation of a new army. And even Lenin when events seemed to preclude any settlement with Germany was grudgingly prepared to accept "potatoes and arms from the robbers of Anglo-French imperialism."[17] On this limited basis Trotsky and Niessel discussed the possibilities of co-operation against the Germans. But the two men did not get along and nothing concrete developed from their meetings. In the end, the Bolsheviks, whipped along by Lenin, signed a peace at Brest-Litovsk on 3 March.

In spite of the Bolshevik capitulation to the Central Powers, the French general staff continued to favour a policy of military collaboration with the Soviet regime. The ministry of war argued that the Bolshevik acceptance of German peace conditions would not modify the military situation in the east. In fact, the general staff believed that the Soviet government intended to use the peace to extend and consolidate its authority in the rest of Russia. Germany would therefore have to occupy the areas it desired to annex or exploit since the Bolsheviks could be expected to resist the German presence wherever possible. Because of the large expanse of territory involved and the complete disorganization of transportation and communications, such an occupation would be difficult, even if unopposed by organized resistance, and would require, at least for a time, the immobilization of a "sizeable" part of German forces in the east.[18] Although this argument was initially envisaged as a means of persuading Rumania not to make peace, it actually constituted the reasoning by which the ministry of war sought to support even minimal Soviet resistance to the German occupation. In effect, the general staff regarded the Bolsheviks as a force for Russian unity and, as such, an obstacle to German expansion in Russia.[19]

Because of the ministry of war's ongoing support for a *rapprochement* with the Bolsheviks, Franco-Soviet relations continued to improve. War directives were sent to Niessel on 8 and 11 March instructing him to encourage Soviet resistance against Germany.[20] On 20 March Trotsky, newly appointed commissar of war, formally requested the co-operation of the French military mission in the rebuilding of the Russian army. Lavergne, who had replaced Niessel as chief of the French mission a few days earlier, responded favourably, and by the beginning of April French officers were ready to assume advisory functions in the Red Army.[21] The ministry of war approved Lavergne's actions, and left the application of French assistance to his discretion.[22] This policy received further confirmation in a war directive of 29 March rejecting a Niessel recommendation that Paris choose between a posture of outright hostility or of *rapprochement* with the Bolshevik government. The circumstances, said this directive, were too ambiguous for such a course of action. Nevertheless, the ministry of war affirmed in unequivocal terms that French policy "must, above all, seek to support the Bolshevik government" in its attempted resistance to Germany. But Lavergne was warned not to expect "any outside support whatsoever" in the pursuance of this mission.[23] The limits of French co-operation with the Bolsheviks were thus drawn. Lavergne could prudently offer his assistance to Trotsky, but he would have to make use of the resources he could find in Russia.

In spite of the limited scope of the Franco-Soviet *rapprochement*, the policy had strong support in the ministry of war. On 5 April the Groupe de l'Avant circulated a forceful note defending the accommodation with Moscow. The "French general staff," it was stated, opposed the idea that the Allies should support "Russian patriotic elements" and turn openly against the Bolsheviks. These "so-called patriotic groups," the memorandum asserted, were discredited and lifeless. The few men who had tried to act were beaten and in flight. As for the rest, either they had supported Kerensky, who had prepared the Russian defeat, or they favoured German occupation to protect their expropriated material interests. Under the circumstances, it had in no way been established that the war against the Germans could be waged more effectively by an anti-Bolshevik government.[24] On the contrary, it was possible to think that it was the Bolsheviks, "duped by the Central Powers and perhaps aware of past errors," who offered the best chance of organizing the last few partisans of resistance against Germany. Significantly, this note stressed that the German offensive, which had begun on the Western Front on 21 March, was reason to *support* the Bolsheviks in that only a revolutionary army could offer hope of posing even a minimal threat to the enemy in the east.[25]

### OPPOSITION TO FRANCO-SOVIET
### CO-OPERATION

As the ministry of war committed itself to a limited *rapprochement* with the Bolsheviks, opposition began to boil up in other quarters of the French government. In the first place Noulens, who had initially opposed a complete rupture with the Soviet regime in hopes of preventing the conclusion of peace, turned openly against *rapprochement* after the signature of the treaty of Brest-Litovsk. In a series of cables commencing on 9 March, he began to condemn the Bolsheviks as an obstacle to the reconstitution of Russia, unlike the ministry of war, and as a serious menace to French economic holdings. Noulens favoured a policy of intervention against the Soviet regime. He recommended that military action by even small-sized inter-Allied units should be undertaken to encourage centres of resistance around which indigenous elements favourable to French influence could form. To this end, Arkhangelsk and the railroad as far south as Vologda should be seized. The intervention of American and Japanese forces in Siberia should also be encouraged. Noulens believed that French policy ought to have two principal objectives: to obstruct the German penetration of Russia and to protect French economic interests. He concluded that the formation of a Russian government favouring the Allies behind the protective cover of intervention would be the most effective way to secure these aims.[26]

Noulens, who left Petrograd for France after the Bolshevik capitulation to the Germans, found his passage blocked in Finland by civil war. As a result, he suggested to Paris that his party return to Russia and establish itself at Vologda where contact could be made with Russian parties favourable to the Allies. While awaiting approval of this proposal, he continued to denounce the idea of a *rapprochement*, and expressed concern that the French military mission might be helping to organize Soviet military forces. It was certain, he said, that such an army would only be used to perpetuate disorder or to oppose intervention. It would never wage war against Germany.[27]

Noulens' views concerning collaboration with the Bolsheviks were remarkably similar to views expressed earlier by the comte Paul François de Chevilly, head of the French propaganda office in Petrograd and an influential businessman associated with the Parisian Banque Privée.[28] Chevilly had close relations with Noulens and began very early to lobby against an accommodation with the Bolsheviks. On 19 February he wrote to Albert Thomas complaining about "certain circles" in Paris and at the French embassy in Petrograd which favoured supporting the efforts of the Soviet government to organize a Red Army to oppose Germany. Chevilly admitted that the question of the war took priority over all others including the "social risk" of Bolshevism. If the Soviet government, he wrote, could really organize further resistance to the Central Powers then France would be compelled to support it. After defeating Germany, there would be time enough to worry about "the peril of Bolshevism." But Chevilly argued that the Bolsheviks could not pose a serious threat to Germany because, as he put it, "Russia no longer wants to fight." In fact, the Red Army was intended as a weapon "of civil war" to be used against internal enemies. If the French government supported the Bolsheviks in this endeavour, it would only succeed in reinforcing the authority of the Soviet regime and eventually in facilitating the penetration of its influence in France where it could spread the "germs of class hatred, civil war, and national disintegration."[29]

The arguments put forth by Chevilly against co-operation with the Bolsheviks soon began to find their way into the outgoing cables of the Quai d'Orsay. On 8 March Philippe Berthelot, the influential deputy political director of the Quai d'Orsay, prepared a dispatch for Cambon in London, which condemned the activities of the British agent Lockhart aimed at achieving an entente with the Soviet regime. The Quai d'Orsay dispatch characterized his work as pernicious and British policy as weak. Berthelot criticized the Soviet government for having signed a separate peace with Germany and expressed the opinion that the Allies should intervene against the Bolsheviks rather than continue a policy of *rapprochement* with their regime.[30] Berthelot's cable, which was not dispatched, was dated the same day as the war directive to Niessel instructing him to encourage Soviet resistance to Germany. Apparently the ministry of war did not share Berthelot's views.

The Quai d'Orsay, however, did not keep silent. On 30 March, taking advantage of Noulens's return to Russia the previous day, it dispatched a cable which openly contradicted the substance and intent of the war directive of 29 March approving French military assistance for the Soviets. The Quai d'Orsay instructed Noulens to begin a re-examination of French options in Russia. Pichon observed that the government continued to reject recognition of the Soviet regime. Although one could not refuse out of hand Trotsky's requests for assistance since it was a question of the struggle against Germany, the "tainted origins" of the regime and the many disappointments the Bolsheviks had caused, made it necessary for French agents to use prudence in giving assistance. Besides the Bolsheviks there were groups with whom France had a common interest in preventing the ruin of Russia's economic future. French policy should therefore have two objectives: (1) to protect the "menaced" economic holdings of France, and (2) to encourage the organization of those parties "favourable to the reconstitution of a Russia where [French] diplomatic and economic influence would play its necessary part for the well-being of both countries." Nevertheless, Pichon indicated that a military intervention in northern Russia, however desirable, was impossible at that moment because of the German offensive on the Western Front and the exigencies of submarine warfare.[31] To be sure, this was not to say that the Quai d'Orsay disagreed with Noulens's general conclusion that the *rapprochement* with the Soviets should be terminated. On the contrary, Berthelot's 8 March draft indicates that sentiment in the Quai d'Orsay had begun to turn against the policy of military collaboration even before the dispatch of Noulens's first unambiguously hostile cable on the Bolsheviks (on 9 March).

Two days later, in even stronger language, the Quai d'Orsay warned openly against the dangers of collaborating with the Soviet regime. It was to be presumed, said Pichon, echoing the argument of Chevilly, that Trotsky was "less preoccupied in organizing a serious resistance against the Germans than in seeking to maintain Bolshevik domination." Collaboration in the constitution of a Red Army, he added, could lead to a French association "with the creation of an instrument of *guerre sociale* designed to break opposition" to the Soviets. The government did not want to give the anti-Bolshevik parties who remained favourable to France reasons to reproach it for having consolidated the dictatorship of their enemies.[32] Because the Quai d'Orsay was reluctant to facilitate the creation of an army intended to serve the interests of social revolution "in Russia and in Europe," it opposed the extension of real assistance to Trotsky until the French government had obtained the necessary guarantees.[33]

These foreign ministry cables were the first in six weeks to comment on the policy of military collaboration. The misgivings raised by the Quai d'Orsay must therefore constitute the primary reasons for its opposition to a Franco-Soviet *rapprochement*. Moreover, until the question of military collaboration had been settled, the issues discussed in the above cables were brought up repeatedly in outgoing Quai d'Orsay correspondence. To be sure, the danger of war supplies stockpiled at Arkhangelsk and Vladivostok falling into enemy hands, the menace of armed Austro-German prisoners of war on the loose in Siberia, and other related factors were invoked from time to time to hasten Allied military action in Russia. However, these issues commonly associated with the decision to intervene were in most cases not raised, or were relegated to secondary importance in the series of foreign ministry cables aimed at halting the Franco-Soviet *détente*. Quite often, in fact, these questions were subordinated to the maintenance of the *rapprochement*. The ministry of war, for example, estimated that any Allied military action undertaken in northern Russia should have Bolshevik approval and should not be the source of new conflicts with the Soviet government.[34] Niessel observed that if the Allies continued to pursue a policy of co-operation, they would be obligated to leave the stockpiled supplies at Arkhangelsk in Bolshevik possession.[35] In early April Lavergne observed that many of the chiefs named to command the Red Army were former tsarist officers who would guarantee, presumably along with French advisers, that the new military forces being raised by Trotsky would not be used as an instrument of *guerre sociale*. Whether or not Lavergne was correct in this regard, he did rightly observe that the nucleus of forces which could be organized in European Russia to oppose Germany would not constitute a threat to Japanese intervention in Siberia (then being discussed by the Allies).[36] In any case, the Quai d'Orsay chose to disregard these observations and pressed the acceptance of its own views.

The Quai d'Orsay cables of 30 March–1 April remained in contradiction with Clemenceau's directive of 29 March for five days until the ministry of war acted to end the inconsistencies of French policy. A war directive to Lavergne, dated 5 April and signed by the new chief of staff, General Henri Édouard Alby, referred to Pichon's recent communications with Noulens, and warned of "the dangers which could develop from the creation of a Bolshevik army used as an instrument of *guerre sociale* or as a weapon against Japanese intervention. Alby ordered Lavergne to Vologda to consult with Noulens and, although not suspending earlier war directives on military collaboration, instructed Lavergne to act "with extreme circumspection" toward the Bolsheviks.[37] This new directive appears to have signalled the beginning of a reversal in policy. The dispatch was more cautious in its endorsement of military collaboration and introduced two new elements never mentioned in prior orders: to wit, the fear of creating an instrument of *guerre sociale* or an obstacle to Japanese intervention.[38]

The general staff, however, was not quite ready to abandon its policy of accommodation. On 5 April it asked the Quai d'Orsay to permit Lavergne to retain "a certain freedom of action" *vis-à-vis* the French embassy so that he could pursue more easily his "important mission" in Russia.[39] The general staff, sensing a growing opposition within the government to the *rapprochement*, appears to have sought to save its policy in Russia by preserving for Lavergne at least a degree of independence from Noulens. In this way, the French ambassador could be prevented from gaining control over the implementation of French policy on the spot and from blocking the *détente*. The continuation of the *rapprochement* therefore came to hinge on the delimitation of authority between Noulens and Lavergne. Lavergne's inclination to assist Trotsky (although it should be emphasized that he had full authority to do so) put him in direct conflict with Noulens, and mirrored the dispute on policy in Paris. Undoubtedly aware of the obstacle Lavergne represented, Noulens began to press for a curtailment of his activities. On 9 April he requested that the military mission be officially disbanded and that Lavergne be put strictly under his authority.[40] By ending Lavergne's independence, Noulens would gain a free hand, and would remove a potentially powerful influence for military collaboration with the Bolsheviks.

Although it took six days for Noulens's cable to reach Paris, the Quai d'Orsay acted overnight on his request. In a letter to Clemenceau on 16 April, Pichon requested that Lavergne be placed under Noulens's orders, and that in the future the French ambassador have sole authority, conditional on government approbation, to determine the efficacy of extending military assistance to the Bolsheviks.[41] The same day the general staff complied with Pichon's request.[42]

The decision to abandon military collaboration thus effectively took place between 5 and 16 April. Although it is not possible to establish with certainty the actual chain of events leading to this reversal of policy, the circumstances suggest that Clemenceau intervened in some way to end the dispute. Probably not as committed as the general staff to the *rapprochement*, Clemenceau, pressed by the Quai d'Orsay, must certainly have authorized the 5 April order pulling the government back from military collaboration with Trotsky. General Alby, who actually signed this directive, did not have the authority or prestige to make a major revision in policy independently. In fact, it would appear that when Foch gave up his functions as chief of staff to become commander of the Allied armies in France, the policy of *rapprochement* lost its most important advocate. Foch signed most of the orders dispatched on military collaboration, while Clemenceau, preoccupied with internal political problems, was only sporadically interested in military affairs.[43] It is likely, therefore, that Clemenceau resolved the dispute over the government's attitude toward the Bolsheviks, first by taking up the misgivings of the Quai d'Orsay, and then by agreeing to Lavergne's subordination to Noulens. Neither the ministry of war nor the Quai d'Orsay could have been unaware of the implications of the latter decision. To charge the French ambassador with full authority over the extension of military aid to Trotsky was to kill the *rapprochement*. This observation is reinforced by marginal comments apparently made by Colonel Alphonse Joseph Georges, chief of the 3e Bureau of the Groupe de l'Avant, on a memorandum opposed to the *détente* with the Soviets. These marginal notes favoured a continuation of military collaboration, and characterized any action which might be undertaken at Vologda by Niessel, or by implication Noulens, as "negative."[44]

Interestingly enough, Georges was to have a much greater role to play at the outset of World War II when he served as commander-in-chief of the northeastern front. He was one of those held responsible for the collapse of France in May 1940. In 1918 his responsibilities were more modest, but he did exercise some influence on the formulation of French policy toward Russia. Although he defended the policy of Franco-Soviet collaboration in the spring, the following autumn he would prepare a series of policy memoranda calling for military intervention in Russia to prevent an invasion of Europe by revolutionary Bolshevism.

In any event, it is improbable and there is no evidence that the opposing views of the ministry of war and the Quai d'Orsay ever led to an outright dispute. The Bolsheviks were not highly regarded by either department, and the policy of military collaboration really was one of last resort. Furthermore, the general staff was exceeding its authority by involving itself in what the Quai d'Orsay considered a political matter. It is unlikely, therefore, that the ministry of war would have risked a dispute over the question of collaborating with a group of immoderate, dangerous revolutionaries, especially since this issue could raise the sensitive problem of delimiting political and military responsibilities between the two ministries. It is equally improbable that such a dispute would have been permitted to come into the open, given its potentially dangerous repercussions on both right- and left-wing opinion in France.

## THE INFLUENCE OF DOMESTIC FACTORS
## ON FRENCH POLICY

In February 1918 the Soviet government had repudiated the Russian state debt and hence all the issues of tsarist bonds.[45] French citizens had invested enormous sums in these securities – the greatest part, in fact, of the thirteen billions in French investment in Russia.[46] For no little reason, therefore, the Soviet repudiation set off a public outcry in France which became a matter of considerable concern to the French government. In fact, when mere rumours of a Soviet annulation of the state debt first showed up in newspaper copy submitted to the bureau of the censor in Paris during December 1917, the government blocked their publication in order not "to sow ... panic" among French investors.[47] But the Quai d'Orsay and ministry of finance also feared the development of a current of opinion capable of pressuring the state to assume responsibility for the payment of interest on the tsarist bonds. As one *consigne* given to the bureau of the censor put it, the government wished "to be able to make a decision [regarding the payment of interest on the bonds] in complete freedom and not under the pressure of unthinking movements of opinion."[48]

The efforts of the government to suppress or at least to control the discussion of this question in the press were not very successful. The Parisian papers began to demand that the government assume responsibility for the interest on the bonds. The financial press argued that the state had a moral, if not a legal responsibility to pay the coupon, the interest on the Russian securities, because the government had encouraged the purchase of bonds to reinforce the Franco-Russian alliance. To invest in Russia had been a patriotic act because it had supported the government's foreign policy and, in a sense, had "financed the alliance." Moreover, it was because of government encouragement that the French public had purchased and then held on to the Russian bonds, especially during the Revolution of 1905.[49] One financial journal in Paris, the *Cote Vidal*, even threatened the government with a scandal on the scale of Panama (during the 1890s), if it did not protect the interests of French investors.[50]

Nor was the discussion of the Soviet repudiation of the tsarist bonds limited to the financial press. The great circulation dailies like *Le Petit*

*Parisien, Le Petit Journal,* and *Le Journal,* as well as the influential journals of opinion *Le Figaro* and *Le Temps* began to comment on the issue.[51] And not without a certain irony, French Socialists began to take a stand – with the government and against payment of the coupon.[52] The debate even spilled over into the Chamber of Deputies in January 1918 where a somewhat heated exchange took place.[53]

There was thus heavy domestic pressure on the government between January and June and again during the late summer of 1918 to take some responsibility for French investments in Russia. The government did not bend to this pressure initially, and in April it suspended the payment of interest on the Russian bonds, a responsibility it had assumed in a wartime agreement with the tsarist government in October 1915.[54] Interestingly enough, this domestic political debate took place precisely when the government was considering military collaboration with the Bolsheviks. To be sure, there is no evidence to indicate that the government connected the two issues; however, French policy-makers could surely not have failed to consider the prospect of an angry public reaction, should it be learned that the government intended to collaborate with a regime which had just dispossessed French citizens of billions in tsarist securities. If French policy-makers were thinking in such terms, then the *rapprochement* with the Bolsheviks would have been seen as an even greater liability which, aside from other disadvantages, risked unchaining the fury of French investors and therefore augmenting pressure on the government to pay the coupon. The interest on the Russian bonds would have been much too high a price to pay for the dubious advantage of maintaining the *détente* with the Soviet regime.

Aside from the potentially dangerous reactions of French business circles to the accommodation with the Bolsheviks, the government also had to be concerned about the response of the socialist left to its foreign policy. The French Socialist and trade union movements had been growing in strength in the years before the war. Both movements favoured pacifism and anti-militarism, ideas forcefully enunciated by the head of the Socialist party, Jean Jaurès. But on the eve of the outbreak of hostilities, Jaurès was assassinated, and left-wing opposition to the war collapsed in a wave of patriotic hysteria. When mobilization orders were issued, Socialists and syndicalists alike shouldered their rifles and dutifully marched off to fight the German army.

There were, however, a few Socialists and union men who were not swept away by this early martial spirit, and their numbers grew as the conflict continued. Like Lenin and the Bolsheviks they viewed the war as a bloody quarrel between rival capitalist states of which the principal victims were the working classes. These French socialists were not Bolsheviks by any means, but their persistent opposition to the war eventually divided the Socialist party into *majoritaire-minoritaire* factions. The anti-war group was in the minority but its strength grew, especially after the outbreak of revolution in Russia gave new enthusiasm to the movement for peace.

The Bolshevik seizure of power only heightened French socialist interest in the revolution in Russia. To be sure, *majoritaires* like Albert Thomas condemned the Bolsheviks and favoured intervention, but *minoritaire* spokesmen did not and began to express their suspicion that the French government's hostility to the Bolsheviks was motivated more by its dislike of social revolution than by the prospect of a Soviet separate peace with Germany.[55] Furthermore, in May 1918 a rash of strikes in France evolved into political demonstrations condemning the war and acclaiming the Russian Revolution.[56] The danger of such strikes was not ignored by the French government. Indeed, there is plentiful evidence in the *consignes* of the bureau of the censor that the government wished to avoid the exacerbation of "class" strife in France. News of strikes and demonstrations was almost completely banned. Moreover, dispatches from Russia concerning revolutionary measures of socialization and property seizures were ordered "largely censored in view of the pernicious influence they could exercise in France."[57]

The government thus found itself in a delicate situation in which it had to wend its way carefully to avoid offending critics of either the right or the left. Domestic politics must therefore be added to the various factors enumerated by the Quai d'Orsay which weighed against the policy of collaboration with the Bolsheviks. Although the left would have been placated by such a policy, financial circles would have been incensed. Hence, after Noulens took complete charge of the French diplomatic and military mission in Russia, the *détente* with the Bolsheviks was allowed to die quietly. As for the general staff, it moved rapidly into conformity with Quai d'Orsay opinion. A late April memorandum from the 3e Bureau noted that because of the dangers involved in the creation of a Red Army, it would be impossible "to give the Bolshevik government the effective assistance in the reorganization of its army which it appeared to desire."[58]

## NOULENS'S OPPOSITION TO
## THE BOLSHEVIKS

While the French government decided to end the *rapprochement* with the Bolsheviks, London appeared to take a greater interest in an accommodation in order to gain Soviet consent for intervention. In spite of Noulens's activities aimed at sabotaging the *détente*, some important negotiations continued to take place in Moscow during April and early

May, principally between Lockhart and Trotsky. Although the Quai d'Orsay did not respond favourably to these talks, London seemed prepared to negotiate. Trotsky, for his part, wished to pursue this option, but stated that he could not invite the Allies into Russia without adequate guarantees. A certain exchange of views took place, and the British were sufficiently satisfied with the progress of the talks to ask Paris to curb the activities of Noulens. A.J. Balfour, the British foreign secretary, felt that Noulens's interest in protecting French investments in Russia was diverting his attention from the purely "military question affecting the policy of intervention."[59] In an interview with Cambon, Balfour explained that the British government had never believed in the possibility of an "explicit and sincere entente" with the Bolsheviks against Germany. However, he believed that it would be imprudent to provoke a rupture which would throw the Bolsheviks into the arms of the Central Powers. The situation was not clear, and would undoubtedly expose the Allies to disagreeable incidents. But this was preferable to a clear situation where the Entente would watch the Soviets come to terms with the Germans. "If one did not want either rupture or accord with the [Soviet government], it [was] necessary to resign oneself to poorly defined relations full of disadvantages, but which in the present circumstances offered a minimum of security."[60]

Noulens reacted with disdain to the exchanges between the British and Trotsky. He pointed out that the conditions under discussion gave advantages to the Bolsheviks but furnished none to the Allies. In fact, the guarantees of territorial integrity and non-interference proposed by the British would only reinforce the power of the Bolsheviks against those parties most favourable to the Allied cause without giving the Soviet government the real force of which the Entente could make use. To this end Trotsky had made only "vague" promises, such as to constitute an army, oppose exports to Germany, and generally to accept Allied aid only in the measure that it was consistent with the interests of Russia. Furthermore, while the French were asked not to intervene in the domestic affairs of Russia, no similar engagement had been required of the Bolsheviks who openly declared their intention to foster social revolution in other countries.[61]

Noulens's opposition to collaboration was closely connected with his wish to prevent the anti-Bolshevik opposition from moving into the German camp. According to his cable of 7 April, Allied representatives in Russia had initially agreed to Trotsky's request for military assistance in hopes of provoking rupture between Russia and the Central Powers. However, on 12 April he observed that before Soviet military reorganization could be completed, it would provoke a German counterresponse (that is, it would achieve the ends hoped for by Allied agents in

Russia as stated Noulens's 7 April dispatch). Noulens remarked that the work was condemned from the outset and would only compromise the French in the eyes of their "best friends." The Bolsheviks were not capable of putting up a "serious resistance" to Germany, said Noulens, because "all national sentiment excluded it." Therefore, any force Trotsky succeeded in forming would only serve as "an instrument of domestic oppression" and a weapon of class war. Noulens clearly implied that a resumption of the war in Russia would be undesirable with the Bolsheviks in power at Moscow because any extension of the German occupation would prompt the anti-Bolshevik opposition to come to terms with the Central Powers.[62] This view was reinforced by anti-Bolshevik spokesmen who were alarmed by Allied contacts with the Soviets, and they warned French agents that these ties could well lead to just such an eventuality.[63] In short, Noulens and the Quai d'Orsay were disinclined to treat with a government intending to liquidate those political and economic groups upon which French influence had been based before the war, or likely to drive these oppositionist parties into an accommodation with the Germans. In either case, future French interests in Russia would be ruined. As Noulens put it, if the Allies committed the error of seeking a rapprochement with the Soviets, they would deliver Russia to the enemy and lose any hope of maintaining "their situation" there.[64]

## JAPANESE INTERVENTION

The final link in the chain of circumstances leading to the French decision to oppose the Soviet government was Japanese intervention in Siberia. At the inter-Allied conference of Paris in December 1917, the British and French were eager proponents of such an operation, but agreement was blocked by Japanese-American rivalry. Nevertheless, the question continued to be discussed, and in January 1918 there was talk of an Allied occupation extending gradually to the Ural Mountains. At the same time, however, the Quai d'Orsay was forced to admit that the Allies needed more detailed intelligence before they could formulate a policy for action in Siberia.[65]

In February there was a flurry of activity as the Allies sought to reach agreement on a mutually acceptable policy. By the end of the month the French and British almost succeeded in getting the American president, Woodrow Wilson, to permit Japanese intervention. According to Professor George Kennan, a cable from the French ambassador in Tokyo, Eugène Regnault, was largely responsible for this near reversal in U.S. policy. This dispatch, as forwarded to the American government, reported that the Japanese foreign minister, Viscount Ichiro Motono, "was ready to pledge his country to act so far as the Ural Mts." and to promise a public declaration of disinterestedness (to calm Russian and American misgivings about Japanese intentions).[66] However, Regnault's actual dispatch to Paris states only that Motono had indicated that Japan was prepared to go to Irkutsk and "even beyond."[67] When Philippe Berthelot passed on this information to the French ambassador in Washington, J.J. Jusserand, he misrepresented Motono's declaration in attributing to him the understanding that the Allies would only approve intervention if Japan would give a public guarantee of disinterestedness and would engage to go to the Urals to fight the Germans.[68] "Even beyond" thus became "so far as the Ural Mts.," and a declaration of disinterestedness was imputed to Motono when in fact none appears to have been offered. It would therefore seem that Berthelot and Jusserand were responsible for an intentional distortion of Motono's words, calculated to reduce U.S. misgivings about the efficacy of intervention in Siberia as a menace to Germany and to overcome Washington's reluctance to facilitate the extension of Japanese influence in east Asia.

This incident, as described by Kennan, conveys the impression that the French were thinking of a far-reaching Japanese military operation in Siberia. This was not, however, the case. In the first week of March the Quai d'Orsay received important indications that Japan did not regard intervention in Siberia as urgent, and would not envisage operations beyond Irkutsk except on the formal promise of "territorial and other advantages."[69] The Quai d'Orsay rapidly absorbed this information and passed it on in a major policy review to Jusserand. The French attitude, Pichon noted, was affected first of all by the belief that Japan was bound to intervene in Asia in defence of its interests. If it went ahead without Allied approval, it would act against the interests of the Entente and would not delay in coming to terms with Germany. He maintained that only an inter-Allied accord would permit guarantees assuring that Japanese action would not violate Russian sovereignty, would oppose German expansion, and would assure the maintenance of Russian unity, "which necessarily implies the re-establishment of order." Intervention was essential because indigenous Russian groups were incapable of ending the anarchy running unchecked in the country. Pichon envisaged that Japanese military action would secure the Trans-Siberian to Chita and re-establish the anti-Bolshevik governments at Irkutsk and Tomsk. A wider ranging operation against the Germans in European Russia, on the other hand, was a much more difficult and distant question. The Japanese general staff had indicated that it was ready to study the problem but that any military action beyond Irkutsk would require long preparation and, the financial assistance of the Allies. Pichon observed, however, that Japan could not commit itself to such a vast enterprise without the stipulation of "territorial advantages." Although present negotiations need not be concerned with this matter, the question should be studied since the Allies could not know what the war might yet have in store.[70]

Pichon's cable indicates that the Quai d'Orsay had a relatively realistic understanding of the limits of Japanese intervention, especially in comparison with the British who, according to Professor Richard Ullman, "persistently refused to recognize the purport" of Japanese statements clearly outlining their limited intentions in Siberia.[71] The French more or less took Japanese signals of intent at their face value, hoping eventually to secure a greater commitment. It should also be pointed out that Pichon's directive regarded the "re-establishment of order," which meant the destruction of the Soviet government, as a prerequisite to the reconstitution of a greater Russia. The ministry of war, it will be remembered, considered the Bolsheviks a force for unity, given the successful extension of their authority, and as such a potential menace to the Germans. To be sure, the Quai d'Orsay and the ministry of war were agreed on the importance of intervention in Siberia and even its aims. But the ministry of war tended to ignore the obvious consequences of this policy on their relations with the Bolsheviks, or preferred to treat European Russia and Siberia as two entirely separate theatres of action.[72] Perhaps having recognized the difficulty in reconciling Japanese intervention with collaboration with the Bolsheviks, the ministry of war preferred not to choose between the two policies. The Quai d'Orsay, however, showed no such reticence.

Even in early March Berthelot drew attention to the essential incompatability of seeking both collaboration with the Bolsheviks and intervention by Japan. He characterized Lockhart's attempt to get Soviet consent for a Japanese presence in Siberia as both "contradictory and absurd." Tokyo had taken a clearly hostile position toward the Bolsheviks, he observed, and its intervention would be directed against Bolshevik anarchy to re-establish order and to facilitate the reconstitution of a free Russia.[73] French views in this respect were only reinforced by complaints from Tokyo about the Allied "flirtation" with Moscow.[74] Noulens, whose views accurately reflected those of the Quai d'Orsay, observed that Japan would act with or without Allied support, and he stated plainly that it was better to abandon the idea of a *rapprochement* with the Soviets than to risk alienating the Japanese and the anti-Bolsheviks, both of whom could turn to the Central Powers.[75] In any case, the Bolsheviks hated the Allies as much as the Germans, but feared the latter and thus yielded to their demands. It was impossible to suppose, said Noulens, that a government which abjectly sacrificed national interests to pursue class war, could ever be an ally or represent a real force.[76]

As Berthelot put it in an April memorandum, the oppositionist parties would be incapable of successfully resisting either the Germans or the Bolsheviks without financial and military assistance from the Allies. Japan offered the only hope of providing this support, and the Americans would incur a "grave responsibility" if they continued to oppose Japanese action in Siberia.

It is above all a question of intervening in Siberia in the name of the [anti-Bolshevik] Siberian government, and it is therefore absurd to ask the opinion of the Bolsheviks since it is against them, their violence, their anarchy, and their scornful refusal of any normal consultation of the Russian population, that we would be intervening to re-establish order.

The attitude of the American government has completely confused the issue and led the British government to follow the recommendations of its semi-official agent in Moscow who is pursuing the illusion of an entente with the Bolsheviks....

Only the French and Japanese governments have since the beginning, in agreement with one another, properly defined the terms of the problem, which is not only political and military, but economic as well: we can bring to Russia not only order and liberty, but we can also furnish the manufactured goods which [the Russian population] so desperately needs....

In view of the urgent necessity of pulling Russia out from under Germany's domination, and in view of the probability of unleashing the forces of resistance in Russia and all its healthy elements, it is necessary that the European allies take decisive action in Washington both to denounce the error of attempting to reach an entente with the Bolsheviks ... and to bring about intervention.[77]

If the Quai d'Orsay's *démarches* to Washington and London were not as strongly worded as the above note, it was only because, as Berthelot pointed out, the French wished to allow the British and Americans to recognize themselves "the inanity and danger" of collaboration with the Bolsheviks.[78]

There can be no question that the Berthelot memorandum represented a statement of the Quai d'Orsay's basic attitude toward the Bolsheviks.[79] Berthelot wrote most of the existing draft cables concerning the *détente* with the Soviet government and the need to intervene against it; Pichon simply signed them without revision. Moreover, Berthelot's general influence in the Quai d'Orsay has long been recognized by historians and other political commentators.[80] During Clemenceau's tenure as premier, this influence became all the greater because of the unassertiveness of Pichon, whom Clemenceau later described as "very weak [and] unable to make up his own mind on anything."[81] The British ambassador in Paris, Edward Lord Derby, rather contemptuously observed in late 1918 that Pichon could say "nothing but ditto to his chief [Clemenceau]."[82] Pichon appears to have acted in much the same way with Berthelot. Although the two men were "old friends," Berthelot, at least at this time, dominated their relationship.[83] Derby and his predecessor, Sir Francis Bertie, commented many times on Pichon's weakness and the pervasive, almost diabolical influence of Berthelot at the Quai d'Orsay.[84]

This influence was based on long years of experience and on an aggressive, strongly competitive personality. Berthelot had entered the foreign service in 1889 six years before his father, Marcellin, briefly served as foreign minister. The younger Berthelot's real influence at the Quai d'Orsay appears to have begun in 1914. During the war he fought tenaciously for power with his immediate superior, Margerie, a struggle which did not end until 1918 when the latter fell seriously ill. Berthelot's ascendancy was aided by a prodigious capacity for work. His admirers declared that he rose at four o'clock in the morning and functioned on only three hours' sleep a night. Long hours put in at the Quai d'Orsay enabled him to master all the important questions with which the government had to deal.[85] His detractors, however, described him as an arrogant, ruthless intriguer who sought to draw all power in the Quai d'Orsay exclusively into his own hands.[86]

The *éminence grise* of French foreign policy was also a diplomat of few scruples and with a predilection for "clear solutions."[87] This aversion to ambiguity no doubt increased Berthelot's opposition to any dealings with the Bolsheviks. Interestingly enough, one early Soviet historian stigmatized Noulens as "the father of the intervention" in Russia.[88] But this characterization more appropriately applies to Berthelot, who appears to have been the guiding spirit of Quai d'Orsay opposition to the Allied-Soviet *détente* and who, according to Paul Cambon, deluged French posts abroad with long cables condemning any accommodation with the Bolsheviks.[89]

Berthelot's April memorandum upon which most, if not all, of these cables were based, represented a recapitulation of the arguments already set out in the Quai d'Orsay dispatches of 30 March–1 April and subsequently put forward by Noulens. The Soviet regime was condemned for having signed the treaty of Brest-Litovsk. Yet the Quai d'Orsay was entirely aware that the oppositionist parties, which the French hoped to keep on the Allied side, might well turn to the Central Powers, should the Entente fail to support them against the Bolsheviks. Furthermore, Niessel had reported in March that any government in Moscow would have to submit initially to German military and diplomatic blackmail.[90] Given Niessel's observation and the Quai d'Orsay's own views, its condemnation of the Soviet regime for having signed a German peace was at least partially self-serving since the oppositionist parties were re-garded as even more enfeebled than the Bolsheviks and more partial to the Central Powers. This criticism of the Soviet peace was also some-what disingenuous in view of the previous popularity among certain French generals and politicians, including Pichon, of "a peace on the back of Russia." Moreover, even Noulens did not initially condemn the Bolsheviks as German agents, but rather as revolutionaries trying to manœuvre between two equally hostile great power coalitions.[91] Finally, it is reasonable to assume that Trotsky's "vague" promises, as they were characterized by Noulens, concerning Russian resistance against Ger-many would have sufficed to assure French support, had they been made by an anti-Bolshevik government. Berthelot stated that the French desired to bring Russia "order and liberty," but what they really sought was to save their menaced political and economic interests. The problem posed by the Japanese intervention appears to have acted as a catalyst in the development of this thinking. Japanese pressure against the Allied-Soviet rapprochement and French fears that Japan might act unilaterally reinforced the Quai d'Orsay's opposition to any arrangement with Trotsky.

By the end of April 1918 Paris was thoroughly committed to over-throwing the Bolshevik regime. The basic assumptions underlying this decision remained unchanged: that the reconstitution of an Eastern Front was impossible, and that the anti-Bolsheviks were too weak to challenge the Soviet regime.[92] The central objectives of government pol-icy, as interpreted by the general staff, continued to be (1) the obstruc-tion of German expansion in the east, and (2) the re-establishment of French influence in a "regenerated Russia."[93] Significantly, this final shift of policy in Paris began at the high point of the Allied-Soviet *détente*. Kennan points out that the Bolsheviks, recognizing the need for disciplined armed forces and fearing Japanese intervention "were never more cooperative, correct, and obliging than in their dealings during the last days of March and the first days of April with that portion of the Allied official colony in Moscow which they felt was well inclined towards them and favoured the development of military collabora-tion."[94] Moreover, the general staff's note of 5 April clearly implied a certain confidence in the Bolsheviks, and made the connection between the German offensive in France and the need for even a minimal diver-sion in the east in order to support and not to oppose the policy of military collaboration.

Kennan states that "liberal or left-wing opinion" has been inclined to accuse the Allies of having "spurned either from shortsightedness or from motives of imperialist greed, a perfectly acceptable alternative to the intervention they later undertook against the wishes and resistance of the Soviet government."[95] Although Kennan rejects this point of view, the evidence indicates that the French government did reject a *rapprochement* with the Bolsheviks at a time of improved Soviet-Allied relations. Paradoxically, Trotsky appears to have been best informed of French intentions. In 1925 when asked why these negotiations for collaboration had failed, he replied that "Lavergne had 'apparently' received instructions from Paris that the coming struggle was to be *against*, not *with* the Bolsheviks."[96]

It should also be kept in mind that this rejected policy was not simply the pipe dream of unimportant agents in Russia. Ullman and Kennan, for example, dismiss the concept of Soviet-Allied military collaboration as an ill-conceived idea, or as something built up out of all proportion by unofficial, over-enthusiastic Allied agents.[97] Although this characterization of British and American attitudes may be correct, it does not accurately describe French thinking. Military collaboration was government policy for approximately nine weeks, and the offer of French aid was unconditional as long as the Bolsheviks began to organize against the Central Powers.[98]

Why then did the French abandon a pragmatic policy for one of inflexible hostility toward the Soviet regime? Why was the French government unwilling to settle for an "ambiguous" relationship with the Bolsheviks, as Balfour put it in May? Why did Paris turn from a *rapprochement* at the high point of Allied-Soviet co-operation? The answer would appear to be that from the French perspective much more was at stake than just the question of restored eastern resistance to Germany. Had this not been so, the general staff's policy of military collaboration would in all likelihood have continued, since in its view the Bolsheviks were the only Russian political elements capable of leading further resistance to the Central Powers. Certainly, when it appeared that the Bolsheviks would not sign a peace, the Quai d'Orsay was also prepared, albeit reluctantly, to aid Soviet resistance. However, in a situation where neither the Bolsheviks nor their political opponents could openly continue the war, it became preferable to support the anti-Bolshevik opposition. The Quai d'Orsay, unlike the ministry of war, looked beyond the simple military problem posed by the collapse of Russia. It feared that anti-Bolshevik, so-called patriotic elements would be lost to the Germans or wiped out should the government continue the policy of *rapprochement*. France's former "friends" would be thrown from influence by the Bolsheviks, who, if their government survived, would never permit the French to re-establish their formerly preponderant positions in Russia. If the Soviets did not survive, which was more likely, the French would only succeed in alienating the anti-Bolsheviks, and in fostering co-operation between these elements and the Central

Powers. Even if the Entente should win the war, the anti-Bolsheviks would probably retain power, and thus constitute a potential ally for a resurgent Germany. Essentially, the Quai d'Orsay regarded the future disposition of these anti-Bolshevik parties as central to the French position in Russia, and any limited military advantage to be gained from collaboration with the Bolsheviks was not worth the sacrifice of long-term political, strategic, and economic interests. To be sure, the Quai d'Orsay was not totally uninterested in organizing new resistance to the Central Powers in the east, but from its point of view the Russian question had ceased to be primarily military in nature. To save French influence in Russia, and conversely to fight that of Germany, was essentially a political objective, not served by military collaboration with the Soviet government.

Finally, the French diplomatic and military archives to some degree substantiate early "liberal or left-wing" views concerning the origins of the intervention in Russia. The French example, however, does not entirely fit the old-left stereotype. The French general staff, influenced by military considerations, favoured rather than opposed a *rapprochement* with the Soviet regime. But the Quai d'Orsay regarded the policy of military collaboration as incompatible with the restoration of French diplomatic and economic influence in Russia, and therefore prevailed upon the ministry of war to end the *détente*. The French government finally concluded that to save its interests in Russia, it must overthrow the Bolsheviks and put down the *jacquerie*. The intervention was the fruit of this presupposition.

## CHAPTER FOUR

# Intervention, *MAY-JULY 1918:*
# The Enemy Engaged

April 1918 was the turning point for the French government in the development of its interventionist policy against Soviet Russia. But the French decision to intervene remained largely one of principle since London and Washington were both still divided and appeared desirous of avoiding an irreparable break with the Soviet regime. The Quai d'Orsay therefore made every effort to persuade its allies to adopt the French policy of hostility to the Bolsheviks. At the same time the Quai d'Orsay sought to locate and encourage those anti-Bolshevik groups in Russia capable of opposing Soviet authority. This was not a very aggressive policy, but the French government was too preoccupied by the German offensive and too dependent on its allies to undertake more direct action against the Bolsheviks. The Quai d'Orsay hoped that events in Russia, if not its own diplomatic efforts, would lead the Americans and British to adopt an aggressively interventionist policy in which the French could then take a hand.

The event which soon led to this development was the rebellion in Siberia of the pro-Allied Czechoslovak Legion. These Czech troops, who were organized to fight the Germans, rose instead against the Bolsheviks and in June and July seized control of most of the Trans-Siberian Railway. The French government was of course encouraged by the news of the spreading rebellion against the Soviets and moved to support Czech resistance. At the same time French agents in Moscow, where the capital had been moved in March, gave money to local anti-Bolshevik groups and tried to co-ordinate their actions to topple the Soviet government. The revolts launched by these groups in July were not successful, but the Soviets, assailed on all sides, appeared staggered and moribund.

## EARLY FRENCH CONTACTS WITH THE
## ANTI-BOLSHEVIK OPPOSITION

The first efforts of the French government to encourage the anti-Bolshevik parties came in early April. At this time the Quai d'Orsay authorized its consul general in Moscow, Fernand Grenard, to enter into contact with anti-Bolshevik groups and to encourage any signs of pro-Allied activity on their part.[1] In the following weeks Grenard duly entered into relations with Socialist Revolutionaries N.D. Avksent'ev and B.V. Savinkov; Kadets N.M. Kishkin and N.I. Astrov; conservatives E.N. Trubetskoi, A.V. Krivoshein, V.I. Gurko; and the former Marxist turned conservative P.B. Struve. These men were representatives of the four major opposition groups then operating in Moscow. Avksent'ev spoke for the Left Centre, later known as the Union for the Regeneration of Russia which represented mostly SR and Left Kadet opinion. Savinkov, an SR terrorist before the revolution, formed his own group called the Union for the Defence of Fatherland and Freedom which was essentially a military organization made up of officers and cadets. Trubetskoi and Krivoshein spoke in the name of the Right Centre, a conservative, monarchist grouping which tended to look to Germany for salvation from Bolshevism. Indeed, the predominantly pro-German attitude of the Right Centre led to a split in which its left wing, composed largely of Kadets, formed a new organization called the National Centre. Astrov and Kishkin appeared to speak in the name of this group with which Savinkov would subsequently associate his own organization.[2]

From the numerous conversations which Grenard had with these men, the Quai d'Orsay learned that Savinkov had formed a military organization in Moscow whose aim was to infiltrate and eventually overthrow the Bolshevik government. The more left-leaning of these organizations envisaged the formation of a provisional "socialist-bourgeois" government intended to re-establish order and to co-operate with the Allies "as soon as possible" in the struggle against Germany.[3] Avksent'ev in his conversations with Grenard seemed to hold out the prospect of a renewed Russian war effort as an incentive to obtain Allied support for his group. The conservatives, however, were more candid in this regard. Trubetskoi told Grenard that the Allies ought to give up the "illusion" that Russia could rejoin the war. No Russian government would undertake such a commitment. In any case, both Trubetskoi and Avksent'ev expressed the hope that the Allies would stop their aid to the Red Army. Trubetskoi warned that, if they did not, the Central Powers would gain influence at the expense of the Entente because the anti-Bolsheviks would turn to Germany for support.[4]

All the anti-Bolshevik factions wanted Allied military and financial support. Avksent'ev indicated that his organization lacked arms and was having difficulty raising troops. He stated that the anti-Bolsheviks needed a reliable force around which to unite, and thought that an Allied occupation of Arkhangelsk could provide this support. For his part, Trubetskoi believed that the disorder of the revolution would eventually undermine Bolshevik popularity and make possible a *coup de main* in Moscow. He felt that Allied financial backing would assure the success of such an operation and asked Grenard for fifteen to twenty million roubles in aid. Just so the French might know what would happen if this assistance was not forthcoming, Krivoshein told Grenard that they would overthrow the Soviets with or without Allied support, and, if need be, with the help of the Germans.[5]

The Quai d'Orsay was alarmed by these threats and became all the more anxious to end the *rapprochement* with the Bolsheviks. But French agents were not greatly impressed by the men and organizations with which they came into contact. Grenard regarded the Trubetskoi group as much too conservative to gain popular support. Even among the left-leaning groups Grenard thought only Savinkov had any hope of taking power.[6] He reported that the former terrorist had gathered a few thousand men in Moscow. Grenard warned that because of the weakness of the individual anti-Bolshevik parties a union of opposition forces would be necessary for any success against the Bolsheviks. He observed, however, that such a union had yet to be formed.[7]

Noulens shared Grenard's views. The ambassador regarded Trubetskoi and Avksent'ev as typical of liberal and SR opinion, which he characterized as weak, indecisive, and responsible for the Russian defection from the war. Noulens commented that Trubetskoi and Avksent'ev spoke as though they represented a real force, which was not in fact the case. These groups were incompetent and leaderless and would unite only under strong Allied or German influence. Noulens warned that the Entente should act quickly to prevent the anti-Bolsheviks from going over to the enemy.[8]

But what could the Allies do? This became the key question which all the anti-Bolshevik groups posed, and to which French agents were hard put to supply an answer. As Grenard observed, "our fault is that we are far away. We are reproached for not aiding our friends."[9] Anti-Bolshevik spokesmen like Gurko and Krivoshein "were pushed," said Grenard, "by their troops, the bourgeoisie which counted on the Germans to re-establish order and mistrusted the Allies ... because of their hesitations and their inability to agree among themselves." Given the circumstances, Grenard concluded that Russia could be saved from Bolshevism and Germany only by Allied intervention.[10]

Grenard therefore requested that 4 to 5 million roubles be put at his disposal to aid the anti-Bolshevik opposition. He cautioned, however, that the government should not expect too much from the Russians who were afflicted by a "profound and universal malaise."[11] Noulens approved Grenard's conclusions which confirmed his own about "the incapacity" of the Russians and the necessity for armed intervention. It was evident, he said, that the Entente should make use of those Russian elements favourable to the Allied cause, giving them financial support in anticipation of military intervention. But Noulens regarded the anti-Bolsheviks with venomous contempt, treating them as little better than spoilt, incapable children, "always given to exaggeration," who could be pacified with a more modest subvention than the 4 to 5 million proposed by Grenard. Consequently, he authorized Grenard to put 500,000 roubles at Savinkov's disposal to be paid out in two or three installments by the end of June.[12]

Later on, after the revolution, Noulens wrote in his memoirs that he had not compromised himself or his staff in Savinkov's activities.[13] The evidence, however, tells a different story and shows that Noulens did authorize subsidies for Savinkov and later on for other anti-Bolshevik groups as well. Grenard indicated after his return from Russia that he had, on the authorization of Noulens, given 250,000 roubles to Avksent'ev and Kishkin. When the Russians were offended by the modesty of this sum, the ambassador had agreed to increase the subvention to 1½ millions.[14] Grenard was also in contact with other SR groups and asked for authorization to provide them with 100,000 roubles for propaganda.[15] Berthelot agreed three days later.[16] Finally, on 7 May, Pichon authorized Noulens, in the event that communications broke down with Paris, to make disbursements for which he could not obtain prior approval. The French ambassador was also authorized to give Grenard this same privilege, should their own communications break down.[17]

Armed with these authorizations, Noulens allowed Grenard to encourage the widest possible union of anti-Bolshevik groups based on a program of coalition government and Allied intervention.[18] But Grenard was careful to remain in the background and would not make any far-reaching commitments to his anti-Bolshevik contacts. Noulens approved of Grenard's discretion but continued to press hard for Allied intervention.[19] The ambassador also kept Paris informed of SR plans for an insurrection against the Bolsheviks. On 9 May he reported that Savinkov had increased the strength of his organization and, if need be, could immediately begin an uprising; however, he wanted assurances that the Allies would support him by occupying Vologda.[20] Two weeks later Noulens learned from Grenard that the SRs and Savinkov were preparing to launch an insurrection in the Volga region in the middle of June if circumstances permitted.[21]

In spite of this news, there was little Paris could do to aid Savinkov's cause.[22] With war raging on the Western Front, the French general staff could not spare troops for action in Russia against the Soviets. Moreover, Berthelot's campaign against an accommodation with Moscow and for Japanese intervention was not producing results. As long as this situation persisted, the Quai d'Orsay had to act cautiously in regard to Russia; it could not risk offending its allies when the outcome of fighting on the Western Front depended on British and especially fresh American troops.[23]

At the beginning of May 1918 the French government was largely incapable of influencing events in Russia. Within weeks, however, this situation suddenly began to change to French advantage. In the first place, the British government, to the great relief of the Quai d'Orsay, lost interest in the policy of *rapprochement*. Even Lockhart, the French *bête noire*, who had tried to gain Bolshevik consent for intervention, changed his colours and began to support the anti-Bolshevik opposition.[24]

At the same time other events in Russia were developing in a manner favourable to the interests of the interventionists in Paris. Noulens continued his efforts to disrupt relations between the Allies and the Soviet government. The ambassador made an extremely hostile public statement on 23 April attacking the Bolsheviks and seeking to justify Allied intervention against them. Naturally, Bolshevik leaders were angered, viewing this statement as an effort to break up their talks with the British and as a sign of the deterioration of their relations with the Allied powers. The commissar for foreign affairs, Chicherin, demanded the recall of Noulens while expressing the hope that the ambassador's remarks did not represent the views of the French government. The Quai d'Orsay ignored Chicherin's *démarche* and the Bolsheviks concluded that no further co-operation with the Allies could be expected. Consequently, in early May Lenin moved his party to accept a policy of appeasing Germany which continued to press demands on the Soviet government. Such a policy would certainly antagonize the Allies, but the Bolsheviks considered them a lesser enemy, whose danger to Soviet power could be contained.[25] This was very nearly a fatal miscalculation because the Allied menace soon proved more formidable than Lenin had anticipated. Allied-organized Czech troops, *en route* from the Ukraine to Vladivostok on the Trans-Siberian Railway, rose in revolt against the Bolsheviks, opening all Siberia to the counter-revolution.

## THE CZECHOSLOVAK LEGION

The Czech Legion was formed in Russia in 1917 largely from Czech and Slovak prisoners of war from the Austro-Hungarian army. It was initially intended for action on the Eastern Front as an arm of the Czech independence movement led by T.G. Masaryk and Eduard Beneš. But the collapse of the Russian army in 1917 prompted the Czech National Council in Paris to press for the transfer of the Czech Legion to France. The French government became the principal interested party in this matter because in December 1917 all Czech military forces being organized by the Allies were placed under the direct authority of the French high command. Consequently, it was French representatives who began to talk with Moscow about the evacuation of the Czechs to France. In the beginning these conversations were inconclusive because the French government initially considered using the legion as part of a southern coalition against the Bolsheviks and then, when the policy of accommodation was adopted, with the Soviet regime against Germany.[26] This latter policy was short-lived, however, and in early April, on the insistence of the Czech National Council, the French government decided to evacuate the legion from Russia via Vladivostok, initially the only possible route of escape.[27]

To secure transportation to Vladivostok, Czech representatives concluded agreements with both Moscow and local Soviet authorities. The local arrangements provided that the Czechs would give up the greater part of their arms in exchange for authorization to cross Siberia.[28] Yet neither side appears to have acted entirely in good faith in carrying out these agreements. The Czechs concealed quantities of arms in excess of those allowed by the Bolsheviks, and Moscow, and especially local Soviet authorities, began to have serious misgivings about allowing disciplined armed forces not under their control to move into Siberia. The disarmament question, as events would show, played into the hands of the interventionist Noulens and provided the spark which ignited the Czech uprising in late May.

Just as the French government and the Czech National Council were reaching agreement on the evacuation of the legion, London began to complicate matters by proposing that the Czechs be left in Russia. The British War Office thought that the Czech Legion would be of greater use to the Allied cause either in Siberia or at Arkhangelsk and Murmansk in the north. But for what purpose the Czechs were to be maintained in Russia, British representatives did not make clear.[29] The French general staff opposed the British proposals essentially because, in its view, Russia had a low priority in the distribution of Allied military resources. The general staff considered it a waste of manpower to leave the Czechs in Russia when there was little prospect of Japanese intervention or the formation of new Russian military forces.[30] Moreover, while the German army still threatened the Western Front, the French government was determined to move every available man, including the Czechs, to the defence of France.[31]

The French and British governments argued over this question for several weeks and finally met at Abbeville in early May to try to resolve their differences. A compromise proposal was worked out whereby part of the legion would be moved to Vladivostok and the rest to Murmansk and Arkhangelsk. The French believed their ultimate destination was still the Western Front, but the War Office apparently remained committed to maintaining the Czechs in Russia.[32]

These decisions were all taken without consultation with Czech commanders in Russia, who were against moving into northern Russia. The troops feared being bottled up there and becoming easy prey for the Germans.[33] Indeed, the idea of turning back toward northern Russia was strongly disliked by the young officers who commanded the legion and contributed to the tension that began to develop between them and local Soviet authorities. This growing antagonism, however, seems to have been caused primarily by the slowness of the Czech evacuation and the desire of various Soviet authorities, both local and in Moscow, to limit the quantity of arms the Czechs were carrying. Moreover, the Czech command was alarmed by Bolshevik agitators operating among its troops, and the Czechs themselves "behav[ed] provocatively towards Russian civilians and Soviet representatives."[34] As tensions increased, so did Czech belligerence. On 14 April battalion and company commanders of the First Czech Division meeting at Kirsanov, west of the Urals, decided that no further arms should be given up and that they ought to be prepared to force their passage eastward.[35]

Because of the increasing hostility between the Czechs and Soviet authorities, it did not take much to set off a clash of arms. On 14 May a brief fight broke out at the railroad station in Cheliabinsk, in western Siberia, between Czech soldiers and Hungarian prisoners of war returning home. One of the latter was killed, and local Soviet authorities intervened, arresting a number of Czech legionnaires. Three days later armed Czech soldiers marched into town, released the prisoners, and disarmed the local Red Guard detachment. The incident was settled locally a few days later, but, when Moscow learned of what had happened, it ordered Czech trains to be stopped and the occupants disarmed.

As these events unfolded, a "Congress of the Czechoslovak Revolutionary Army" was meeting in Cheliabinsk. When delegates of the congress heard of the Moscow directive, they voted on 23 May to defy the

Bolsheviks and shoot their way to Vladivostok if necessary. Trotsky responded, on 25 May, by ordering "every armed Czechoslovak found on the railway ... to be shot on the spot." The following day fighting broke out at several points along the Trans-Siberian.[36]

The open fighting between the Czechs and Bolsheviks completely altered the situation in Russia. Although Paris was slow to grasp the consequences of the revolt, Noulens hastened to urge French support of Czech action. Indeed, the French ambassador had recognized the value of the Czechs as an anti-Bolshevik force many weeks before. On 18 April, for example, Noulens had written to the minister of armaments, Louis Loucheur, suggesting that Czech troops remain in Russia to co-operate with the anti-Bolshevik Volunteer Army of General M.V. Alekseev.[37] Similarly, the ambassador reported on 1 May that a delegation of anti-Bolsheviks from Saratov (the group was not further identified) had suggested in a meeting with Grenard that the Czechs could probably furnish "decisive" aid in any uprising against the Soviets. Noulens indicated that he was not advocating such a scheme, but he thought it worth considering "if the circumstances did not permit a Czech transfer in good time to Arkhangelsk."[38] Nine days later Noulens stressed again that it might be useful to leave the Czechs in Russia. "I simply point out," he said, that the Czechs "would represent a force superior to any which the Allies could divert from the French front to Russia."[39] In mid-May Noulens learned that Czech troops were defying Soviet orders to give up their weapons.[40] The ambassador encouraged this defiance and received a promise from a member of the Czech National Council in Russia to do "everything possible" to prevent his compatriots from surrendering their arms to Soviet authorities. Noulens surmised that the Czechs might defy the Bolsheviks if the latter became too demanding over the conditions of their transportation out of Russia.[41]

Noulens's correspondence indicates that he had some knowledge of the Czech disposition to challenge Soviet authority, and that he appears to have encouraged Czech intransigence on the disarmament issue in order to embroil the legion with the Soviet government. The French ambassador could not do this openly, however, since it would have contravened direct orders from Paris. Nevertheless, the gap between the positions of Clemenceau and Noulens on the Czech issue began to narrow. Although the ministry of war had authorized Lavergne on 27 April to approach the Bolsheviks about the evacuation of the Czechs via the north, its position on this matter hardened in May. On 22 May just before the Czech rising, Clemenceau informed Lavergne that he had come to agree with Noulens's view that it would be "useless" and "dangerous" to seek assistance from Trotsky in the matter of transportation

for the Czechs and that they would eventually have to "dispense" with
Soviet authority.[42] To be sure, Clemenceau still pressed for a Czech
evacuation, but he did not seem to understand that "dispensing" with
Soviet authority would mean embroiling the Czechs in Russia and preventing their evacuation to France. However, if Noulens understood
this point, and it is probable that he did, Clemenceau's 22 May directive
made it easier for the French ambassador to proceed with his own plans
without seeming to oppose the government's desire to evacuate the
Czechs.

In any case, after the Czech rebellion began, the Soviet government
sought assistance from the French military mission in bringing an end to
hostilities. Lavergne at first seemed disposed to try to stop the fighting
and sent out officers to mediate.[43] Noulens, however, was not anxious to
halt the conflict and directed Lavergne to refrain from any action which
might lead to the disarmament of the Czechs.[44] Indeed, when the
ambassador learned that mediation attempts might be successful, he
quickly squelched these efforts. Noulens ordered Lavergne "to warn [his
officers] against any inopportune concessions which risked to turn to the
detriment of the Czechs at the moment when they appeared to command at Syzran [west of the Urals] the course of the Volga and the line
of the Trans-Siberian."[45] Again on 8 June Noulens complained to Grenard about French officers involved in mediation efforts who were
apparently disposed to accept a partial disarmament of Czech troops.
Noulens ordered Lavergne to stipulate to his men that they should show
themselves "intransigent on the question of disarmament and should
not encourage the Czechs ... to give up any part whatsoever of their
[arms].... We do not have any interest," he said, "in hastening a solution
which does not completely satisfy us."[46] Noulens also asked the ministry
of war to give Lavergne unambiguous instructions concerning the conduct of those French officers attached to the legion. The ambassador
expressed the fear that the military mission might still be under the
influence of certain "Soviet *milieux*."[47]

These few cables suggest that members of the French military mission
thought the conflict between the Czechs and Bolsheviks could be medi-
ated and that in fact they set out to do so. Moreover, a settlement was
not completely out of the question since a local armistice was arranged
through Allied agents in the area around Irkutsk on 27 May.[48] The fact
that Noulens still found it necessary to reiterate his orders to Lavergne
on the question of Czech disarmament indicates that French officers on
the spot favoured a compromise, probably because it was the only way
to stop hostilities. Whether these officers could ultimately have succeeded in ending the conflict is perhaps doubtful, but the fact is that

they were disposed to try, and Noulens, who understood the significance of the Czech uprising, obstructed their efforts.

The ambassador's activities are the more important because the Quai d'Orsay gave him considerable freedom of action. Berthelot minuted on a Clemenceau letter of 29 May that Margerie thought it best in view of the uncertain situation in Russia concerning the Czech Legion "not to intervene from Paris" and to give authority to Noulens and Lavergne to direct Czech action as best they could.[49] Since Lavergne could not act independently of Noulens, the ambassador was able to work surreptitiously against Clemenceau's desire to bring the Czech Legion to France.[50] One can only conjecture as to whether Berthelot's minute is an indication that Noulens had sympathizers in the Quai d'Orsay who understood his motives and sought to shield him from the general staff. As for Lavergne, although he may have deplored the Czech rebellion, his efforts to stop it were completely stymied by the intransigence of Noulens.[51] In the end, already out of favour in Paris because of his support for the *rapprochement* with Moscow, Lavergne succumbed to the force of circumstances and gradually became an advocate of intervention.[52]

On 1 June Lavergne reported that fighting was raging between the legion and Bolshevik forces all along the Trans-Siberian and that the Czech rebellion made opportune an Allied military intervention. He indicated that relations had been established between Czech units and an anti-Bolshevik provisional Siberian government.[53] But Lavergne warned Paris a few days later that the Czechs could be isolated if they did not receive military support from an Allied intervention in Siberia or from indigenous anti-Bolshevik groups. Although Lavergne did not express much confidence in the anti-Bolshevik parties, he thought the Cossacks of Orenburg and the Urals could offer useful assistance. If Allied military action were imminent, he recommended that the Czechs be used as a spearhead of intervention.[54] Noulens, who saw events going in a direction favourable to his own policies, pressed insistently for immediate Allied action. Even a symbolic landing at Arkhangelsk, he said, should be undertaken to give the Czechs some proof of Allied support.[55] Similarly, Grenard recommended that financial assistance be extended to various anti-Bolshevik groups. Noulens instructed Grenard to enlist Cossack support and informed Paris that "arrangements had already been made" for financial assistance to the SRs, Alekseev, and Savinkov.[56]

The French government, however, initially rejected pleas from Noulens and Lavergne recommending that the Czech Legion be left in Russia. The general staff continued to think that such action would not be useful as long as an Allied intervention in Siberia and the organization of Russian anti-Bolshevik forces remained in doubt.[57] Intervention and indigenous military support were still considered essential to the success of any Czech operation in Russia.[58]

Nevertheless, both Noulens and Lavergne persisted in pressing their own views. Lavergne reported that Czech forces were overwhelming the Bolsheviks all along the Trans-Siberian. At the beginning, he said, the Czechs intended only to make their way to Vladivostok, but the revolt had given birth to a movement against the Bolsheviks. A government had formed at Omsk which was in liaison with the anti-Bolsheviks at Harbin, in northern Manchuria, and sought to sweep the Soviets out of Siberia. Lavergne recommended that, if intervention were imminent, the Czechs should be instructed to maintain control of the Trans-Siberian and to form a covering zone on the Volga where all the anti-Bolshevik organizations in Russia could gather their forces. While awaiting instructions, Lavergne said he would advise the Czechs to hold their positions.[59]

Under this mounting pressure, French policy began to shift: On 20 June Clemenceau informed Lavergne that, if previous directives concerning the Czechs proved unworkable, the legion could be left temporarily in Russia. Their objectives would be "to constitute a centre of resistance around which Siberian and Cossack elements could gather; to complete the seizure of the Trans-Siberian; [and] to prepare the way for an eventual Allied intervention from the east."[60] As the ministry of war put it a fortnight later, French action in Siberia should not be "paralysed by considerations based on the principle of non-intervention in Russian domestic affairs," but, on the contrary, should seek "to crush anarchistic elements, [and] to develop ... forces capable of impeding the German advance."[61]

These objectives became firm French policy on 12 July when the ministry of war directed the Quai d'Orsay to suspend its efforts to find transportation for the Czechs to France.[62] To the French government it seemed possible that the Czech Legion might after all be of use in Russia both as a vanguard of intervention and as an instrument of French political influence.[63] Noulens had affirmed that Bolshevik authority was crumbling, and intelligence reports from various sources indicated a noticeable increase in the activities of the anti-Bolshevik opposition.[64] Moreover, the general staff, which for a time had regarded the Bolsheviks as the only political party in Russia capable of resisting Germany, now came to view them as agents of the German government.[65] As French historian Jean Delmas put it, the Czech uprising "had the merit of dissipating the ambiguities [which existed] concerning the definition of the enemy in Russia...."[66] Henceforth, the Bolsheviks were considered to be "enfeoffed" to Germany and for the duration of the war were referred to as "Germano-Bolsheviks."[67]

## THE SR UPRISING AT IAROSLAVL

The Czech rebellion gave new impetus to the anti-Bolshevik organizations and in July they rose in open revolt. On 4 July the fifth All-Russian Congress of Soviets met in Moscow. The only parties represented were the Bolsheviks and the Left SRs even though the latter had withdrawn their support from the Soviet government after the ratification of the treaty of Brest-Litovsk. During the congress Left SR delegates denounced the Germans and condemned the Bolsheviks for having concluded a capitulatory peace. On 6 July after an SR resolution calling for a renunciation of the treaty of Brest-Litovsk was voted down, the SRs precipitated a short-lived uprising. The assassination of the German ambassador in Moscow, Count Wilhelm von Mirbach, marked the beginning of the revolt, which collapsed the following day. A more serious anti-Bolshevik rebellion broke out at Iaroslavl on 6 July. Three days later there were further risings at Murom, Rybinsk, and Arzamas. The towns had great strategic importance in any operation trying to link the Czechs with Allied units descending from Arkhangelsk. As historian and journalist Louis Fischer observed,

It is almost a straight north-south line from Archangel to Moscow. The only important towns on the route are Vologda and Jaroslav. Ribinsk is near Jaroslav. It is almost a straight east-west line from Kazan to Moscow. The only important towns on the route are Arzamas and Murom. If all these points fell into the hands of the Allies or their Russian supporters, Moscow and with it the Bolshevik regime were doomed.[68]

French agents had at least a week's notice of the impending revolt with Lavergne reporting it on 29 June. Savinkov and his men would act shortly, Lavergne said, and "they count on being morally supported by the arrival of Allied troops at Arkhangelsk." Although Savinkov had only 5,000 men at his disposal, intervention would mask his weakness and encourage new partisans to join his ranks. Lavergne warned that any delay in the landing would give the Bolsheviks time to act against Allied "friends" in Arkhangelsk.[69] Noulens warned of the same danger. Anti-Bolshevik groups, he said, would be forced to disband if Allied troops did not soon arrive.[70]

In spite of the French ambassador's urgent pleas, the landing at Arkhangelsk – which took place on 2 August – was too little and too late to help the last of Savinkov's partisans, who had been brought to bay in Iaroslavl on 23 July. In any case, the fate of the rebellion was out of French hands. The small-scale intervention in the north, finally approved by the Supreme War Council on 3 June, had been put under overall British command. Even if the circumstances had been different, however, Paris was not well informed (because of erratic communications) about the development of the political and military situation in Russia, and therefore could not have directed events. Indeed, when Alexander Kerensky, who had escaped from Russia some weeks before, came to Paris in early July, he seemed to know more about relations between the anti-Bolshevik parties and French agents than the Quai d'Orsay. He told Clemenceau and Pichon that an organization had been formed in Moscow which hoped to unite all the anti-Bolshevik, pro-Allied parties and which had been promised financial and military support by agents of the Entente through Grenard. The Quai d'Orsay responded that the French government knew nothing of these activities. Grenard had sought information about the morale of the anti-Bolshevik parties and their plans against the Soviets, but he had not spoken of any specific agreements with a united anti-Bolshevik organization.[71] Nor did he appear to have given any large sums of money to these parties, although, as one Quai d'Orsay official put it, "no credits would have been refused him" by the government.[72]

To obtain more information, the Quai d'Orsay authorized the deposed Russian leader to communicate with Avksent'ev and Kishkin in Moscow through Grenard. Kerensky told them that Paris and London had no knowledge of their activities and that they should forward some report as soon as possible.[73] The uprising in Iaroslavl was eight days old before Paris had an answer. Grenard reported that groups loyal to Alekseev and Savinkov had agreed to follow a common line of action and to subordinate their respective military units to a unified command. The accord, however, had been "more theoretical than real." Grenard added that the people associated with Kerensky wanted to work out military plans with the Entente and to conclude a financial agreement. But Noulens did not approve of these proposals and had only authorized the disbursement of 1½ million roubles to Avksent'ev and Kishkin.[74]

In fact, French agents in Russia paid out 12,313,000 roubles to the anti-Bolshevik opposition between May and August, apparently without direct authorization from Paris. The French military mission also disposed of a further 4 million francs for unspecified purposes. Unfortunately, it has not been possible to determine who received most of these sums.[75] Aside from the money given to Avksent'ev and Kishkin, Lavergne turned over 1½ million roubles to Captain Pierre Théodore Laurent of the French military mission.[76] Apparently this officer was in contact with both the Left and Right SRs and supplied them, among other things, with explosives for sabotage against Soviet rail facilities.[77] Lockhart reported that the French had given the National Centre (to which the organizations of Savinkov and Alekseev were both affiliated) 2½ million roubles and that he and his French colleagues had forwarded by courier 10 millions to Alekseev in the Don region.[78] Savinkov claimed to have received some 2½ million roubles from the French with 2 million received "in one payment specially earmarked for the risings."[79]

Although it can be determined that French representatives maintained close contacts with the anti-Bolshevik opposition and supported it with modest financial subsidies, Noulens's exact role in the Iaroslavl rebellion remains unclear. Savinkov claimed in 1924, after being arrested by the Soviet secret police and brought before a revolutionary tribunal, that Noulens's role was crucial. Indeed, the focus of the rebellion had been moved from Moscow to the upper Volga at French urging to provide for a possible link-up with Allied forces landing at Arkhangelsk.[80] Savinkov claimed as well that he had received a cable from Noulens in Vologda by way of Grenard,

in which he positively assured me that the landing would take place between the 5th and 10th of July, or excuse me, perhaps it was between the 3rd and the 8th of July, and he urged me strongly to begin the uprising along the Upper Volga in those days and not later because it might happen that "the landing takes place and you will not have risen." It was this telegram which forced me to attack ... on the 6th in Jaroslav.[81]

In any event, Savinkov remarked that "the French deceived us. The landing at Arkhangelsk did not [then] take place, and we were left hanging in the air at Iaroslavl."[82]

The latter portion of Savinkov's testimony is the least believable. There is no indication that Noulens expected an Allied landing on the dates mentioned. Indeed, Noulens complained the very day the Iaroslavl rebellion broke out that he had no information at all on British plans to occupy Arkhangelsk. Word arrived only on 17 July, eleven days after the revolt began.[83] Hence, either Noulens lied to Savinkov to set off the revolt or, more likely, he created the general impression that the intervention was imminent without giving any specific date for an Allied landing.

Savinkov may then have started the rising on his own initiative to steal a march on Alekseev, a political rival, and to place himself in the key position once the intervention had gotten underway. The former terrorist probably gambled that he could hold out until the Allies moved down from Arkhangelsk. In this respect, Lavergne reported in August that Alekseev had reproached Savinkov for having launched the

Iaroslavl revolt "without authorization" and for wanting "to play a personal role."[84] Grenard, writing in the 1930s, stated that Savinkov had acted "in complete independence ... on his own initiative, [and] in violation of commitments which he had made to attempt nothing except in agreement with the other Russian parties."[85] But if this were the case, it is difficult to understand why Lavergne apparently made no effort to hold back Savinkov, since he knew of the imminence of the revolt at least a full week before it broke out. In this regard, Savinkov speculated at his trial that the French, being informed of Left SR plans for an uprising in Moscow, sought to time the revolt at Iaroslavl to coincide with the one in the capital.[86] On the other hand, circumstances may have worked against a delay in the uprising. Noulens, it will be remembered, had warned that if intervention did not occur quickly, the anti-Bolsheviks in Arkhangelsk might have to disband because of Soviet countermeasures. For the same reasons, Savinkov may have had to start the Iaroslavl rising at once or not at all.[87]

In any event, Noulens's unbounded encouragement of the anti-Bolsheviks is difficult to understand since he must have known from incoming dispatches that the intervention planned for Arkhangelsk was quite limited in scope.[88] Furthermore, the French ambassador never believed that the anti-Bolsheviks by themselves could overthrow the Soviet regime.[89] It is true that he thought that Bolshevik authority was crumbling, but in his mind intervention would still be necessary to deliver the *coup de grâce* and to prevent the Germans from gaining the sympathies of the Russian privileged classes.[90] Whatever his calculations, Noulens soon discovered that a few million roubles and the mere appearance of a handful of Allied troops at Arkhangelsk would not suffice to topple the Soviet regime.

Nevertheless, the possibility of an accommodation with the Bolsheviks was quite dead, and before the end of the summer the western Allies had committed themselves to an intervention against the Soviets. Noulens played an important role in precipitating these events. In the spring of 1918 he had an influential voice in the Quai d'Orsay and almost a free hand in Russia, and he did his best to embroil the Allies in armed conflict with the Soviet government. It should be kept in mind, however, that the French ambassador's ability to shape events stemmed directly from the decision taken in Paris during April to break off the *rapprochement* with the Bolsheviks. Had the policy of military collaboration continued, Noulens could not have acted as he did and indeed might well have been recalled.

This did not happen, of course, and the Allied powers were soon deeply involved in the Russian civil war. Although Noulens's encouragement of an anti-Bolshevik rebellion in central Russia proved unproductive, Soviet authority had been badly shaken and seemed on the brink of collapse. The failure of the Savinkov revolt was therefore not particularly discouraging to French policy-makers. Paris simply turned its attention to another more promising theatre of operations. From July until early October the focus of French attention was in Siberia.

CHAPTER FIVE

# The French Interest in Siberia

While French agents in central Russia pressed their government to take advantage of the Czech rebellion to overthrow the Bolsheviks, the Quai d'Orsay continued to be preoccupied with Japanese intervention. The French government had maintained a keen interest in Japanese military action in Siberia, but the question remained blocked by Woodrow Wilson's opposition. Throughout the early summer of 1918, the Quai d'Orsay laboured to overcome this obstacle. The uprising of the Czech Legion finally broke the deadlock and forced Wilson to act. After much wrangling, Japanese and smaller units of American and Allied troops landed at Vladivostok in August. The French government was pleased by these developments, but it was also concerned to acquire an influential role in the direction of the intervention.

Until the autumn of 1918 the French government assumed that Siberia would be the principal arena of intervention and it therefore sought to assure itself a position from which it could protect French vital interests. The other Allies were also doing much the same thing, only unlike the French they had greater strength to implement their policies. As a result, the French government, though it manœuvred for political influence, came away empty-handed.

## JAPANESE INTERVENTION

It was otherwise with the Japanese who had the manpower and resources to mount a considerable military effort in Siberia. Although Tokyo had indicated in March that it would not intervene without American consent, members of the Japanese general staff tried to sound out the French about their attitude toward unilateral Japanese action. First, the influential deputy chief of staff, General Gi'ichi Tanaka, and later a bureau chief asked the French naval attaché, Captain Roger Auguste Brylinski, what the position of the French government would be in the event that Japan felt compelled to intervene without American approval. Would the French government, they asked, be prepared "to march with the Japanese in spite of the opposition of the other Allied governments?" Brylinski did not know how to respond and asked for instructions.[1] But before Paris could reply, Ambassador Jusserand sounded the alarm from Washington against such conversations. Jusserand doubted the authority of these Japanese officers and did not believe that an entente with them would really lead to large-scale intervention in Siberia. Moreover, such queries, he said, could only lead to the most serious difficulties with the British and American governments.[2] "We would run the gravest risk," warned Jusserand in a subsequent cable, "if we alienated ... President Wilson at the same time as we, so to speak, put into his hands our military and financial ... salvation." Whatever the importance of Japanese intervention, it could not take precedence over the maintenance of Wilson's "unreserved good will" concerning the Western Front.[3] Pichon, who personally drafted the reply to Jusserand, commented that the government "entirely" agreed with his views on this matter.[4] Earlier, the Quai d'Orsay had informed the ministry of war that it disapproved of any negotiations with members of the Japanese general staff concerning the intervention in Siberia. Such talks could jeopardize Allied unity.[5]

The French government thus kept the Japanese intervention in proper perspective. Paris would pursue the matter as energetically as possible, but not at the risk of alienating Wilson. Nevertheless, the French did not sit with folded hands while Wilson dallied, as they saw it, in Washington. They continued to look for a basis of agreement on Japanese intervention. Moreover, the French as well as their British allies were encouraged when the American government consented at a meeting of the Supreme War Council in early June to agree to an Allied landing at Arkhangelsk. As a result, both the French and British governments could begin to envisage a combined military operation from the north and from Vladivostok in the east. With the Czechs in control of a large portion of the Trans-Siberian Railway, the Siberian phase of this operation became more feasible. The Americans, however, still hesitated. They had gone along with the intervention in northern Russia because it did not involve any great diversion of resources and because a seemingly viable military argument could be made that the area was menaced by the enemy and that, if possible, it ought to be kept out of his hands.[6] But the American government did not see the Siberian intervention in the same light. Wilson as well as the Department of War had long held that Japanese action in Siberia would alienate Russian opinion and drive the Russian government into the arms of the Central Powers. Moreover, even if an intervention did take place, it would not cause any concern to the German command because of the enormous distance across Siberia and the logistical problems of trying to supply an army over such long and fragile lines of communication.[7]

On the other hand, the Japanese government, though divided over the timing and objectives of intervention, wished to act and therefore wanted Allied consent to put Japanese forces into Siberia. In view of their position, the Japanese continued to complain about the apparent British interest in securing a Bolshevik invitation for intervention.[8] British policy had already had a rippling effect in the far east where the Foreign Office had tried to advance Lockhart's work in Moscow by restraining the military activities of Captain Grigorii Semenov, an anti-Bolshevik freebooter and client of Japan. Semenov had organized a small band of Cossacks, Chinese, and other desperadoes to raid Bolshevik positions south of the important rail centre of Chita, near Irkutsk. The Japanese believed that these activities were useful in destabilizing eastern Siberia and they therefore sought to prevent the British or other Allies from interfering in Semenov's operations.[9]

In May Japanese complaints concerning these matters began to be listened to by the British government which had abandoned any consideration of co-operating with the Bolsheviks. London then wanted to get on with intervention in Siberia; and Semenov, the Czechs, and Japanese might all play a useful part in this policy. To make a Japanese presence in Siberia more acceptable to the United States, the British sought a firm commitment to an extensive military occupation reaching Cheliabinsk in western Siberia as well as to a pledge of territorial and economic disinterestedness in Russia.[10] The Japanese replied evasively though they continued to tease the British with hopes of a Japanese advance beyond Irkutsk. Tokyo never seems to have taken this approach with the French since it must have known that Paris would have been quite happy to see the Bolsheviks chased out of even limited areas of eastern Siberia.

Negotiations continued throughout June, and toward month's end the Japanese government, replying to a joint Anglo-French and Italian *démarche*, indicated that it was prepared to respect Russian sovereignty but that it could not commit itself to a military advance beyond eastern Siberia. The logistical problems involved in any such operation would be too great.[11] The British did not accept this response as the last word and continued to press the Japanese for a further westward advance. The French, on the other hand, sought to find ways of reconciling the Japanese and Americans since Wilson was still unprepared to sanction Japanese intervention. In any case, the Quai d'Orsay did not envisage a large-scale Allied military venture in Siberia initially, and it certainly did not favour any significant diversion of American troops from the Western Front.[12]

What the French wanted was a limited commitment of Japanese troops to eastern Siberia along with smaller units of American and Allied forces. These objectives were clearly laid out in a memorandum, written by Philippe Berthelot in early June. In this memorandum Berthelot envisaged the landing of a Japanese force of some four divisions whose objective would be to secure Vladivostok, Harbin, Chita, and Irkutsk. Allied contingents including a few thousand Americans and those British, French, and Italian troops available in Asia would be attached to the Japanese force. The Japanese would have overall command of Allied troops, but the Americans would garrison the cities and assure protection of the civilian population. Moreover, an Allied high commissioner, preferably French or American, would be appointed to take general control of the intervention. Local Russian groups would be free to organize military forces which might reinforce and eventually replace the Japanese. At the same time, a "mission of economic reconstruction," including technicians, engineers, and other specialists provided with the necessary *matériel*, would reorganize the economic life of those areas shielded from the Bolsheviks. Manufactured goods could then be exchanged for agricultural products found in these areas. With such limited means, Berthelot hoped that the Allies could rid the region of Bolsheviks and re-establish a pro-Allied, anti-German Russian government.[13]

At the same time that Berthelot was formulating this new pitch for American participation, Washington began of its own accord to move toward intervention in Siberia. Reports were beginning to reach the United States about the Czech rebellion. Moreover, pressure both from the Allies and from within the American government, especially from the rabidly anti-Bolshevik Department of State, had started to wear down Wilson's resistance.[14]

Interestingly enough, the Quai d'Orsay was not aware of the strongly anti-Bolshevik feeling prevalent in the Department of State. Yet from the beginning of the Bolshevik revolution Robert Lansing, the secretary of state, and his principal advisers proved to be intransigent toward the Soviet government and considered any arrangement with it as "politically and morally inconceivable."[15] Lansing's ideological hatred was shared by Wilson, according to some American historians, and in February the two men opposed the French proposal to co-operate with the Bolsheviks "even on the basis of wartime expediency."[16] In Lansing's view, collaboration was "out of the question" because the Bolsheviks' revolutionary ideology ultimately represented a greater danger to American security than did Germany.[17] Indeed, the Department of State and its consul general in Moscow, Madden Summers, used some of the same arguments employed by the Quai d'Orsay and Noulens to block the *rapprochement* with the Bolsheviks. For example, Summers reported that the Soviet government would be incapable of organizing a national resistance against Germany, and that collaboration with Moscow would only drive the anti-Bolshevik parties into the arms of the Central Powers.[18] The Department of State also expressed the fear that the Red Army "might be used to promote social revolution."[19] All of these arguments were familiar to the French, and Berthelot would have been pleased to know of the Department of State's use of them. That he did not was initially due to the American desire to conceal its attitude toward the Bolsheviks in order not to precipitate a separate peace or to appear to be opposing Soviet efforts to end the World War.[20] Later on, when Wilson opposed Japanese intervention, it was not because of moral aversion, but rather on the practical grounds that it menaced American interests or that the time was not right for action.[21]

The rising of the Czech Legion, however, appeared to offer Wilson a suitable opportunity for intervention.[22] Moreover, if the American president still harboured any doubts, the French and British sought to back him into a corner from which he could not escape. This was done in part through the Supreme War Council which met on 2 July to discuss Siberian intervention. The council issued an appeal to Wilson which more or less rehashed previous arguments – except that on this occasion the appeal drew attention to the Czechs and implied that their fate lay in Allied and particularly American hands.[23]

Although the Czech Legion's military position was strong, it was by no means secure. Since the initial uprising at the end of May, Czech troops had taken control of the Trans-Siberian Railway from Penza, west of the Urals, to Irkutsk in eastern Siberia.[24] There were also some 15,000 Czechs in Vladivostok. Bolshevik forces still held the railway, however, between Vladivostok and Irkutsk, cutting off the two Czech groups from one another. Hence, on 25 June Czech representatives informed Allied authorities in Vladivostok that they were sending forces west to open the way to their entrapped compatriots, and they asked for support in men and *matériel*. A few days later, on 29 June, Czech forces seized control of Vladivostok from the local Soviet. Allied naval commanders, whose ships had been sitting in the harbour there for several months, put ashore small contingents of marines as a show of support. It was this local commitment of troops which apparently triggered Wilson's decision to approve an Allied intervention in Siberia.[25]

On 6 July Wilson called together the members of his war cabinet to discuss a change in American policy toward Russia. The president made it clear at the outset that he continued to regard the idea of a re-established Eastern Front an impossibility. Hence, he would not consider any military advance west of Irkutsk. But he acknowledged that the American government would be held responsible if it refused to intervene and the Czechs subsequently came to harm. It therefore seemed impossible to continue to oppose a Siberian intervention. The war cabinet agreed to propose to the Japanese that an expeditionary force of approximately 7,000 Americans and 7,000 Japanese be sent to guard Czech lines of communication toward Irkutsk and to co-operate with them in the occupation of Vladivostok. The United States, along with Japan, would also assist in supplying arms to Czech forces.[26] Wilson made it clear to the Allies, however, that he would not allow American troops to be used for other purposes than to aid the Czechs, and that he was not prepared to engage American forces in a large-scale intervention mounted from Vladivostok. Nevertheless, American policy remained somewhat ambiguous since Washington did not seem to put any restriction on the use of Czech troops in Russia.[27]

For the Quai d'Orsay, this ambiguity offered a convenient means of circumventing the restrictiveness of American policy. Berthelot observed that even the introduction of 14,000 Japanese and American troops would greatly facilitate the struggle against the Bolsheviks in Siberia. He also noted that while the Americans had refused to envisage an extension of their own participation in the intervention, they had not tied the hands of the other Allied powers. As he saw it, the other Allies could therefore take up "the Czech mask" to pursue a more far-reaching course of action. "Such an arrangement," said Berthelot, "will in fact favour the French direction of the entire operation" because of French command of the Czech Legion.[28]

The French government presumed that the Americans would oppose any Allied involvement in the political and economic reorganization of Siberia, because of Wilson's touting of the ideals of self-determination and non-intervention which were enunciated most forcefully in his Fourteen Points of January 1918.[29] But this French appraisal of American policy was not entirely accurate. Indeed, Wilson himself favoured the "reorganization" of Siberia and the creation of a liberal anti-Bolshevik government supported by the Czech Legion. However, the president wanted to limit the scope of the intervention to prevent the Japanese or the other Allies from pursuing their own narrow interests in Siberia and to avoid antagonizing Russian national sentiment.[30] The Quai d'Orsay, on the other hand, had no intention of being excluded from the intervention in Siberia, and in spite of the need to conciliate Wilson, intended to benefit as much as possible from the ambiguities of American policy to establish French influence over the intervention.

## THE FRENCH STRUGGLE FOR INFLUENCE
## OVER THE INTERVENTION

Although there are numerous references in French documents of the late summer of 1918 to the anti-German aims of the intervention and even to a limited reconstitution of the Eastern Front, the Quai d'Orsay was no longer overly worried about an extension of German influence in Russia.[31] The tide of battle was beginning to turn on the Western Front and the Germans appeared to be encountering serious problems in the east. In a long cable intended for Jusserand, Berthelot noted that intelligence reports indicated that German troops were being tied down in Russia by rising popular unrest and resistance – encouraged, so Berthelot thought, by German setbacks on the Western Front and the weakening of the Bolsheviks. The oppositionist parties were still weak, conceded Berthelot, but this was not overly disquieting with Allied military intervention looming in Siberia.[32]

The French government's real concern, once Wilson had approved the intervention in Siberia, was to establish a position of influence equal to that of its allies. Paris sought to achieve this end through its command of the Czech Legion and through the establishment of an inter-Allied high commission. The Quai d'Orsay feared that the senior ranking French officer attached to the Czechs, General Robert Paris, did not have sufficient stature to impose his authority on the various Czech echelons strung out along the Trans-Siberian. Berthelot therefore recommended to the ministry of war that General Janin, the former chief of the French military mission in Petrograd, be sent to Siberia to take command of the legion.[33] The Quai d'Orsay believed that Janin, who had been selected to command the Czech National Army several months before, would have sufficient prestige to impose his authority on headstrong Czech officers. To this same end, the French government arranged to have General Milan R. Stefanik, a leader of the Czech National Council in Paris, accompany Janin.[34]

The Quai d'Orsay was extremely anxious to get the Janin mission moving toward Vladivostok since it appeared that the other Allies were hastening to establish themselves in Siberia. Berthelot sent a stream of letters to the ministry of war warning that if Janin and Stefanik did not leave immediately, the French government might find itself left out of a directing role in the intervention. Berthelot warned, however, that the size of the Janin mission should be kept down in order not to disquiet Wilson, who regarded the Siberian intervention as essentially a U.S.-Japanese affair. "If we were to give the impression, however slight, that we sought to play the first role, we would awaken [American] suspicions and jeopardize the result." Nevertheless, it was essential to act quickly, concluded Berthelot, "I cannot insist on this too much."[35]

While trying to hasten the departure of Janin and the formation of a French military mission, the Quai d'Orsay also proposed to its allies the creation of an Allied high commission. The initial efforts of the French government to gain acceptance for the appointment of an Allied high commissioner do not appear to have brought any response from Washington. Berthelot then went further to propose the formation of a full-fledged high commission on which a representative from each of the intervening Allied powers would sit. This commission was intended to have authority over all political and economic questions arising from the intervention. The Quai d'Orsay favoured an American as president of the high commission to provide a counterweight to the influence of the Japanese.[36]

Berthelot no doubt reasoned that an inter-Allied council would preserve a political and economic influence for France which it could not have maintained in the event of an uncontrolled Allied struggle for power in Siberia. Offering the presidency of the high commission to the United States was thought to be the best way of assuring the project's success. The Quai d'Orsay hoped that a strong American presence would discourage Japanese attempts to establish a pre-eminent position in the Russian far east. Japanese dominance would upset the French government's efforts to establish its own influence in Siberia and might weaken the Russian administration which Paris hoped to set up under its patronage. Moreover, aside from the restraint on the Japanese, the Quai d'Orsay probably also felt that the Americans would exercise a similar control over the British who were making unilateral plans to send troops and a large military mission to Siberia.[37]

The first American response to the French proposal for an Allied high commission was favourable. Jusserand broached the subject with Lansing, who indicated that he would put the idea before Wilson. Lansing himself considered the project "very useful" and favoured having an American president of the council.[38] Nevertheless, Lansing's attitude soon soured apparently because of unilateral actions taken in Siberia by the British and especially by the Japanese.

On 24 July the Japanese ambassador in Washington, Viscount Kikujiro Ishii, replied to the American proposals on intervention. He told the acting secretary of state, Frank Polk, that the Japanese government could not agree to limit its forces to 7,000 men. It was prepared to send a division, about 12,000 men, and would dispatch additional troops if the circumstances so required.[39] Ishii's *démarche*, implying as it did the prospect of unilateral, open-ended action in Siberia, was not well received by the American government. Indeed, Wilson considered withdrawing American approval for the venture, but in the end he accepted an ambiguous Japanese promise to limit the number of troops involved to those necessary to protect the Czechs.[40] Tokyo finally forced Wilson's hand by publishing on 2 August a declaration of policy concerning the intervention. Washington could not then back out without appearing to leave the Czechs to their own devices and without revealing a serious conflict of opinion between the American and Japanese governments.[41] Hence, on 3 August Japanese and British troops began to go ashore at Vladivostok, and the Americans were quick to follow on 16 August.

In the aftermath of these events, Washington was indisposed to endorse the French plan. Jusserand reported that Lansing and Wilson were highly "irritated" by the *faits accomplis* of their allies, and that the president would almost certainly refuse to appoint an American representative to head the council of high commissioners.[42] The French persisted in their efforts to gain U.S. assent, but to no avail.[43] Indeed, none of the intervening powers would go along with the French plan. The Americans remained indisposed toward their allies, while the British and Japanese would not agree to tie their hands.[44] The Quai d'Orsay reacted to the every-man-for-himself attitude of its allies by adopting a like posture. Berthelot commented that the American refusal to cooperate presented certain advantages since it gave the French government a free hand, and would permit Paris through the Czechs "to play discreetly the preponderant role" in the intervention.[45]

### FRENCH ATTITUDES TOWARDS THE SIBERIAN ANTI-BOLSHEVIKS

While the Quai d'Orsay was preoccupied with establishing a French voice in the direction of the Siberian intervention, Paris was much less concerned about its relations with the anti-Bolshevik Russians. Indeed, the French considered the latter as scarcely more than a nuisance to be consulted perfunctorily and then ignored. For example, the anti-Bolshevik Russians figured little in the Quai d'Orsay's high commission. As Berthelot put it, "several eminent Russian personalities chosen by the Allies might be joined to [the] council in a consultative role."[46] Berthelot in fact viewed the high commission more as an instrument to impose order on the quarrelling Russian factions than as an organ in which they should participate in any meaningful way.

These anti-Bolshevik groups were proving particularly unco-operative on the eve of the Allied landing at Vladivostok. In early July General D.L. Horvat, general manager of the Chinese Eastern Railway, a Manchurian line under Russian control before the war, sought to take advantage of the Czech suppression of Soviet authority in Siberia to make a bid for power. Similarly, an SR faction in Vladivostok, headed by Peter Derber, attempted to establish itself as the "provisional government of autonomous Siberia." Horvat left Harbin for Vladivostok to challenge Derber's fledgling "government," but the Czech Legion, which was caught in the middle of this dispute, blocked Horvat at the Manchurian border.[47]

Characteristically, the French did not have a high opinion of either of these men. When in April 1918 there was some discussion among Allied representatives in the far east about establishing an anti-Bolshevik government under Horvat, the Quai d'Orsay had responded unfavourably. Margerie and Jean Gout, chief of the Asia sub-division of the Quai d'Orsay, characterized him as pusillanimous, irresolute, and self-seeking. "We must ask the question," minuted Margerie, "whether we are not dealing with a small clique, which on the pretext of beginning the reconstruction of a healthy Russia in eastern Siberia, is merely seeking to advance its own narrow interests." It was, said Gout, "a ridiculous idea to put forward such an individual."[48]

The French view of Horvat and his followers matched that of other observers. A Dutch journalist on the scene, L.H. Grondijs, noted that most of the Russian officers who had taken refuge in Manchuria and served Horvat were involved in opium smuggling and speculation. They had become corrupted, he said, by the seamy life of Harbin and were content to posture in the streets wearing "newly invented uniforms" and noisily clanging swords so as to impress passers-by.[49]

As for Peter Derber, French intelligence reports dismissed him as "a Jew without roots or influence in Siberia, [and] as an SR of the extreme left [who] reject[ed] collaboration with the bourgeois parties."[50] The freebooter Semenov rated little higher in French eyes. It was reported that the Bolsheviks had driven him into Manchuria and that his bands had been reduced to a few hundred men.[51] As for the rest of the anti-Bolsheviks, General Paris commented that "local experience" had proven that they were incapable of maintaining power and would be overthrown by the Bolsheviks as soon as the Czechs departed.[52] Although the French were occasionally more charitable toward some of the other Russian factions, and desired to foster the broadest possible grouping of Russian political elements, it was only to provide a "screen for Allied action."[53]

French disregard for the Siberian anti-Bolsheviks did not dispose the Quai d'Orsay to tolerate Horvat's attempt to take power in Vladivostok. Indeed, the French and other Allied ministers in Peking sought to discourage his ambitions.[54] But Horvat proved unco-operative and told the Czechs that he would not permit them to make use of the strategic Chinese Eastern Railway unless they disavowed the Derber government.[55] In the end, Allied agents in Peking were able to persuade Horvat to give up his plans and to return to Harbin. The Quai d'Orsay fully endorsed this action and informed the French minister in Peking, Auguste Boppe, that the government did not intend to single out for support any one Russian political party.[56] The Quai d'Orsay did not want Horvat to profit from the presence of Allied troops to establish himself and to eliminate his political rivals. On the other hand, since Horvat seemed to have the support of the Japanese and of certain Russian politicians, the Quai d'Orsay preferred not to fight him, if he ceased his efforts to take power in Vladivostok.[57] Berthelot put this message out in a series of cables which the Quai d'Orsay claimed to be forwarding from V.A. Maklakov, the Russian ambassador in Paris, to several anti-Bolshevik representatives in the far east and to Horvat himself. These cables urged the Russians to join together and co-operate with the Allies "to liberate" their country from the Bolsheviks. "Disunion," these messages warned, "would lead to ruin and the partition of Russia."[58]

The Quai d'Orsay's attitude toward the political rivalries of the Siberian anti-Bolsheviks presaged the French government's attitude toward all the anti-Bolshevik groups vying for power in Russia or on its frontiers. In refusing to take sides, the Quai d'Orsay could avoid becoming embroiled in internal Russian political rivalries, and could simply support the group or groups that eventually were victorious. Moreover, the French government felt compelled to move carefully in its relations with the Siberian anti-Bolshevik factions in order not to offend Wilson's apparent scruples about the principle of self-determination.[59]

This latter concern emerged clearly in the aftermath of elections held at the end of July in Vladivostok. In spite of the fact that the city was under Czech and Allied control, the Bolsheviks, to the consternation of the Quai d'Orsay, won a majority. Berthelot was quite disturbed by this outcome, and in a long note to Pichon was highly critical of Allied policy. As he saw it, the Vladivostok elections were "a good example of the serious disadvantages arising from the diplomatic position [concerning non-intervention and self-determination] which the Allies had been forced to adopt in Siberia in order not to run up against the ideas of President Wilson." Berthelot warned that the concept of non-intervention was being carried too far. The Allies could not simply sit back while the anti-Bolshevik factions in Siberia, none of which had any real force, indulged in partisan struggles for power. To do so would only delay the creation of a stable government. Berthelot concluded that the Allies would have "to destroy, either by supporting Russian groups, or directly themselves, Bolshevik elements wherever they were found...." Similarly, "certain Russian non-Bolshevik authorities, espousing ... excessive or revolutionary principles, should not be supported or tolerated." Berthelot commented that some effort would have to be made to reconcile "the publicly accepted principle of non-intervention ... [with] the necessity to remain practical and not to succumb to ideology." He recommended that Janin, who was preparing to leave for the far east, be apprised of the government's attitude concerning this question. As commander of Czech troops, Janin could favour certain local political factions over others and thus facilitate their success without appearing to take sides. Berthelot stressed that Janin should not be allowed to leave Paris with the idea that he could do nothing to influence events in Siberia which might otherwise move in a direction harmful to French interests.[60]

Berthelot's anxiety over the negative effects of Wilsonian policy stemmed largely from his recognition of the extreme weakness of the anti-Bolshevik parties. Without strong opposition groups in Siberia, Wilsonian slogans became a formula for chaos and disaster. In such an environment, either the forces of revolution or the other Allies would gain the upper hand. In either case, the French government would be the principal loser.

Berthelot, however, may not have fully understood Wilson's interpretation of self-determination, which in Russia meant neutrality *vis-à-vis* the various anti-Bolshevik factions but hostility toward Moscow.[61] In the mind of the president, American opposition to Bolshevism did not violate his highly publicized principles. Wilson after all regarded the Bolsheviks as a small minority which had usurped power and prevented the Russian people from exercising their right to choose a government of "liberal institutions" more conducive to American ideals and interests.[62] The Quai d'Orsay would not have quarrelled with the latter part of Wilson's formula but obviously disliked his hands-off policy toward the weak and disorganized anti-Bolsheviks. At any rate, Berthelot may have confused Wilson's pragmatic manœuvring for moral scruples probably because he was misled, like others, by American propaganda.

The confusion of Berthelot and the Quai d'Orsay about American policy is evidence of a certain lack of candor between the two allies. Neither the Department of State nor the Quai d'Orsay was properly informed about the other's Russian policy, essentially because of distrust, but also because both the French and American governments were initially divided on what policy to adopt toward the Bolsheviks. Wilson believed that all the Allies, with the exception of the United States, had self-interested motives in Russia and that they would re-establish a reactionary, monarchist regime if not kept in check. The Quai d'Orsay was aware of these somewhat messianic American attitudes and therefore sought to cloak its profoundly anti-Bolshevik views. On the other hand, the Department of State, which chafed under Wilson's restraints but shared his mistrust of the other Allies, could not be overly forthcoming with the Quai d'Orsay without seeming to go behind the back of the president and without incurring criticism from the anti-interventionist Department of War. In the early spring the Quai d'Orsay had acted under similar restraints because the ministry of war, whose chief, Clemenceau, was also premier, favoured a policy of collaboration with the Bolsheviks. Neither government was prepared to air out internal policy disputes before its allies, and of course neither could say outright that it mistrusted the other's motives in Russia.

## THE "AUGUST ACCORD": ANGLO-FRENCH NEGOTIATIONS OVER RUSSIA

Berthelot's preoccupation with American policy and with events in Vladivostok was due principally to the fact that by mid-summer Siberia represented the main focus of French attention in Russia.[63] This interest developed because of the inaccessibility of other, nearer regions of Russia and because of commitments to the Czech Legion. The Black Sea was closed to French penetration and the British had overall command of Allied operations in northern Russia. Moreover, the French government had agreed at the Abbeville conference of 2 May to undertake responsibility for the supply and maintenance of the Czech Legion until it left Russia.[64] At a further meeting between British and French representatives on 2 July in Paris, the Abbeville agreement was confirmed.[65] The British government, however, wanted to extend these arrangements even further. On 16 July Sir George Grahame, a member of the British embassy in Paris, informed the Quai d'Orsay that London "consider[ed] desirable" the conclusion of "a general agreement covering the expenses of Allied activities in Russia."

Mr. Grahame is to suggest that H.M. government should be made responsible for expenditure in the first place involved in the activities in Russia from Murmansk to Archangel; that the French government should be responsible for expenditure in the first place involved a) in the financing of pro-ally activities in the Moscow area; b) by maintenance of Polish, Serbian, and Czechoslovak forces in Russia. H.M. government being responsible for eventual transport to the west from Russia of any such forces; that all such expenditure, other than on the French and U.S. forces engaged in Russia should later be pooled.

Furthermore, the British government supported by France should invite the United States to take a one-third burden, "but that if the U.S. government be unwilling to pay their quota, then the whole expenditure should be borne in equal parts by the French government and H.M. government."[66] The Quai d'Orsay accepted the terms of Grahame's note on 15 August with the proviso that this arrangement could be altered if French expenditures became disproportionately high. Pichon's letter indicated that the French government understood the agreement to cover "all expenses which have been made in order to maintain the influence of the Allies in Russia, to struggle against the German invasion, and ... to prepare the actual intervention...."[67]

The Foreign Office thus took the initiative in extending the agreement of 2 July by way of Grahame's note of 16 July to include an arrangement whereby the British took responsibility for the Arkhangelsk-Murmansk region and the French, the Moscow area. The Grahame note also added the Polish and Serbian detachments in Russia to the body of troops under French responsibility. Pichon's letter of 15 August appears to have taken the "agreement" beyond the scope of the earlier British note by assuming that all expenses incurred by the Allied intervention in Russia would eventually be divided and borne equally.

The British responded to the French note only two months later. In a letter of 7 October, Lord Derby indicated that the British government considered the "understanding for distribution of expenditure in Russia 'to be— limited under the agreement of December 23, 1917 to activities in the Ukraine and the Southeast Russia areas." If France wished to extend this agreement, the British government, said the note, would require a statement "to date of the amount and purpose of such expenditure."[68] In short, Derby appeared to repudiate the British note of 16 July. As the Groupe de l'Avant subsequently remarked, the 7 October letter undid certain points previously thought secured by the French government.[69] In spite of the ambiguity concerning what had been agreed to, the French subsequently referred to this "understanding" as the "August accord."[70] In the Quai d'Orsay's view, these so-called agreements had the advantage of simplifying Allied action by permitting each country to act in its own "sphere" without having to demand each time the assent of the other party.[71]

This exchange of letters sheds light on the controversy concerning the alleged conclusion of an Allied agreement aiming at the dismemberment of Russia. The 23 December Anglo-French convention has been assumed to have contained other clauses or been part of other collateral agreements dividing up the rest of Russia among the Allies.[72] This was not precisely the case, but there were in fact subsequent agreements or proposals made between London and Paris concerning Russia. They were not clauses of the 23 December convention, but they were considered a follow-up to this accord. The Anglo-French exchanges in July and August covered northern and central Russia, and the French would later seek unilaterally to extend the "August accord" into Siberia where they wished to control the reorganization of the Russian army. Moreover, in February 1919 Clemenceau directed Pichon to suggest to the British government a division of the Baltic area into "zones of action" similar to those established by the 23 December convention.[73] The Quai d'Orsay duly proposed such an accord to the British on 14 February 1919. Pichon wrote to Derby that this new arrangement would represent "simply a repetition in the Baltic Sea area of the method applied to good purpose in the rest of Russia and sanctioned by the accord of December 23, 1917 and by the subsequent accords which attributed action in Siberia to France and [action] in the territories of the Don, Caucasus, and northern Russia to Britain." Pichon proposed a formalization of the *de facto* situation in the Baltic and in northeastern and central Europe. Britain should take responsibility for the material support of Estonia, Latvia, Lithuania, and "eventually" Finland, while France "would continue to be charged" with the responsibility for supplying Poland and Czechoslovakia.[74] The British responded indifferently to the French proposals, and the ministry of war eventually decided not to pursue the matter because of France's inability to bear the entire burden of supplying the Poles.[75]

Although the French proposal concerning the Baltic dealt only with the material support of the anti-Bolshevik states in central and eastern Europe, Paris tended to regard such agreements as establishing zones of political and economic influence. For example, in the Quai d'Orsay's 14 February note to Derby, Siberia was referred to as part of the French zone of action. In fact, this was not the case, and in the Quai d'Orsay's subsequent letter to Derby concerning the Baltic, the reference to Siberia as part of the French sphere was dropped. The fact remains, however, that the Quai d'Orsay tended to interpret its agreements with Britain very broadly and often referred to the areas attributed to its sphere by these accords as "zones of influence."[76]

In regard to Siberia, the French government began to assume this area to be within its sphere of action largely on the basis of the "August accord." Paris was therefore annoyed when it perceived that the British were moving into this region as well. Berthelot, it will be remembered, had urged the prompt dispatch of Janin to Siberia to preserve for France the same prerogatives as the other great powers. When London appointed Sir Charles Eliot as high commissioner in Siberia, the Quai d'Orsay responded by selecting Eugène Regnault for an equivalent position "to safeguard French interests."[77] And when the British government ordered General Alfred W.F. Knox in late August to begin organizing and training a Russian army, Paris strongly objected. The Quai d'Orsay assumed that Janin's command of the Czech Legion "would probably lead him to take *de facto* command of Russian troops operating conjointly with the Czechs on the entirety of the Trans-Siberian" – especially in view of the fact that the Japanese would probably not go beyond Irkutsk.[78] Finally, the French government believed that it had "a special position" in Russia by virtue of the Franco-Russian alliance – a position to which the

British should yield.[79] Knox characterized the French case for Janin's appointment as commander-in-chief of Russian forces as a "weak and dishonest ... piece of pleading."[80] And so it was, but the French general staff in turn regarded the Knox mission as a ploy intended to assure London "a predominant influence in Russia."[81] Obviously, this was a development the French hoped to avert.

In spite of competitive British plans for Siberia, the French government pursued its efforts to put Janin at the head of a reorganized Russian army. At a meeting of the council of ministers at the end of September, it was decided to undertake responsibility for the organization of Russian troops in Siberia by means of a unilateral extension of the August accord.[82] The ministry of finance, however, soon notified the Quai d'Orsay that France could not afford the costs of such an undertaking and that the government would have to seek the aid of its allies to meet its commitments. The Quai d'Orsay had to comply and so informed the other Allied governments.[83] Although the dispute between London and Paris over the attributions of Janin and Knox lingered on for several months, the French interest in Siberia began to diminish after the reopening of the Black Sea.[84]

The outlook and actions of the French government in regard to Siberia during the summer of 1918 highlight a bourgeoning rivalry with Britain and the other intervening Allies in Russia. The Quai d'Orsay's efforts to create an Allied high commission were intended to preserve political and economic influence for France *vis-à-vis* its more powerful allies. Similarly, the series of exchanges culminating in the "August accord" were viewed by the Quai d'Orsay as a means of keeping Anglo-French rivalries within bounds. But neither arrangement worked. In Siberia the British acted on their own account, and the Franco-British exchanges of July and August were largely undone by the Foreign Office in October. The Quai d'Orsay, which was also conscious of the potential danger of Japanese action to French interests, sought to encourage American participation in the intervention to restrain Tokyo. But Washington jibbed at the precipitous and unilateral actions of its allies and would not co-operate with Paris in any active way.

These Allied rivalries did not go unnoticed in Moscow. During May Lenin began to comment on the conflicting interests of the United States and Japan and the possibility of a German-Japanese *rapprochement*. His terms of reference were scarcely different from those Pichon and Berthelot had used earlier in the year when discussing the problem of Japanese intervention.[85] Some western historians tend to dismiss Soviet claims that the Allies were rival "imperialists" who meant to exploit Russia in their own interests.[86] As will be demonstrated in subsequent chapters, the Soviet view, at least in regard to the French, should not be taken so lightly. Paris was keenly aware of the dangers to its political and economic interests in Russia not only from the Bolsheviks, but also from its own allies, and sought to defend them with all the means at its disposal.

To this end the Quai d'Orsay hoped to employ the Czech Legion as an instrument of political and economic influence. This effort collapsed, however, when the Red Army began in late August to roll back Czech forces to the east. Czech morale disintegrated, while the Allies proved unable to give the legion any meaningful support. By October the Czechs had ceased to represent a serious military force, and Paris had lost its anticipated tool of influence. Consequently, when the prospect of the reopening of the Black Sea arose in early October, the French quickly turned their attention to southern Russia. But before examining the development of the intervention in the Ukraine, it is necessary to look at the economic policies and projects that began to crystalize within the French government in the aftermath of the Bolshevik seizure of power.

## CHAPTER SIX

# The Early Development of
# French Economic Policy
# in Russia

After the Bolsheviks took power, they did not wait long before putting their ideas on state ownership of the means of production into practice. The Soviet government quickly enacted measures expropriating private property and repudiating state obligations contracted by the tsarist regime. The Quai d'Orsay viewed with growing anger and alarm these Soviet domestic policies which threatened, at a stroke, to wipe out thirty-five years of French investment in Russia. But the French government's preoccupation with the military situation on the Western Front prevented a rapid response. This relative neglect persisted until the late spring when French policy-makers began serious discussions on the objectives of French economic policy toward Russia. They assumed from the outset that the government should make every effort to protect French investments. But it was not easy to determine just how this could be done. French resources were almost totally committed to the war on the Western Front. Moreover, Siberia, which seemed destined for a time to be the main theatre of operations against the Bolsheviks, was far away and much beyond the range of effective French power. Nevertheless, something had to be done and French policy-makers began to cast about for solutions. They eventually came up with the idea of creating a *banque d'émission* to produce an Allied currency in Russia to replace the old depreciated issues of roubles still circulated by the Soviet and anti-Bolshevik governments. To force these old roubles out of circulation would be a damaging blow to the Bolsheviks, and would give the intervening powers who controlled the bank levers of influence to protect their interests in Russia.

Governmental discussions concerning the protection of French economic interests in Russia progressed altogether too slowly for French businessmen who decried the ruin of their enterprises by nationalizations and expropriations. Shortly after the Bolshevik seizure of power they organized themselves into a defence committee to lobby the government for action against the Soviet regime. However, French bankers and industrialists on the committee soon began quarrelling among themselves, and the government pleaded that for the moment it could do little to stop the Bolshevik "spoliation" of French investments.

These losses were considerable since French investments in Russia totalled more than 13 billion gold francs. Most of this sum, 11.5 billion, was invested in various types of bonds issued or guaranteed by the tsarist government. Although only 1.7 billion gold francs were placed in industrial and financial enterprises, the concentration of French investment in the heavy industrial sector of the Russian economy was very high: 80 per cent of investment capital in iron mining, 75 per cent in coal extraction, and 60 per cent in metallurgy. Most of the Russian mining and metallurgical industry was located in the Ukraine and the Donetz basin; French capital represented from 51 to 97 per cent of total investment in these areas.[1]

French capital was also important in the banking sector of the Russian economy where French financial establishments like the Société Générale, the Banque de Paris et des Pays-Bas, and the Banque de l'Union parisienne had very large interests. Indeed, these investments gave French bankers important leverage in aiding French industrial concerns in Russia.[2]

It is therefore not surprising that French investors were distressed by the economic policies of the Soviet government. Indeed, even before the Bolshevik seizure of power, they had begun to worry about the security of their investments. French industrialists were the first to raise the alarm as strikes and demands for higher wages and workers' control began to disrupt production and profits. This growing working-class militancy led to the organization in 1917 of the Bureau industriel in Petrograd. It was set up on the initiative of the French commercial attaché, F. de Poulpiquet Du Halgouet, and the president of the French chamber of commerce in Petrograd, Pierre Darcy.[3] The Bureau was intended to gather information on economic conditions in Russia and to defend French industrial interests. Halgouet, in his capacity as commercial attaché, took up the complaints of the Bureau with the Provisional Government. However, these representations did little good because of the weakness of the Kerensky regime.[4] In Paris, a Groupe industriel was also organized under the leadership of Édouard Gruner, the director general of the Société des minerais de fer de Krivoi-Rog, and included representatives of about thirty French firms operating in Russia. But the Gruner committee was no more successful than its Petrograd counterpart in protecting industrial interests.[5]

The Bolshevik seizure of power generalized the menace to French economic interests and provided the incentive for the formation of a group representing all those industrial, commercial, and financial elements having investments in Russia. The Office national des valeurs mobilières, an organization for the protection of French economic holdings abroad, took the lead in setting up this new group and sought government support from the ministry of finance and the Quai d'Orsay. During January 1918, Gruner, Jules Chevalier, director of the Office national, and several others met with F.A. Kammerer, chief of the Service financier of the Quai d'Orsay, and Charles Sergent, under-secretary of state in the ministry of finance, to discuss the organization of the committee.[6]

Although the government did not wish to lead the commission openly, it sought to exercise a guiding influence.[7] It also selected the president of the new organization. Kammerer wanted a political personality to head the committee who would be above the particular interests of any one of its member groups. He was particularly anxious that an individual representing the interests of the *Bourse* or banks did not become president.[8] Although Kammerer did not record his reasons for this attitude, he appears to have feared that the latter elements might furnish leadership to any committee of French investors holding Russian bonds. As it turned out, Kammerer's wishes were not respected. Maurice de Verneuil, former head of the Paris stockbrokers and one of those chiefly responsible for selling Russian securities in France, was eventually chosen to lead the committee.[9] The ministry of finance favoured Verneuil's appointment in spite of Kammerer's strong opposition.[10]

The Commission générale de protection des intérêts français en Russie constituted itself in the middle of February. The commission informed the government that among other things it would seek to formulate measures designed to protect French interests and to compile a list of claims for damages against the Russian state.[11] The commission was composed of three main groups: Gruner's; a *groupe financier*, actually the Comité des emprunts russes, the consortium of banks that had handled the tsarist bond issues in France; and an unimportant commercial grouping headed by David-Mennet, the president of the French Chamber of Commerce. Among those representing the industrialists were Maurice Devies, secretary general of Schneider et Compagnie, and Joseph Chanove, a member of the board of directors of the Société des forges et aciéries du Donetz.[12] The large holding company, Giros et Compagnie, or the Société générale d'entreprises, was also represented in the industrialist group.[13] Louis Loucheur, Clemenceau's minister of armaments, was closely associated with this conglomerate, as was Joseph

Noulens, who eventually succeeded Verneuil as president of the Commission générale in January 1920.[14]

The *groupe financier* represented the most powerful banks in France: the Banque de Paris et des Pays-Bas, the Banque de l'Union parisienne, the Crédit Lyonnais, the Société Générale, the Comptoir national d'escompte, and the Société Générale de Crédit industriel et commercial.[15] Its president was André Bénac, former director of the Mouvement des fonds in the ministry of finance and "right arm" of the minister of finance before the war, Joseph Caillaux.[16] Bénac also sat as a member of the boards of directors of the Banque de Paris et des Pays-Bas, the Société Générale, and the Banque Russo-Asiatique.[17]

The connections of many of the men on the commission were far-reaching. Louis Lion, for example, was president of the Société normande de constructions navales and sat on the board of directors of the Banque de l'Union parisienne.[18] René Boudon was president of the Société française et italienne des houillères de Dombrowa. Gabriel Brizon was director general of the Banque des Pays du Nord and a member of the board of directors of the important Compagnie des forges et aciéries de la marine et d'Homécourt.

In spite of the importance of its membership, the Commission générale during the first few months of its existence does not appear to have made any serious attempt to influence government policy. At the time, however, there was little the Verneuil committee or the Quai d'Orsay could do about Bolshevik expropriations. In early December 1917 the government had formed the Commission interministérielle des affaires financières russes et roumaines (CIAF). The commission was composed of representatives of all government ministries and agencies concerned with Russian affairs. Although its size and composition varied from week to week, during this period Kammerer usually represented the Quai d'Orsay; Alby, the ministry of war; Frédéric François-Marsal, the Présidence du Conseil; and Sergent, the committee's chairman, and Alexandre Celier, director of the Mouvement des fonds, the ministry of finance. The CIAF was formed to study various economic problems concerning Russia and Rumania and to formulate policy to deal with them. During the early months of 1918, it was preoccupied by how to obtain roubles to finance French political action in Russia, prevent the Germans from taking over French-controlled industrial enterprises, and maintain French economic influence in Russia. In the realm of concrete action, however, the government was practically helpless. In a letter to the Crédit Lyonnais on 15 January, Pichon stated frankly that while the government would do everything possible to protect French interests, circumstances did not permit it to take action beyond making a formal protest against Bolshevik property seizures.[19]

## THE OUTLOOK OF THE
## COMMISSION GÉNÉRALE

French helplessness in Russia soon led to quarrelling in the Commission générale. Gruner and Verneuil became involved in a heated dispute over the organization and objectives of the commission. The disagreement appears to have arisen over budgetary questions, but rapidly spread to other matters. Essentially, the Groupe industriel wished the commission simply to transmit damage claims from its member groups to the government.[20] Gruner did not want the central committee to deal with questions concerning solely the Groupe industriel, evidently because he feared that industrialist claims against the Russian government might be weakened by the divergent interests of other elements within the commission.[21] Verneuil, on the other hand, felt that the central organization should concentrate on plans for the expansion of French economic activity in Russia rather than on claims for damages against the Russian state.[22] This approach, however, did not have much appeal to the industrialists, who were counting their losses and wanted action taken to protect their holdings. But Verneuil apparently thought that by giving the Commission générale a major planning role, he could place it in a position to direct French economic activity in Russia after the destruction of the Bolshevik regime.

In May the dispute between Gruner and Verneuil reached the point where the latter temporarily resigned as president. Other members of the commission sought to conciliate the dispute to prevent the organization from breaking up. They argued that private French economic groups would need to unite in the broadest possible coalition to influence public and parliamentary opinion, and that the industrialist program would be inadequate for this purpose.[23] Eventually, these views prevailed, and a compromise was worked out whereby the Groupe industriel gained a larger representation on the commission presumably in exchange for its agreement to co-operate more fully with the larger group.[24]

Verneuil and the Commission générale also came under heavy criticism in mid-March from the financial daily, *La Cote Vidal*. Its editor, Emmanuel Vidal, thought it highly inappropriate that Verneuil and his colleagues from the big banks should be taking a prominent role in the commission, given that they had acted as the principal middlemen in the sale of Russian bonds in France. They had led the French public down the garden path and thus shared the responsibility for the ruin of so many French investors.[25] Verneuil and his friends were participating in the commission, thought Vidal, to atone for past sins and to undercut criticism of their previous roles. Vidal concluded in somewhat ambiguous terms that Verneuil's position was compromised and that he could not be depended on to defend fully the interests of French investors.[26]

This, of course, was also the view of Gruner, whose misgivings concerning the Commission générale were matched by his dissatisfaction with government policy. In the latter part of June Gruner gained an interview with Clemenceau to complain of the government's inaction and of the irreparable damage being done to the interests of French industrialists in Russia.[27] Shortly thereafter, the Groupe industriel sent a note to the Quai d'Orsay demanding that France and its allies take "energetic measures" to organize anti-Bolshevik elements in those areas of Russia which were or would shortly be in the hands of the Entente. It demanded as well that the government appoint a high-ranking official in Paris to co-ordinate action taken to safeguard French interests in Russia.[28] In late July Gruner also requested a subvention from the government to maintain the Bureau industriel in Petrograd headed by Darcy.[29]

The Gruner démarche prompted a good deal of criticism in the Commission générale. Many commission members did not wish to see the government direct, as Gruner recommended, the defence of private French economic interests. Verneuil was particularly opposed to such a solution because he did not believe that the state could be trusted on its own to protect French interests adequately. "What is necessary," said Verneuil, "is a solidly based organization which could, outside the government but with its support, defend private interests." André Bénac, another important member of the commission, strongly supported this position. He stressed that the Commission générale offered the best means of protecting private interests and that the government would be compelled to yield to its wishes. To be successful, however, the group would have to remain united. Bénac and Verneuil seemed to speak for the majority of the commission in hoping that the Groupe industriel would co-operate more fully with the central organization. The industrialists acknowledged the justice of these views, but explained that they were without funds and had no alternative but to turn to the government.[30]

The fear of government interference in the Commission générale, ignited by the Gruner démarche to the Quai d'Orsay, appears to have prompted Verneuil to press for the formation of a separate defence committee to protect the interests of French nationals holding Russian bonds.[31] The formation of this new group, called the Comité de défense des porteurs français de fonds d'état russes, was handled by the Office national. Aside from the desire to forestall any government initiative in this regard, the Office national also wished to prevent the establishment of other rival committees.[32] It therefore approached the ministry of finance for government patronage of the new organization. On the face of it, this posture was contradictory in so far as the Office national mistrusted the government but looked for its support to strengthen the position of the Comité de défense. Yet the contradiction was more apparent than real since these committees simply sought to avoid being dominated by the government while still soliciting state support. The government, on the other hand, does not seem to have been unaware of these motives and tried to keep these committees under control. The ministry of finance pointedly asked the Office national to remove certain clauses from its statement of principles holding the state responsible for payment of the coupon.[33]

Beyond forming committees and arguing among themselves, the member groups of the Commission générale could only sit by impatiently as the Bolsheviks continued to expropriate and confiscate private property. Members of the commission recognized, in spite of the industrialist clamour for action, that for the moment the state could do little. Darcy, who maintained a sporadic correspondence with Gruner in Paris, noted in June that all they could do was mark time and prepare claims for future compensation.[34]

In July Verneuil informed Darcy of the formation of the Commission générale and invited him to collaborate with its activities.[35] In a long letter of acceptance, Darcy was critical of what he regarded as the narrow orientation of the commission and of French business in general toward Russia. He complained that the Verneuil committee seemed interested only in protecting existing French investments. Similarly, certain French nationals appeared uniquely concerned with salvaging what they could of previous investments and then pulling out of Russia. Others hoped that French enterprises in the Ukraine would be seized by the Germans because French shareholders would then be indemnified when peace was concluded. Darcy thought these attitudes inconsistent with the long-term economic interests of France. War was not being waged against Germany, he wrote, simply to allow Russia to become a German colony after the conclusion of peace. Darcy urged that the French economic presence be maintained whatever the cost. Undoubtedly the immediate future would be difficult, but the prospective economic development of Russia was so promising, said Darcy, that it would be folly to abandon the field to another power. The French position in Russia must be held and expanded. To this end, Darcy recommended the organization of a financial consortium capable of providing funds to French industrial enterprises seeking to resume production. He suggested as well the grouping of French industries into trusts to facilitate recovery and expansion.[36]

Darcy's proposals were not favourably received by the members of the Commission générale, who either did not have or were not prepared to commit the funds necessary to realize these aims. Kammerer commented in an August memorandum that French industrialists "felt ruined" by the revolution in Russia and did not wish "to throw good money after bad" in hopes of saving their holdings.[37] The Parisian banks were also reluctant to invest in Russia and rejected out of hand Darcy's proposal for a financial consortium.[38]

The negative reaction to Darcy's proposals as well as the Gruner-Verneuil dispute in the Commission générale indicate that there was no united monolith of finance and industrial capital seeking to tighten its loosened grip on the Russian economy. There were only squabbling individual groups, eyeing each other suspiciously, trying to save their investments, but leery of making new commitments in a country torn by revolution and civil war. Neither French industrialists nor Parisian bankers were prepared to subordinate their respective interests to the long-range good, as Darcy saw it, of preserving French economic holdings in Russia – unless, of course, the government was prepared to pay for it by a policy of military and financial intervention.

### THE FRENCH GOVERNMENT AND
### THE COMMISSION GÉNÉRALE

Like the Gruner committee, the government was dissatisfied with the inaction of the Commission générale. But the government's discontent stemmed from the fear that dissatisfaction with the Commission générale might lead to the formation of rival groups not under state influence. The government wanted to prevent the emergence of a number of rival organizations each jockeying for position and practising a *politique de surenchère* of making gradually more strident demands upon the state.[39] This kind of competitive jostling could lead to irresistible pressures on the government to take responsibility for defaulted French investments in Russia. The CIAF discussed this problem on several occasions and recognized that the government would have to take the Verneuil committee in hand. This could best be done, it was believed, by appointing a government representative to sit on the commission in a semi-official capacity or by giving it some specific tasks to perform. But the CIAF could never decide which alternative to pursue, basically because of reluctance to be drawn into any far-reaching commitments to the Verneuil committee.[40]

The controversies surrounding the Commission générale illustrate the feelings of wariness and suspicion that existed between the government and business groups. Neither side wanted to become too committed to the other. The Commission générale did not believe the government would defend its interests fully except in response to outside pressure.

The government, on the other hand, sought to avoid responsibility for defaulted investments in Russia. Yet both sides had need of the other to prevent the emergence of rival defence committees which would jeopardize their respective, but somewhat contradictory interests. The Verneuil committee sought to maintain its prominent position no doubt in hopes of profiting handsomely when the Bolsheviks were finally overthrown and economic reconstruction began. By contrast, the government, in bestowing "semi-official" status on the Commission générale, sought to maintain these economic groups close enough to the state to control them, but at the same time far enough away to avoid any real commitments to them. To be sure, relations remained deferential between the two sides, but beneath the surface each manœuvred against the other.

### THE EMERGENCE OF FRENCH ECONOMIC OBJECTIVES IN RUSSIA

Although the government sought to avoid any extensive financial commitments to the Commission générale, its first actions to protect French economic interests appear to have come in response to pressure from the Groupe industriel. Berthelot and ultimately Pichon approved the subsidy requested by Gruner in July for the Bureau industriel in Petrograd so as not to justify "certain attacks" from industrialist circles "to the effect that the government had failed to defend French economic interests in Russia."[41] Similarly, Kammerer noted in August that certain measures taken to strengthen the economic section of the Arkhangelsk embassy were a response to attacks from private groups, especially the large industrialists, and from parliament about the government's lack of action in Russia. These measures were also necessitated in Kammerer's view because French industrialists were unwilling to make new financial commitments in Russia, and because it was the role of the state to take the initiative in protecting French economic interests.[42] Kammerer did not elaborate, but he must have felt that nothing would be done unless the state intervened.

Berthelot gave an earlier hint of Quai d'Orsay thinking when he prepared the blueprint for the reorganization of the French foreign ministry in 1907. He favoured a fusion of the political and commercial services of the Quai d'Orsay because of the difficulty in distinguishing between political interests of the state and economic interests of its nationals. Economic and political issues, he noted, were linked together and interacted. Indeed, international political rivalries were often hidden behind private commercial ventures.[43] It was probably this type of reasoning which led Kammerer, Berthelot's admirer and *alter ego*, to propose the creation of a high level "autonomous service" attached to the French embassy in Russia which could deal with economic problems arising in those areas occupied by the Allies.[44]

The impetus for this action came not only from the disgruntled Groupe industriel but also from Noulens who in July began to inundate Paris with cables insisting on government action. By this time, Noulens had begun to sound like a double-dyed imperialist, clamouring for economic concessions and warning of the danger to France's economic position in Russia which could arise from the activities of the other Allied powers.[45] Noulens argued that since the Bolshevik regime was on the point of collapse, Paris should act "to guarantee French industry a favourable position in the economic and financial reorganization [of Russia] which any [succeeding] government of order would have to undertake." To this end, he recommended the formation of an industrial consortium which could seek concessions and establish a firm French position in the north.[46] The government hastened to give some satisfaction to Noulens and also undertook negotiations with the Crédit Lyonnais for the establishment of a branch bank at Arkhangelsk to strengthen the French financial presence in that area.[47] Moreover, by the end of the summer the consortium recommended by Noulens had been formed by Schneider et Compagnie, the Société des grands travaux de Marseilles, Fougerolle Frères, and Giros et Compagnie.[48]

As it turned out, these projects were only indifferently followed up because of the relative unimportance of the north Russian theatre. The Commission générale wanted government action, but northern Russia held little interest for it. The French consortium organized on Noulens's recommendation, for example, suspended plans to send a mission to Murmansk to look for concessions.[49] Moreover, the Quai d'Orsay's negotiations with the Crédit Lyonnais and subsequently with the Comptoir d'escompte for the establishment of a branch bank at Arkhangelsk proved unsuccessful. James Rosselli, a member of the board of directors of the Crédit Lyonnais, told Kammerer in early August that he saw no point in establishing a bank in northern Russia since the British were taking principal financial responsibility for the area. He added, however, that it was pointless to make ambitious economic plans for Russia without a recognized central or even regional government with which to negotiate concessions and other such arrangements.[50]

THE BANQUE RUSSO-ASIATIQUE

Although the French government was relatively uninterested in northern Russia as a sphere of economic activity, this was not the case elsewhere. In May 1918 the CIAF began to discuss the creation of a *banque d'émission* in Russia. The concept of an inter-Allied *banque d'émission*, it will be remembered, had been raised as early as December 1917 in the context of efforts to retain the anti-Bolshevik Ukrainian Rada on the Allied side. Although this proposal was abandoned because of the Ukrainian peace with the Central Powers, the idea began to circulate again during the summer in meetings of the CIAF. The focus of this discussion centred on the Banque Russo-Asiatique. This bank, in which the powerful Société Générale and Banque de Paris et des Pays-Bas had important interests, was formed in 1910 from a merger of the Banque du Nord (or Severnyi bank) and the Banque Russo-Chinoise. The former, though a Russian institution, was controlled by the Société Générale, while the latter, whose foundation capital was more than 50 per cent French, had been established in 1896 as an instrument of both French and Russian economic penetration in China.[51] The new Russo-Asiatique became the largest banking institution in total assets in tsarist Russia.[52]

In early January 1918 André Bénac, a member of the Russo-Asiatique's board of directors, had written to the Quai d'Orsay offering to put his institution entirely at the disposal of the French government in exchange for protection of the bank's interests.[53] The Russo-Asiatique needed French diplomatic support to compel the Chinese government in Peking to continue to pay the Boxer indemnity (the Russo-Asiatique acted as the agent of the Russian government in this regard), which was indispensable for the bank's continued operation and for the maintenance of the Russian embassies in Peking and Tokyo.[54] The Quai d'Orsay, for its part, was disposed to help the Russo-Asiatique in order to employ it as an instrument of French policy both in China and in Russia.[55] Thus the Quai d'Orsay supported a plan whereby the Russo-Asiatique would take over the Chinese Eastern Railway across Manchuria, which the Russo-Chinoise had financed, as security for French stockholders in the bank and as an instrument of French political influence.[56] But General Horvat, who controlled the railway, along with officials of the Russo-Asiatique in Peking, tried to block the French plan by presenting counter-proposals to the Chinese government.[57] The French legation in Peking reacted angrily to these Russian efforts, and the French chargé d'affaires, Charles de Martel, tried to have one bank official removed and French agents placed in the administration of the Russo-Asiatique in order to assure French control.[58] The Quai d'Orsay supported Martel's proposal, and instructed him to inform the Chinese government in Peking that, in the absence of any legal authority in Russia and in view of the threat to French capital in the Russo-Asiatique, the French government would have the last word in matters concerning the bank in China.[59]

Martel informed the Peking regime of the contents of the Quai d'Orsay note, but the *démarche* backfired because it undermined the authority of the Russian agents of the Russo-Asiatique and of the Russian legation *vis-à-vis* the Chinese government.[60] This in turn encouraged the Chinese to refuse to pay the Boxer indemnity and to try to take control of the Chinese Eastern Railway. The Quai d'Orsay was then forced to beat a hasty retreat since it risked delivering the Chinese Eastern Railway to the Peking government and through it to the Japanese whose influence in southern Manchuria was already predominant. Consequently, Paris recommended to Martel that Horvat, in spite of his shortcomings, be left in control of the railway and that the authority of the Russian legation be supported by French representatives. The French government, observed the Quai d'Orsay, wished to obtain more direct control over the Russo-Asiatique, but it would have to do so without weakening the position of the former agents of the Russian government *vis-à-vis* the Peking regime.[61] The Quai d'Orsay therefore acted to assure the continued payment of the Boxer indemnity and also to free assets of the Russo-Asiatique blocked in the United States because of the bank's uncertain status after the Bolshevik seizure of power.[62]

While these events unfolded in the far east, the European board of directors of the Russo-Asiatique, divided between Paris and Petrograd, found itself at odds over the bank's future. Two members of the Petrograd executive, Maurice Verstraete and M. Boutry, were impressed by the strength of the Bolsheviks and favoured coming to terms with them, apparently to disengage at least some of the bank's assets and set up a purely French establishment in China. In general, Verstraete, like Chevilly, believed that the French government faced the two alternatives of either ignoring the revolutionary danger of Bolshevism and co-operating with Moscow against Germany, or of crushing the revolution perhaps in co-operation with the Central Powers (by means of a peace at the expense of Russia). In the first case, Verstraete noted that the government could always turn on the Bolsheviks after the end of the war in order to protect threatened French economic interests.[63] Unlike Chevilly, however, Verstraete tended to favour the former rather than the latter course of action.

The Quai d'Orsay was extremely alarmed by Verstraete's views, which, if put into effect, would liquidate French influence in one of the most powerful financial institutions in Russia. Moreover, by this time the government regarded any contact with the Soviets as undesirable since, as Sergent put it, Bolshevik policy aimed only at the "spoliation" of French interests.[64] Bénac, who was invited to the CIAF meeting of 19 June, explained that the Paris executive had not been able to contact Verstraete to warn him of the dangers of liquidating the Russo-Asiatique as a Russian institution. If this were to happen, said Bénac, the bank would lose it authority to act as agent for the Russian government in the collection of the Boxer indemnity and the interest on the 1895

Russo-Chinese loan. The Russo-Asiatique would also forfeit its concession on the Chinese Eastern Railway. But even if these problems could be solved, Bénac stressed that he could not be certain whether a majority of the bank's stock remained in French hands, an important consideration if Paris were to be assured of control over the bank.[65] In the aftermath of this meeting, the Quai d'Orsay directed Noulens to approach Verstraete in order to stop his conversations with the Bolsheviks and to prevent the liquidation of the bank. As the Quai d'Orsay told Noulens, the government intended to exercise "a sort of protectorate" over the Russo-Asiatique to safeguard French capital and France's "legitimate" influence in the bank.[66]

THE BANQUE RUSSO-ASIATIQUE
AS BANQUE D'ÉMISSION

During the summer of 1918 the Russo-Asiatique figured very largely in the French government's plans for the recovery of its economic interests in Russia. With military intervention soon to take place in Siberia, the CIAF recognized that the Allied command would need an acceptable medium of exchange with which to obtain provisions and pay its troops. The creation of a new currency would provide for these needs and would also precipitate the final collapse of the old roubles, thus weakening the Bolshevik regime. But in the view of the CIAF, a new currency would also be a potentially powerful instrument of economic influence which could serve to protect French interests in Russia. Indeed, French policy-makers were fearful that the government might be excluded from a share in the "guarantees and concessions" which would devolve upon those powers circulating a new currency in Russia. Discussions in the CIAF centred for several weeks on this problem and on the need to prevent Russia from coming under the preponderant influence of one of the other Allies. Frédéric François-Marsal believed that France could avert this outcome by mediating between conflicting Japanese and American interests. The Russo-Asiatique, he thought, could serve a role in this sense, and should therefore be brought quickly under French control.[67]

François-Marsal, who became minister of finance in 1920, was the most aggressive advocate in the CIAF of a strong French economic presence in Siberia. The government, he said, should put itself "on a footing equal to that of the Americans, Japanese, and British," and should quickly send an economic mission to Siberia to watch over French interests. Kammerer made the most direct response to François-Marsal's remarks. Although not disagreeing with their substance, he pointed out that France could not act independently of its allies, especially the

United States. Moreover, French means of action were extremely limited in the supplies and tonnage necessary to give purchasing power to a new currency and influence to an economic mission. As for past French interests, Kammerer observed that they counted for little in the actual balance of forces. In spite of such arguments, it was François-Marsal's position which prevailed and the CIAF recommended that the government take an active part in any economic intervention in Russia.[68]

The Russo-Asiatique interested the CIAF not only as a possible *banque d'émission*, but also as an instrument which could assist in the rebuilding of French industrial enterprises after the war. These industries would require large amounts of new capital to resume production. The Russo-Asiatique, in providing these funds, could co-ordinate reorganization and consolidation. Moreover, with its large network of branch outlets, the bank could also facilitate the development of French commercial relations with Russia.[69]

All these plans remained in abeyance because the government encountered difficulties in reorganizing the Russo-Asiatique to its liking. The main problem seemed to be that the government could not determine whether French nationals or institutions retained a majority of the bank's stock. In addition, the Verstraete affair had yet to be cleared up, and apparently the bank's administrators in Paris were not entirely agreed among themselves.[70]

In spite of the impasse in negotiations, Nicholas Raffalovich, a member of the Paris directorate, renewed the bank's offer of co-operation. Raffalovich proposed as a basis for discussion to concentrate administration of the Russo-Asiatique in Paris and to allow certain positions on the bank's directorate to be filled in accordance with the wishes of the French government. It would also agree to furnish financial support to industrial enterprises in Russia in which the French were interested, and generally would put its services at the disposal of the Allies.[71] The Quai d'Orsay responded, as it had previously, that such an arrangement could not be envisaged until it had been established that a French majority in the capital of the Russo-Asiatique could be maintained and before the directorate of the bank had been reorganized to assure the French government of a "preponderant influence." Even if the bank should remain a Russian institution, a majority of its executive would have to be filled by French nationals approved by the government.[72]

Because negotiations with the Russo-Asiatique continued to be inconclusive, the government began to consider other means of protecting its economic interests in Russia. It pressed for the formation of an inter-Allied high commission which would have political and economic direction over the intervention and, subsequently, it proposed on 5 September the organization of an inter-Allied *banque d'émission*.[73] The

project for the inter-Allied bank was the outcome of discussions in the
CIAF and between the Quai d'Orsay and the ministry of finance. The
French proposal envisaged the issue of a new currency backed by the
treasuries of the interested Allied powers. Britain, the United States,
Japan, and France would each furnish a quarter of an initially modest
capital of 40 million roubles. The administration of the bank would be
directed by mandatories of the four governments, to which Russian
representatives could eventually be added. As with the proposal for the
high commission, the Quai d'Orsay was prepared to offer the presidency
of the bank to an American, though it wanted the central offices of the
new financial institution to be established in Paris. According to the
minister of finance, L.L. Klotz, the new currency would be "an instrument of payment of the first order" both for the maintenance of Allied
troops in Russia, and for use in loans to regional governments established under Allied protection – "loans in compensation of which the
Allies should demand all the necessary securities...." In a sense summing
up the conclusions of the CIAF, Klotz wrote to Pichon that the *banque
d'émission* would serve as a major instrument in "the safeguarding of our
economic, financial, and industrial interests in Russia."[74]

As with Berthelot's proposal for an Allied high commission, the
French government's interest in an Allied *banque d'émission* stemmed
from the recognition of its own weakness. Such a bank would prevent
economic competition between allies in which the French government
could not hold its own and which might jeopardize the re-establishment
of France's pre-war influence in Russia.[75] As a member of the CIAF
observed, one role of the bank would be to distribute fairly among the
Allies the economic influence they would acquire through intervention.[76] France would get its share only if it could reach agreement with
the other powers.

As in the political sphere, therefore, the French government was
afraid of losing its once pre-eminent economic position in Russia to its
allies. But the need to avoid difficulties with Wilson and, above all,
weakness caused by the exhausting struggle of the World War prevented Paris from acting independently. The French were therefore
compelled to hide behind the skirts of their allies, hoping to dash out at
a propitious moment and snatch back lost economic advantages in Russia. The principal instrument of this subterfuge was the *banque d'émission*.
The purposes of the bank were manifold. Aside from seeking a means of
payment for an Allied army of occupation, Paris also sought to establish
an economic influence over the future Russian government. Klotz, for
example, viewed the inter-Allied bank's function of issuing loans to
local Russian client regimes as a means of extracting "guarantees" and
therefore of exerting control over these administrations.[77] If the old

issues of roubles collapsed, the anti-Bolsheviks would have no choice but to turn to the Allies for financial support.[78] And as Noulens had put it so succinctly during the spring, he "who pays the piper calls the tune."[79] If the French and Allies paid the costs of intervention, they would expect their anti-Bolshevik protégés to dance to Allied music. But the *banque d'émission* was not only a tool of influence, it also represented a direct means of saving previous French investments. Such a bank could serve as an excellent financial instrument with which to restart French industry in Russia and to facilitate the expansion of Franco-Russian commercial exchanges.

The French government, of course, could hardly do otherwise than protect its special interests in Russia. Indeed, action in this sense became all the more urgent because a power vacuum created by the weakness of the anti-Bolsheviks seemed to be developing and threatened to draw in the other Allies and jeopardize French pre-war influence. As a result, the objectives of French policy in Russia became gradually more acquisitive. In this sense, it is symbolic that the French government wanted to use the Boxer indemnity and the revenue from the 1895 Russo-Chinese loan, both the ill-gotten gains of western imperialism in China, to advance the cause of the counter-revolution in Russia and to protect its economic interests there. If the nature of French objectives was not fully apparent in the summer of 1918, it would become so during the coming autumn and winter. But before turning to these developments, the shift of French attention from Siberia to the Ukraine needs to be examined.

## CHAPTER SEVEN

# Intervention in the Ukraine

## OCTOBER–DECEMBER 1918

The autumn of 1918 was a dramatic period in the history of the early twentieth century. The World War, of course, ended in victory for the Allied coalition. The Habsburg and Hohenzollern monarchies collapsed, but, more than that, Soviet-style revolution seemed ready to engulf all central Europe. Even in the Allied states the tremors of revolution were felt. Bitter soldiers came home from the war muttering of vengeance against their own governments which had sent them off to more than four years of senseless and infernal slaughter.

The French government, fearing revolution and wanting to recover its pre-war political and economic advantages in Russia, began to entertain thoughts of direct military intervention against the Bolsheviks. The collapse of the Central Powers would free troops for action in Russia and allow access to the Soviet heartland through the reopened Straits and the Black Sea. The French general staff spent the autumn months planning for a military occupation of the Ukraine and Crimea. These plans were initially ambitious but had to be whittled down because of public demands for rapid demobilization and outright opposition to the intervention. This opposition was fanned by French Socialists who pointed long, shaking fingers at the government, accusing it of preparing a capitalist expedition against the Bolsheviks. The French government would not be deterred, however, and in December it ordered the landing of troops in southern Russia.

The military collapse of the Central Powers which permitted the French government to contemplate intervention in the Ukraine came about with startling rapidity. In May the German army seemed to threaten Paris, but in July what was to be the last German offensive misfired. Within days troops under the command of General Charles Mangin successfully counter-attacked German lines in the forest of Villers-Cotterêts. In a matter of weeks the Allies were rolling back the

German armies all along the Western Front. In the east on the Salonika front the Armée d'Orient under General Louis François Franchet d'Esperey commenced a general offensive on 15 September which within a fortnight led to the capitulation of the Bulgarian army and punched a gaping hole in the defences of the Central Powers. Turkey was also on its last legs. British forces led by General Sir Edmund Allenby entered Damascus on 1 October, and the Turkish government was soon compelled to ask for an armistice. These events, portending a rapid end to the war, reawakened French interest in the Ukraine.

In the early autumn of 1918 the French government still devoted its main attention in Russia to the Siberian theatre of operations. Indeed, the French general staff was prepared to leave southern Russia to the British who had troops in Mesopotamia and could reach the Don and Caucasus more easily than French forces.[1] But at the beginning of October the general staff's 3e Bureau began to examine the possibility of French penetration into the Ukraine since the capitulation of Bulgaria and Turkey would allow access to southern Russia by way of Rumania and the Black Sea.[2] Renewed contacts with the anti-Bolshevik Russians in the Caucasus and Don were also contemplated.[3] French interest in these areas grew rapidly as the defences of the Central Powers continued to disintegrate.

THE RISING SPECTRE OF BOLSHEVISM

Military opportunity was not the only motive behind the renewed French interest in the Ukraine. In October 1918 apprehension about the growing strength of the Bolsheviks suddenly erupted in the French capital. During the past summer, in the aftermath of the Czech rebellion, Paris had taken the imminent collapse of the Soviet regime for granted. But in the autumn, because of the military reverses suffered by the Czechs and the continued weakness of the anti-Bolshevik opposition, the situation in Russia appeared to revert to the days of the brief Franco-Soviet détente when the Bolsheviks seemed to hold the upper hand.

French fears concerning the new power of the Bolsheviks appear to have been ignited by an early October report from General Lavergne in Stockholm on his way back to France from Russia. This report warned in no uncertain terms of the growing strength of the Soviet regime. The Bolsheviks, said Lavergne, were becoming bolder and now threatened to back their agitation for world revolution with the force of arms. This consolidation of Soviet power deserved immediate attention because Allied military intervention had been contained or thrown back by Soviet troops. The Allies would therefore have to decide whether to reinforce their military effort in Russia or treat with the Bolshevik regime. Lavergne cautioned, however, that the survival of the Soviets would mean exposing western Europe and Germany to a heavy infestation of the "virus" of revolution. Could the Entente run this risk, he asked? If not, the Allied would have to act quickly and with sufficient forces "because each new day added to [Bolshevik] power." Lavergne estimated that it would take half a million men to overthrow the Soviets, and warned the government not to count on the anti-Bolsheviks who remained disorganized and leaderless.[4]

The continued weakness of the anti-Bolsheviks only augmented the alarm over the growing power of the Soviet regime. Noulens, for example, although strongly disagreeing with Lavergne's assessment of Bolshevik strength, recommended that Austro-German troops not be removed too quickly from occupied Russia lest these areas, for want of indigenous troops to defend them, fall immediately into the hands of the Red Army.[5] Similar recommendations were received in all the capitals of the Entente, and Allied statesmen began to contemplate using the German army as a temporary bulwark against the spread of Bolshevism.[6]

The French government responded immediately to these signs of danger, informing its ambassadors in London and Washington of the "dangerous reinforcement" of Bolshevik power and warning of the likely consequences of a precipitous German evacuation of occupied Russia. The spread of Bolshevism, in the view of the Quai d'Orsay, would menace "all civilization" and required immediate preventive action by the Allies.[7]

Lord Derby recounted a conversation with Pichon on 18 October in which the French foreign minister said that his government was

very much disturbed by certain information that they had got from Germany as to that country being on the eve of a revolution. He [Pichon] says that they are as full of Bolshevism as Russia itself was before the revolution, and it may break out at any time.... What frightens him is the fact, as he says, that Bolshevism is very contagious and he is evidently considerably alarmed as to what may happen in this country.

Derby asked if there were "any signs of trouble" in France, Pichon responded negatively, but said that he remained "gravely anxious" about the situation.[8] Derby commented the following month that the French ministers with whom he had spoken were "none of them very much afraid of Bolshevism here [in France] although they do not like to see it creeping so close...."[9] Nevertheless, the direction of events was sufficiently alarming for the Quai d'Orsay to characterize the Bolshevik menace as "more fearful for humanity" than Germany had been during the war.[10]

The general staff shared the Quai d'Orsay's concern. Colonel Georges, chief of the 3e Bureau, in two notes prepared during the third week of October also stressed the dangers of a German withdrawal from Russia which, as he put it, risked turning the former tsarist empire into "an immense hotbed of anarchist propaganda." Referring to Lavergne's report, Georges wrote that Soviet power was steadily growing both because of increasing popular support, attracted by the 'demagogic expedients" of Bolshevism, and because of the weakening of its enemies, broken by the Red Terror. According to Georges, the Red Army had grown to 300,000 men whose morale had improved with their victories over the Czechs and whose leadership had proven its competence in battle. This burgeoning menace, concluded Georges, should be destroyed before it became too strong.[11]

The Georges memoranda were quickly adopted into a war directive to Pichon signed by Clemenceau. This letter, dated 23 October, laid out the basic reasoning behind the government's determination to pursue its struggle against the Soviet regime. The collapse of Germany and the inadequacy of the intervention in Russia, the letter observed, had contributed to the growth of Soviet power. The Red Army, whose strength Moscow sought to raise to a million men, threatened to extend Soviet authority to all the former territories of the Russian empire "and then to the rest of Europe.... This new and monstrous form of imperialism represented a danger all the more fearful as it arose at the precise moment when the impending end of the war would inevitably provoke in every country a grave social and economic crisis." Clemenceau warned as well that if the Entente left the task of overthrowing the Bolsheviks to Germany, the German government could in a brief time compensate for its defeat in the west by creating a Russian state subservient to it and open to its economic influence. Yet this was not the only danger because Bolshevism was a double-edged sword. Germany itself could be directly threatened by Soviet-style revolution. The German government might become a victim of its own creation since it had encouraged revolutionary activity in Russia during the war and tolerated the survival of the Soviet regime.[12]

If the French general staff worried about future German political and economic penetration of Russia, it was incomparably more alarmed by the immediate threat of revolutionary Bolshevism. Although the government appears not to have been unduly concerned about any danger from the French left, it was fearful that the Soviet regime might try to spread Bolshevism into Europe by military force and use its propaganda to spark unrest and rebellion ahead of an advancing Red Army. It is not surprising, therefore, that the Quai d'Orsay was unreceptive to a strong Soviet peace effort in November that attempted to forestall a deepening of the intervention. Lenin feared that with the war over in Europe, the Allies might turn their full military strength against Soviet Russia. He hoped, however, that rivalries between the Allied powers would hamper their efforts to launch a fully co-ordinated, anti-Bolshevik campaign. Lenin sought to exploit these rivalries and divide the Allied camp by proposing peace negotiations along with substantial political and economic concessions.[13] Having appeased the Germans through the summer, Lenin now sought to do the same with the Allies, hoping to gain a further "breathing spell" to consolidate the authority of the Soviet government.

It was with these objectives in mind that in early November Chicherin, commissar for foreign affairs, approached the Norwegian chargé d'affaires in Petrograd to act as an intermediary between the Soviet government and the Entente. Chicherin stated that the Bolsheviks were prepared to make large concessions to reach a peace agreement. The French response to this Soviet initiative was entirely negative. Berthelot minuted on the cable reporting Chicherin's *démarche*, "we do not have the slightest intention of entering into conversations with the Bolsheviks."[14] This response was confirmed a few days later when Pichon told his minister in Christiania, Edmond Bapst, "I scarcely need tell you that no response can be given to the Bolshevik attempt to enter into discussions with us, even in the case of the most extensive concessions."[15] Pichon gave no reasons for his attitude, but in a subsequent cable he indicated that it would be impossible for the French government to negotiate with a regime which "did not cease to violate the rights of men and ... the most elemental principles of humanity."[16] In more practical terms, of course, the Quai d'Orsay did not want, by negotiating with the Soviet government, to reinforce the latter's authority *vis-à-vis* the Russian people. Nor did it wish to permit the Bolsheviks to send agents to western Europe where, under the guise of negotiating with the Allies, they could spread their "criminal" revolutionary propaganda.[17]

The Quai d'Orsay's cables were short and to the point, and few explanations were given for the government's decision to reject the Soviet offer of negotiations. But at the time, none were needed. The French were alarmed by the growing threat of the Bolsheviks. French apprehension was so great, in fact, that it began to take precedence over other factors affecting the attitude of Paris toward the Soviet regime. This development represented a definite change from earlier French policy. The government's decision in the spring of 1918 to break off the *rapprochement* with Moscow seemed motivated more by the determination to preserve French political and economic interests in Russia than by fear of Bolshevism spreading destabilization in Europe. However, in the spring the Red Army existed only on paper or in the imagination of L.D. Trotsky. The following autumn, it was becoming a formidable force, one that could spread revolution into Europe. In these circumstances, stopping the expansion of Bolshevism became the principal concern of the French government. Otherwise, the Quai d'Orsay might have proved more receptive to Bolshevik offers of substantial political and economic concessions in exchange for peace.[18]

The somewhat panicky French reaction to growing Soviet strength was also repeated in the other capitals of the Allied coalition. Both Lloyd George and Wilson were apprehensive about the potential influence of Bolshevism on the war-weary and disaffected populations of Europe. Their minds were not put more at ease by the collapse, in the last days of the war, of the German and Austro-Hungarian monarchies. The old multi-national Habsburg empire broke up into states of uncertain stability, led by bumptious, quarrelling leaders. In Berlin, armed soldiers with woolly ideas and Red flags began to form Workers' and Soldiers' Councils and to talk of socialist revolution. Ironically, these popular discontents were exacerbated by the Allied maritime blockade which had been intended to starve out the enemy. But the blockade worked too well as rumours flew of the spread of Bolshevism in Germany. At first it was hard to know what was going on and sobering visions of a revolutionary Armageddon began to trouble British and American statesmen. Shortly before the Armistice Wilson told his cabinet that he was extremely concerned about the danger of revolution in Europe. "The spirit of the Bolsheviki," he later remarked, "is lurking everywhere."[19] Even in London the British government was nervous about the building revolutionary danger.[20] The problem of the "Bolshies," not the *Boche* began to preoccupy the Allied governments.

To fight the spread of revolution meant striking at its heart in Russia. The French and Allied governments therefore sought to prevent the extension of Bolshevik authority into the areas of southern Russia occupied by the Austro-Hungarian and German armies. It was decided to order these troops to hold their positions until Allied units could be sent to replace them. On 10 November Foch approved this arrangement which was formalized in Article XII of the Armistice agreement.[21] In so doing, the Allies could prevent the creation of a power vacuum in southern Russia into which the Bolsheviks could quickly move. Such a provision implied, however, a widening of the intervention since the French at least had no intention of permitting the Germans to remain indefinitely in Russia.

## FRENCH PLANNING FOR INTERVENTION

Military planning for the intervention in southern Russia picked up rapidly as the war drew to a close. Clemenceau's directive of 23 October, after discussing the necessity for intervention, outlined a plan of action for crushing the Bolshevik regime. The French government sought to tighten the Allied blockade of Russia, imposed after the Bolsheviks took power from Kerensky. As the directive of 23 October put it, the Allies should envisage an "economic encirclement of Bolshevism in order to bring about its collapse." This objective would be accomplished in the north from bases on the Arctic Ocean and eventually from Finland, depriving the Bolsheviks of access to the sea. In the east, the resources of Siberia would be denied central Russia through the operations of Japanese, Czech, and anti-Bolshevik Russian military forces. In the southeast, elements of the British army moving up from Mesopotamia and Armenian contingents would separate the Caucasus, the Trans-Caspia region, and Asia Minor from the Bolshevik grasp. In the south and southwest, the landing of Allied forces would deprive the Soviet regime of access to the grain and mineral areas of the Ukraine and Don region. The Clemenceau directive anticipated that the Armée d'Orient and British forces operating in Asia Minor would "easily" furnish the divisions necessary both for the construction of a cordon sanitaire to isolate the Bolsheviks and for the establishment of a military nucleus around which anti-Bolshevik elements could gather.[22]

The initial plans drawn up by the French general staff for operations in the south were relatively ambitious. It was believed that eighteen to twenty divisions from the French, British, and Rumanian armies would be available for action in the Ukraine and the Don valley. Their military objectives would be to occupy Odessa, the Crimea, and then progressively the grain- and mineral-bearing areas of southern Russia. Allied forces would also seek to establish liaison with the anti-Bolshevik armies of Generals A.I. Denikin and P.N. Krasnov.[23] Finally, many war directives of this period emphasized that intervention would have the economic objective of taking control of those areas of southern Russia which could provide collateral to secure French investments.[24]

Almost immediately, the general staff was forced to whittle down the scale of the intervention. By the middle of November the number of divisions for action in the Ukraine and Don was cut from eighteen to twelve – five French, two British, two Italian, and three Greek. Five British divisions were also allotted for the occupation of the Caucasus. The 3e Bureau conceded that these forces were not as strong as those the Central Powers had previously maintained in Russia. But it believed that Allied prestige gained from the victory over Germany and popular support from the local Russian population would make up for the difference in numbers.[25] Nevertheless, even these figures had to be reduced. A week later a war directive signed by Clemenceau indicated that only six divisions would be committed to the intervention: three French and three Greek. The addition of some Rumanian troops was also envisaged.[26]

The French general staff thus encountered serious difficulties in finding troops to make up its army of intervention. The 3e Bureau had stressed even before the Armistice that after four years of uninterrupted war it would be "difficult, if not impossible, once the magic word of peace had been pronounced" to resume military operations. After the troops had once put down their arms, they would not take them up again.[27] These views were only reinforced by reports of French representatives abroad concerning the dangers of intervention.

Franchet d'Esperey is the best known of these reluctant interventionists. He informed Paris in mid-November that a military occupation in southern Russia would be unwise because of the war-weariness of his soldiers. "I must tell you," he said, "that whereas during the war our troops accepted their prolonged stay in the east in a spirit of patriotic resignation ... operations or occupation of the Ukraine and Russia would be viewed unfavourably and might lead to deplorable incidents because of [troop] exposure to Bolshevik propaganda." For these reasons, he thought that the Allies should help the anti-Bolshevik Russians to overthrow the Soviet regime.[28] However, if the government did decide to intervene directly, he stressed that it should do so in force and should treat the conflict as a colonial war, using volunteers and young conscripts.[29] Franchet d'Esperey was not alone in holding such views. General Philippe Henri d'Anselme, who would command French and Allied troops in the Ukraine, was altogether opposed to the intervention. Indeed, many French officers in the Armée d'Orient felt that spent troops awaiting demobilization and stricken by a raging epidemic of influenza would not perform well in Russia.[30]

A. de Fleuriau, the French chargé d'affaires in London and long associated with Paul Cambon, also opposed further military action in Russia. He warned that it would be a mistake to transform the intervention, justified by the struggle against Germany, into a war against the Russian Revolution. Such a policy would be unpopular in France and destined to certain defeat. Similarly the government should not be lured into seizing small-scale collateral to guarantee French economic interests. "The enterprise is too vast," he said, "it must be undertaken on a grand scale, or it will fail." The best alternative, Fleuriau thought, was to hold back and to treat with the government that emerged from the disorder of the revolution.[31] Although the Quai d'Orsay was not disposed to follow such advice, low morale in the army and the skepticism of Franchet d'Esperey would incline the ministry of war to scale down its plans for intervention.

Not all the advice coming into Paris concerning the intervention was negative. Noulens, for example, debunked Lavergne's October observations regarding the strength of the Red Army. Bolshevik troops, he asserted, were weak and undisciplined and would be swept away by the Allies.[32] In Rumania Saint-Aulaire also pressed hard for intervention. He too warned of the rapid spread of Bolshevism if German troops were not immediately replaced by Allied contingents. The moral effect of an Allied presence, he said, would produce important results even with small numbers of troops.[33] Saint-Aulaire's enthusiasm seems to have been influenced by the urgent pleas for Allied action from anti-Bolshevik circles in Rumania. Even Franchet d'Esperey, though less impressionable than Saint-Aulaire, was not immune to these appeals and in response to one made in November by anti-Bolshevik representatives meeting in Jassy, advised Paris not to delay further the intervention.[34]

General Henri Berthelot, who had contributed to the ill-starred French recognition of the Ukraine in January 1918 and who took command of the Armée du Danube intended for action in Russia and Rumania, was another strong partisan of intervention. But General Berthelot complained that the government had not given him sufficient troops to fulfil his mission, and that, of the three French divisions at his disposal, only one could immediately be put into the field. To make up for the shortage of French troops, he asked for authorization in late November to organize seven to nine Franco-Rumanian mixed divisions which along with Greek troops would provide an adequate force for intervention.[35] Ten days later Berthelot warned flatly that, if the Allies intervened in Russia, they should do so with the necessary means or, he implied, face unhappy consequences.[36]

Franchet d'Esperey, who thought that Berthelot's plans were too ambitious, argued for the deployment of a smaller force which would be sufficient to re-establish order in limited areas of southern Russia and would allow for new Russian and Allied troops to be organized.[37] The general staff tended to agree, primarily because General Berthelot's proposals went well beyond Clemenceau's directive of 21 November limiting the army of intervention to six divisions. In any case, the general staff considered these forces adequate for initial operations. Moreover, the strength of this army would be augmented by airplanes, tanks, and armoured trains. The full application of these modern weapons, the general staff believed, would make up for shortages in manpower. Plans were also initiated to buttress Berthelot's forces with colonial troops and volunteers.[38]

Orders to this effect, which were sent to Franchet d'Esperey on 18 December, indicated that the 156th, 30th, and 16th Infantry Divisions as well as the 1st Corps of the Greek army were being put at the disposal of General Berthelot. It was anticipated that the occupation in southern Russia would initially extend to Odessa, Sevastopol, Nikolaev, Taganrog, and then gradually inland toward Kiev and Kharkov. Expansion of the occupied zone would be left to the discretion of General Berthelot but depended on the availability of reinforcements.[39]

This was as far as the general staff felt it could go, especially in view of the disintegrating morale of the French army. From the reports of Franchet d'Esperey and other officers of the Armée d'Orient, only one conclusion could be drawn. As General Alby reported in early December, the fight had gone out of French troops who would take a dim view of even police duty in Russia. Alby surmised that Bolshevik propagandists would not fail to be active among French soldiers and indeed "would find fertile ground among troops brought to Russia against their will...."[40] For a high command that could scarcely have forgotten the mutinies of 1917, this was a danger not to be ignored.

Whatever the reasons for limiting the scope of the intervention in southern Russia, the decision did not sit well with certain French representatives abroad. Saint-Aulaire was particularly vocal in demanding a larger French military commitment. The French minister, who had earlier said that a symbolic presence of Allied forces would suffice, now warned that the government was courting disaster by not sending enough troops to Russia.[41] The persistence with which Saint-Aulaire pressed his views only exasperated Clemenceau who regarded these calls for intervention in force as completely unrealistic.[42]

The Quai d'Orsay, or rather its minister Pichon, had to bear the brunt of Clemenceau's formidable exasperation and he in turn took it out on Saint-Aulaire. Pichon twitted his minister for insubordination and in effect directed him to be silent.[43] The Quai d'Orsay, however, could not silence all its agents abroad and soon felt compelled to respond to other complaints from its chargé d'affaires in Arkhangelsk, Marcel Guiard.[44]

In a long dispatch prepared by Philippe Berthelot, the Quai d'Orsay tried to respond to all the criticisms of French policy from its representatives abroad. Berthelot indicated that the government was fully aware of the menace of Bolshevism and the weakness of its opponents, but had itself only limited means with which to respond to these dangers. None of the other Allies was prepared to undertake a large-scale intervention in Russia, and because of French losses in the war, it was in no position to launch such an operation by itself. Moreover, neither public opinion nor parliament would approve a far-reaching and hazardous military expedition to Russia. "This is not to say in any sense," wrote Berthelot, that we are uninterested in the Russian problem but we limit our action to our means....

No doubt it is more seductive to imagine the thundering march of an army of 200,000 men provided with all the engines [of modern war], supported by powerful logistics and economic aid, and certain of sweeping away a Red Army which, though numerous, lacks real cohesion and is incapable of resisting organized troops.

But such a policy is a function of the imagination rather than of a careful assessment of realities. It cannot stand critical analysis.[45]

Berthelot's reference to opposition from public and parliamentary opinion was quite to the point. Since the early summer, *minoritaire* Socialists had begun increasingly to condemn the intervention as a mean effort by French and Russian capitalists to recover their lost investments and expropriated property.[46] By the end of the war, the *minoritaires* controlled the Socialist party and their attacks became even more vitriolic. Socialist papers like *Le Populaire*, *L'Humanité*, and *Le Journal du Peuple* began to express fears that the government intended to send troops, freed by the Armistice in Europe, to crush the Soviet republic. Angry charges were levelled that the government was delaying demobilization in order to maintain sufficient forces for a new campaign against the Bolsheviks.[47] Socialist Jean Longuet warned in *L'Humanité* that French soldiers would not fight their "brothers in Russia" to re-establish the old capitalist order.[48] And Paul Faure, writing in *Le Populaire*, commented that Socialists and syndicalists in "all corners of France" were organizing to protest against the government's new war in Russia.[49]

This Socialist agitation against the intervention had an inflammatory effect on an already highly discontented population.[50] Workers and returning soldiers, alienated and brutalized by four years of war, were openly hostile to the government's trumpeting of a new call to arms against the Bolsheviks. The "war to end all wars" was hardly over and instead of tending to business at home, proceeding with demobilization and reconstruction, the government planned a new "capitalist expedition" to Russia. Moreover, the Russian Revolution was popular in France, as it was elsewhere in Europe. The Red Army had bearded the Allies, and the Soviet regime had survived in spite of all its enemies. For French workers and soldiers, who disliked their own bourgeois government, the image of Bolshevik defiance was inspiring.[51] This popular sympathy for the Soviets added weight to the Socialist campaign against the intervention which carried into the Chamber of Deputies at the end of December.

The Socialists pushed the government into a two-day foreign policy debate to force it to make some public statement about its intentions in

Russia. Several Socialist speakers condemned the intervention, drawing uncomplimentary analogies with the efforts of aristocratic Europe to crush the French Revolution. Socialist deputies Alexandre Blanc and Ernest Lafont rose to challenge the legality of sending French troops to fight in Russia without the approval of parliament.[52] And Lafont accused the government of ignoring Wilsonian principles to adhere to a policy based on force and the right of the strongest.[53] Both Pichon and Clemenceau rose to respond to these attacks, vigorously defending the government's policy, and obtaining a strong vote of confidence.

In spite of its majority in parliament, the government's freedom of action was limited to some degree, as Berthelot himself admitted, by public opposition to the intervention. But it was also limited by French dependence on the British and American governments. Neither Lloyd George nor Wilson was eager to become entangled in a far-reaching military involvement in Russia. Although both men intensely disliked the Bolsheviks, both were hampered by domestic considerations. In the United States Senator Hiram Johnson of California began to attack Wilson's policy in Russia and to demand the withdrawal of American troops. Johnson's attacks touched off an important movement of opposition to any further U.S. involvement.[54] In Britain Lloyd George had to be mindful of left-wing opposition which began to organize around the slogan of "Hands off Russia." The British government also had to contend with growing unrest and insubordination in the army. Like the French *poilus*, British soldiers were sick of war and looked forward to immediate demobilization. When it was not forthcoming, unrest and mutiny broke out among troops on both sides of the Channel. Soldiers' grievances were sharpened by fears that the delay in demobilization meant that the government was contemplating the dispatch of troops to Russia.[55] Under the circumstances Wilson and Lloyd George began to consider the option of coming to terms with Moscow. Wilson, unlike the French, was responsive to the Soviet peace initiatives of November and December, and decided on New Year's Day 1919 to send an envoy to Stockholm to sound out the Bolshevik representative there, Maxim Litvinov. Wilson also seemed to gain the ear of Lloyd George, who was moving in the same direction and was interested by Soviet offers of generous trade concessions.[56]

With Wilson and Lloyd George flirting with Moscow and without sufficient troops or wide popular support, the French government was compelled to back away from a large-scale military campaign against the Bolsheviks. As it did so, an important, if not entirely perceptible, change came over French policy. It will be remembered that during the spring and summer the principal rationale for intervention had been the weakness of anti-Bolshevik Russians. Since they could not overthrow the Soviet regime, Allied troops would have to undertake this task. But in the autumn of 1918, it rapidly became apparent in Paris that there would be few French or Allied troops available for duty in Russia. The rationale for intervention, therefore, had to change because if the Allies could not themselves intervene in force and if the anti-Bolsheviks were too weak to act alone, then the Soviet regime would survive. Instead of conceding victory to the Bolsheviks, however, the French government decided to adopt a new defensive strategy intended to give the anti-Bolsheviks, by way of a limited intervention, the protection necessary so they could organize themselves the armies to crush the Soviet regime. In December Clemenceau stressed to Janin that he must impress upon the anti-Bolsheviks that they, and not the Allies, would have to take the offensive to overthrow the Bolsheviks.[57] Thus, the keystone of French strategy against Bolshevism became the heretofore scorned anti-Bolshevik opposition. To be sure, Paris at this time expressed a certain amount of confidence in Admiral A.V. Kolchak, who had come to power in Siberia during November, and in General A.I. Denikin, but this confidence did not go very deep.

In a sense, the French government adopted a policy which was condemned from the outset. Yet, with the exception of A. de Fleuriau, no one in the ministry of war or in the Quai d'Orsay, not even Berthelot, the supreme practitioner of *realpolitik*, appears to have perceived this fundamental weakness of French policy. Franchet d'Esperey and others in the Armée d'Orient were reluctant to send their troops into Russia; yet in November Franchet d'Esperey had himself advised against further delays in undertaking military operations in the Ukraine.[58] Support for this policy represented more than just a good soldier's obedience to orders; it was an expression of alarm at the rapid spread of Bolshevism. Had Franchet d'Esperey considered solely the military merits of the case, he might well have opposed intervention altogether.

Similarly, the general staff, had it followed the logic of its own misgivings, might not have approved the commitment of troops to Russia. But the Quai d'Orsay and Clemenceau apparently put such doubts aside and went ahead with plans which were, Philippe Berthelot's avowals to the contrary notwithstanding, beyond French means to carry out. The government proceeded because it would not follow the October advice of Lavergne that the Allies either intervene in force or treat with the Soviet regime. The risk of allowing Europe to become "infested" with the "virus" of Bolshevism was too great. Paris was thus caught between permitting the survival of the Soviet regime with all the incumbent risks and disadvantages on the one hand, and sending a makeshift force of unwilling soldiers to fight the Bolsheviks on the other. In the climate of revolutionary hysteria which possessed the continent in the autumn of

1918, the grumblings of the war-weary *poilus* were much less a worry than the barking of revolutionary Bolsheviks who sought to turn Europe on its head.

## THE FRENCH LANDING AT ODESSA

Although a decision in principle to intervene directly in Russia was taken in October, the actual order to send in French troops came only on 5 December.[59] A few days earlier French naval units had appeared in the roads of Odessa harbour to gather intelligence and prepare the way for a military occupation should it be ordered by Paris. What they found there was not altogether encouraging.

The Ukrainian government of P.P. Skoropadskii, a puppet regime set up by the Germans in April to take the place of the unco-operative Rada, was itself disintegrating because of the military collapse of Germany. Skoropadskii had attempted to shed his pro-German, separatist image and to gain Allied support, but the sudden change of colours did not suffice to save him. V.V. Vinnichenko and Simon Petliura, formerly members of the Ukrainian Rada, set up a new government known as the Directorate and launched a rebellion against the German-organized regime. By the time French battleships appeared off Odessa, Petliura's insurgents had overthrown Skoropadskii's authority everywhere but in Kiev and Odessa. In the latter city, a Skoropadskii prefect still nominally ruled but had no military forces with which to defend his authority. The only troops in Odessa were a small detachment of Poles and about 1,500 officers of the Volunteer Army loyal to Denikin. These soldiers, however, would not co-operate with the local administration and in any case were incapable of holding the city against Ukrainian insurgents advancing from the north.

This situation was further complicated by the activities of Émile Henno, a so-called French consul who took it upon himself to act in the name of the Entente in the Ukraine. Henno had been a member of the Tabouis mission during early 1918 and had stayed behind to do intelligence work during the German occupation. He was well connected with the anti-Bolshevik great Russians and had absorbed their strongly anti-Ukrainian prejudices. Although Henno was in contact with Saint-Aulaire, he had no direct relations with Paris.[60] Indeed, the Quai d'Orsay had no knowledge of Henno's existence until the repercussions of his activities began to reach back to Paris.

Henno was in Jassy in November, and with the approval of the Allied ministers there, went to Odessa as a spokesman for the Entente. He carried with him a proclamation signed by the British and French ministers appealing to the Ukrainian population to maintain order until the arrival of Allied troops. Once in Odessa, Henno added, on his own initiative, a specific declaration supporting Skoropadskii, promising imminent and large-scale intervention, and threatening Ukrainian insurgents with dire consequences if they disturbed the public order. Henno acted in this manner to hold off Petliura, whom he regarded as a Bolshevik and a separatist, until French troops arrived.[61] But his efforts did not succeed, and, worse still, put Henno and theoretically the Allies into open conflict with the only military force of any consequence in southern Russia.[62]

Henno's conduct was not looked upon with favour either in Paris or by French personnel in Russia. Admiral Jean-François Amet, the commander of the French fleet in the Black Sea, characterized Henno as a "trifling scatter-brain," a view shared by local naval commanders at Odessa.[63] In Paris, the Quai d'Orsay was highly vexed by Henno's declaration promising unlimited intervention and it directed Saint-Aulaire to bring his agent under control.[64] Although Henno did not speak for the French government, his activities created major problems for the local French command and contributed to the serious difficulties which later arose between Paris and Denikin.

On 11 December, several days before the French landing, Ukrainian military forces under Petliura seized Odessa almost without firing a shot. The small group of anti-Bolshevik officers and functionaries in the city "disappeared" at the approach of the insurgents.[65] The local French naval command sent a representative to try to dissuade the Ukrainians from entering Odessa, but without success.[66] Petliura, however, who was also fighting the Bolsheviks advancing from the north toward Kiev, chose not to expel Henno, in hopes of reaching an accommodation with the Allies. Hence, while Petliura occupied most of Odessa, he left a small section of the city to the control of 400 French marines, some Poles, and those anti-Bolshevik Russians who were not "hiding out" on a freighter in the harbour.[67]

In the few days between the arrival of the Ukrainians and the landing of French troops the situation in Odessa remained extremely confused. The local French command was uncertain of Ukrainian intentions with regard to the impending landing. Admiral Amet reported that his intelligence concerning the Ukrainians was very contradictory. Denikin's officers, he said, claimed that Petliura was a Bolshevik, while other observers stated that he was pro-Allied and anti-Bolshevik, and that he was prepared to accept an autonomous, rather than an independent Ukrainian state. However, Petliura favoured breaking up the large estates, which explained, said Amet, why the big landowners regarded him as a Bolshevik.[68] Amet suggested that perhaps an agreement could be reached with the Ukrainians to facilitate the landing of French troops. In any case, he added, since the government had decided "to rush into an adventure," it was best to get on with the landing.[69]

The uncertainty of French commanders continued because of the deportment of Petliura's troops in Odessa. French officers were allowed to circulate freely in the Ukrainian zone of the city during the day, but at night there were occasional exchanges of rifle and machine-gun fire between French and Ukrainian outposts.[70] This confused situation prompted General Albert Borius, commander of the French landing force, to ask whether he should proceed with the debarkation without taking into account the presence of the Ukrainians, or whether he should enter into relations with them before disembarking his troops.[71] General Berthelot responded on 16 December that the landing should be undertaken immediately, and that Borius was not to contact Petliura other than to inform him that he would be held personally responsible for any disorders created by the troops under his command.[72]

Interestingly enough, General Berthelot's attitude toward the Ukrainians was rather more inflexible than that of the French government. Although at the time of the Armistice, the Quai d'Orsay rejected the idea of recognizing a Ukrainian government, it did not rule out this option for the future. As Pichon put it, the constitution of an independent Ukrainian state would only be possible if such a movement had strong indigenous support. "It goes without saying," he remarked, "that no one would propose to the Ukraine that it rejoin a union with Russia as long as the Bolshevik crisis had not been ended."[73] As this last remark suggests, anti-Bolshevism, not anti-separatism, was the immutable principle of French foreign policy toward Russia.

In view of the government's uncompromising anti-Bolshevism, the contradictory intelligence concerning Petliura's political affiliations inclined the Quai d'Orsay to regard the Ukrainian nationalists with distrust. Pichon therefore advised the ministry of war that if local French commanders entered into relations with the insurgents in order to dissociate them from the Bolsheviks they should proceed with extreme caution.[74] Such words of caution were by no means an absolute proscription on contacts with the Ukrainians, unlike General Berthelot's directive to Borius. The ministry of war forwarded these instructions to Franchet d'Esperey, but they did not reach Borius before the landing.[75] Had it been otherwise, he might have had less difficulty in dealing with the still uncertain situation at Odessa.

On the afternoon of 17 December the first elements of the French expeditionary force, approximately 2,400 ill-equipped troops, arrived in the harbour of Odessa. Borius, accompanied by several French officers, went ashore and travelled in an open car across lines of gawking Ukrainian sentinels to a meeting with Henno and anti-Bolshevik Russian officers. At this meeting, which took place at Henno's headquarters, it was decided to issue a public announcement indicating that the city of Odessa would come under French authority the following day. Anti-Bolshevik Russian and Polish detachments in the city were taken under French command, and General A.N. Grishin Almazov, formerly an aid to Kolchak, was named military governor under the orders of Borius. It was also decided to begin landing soldiers and *matériel* that evening. However, it still remained unclear whether French troops would be able to enter the city peaceably, *musique en tête*, or whether the landing would have to be undertaken by force.[76]

The following morning small groups of French troops and Russian officers were organized to take control of strategic positions in the city. These units immediately encountered armed resistance and could not fulfil their missions. Intermittent shooting broke out against French outposts, although this fire was apparently not returned. In the afternoon, new efforts were made to occupy strategic points in Odessa, and in general these objectives were achieved. But the majority of French troops were not engaged and the city appears to have remained at least partially in Ukrainian hands.[77]

While these events were unfolding, Ukrainian delegates attempted throughout 18 December to meet with the French command. During the evening General M. Grekov, soon to be Ukrainian minister of war, requested several times to enter into talks with Borius in order to conclude an armistice. But Borius, not wanting to disobey his instructions from General Berthelot, declined to respond. Instead, he issued an ultimatum calling upon Ukrainian troops to withdraw from Odessa. Late in the evening of 18 December, Grekov complied with this demand in hopes of keeping open the possibility of discussions with the French command.[78]

The following day French troops occupied Odessa without further incident. D'Anselme later commented that there would have been no resistance at all to the landing, had it not been for the actions of the Volunteers.[79] French officers believed that the anti-Bolsheviks had deliberately started the skirmishes to block an entente between the French command and the Directorate.[80] These suspicions of Volunteer intentions did not augur well for the French command, which would soon find it necessary to reach an accommodation with the Ukrainians.

The landing at Odessa, though completed successfully, did not mark an auspicious beginning. Because of shipping shortages, French soldiers came ashore badly ill-equipped. Worse still, the troops had been told before leaving Salonika that they would be welcomed enthusiastically by the indigenous population. Instead, they had been greeted by the small-arms fire of Ukrainian insurgents. Amet observed ominously that

French soldiers had begun to complain about participating in a military expedition intended to save the money of Russian and French capitalists.[81]

The misgivings of the French general staff concerning the inadvisability of a military intervention were thus almost immediately substantiated by reports from Odessa. But the French government ignored these early signs of danger. Pride of place probably contributed to the decision to proceed with the landing in southern Russia. No doubt still caught up in the euphoria of the victory over Germany, the French seemed slow to recognize that their position as a great power had been seriously eroded by the World War. The long struggle had in fact drained French resources to the point of exhaustion. One and a half million French soldiers, or 10 per cent of the active male population, had died. Some of the richest, most highly developed parts of the country had been laid waste by the German occupation, and industrial production stood at only 60 per cent of its pre-war level. French finances were in no better condition. Though a creditor nation before the war, the French government was deeply in debt at war's end. It had contracted huge loans in Britain and the United States, and, instead of relying on taxation, it had resorted to national defence bonds and inflation to finance the war.[82]

The slowness of the French to perceive the crippling effect of these circumstances on their foreign policy was especially marked at the Quai d'Orsay which, unlike the ministries of war and finance, was always one step removed from having to find troops or money to implement government policies. Indeed, with regard to Russia, French diplomats seemed to carry on, in spite of avowals to the contrary, as if they had the resources of pre-war France at their disposal. This was far from being so, though the Quai d'Orsay had some painful lessons to learn before accepting the new limitations on French power. In the interim, however, the French government pressed ahead with its interventionist policy. The Quai d'Orsay and the ministry of finance continued to work on the preparation of economic plans to buttress the occupation of the Ukraine and to protect French investments in Russia. These plans developed along with those concerning the military aspects of the intervention.

## CHAPTER EIGHT

# The Economic Objectives of French Intervention

## SEPTEMBER 1918–APRIL 1919

If the impending defeat of the Central Powers had raised the question of military intervention, it also intensified discussions within the government on ways to salvage French economic interests in Russia. The intervention in a general sense, of course, was expected to achieve this end by obtaining collateral to guarantee the security of defaulted French investments.[1] But a detailed plan of action designed to protect these interests still had to be worked out. During the autumn and winter of 1918–19 the focus of the government's attention came to rest on the organization of a *banque d'émission* in Russia such as had been discussed in the CIAF during the previous summer. Because the British and American governments rejected the French proposal for an inter-Allied bank, the Quai d'Orsay went ahead with plans to circulate a uniquely French currency both in southern Russia and in Siberia. In so doing, the Quai d'Orsay also hoped to obtain economic concessions, expand French trade with Russia, and facilitate the movement of Russian grain and natural resources to France. As these plans developed, the Quai d'Orsay became more willing to dispense with the co-operation of its allies and in fact sought to exclude them from the economic advantages it hoped to acquire in the Ukraine. The French seemed to pursue these objectives with an energy heightened by the belief that the British and Americans were ready to wrench away the privileged economic position France had enjoyed before the World War.

### THE FRENCH GOVERNMENT AND THE COMMISSION GÉNÉRALE, AUTUMN 1918

While the French government formulated a policy for economic intervention in Russia, it also kept a wary eye on the Commission générale. The commission's new satellite organization, the Comité de défense, was impatient to know what the state intended to do about defaulted interest payments on tsarist bond issues. The government, which was still trying to avoid any pressure to pay the coupon, was to some extent prepared to appease the groups represented by the Commission générale. As a gesture to this end, several delegates of the CIAF attended a plenary session of the commission in September and assured its members of continuing state support for French economic interests in Russia.[2]

Some members of the commission, however, were not satisfied with general assurances and wanted to know exactly what the government intended to do about the interest on the tsarist bonds. One member of the Comité de défense expressed the hope that some settlement of the interests left in arrears could be arranged. Charles Sergent, who headed the delegation from the CIAF, made no direct response to these remarks, but commented that the government was pleased to see the formation of the Comité de défense and that it would receive full state support.[3]

In a more important step to quell public discontent over the defaulted tsarist securities, the government made its first and last major concession to the Commission générale. It agreed to accept defaulted Russian coupons for half the value of new national defence bonds (*loi du 19 septembre*). The government's gesture cost the state 264 million francs.[4] This concession, however, was not a sudden reaction to pressures from the Comité de défense. The government had been considering such a measure for several months.[5]

A memorandum circulated in the CIAF during May, for example, had recommended that the state take some temporary measures "to tranquillize" public opinion and to avoid undermining the success of upcoming national defence bond issues.[6] There was no consensus as to what these measures should be, but François-Marsal proposed a partial compensation of French bond holders which appears to have been the basis for the *loi du 19 septembre*.[7] This was done for purely pragmatic reasons since the government rejected the notion of the financial press that it had any permanent obligation to French holders of Russian bonds. François-Marsal acknowledged that the state had a duty to aid French investors but maintained that it was not obligated to free them from all risks and losses.[8] Partial compensation, therefore, was purely a means of maintaining stability in the bond market and avoiding unwanted political debate on the defaulted tsarist securities.

After the passage of the *loi du 19 septembre*, the government felt secure enough to inform the Comité de défense directly that it assumed no responsibility whatever for the compensation of French investors holding tsarist bonds. Pichon complained to A. Machart, the president of the Comité de défense, that his group appeared to regard exerting pressure on the state concerning the indemnification of French bondholders as its only purpose. The foreign minister found this perspective "somewhat limited" and suggested that Machart's group broaden its field of activities.[9]

The Commission générale was angered by the Quai d'Orsay's attempt to limit its role as a pressure group *vis-à-vis* the government. Verneuil observed to a colleague that the Comité de défense obviously did not see itself solely as a lobby group for French investors. However, he noted that Russia would certainly be capable of meeting its foreign obligations at some point in the future, and that only the French government would have the necessary influence to persuade the Russians to honour their commitments.[10] In this respect, Verneuil feared that the government might shirk its responsibilities.

FRENCH "WAR AIMS" IN RUSSIA

Although the Quai d'Orsay was categorical in disclaiming any responsibility for the servicing of tsarist bonds, it was also quick to assure the Comité de défense that France would recognize a future government of Russia only after an express commitment had been given to honour the tsarist debt. The Quai d'Orsay noted, however, that the future Russian government would be hard pressed to meet these obligations. The Russian foreign debt had increased considerably since the beginning of the war. Moreover, the effects of the Bolshevik revolution and German occupation of the Ukraine made it doubtful whether the payment of interest on the Russian national debt could immediately be resumed.[11] Hence, any future Russian government's recognition of the tsarist debt would not necessarily assure satisfaction to French bondholders. The Quai d'Orsay concluded that a series of measures designed to hasten the recovery of French investments would also have to be implemented. The Russian government would have to be persuaded to pursue a policy of exportation to obtain the foreign currency necessary to pay its debts. These measures might also entail the creation of special allocations from future budgets or the extension of concessions and other such privileges.[12]

This was not the first time that the question of indemnification of French investors had been raised. During the summer of 1917 even before the Bolsheviks seized power, the Bureau industriel in Petrograd had begun collecting the inventories of French enterprises so as to be able to substantiate later claims for the "reimbursement of damages" caused by the revolution.[13] Later on, in December 1917, the ministry of finance proposed taking a systematic inventory of all French investments in Russia to support eventual claims for damages.[14] It was still many months before any steps in this direction were taken, but in January 1919 the government approved a law making it mandatory for French nationals to turn over a list of their investments in Russia to the Office des biens et intérêts privés.[15]

In the spring of 1918 the CIAF also discussed a proposal for the formation of a French consortium of Russian bondholders. This scheme provided for an intermediary organization through which the government would continue to pay the coupon. The consortium would unite French bondholders and represent their interests. Although some members of the CIAF regarded this particular proposal as half-baked, they remained interested in the organization of one or more consortia which could exploit concessions or act as agents for the sale of grain and natural resources provided by the Russian government to indemnify French investors.[16] The Quai d'Orsay at first favoured the proposal, but Klotz regarded it as impractical.[17] Such a consortium was, therefore, not formed at this time, but the discussions concerning it remain an early indication of how the government hoped to recover its economic losses in Russia.

The Commission générale was thinking along similar lines. Machart proposed in a reply to Pichon's letter of 23 October that certain revenues of the Russian government be put under the direct or indirect control of its creditors for the servicing and amortization of French-held bonds. Payments in natural resources and the acquisition of concessions, he suggested, should also be considered.[18]

The question of concessions was raised in a concrete way in August and September 1918 when the anti-Bolshevik regime at Arkhangelsk sought to obtain a 15-million-rouble loan from the Allies. The amount of the loan itself was insignificant, but the French government considered the issues of principle involved important enough to submit to the council of ministers. On 3 September it approved French participation. The Quai d'Orsay believed that France should make the loan in exchange for guarantees of even a precarious nature since there was every chance that the Allies could have these guarantees recognized by the future Russian government. Indeed, the Quai d'Orsay intended to condition formal French recognition of such a government on the acceptance of a commitment to honour agreements made by preceding local administrations.[19]

With the loan approved, the Quai d'Orsay instructed Noulens, in the case where the funds were advanced exclusively by the French, to obtain forestry, port, and other concessions – "in order to permit the development of France's future economic and financial position [in Russia]." If, on the other hand, the loan were to be inter-Allied, then collateral should consist only of readily available merchandise or raw materials which entailed no long-term commitments from the Russian government. Pichon indicated that "guarantees and concessions" were the only means by which France and its allies could cover themselves for various industrial, commercial, and other losses suffered during the revolution.[20]

The logic behind the Quai d'Orsay's instructions seems evident. Noulens was not to seek concessions in the case of an inter-Allied loan in order to prevent the economically stronger Allies from gaining an advantage over French interests. If, however, the loan were entirely French, the acquisition of concessions would be desirable. Indeed, as the Quai d'Orsay put it, guarantees for an exclusively French loan "should naturally profit France alone."[21] Nevertheless, Noulens was later instructed to oppose categorically any attempt by the British to gain concessions on a unilateral basis.[22] In short, the French were prepared to take for themselves what they would not allow their allies.

Even though the Quai d'Orsay withdrew its approval for the loan after the government at Arkhangelsk was overthrown in a military *coup d'état* on 5 September, the instructions to Noulens remain an important indication of the government's intentions with regard to safeguarding French economic interests in Russia.[23] It would appear that the Quai d'Orsay viewed the loan less as a means of extending financial support to an ally than as a way of obtaining guarantees for the protection of its own interests. The advance would have constituted a first step toward securing the indemnification of French investors. Indeed, the Quai d'Orsay would inform its allies in the new year that it regarded all the resources of Russia, both developed and undeveloped, as security or collateral for the creditors of the Russian government.[24]

The Commission générale, which does not appear to have been informed of these efforts to protect its interests, continued to be dissatisfied with French policy in Russia. The Groupe industriel was predictably the most vocal in this regard, and wanted to make a direct request to the government for intervention. However, other members of the Commission générale opposed this action. A demand for intervention made by big business, they argued, would be interpreted, no matter how it was worded, as a request for "a capitalist expedition" against the Russian Revolution. It would only succeed in unleashing socialist recriminations and reinforcing opposition to the government. Nevertheless, the industrialists pressed their point, and Verneuil wrote the government in early January 1919 setting out the views of the commission concerning intervention and requesting an audience with Clemenceau.[25]

Verneuil's letter, though moderate in tone, still called for military action against the Soviets both because of the danger of German economic penetration in Russia and because of the threat of "world revolution" represented by Bolshevism. More to the point, Verneuil's letter noted that the expansion of Bolshevik authority into the Ukraine would

lead to the ruin of French enterprises that had survived the war relatively intact. The loss of the Ukraine would also compromise irrevo-
cably the interests of Allied bondholders for whom southern Russia
represented the single area which could provide collateral for their
investments. Given these considerations, Verneuil asked that "energetic
measures" be taken to halt the Bolshevik advance. Moreover, because of
the need to rehabilitate the economy of the areas occupied by the
Entente, the Allied governments should assist commercial groups forming to do business in southern Russia. A central organization should be
created under the authority of Allied representatives to co-ordinate
commercial activities and to exercise price controls and prevent speculation. In addition, Verneuil urged the Allies to create a new monetary
unit for Russia which would facilitate economic recovery and, in so
doing, gain the loyalties of the local population.[26]

The Quai d'Orsay's reaction to this *démarche* is recorded by Kammerer's marginal notations on Verneuil's letter. He remarked that the
German danger in Russia pointed to by the Commission générale was
entirely without substance. "The Germans," minuted Kammerer, "have
no further interest there. They will [first] need to look after their own
reorganization. The Commission weakens its argument which is very
strong by putting forth such a manifestly unfounded idea."[27] This view
was also reflected in the Quai d'Orsay's official correspondence. A few
days later Kammerer noted in a dispatch for Regnault in Omsk that the
danger of German economic penetration in Russia was over and could
not arise again "for years to come."[28]

Kammerer's reaction to the so-called threat of German economic
penetration in Russia was in marked contrast to that of the general staff
some eight weeks before and suggests that the Quai d'Orsay may not
have entirely shared their views on this matter.[29] Kammerer's belittling
of this danger also reinforces the view that the government, or at least
the Quai d'Orsay, sought to pursue the struggle against Bolshevism primarily because of the revolutionary danger it represented to Europe.

In regard to the other points of the Verneuil letter, the Quai d'Orsay
was not optimistic. Concerning the formation of a central trading
organization in southern Russia, Kammerer noted that several efforts
had already been made but had not been successful because of the lack
of manufactured goods. In any case, the Commission générale, he
observed, was better placed than the government to make such efforts.[30]
These views were conveyed to Verneuil by Clemenceau who flatly told
the commission executive during an interview in the second week of
January that the government did not have the means to realize the
objectives of their program, and that they would have to remain patient.
Only the question of a *banque d'émission* could be treated immediately.[31]

The exchanges between the government and the Commission générale during the autumn and early winter of 1918–19 amounted to a
discussion of French "war aims" in Russia after the destruction of the
Soviet regime. These exchanges indicate that even before the Armistice,
Paris envisaged making extensive claims against the future Russian state
for damages suffered by French investors because of the revolution.
Compensation would be sought through economic concessions and
other such privileges. Indeed, the Quai d'Orsay's treatment of the question of a loan for the local anti-Bolshevik government at Arkhangelsk
demonstrates that Paris was prepared to acquire these special rights unilaterally and to the exclusion of the other Allies.

The private economic groups represented in the Commission générale, however, seem to have had little influence on these economic
objectives. The Verneuil committee was too divided and too amorphous
a group to exert such an influence. French bankers were not as heavily
committed in Russia as some of their industrialist colleagues and were
therefore not as aggressive in pushing for intervention. As a result,
domestic political pressure on the government for a more activist policy
against the Bolsheviks was never as great as it might have been, had the
Commission générale been a more cohesive group.

The government's only major concession to the commission générale,
the *loi du 19 septembre*, was a domestic one, and appears to have quieted
public discontent concerning the defaulted tsarist bonds. This concession and the inertia of the Verneuil committee permitted the government to undercut internal political pressures which might conceivably
have forced it to adopt a more aggressive policy against the Bolsheviks
or at least to have assumed a greater responsibility for the servicing of
the Russian debt in France. Although it may not have been so intended,
the *loi du 19 septembre* by paying off French bondholders, appears to have
bought the government something of a free hand in Russia. It was for
this reason that Clemenceau could so easily tell the executive of the
Commission générale that the government's policy options in Russia
were limited and that it would have to be satisfied with action on the
*banque d'émission*.

THE BANQUE D'ÉMISSION

Discussions concerning this project had continued throughout the summer of 1918, and resulted in a Quai d'Orsay proposal on 5 September for
an inter-Allied currency issue in Siberia.[32] Washington and London,
however, showed no interest in the French scheme. The State Department replied in early October with a different proposal, also envisaging
the organization of an inter-Allied bank in conjunction with a commer-

cial venture to be undertaken by the War Trade Board.[33] The Foreign
Office, for its part, submitted a plan to the American government on 5
September for a solely British-administered currency at Arkhangelsk.[34]

The initial reaction in Paris to the British proposal was hostile. As
Kammerer observed to Jusserand in Washington, France was the most
affected by the "financial disaster" in Russia and so could not agree to
the issue of a new currency by its allies alone – especially since this
operation would probably raise the question of guarantees and concessions designed to compensate foreign investors hurt by the revolution.
Kammerer also pointed out that an inter-Allied bank, like the one proposed by France, would have the advantage of dealing with Russian
financial reorganization on the basis of a single currency for the entire
country, and would avert any competition between the Allies. The Quai
d'Orsay, therefore, sought to enlist American support for its position
against the British bank.[35]

Kammerer's cable points to the crucial linkage for the French between the *banque d'émission* and concessions, which the Quai d'Orsay
believed were the only device by which to secure French investments in
Russia.[36] Since an Allied currency would drive the various already badly
depreciated issues of Russian roubles out of circulation, local administrations would become dependent on the Allies for financial support.[37]
In such straits, local anti-Bolshevik governments would have been hard
put to reject French conditions for cash advances. Moreover, the ministry of finance made it clear in December 1918 that these conditions
would include the appropriation of certain revenues of the Russian
state for the amortization of such loans and submission to Allied controls.[38]

Although French protests against the British bank of issue gained
a sympathetic hearing in Washington the Quai d'Orsay eventually
dropped its opposition to the British scheme after receiving assurances
from London that the proposed currency would not circulate outside
northern Russia.[39] All the same, the Quai d'Orsay did not like what it
regarded as the "cavalier" fashion in which the British government had
hurried through its plans.[40] There was no formal protest, however,
because, as Klotz put it, British action left France free to proceed with its
own currency issues elsewhere in Russia.[41] Klotz warned that if the Quai
d'Orsay protested against the British bank, London might well oppose
similar French plans on the basis of a precedent first established by
France itself.[42] Paris also declined to participate in the administration of
the British bank so that London would have no grounds to ask for some
role in future French projects.[43] In short, as Kammerer had implied in an
earlier note, the French planned to pay the British back in something
like their own coin.[44]

## THE BANQUE D'ÉMISSION AND THE
## BANQUE DE L'INDOCHINE

The French proceeded therefore to plan currency issues both for southern Russia and Siberia. This latter project was the result of the earlier French interest in the Siberian theatre of operations and of the commitment to support the Czech Legion. The large cash expenditures for roubles needed to support the Czechs and later the government of Kolchak were seriously depreciating the value of the franc in the far east. The ministry of finance hoped that a French *banque d'émission* in Siberia would put an end to this problem.[45]

It will be remembered that the CIAF had discussed the possibility of using the Banque Russo-Asiatique as the foundation for an inter-Allied bank in Siberia. But the government wanted to be sure that French nationals still controlled a majority of the bank's stock before moving ahead with these plans. Negotiations with the Russo-Asiatique continued during the autumn, but in November the Société Générale, which had tried to trace the Russo-Asiatique stock, reported that majority control of the bank might well have slipped from French hands.[46]

In view of the uncertainty concerning the Russo-Asiatique, the French government began to contemplate the use of the Banque de l'Indochine (BI) as an agency for the circulation of a French currency in Siberia. The first step in this direction was taken during the summer when the government invited the Banque de l'Indochine to establish a branch office at Vladivostok.[47] Then, in November, the CIAF recommended using the bank as a currency-issuing institution.[48] In spite of the acknowledged inability of France to compete economically with its allies in Siberia, the government continued to think it could exploit the rivalry between the United States and Japan to gain their consent for the circulation of a currency by the Banque de l'Indochine.[49] The thinking in Paris appears to have been that since neither the Japanese nor the Americans would permit the other to organize a *banque d'émission*, they might agree to a French bank as an alternative. The French government could then play the role of "honest broker" and at the same time acquire a political and economic influence in Siberia which would have been impossible in other circumstances.

On 1 December the ministry of finance formally invited the Banque de l'Indochine to undertake the issue of a new currency in Siberia. Such action, explained Klotz, was necessitated by the absence of any Russian governmental authority capable of undertaking this function. There were, of course, conditions. Klotz's letter indicated that the government could not convey to the bank any sort of privilege. The new currency would have a "purely commercial character" and would be issued by the bank at its own risk. The notes were to be termed roubles and would be reimbursable in Paris.[50]

The Banque de l'Indochine responded favourably but sought clarification as to the state support it could expect. The bank wanted assurances that the government would ask its allies to use the new money as much as possible and to refrain from setting up competitive currencies. The new monetary issue could only be successful, observed the bank, if it was very largely circulated in eastern Siberia and replaced the depreciated Russian roubles.[51]

The Quai d'Orsay was agreeable to asking the other Allies to use the BI currency, but it doubted whether they would consent "to tie their hands" in regard to the issue of their own banknotes. In any case, the Quai d'Orsay did not think the problem was as serious as the Banque de l'Indochine appeared to believe in view of the commercial activity likely to develop in Siberia, should the monetary situation improve. Given the immensity of Siberia and its poor means of communication, the Quai d'Orsay thought it improbable that a currency subsequently issued by another ally would jeopardize the first put into circulation. Anyway, as Kammerer minuted on a Klotz letter of 17 January, "there is room enough [in Siberia] *pour tout le monde*."[52]

The transformation in the Quai d'Orsay's attitude toward competitive Allied currencies in Russia is striking. Only three months before, Kammerer had told Jusserand that the French government favoured a single new currency in Russia precisely in order to facilitate financial reorganization and to avoid competition between the Allies.[53] Because of its inability to obtain Allied agreement, however, the Quai d'Orsay abandoned this policy. Paris would now risk igniting Allied economic rivalries in Russia. Hence, on 28 January Klotz gave final approval to the plans submitted by the Banque de l'Indochine, but with the stipulation that the government could not guarantee the success of any request to its allies to use the BI banknotes or prevent them from issuing their own currencies.[54] Shortly thereafter, the Banque de l'Indochine placed an order with the American Banknote Company for an initial bloc of 282.5 million "roubles."[55]

## THE BANQUE D'ÉMISSION
## IN THE UKRAINE

Negotiations for the formation of a *banque d'émission* in the Ukraine also proceeded. On the initiative of the ministry of finance and the Quai d'Orsay, the Banque de Paris et des Pays-Bas (Paribas) called a meeting on 28 October of the financial institutions making up the former Comité des emprunts russes.[56] The government's proposal for a currency issue in southern Russia was favourably received at this meeting and the Banque de Paris et des Pays-Bas began to plan the organization of the new bank.[57]

French objectives in undertaking this ambitious project in the Ukraine were basically those the CIAF had outlined during the summer. The French government required an acceptable currency with which to cover the financial needs of an army of occupation. But more than that a *banque d'émission* would facilitate the rapid recovery of French industries in the Ukraine and promote the resumption and expansion of Franco-Russian trade.[58] In the latter regard, the Quai d'Orsay stressed in numerous letters at the end of 1918 the importance of gaining access to Russian grain, petroleum, and other raw materials vital to the restoration of the French economy.[59]

From the importance with which the Quai d'Orsay viewed these objectives, there seems little question that the choice of the Ukraine as the target of a French military landing was at least partially motivated by economic considerations. There are numerous references, for example, in the war memoranda and correspondence of this period to the need to occupy the Ukraine and the Donetz basin where French industrial enterprises were heavily concentrated.[60] The French government obviously meant to protect these industries from the Bolsheviks as well as to seize those grain and mineral-bearing areas capable of supplying the French economy and compensating French investors. To be sure, the accessibility of the Black Sea to the French fleet and to French bases in the Mediterranean was of primary importance, but the lure of Russian grain and raw materials represented a powerful additional incentive to intervention.[61]

The importance of this potential warehouse of resources for the French economy made the Quai d'Orsay impatient for action on the *banque d'émission*.[62] It took a month, however, before Albert Turrettini, vice-president and director general of the Paribas, finally forwarded to the government a preliminary study for a bank of issue in southern Russia.[63] This proposal was much like that of the Banque de l'Indochine except that it called for state guarantees and financial backing. The government regarded such guarantees as unacceptable and preferred a *banque d'émission* in southern Russia based on the same principles as the BI project, to wit, a private bank acting with state support but under its own responsibility.[64] Apart from the state guarantees, the principal difference between this and the BI project was that the former included plans for the formation of a trading syndicate intended to function in close association with the bank of issue.

Negotiations between the Paribas and the French government continued at a sluggish pace, apparently because Parisian bankers had doubts about the extent of the government's commitment to intervention.[65] Moreover, the Paribas continued to press for direct state participation in the proposed bank. Sergent had to tell Horace Finaly, a director of the Paribas, that the government could not participate in the *banque d'émission* because of the impossibility of consulting with parliament.[66] Sergent is not recorded as having elaborated, but government unwillingness to go to parliament was undoubtedly due to its desire to avoid lengthy debates provoked by Socialist opposition to the intervention.

This stymied the government, however, because, as Klotz reminded Pichon, French businessmen were not prepared to invest new capital in Russia until they could be assured that France intended to commit itself to a course of action powerful enough to provide "a minimum of material security" for their holdings. The government, said Klotz, had "a sort of moral obligation" to these groups in this regard. He therefore requested more information on the intended strength of the military intervention, and urged the Quai d'Orsay to seek support from the Allies for the *banque d'émission*.[67]

The Quai d'Orsay did not see the impasse and was therefore little disposed to listen to the more sober reflections and advice of the ministry of finance. Indeed, Pichon continued to be impatient for action on the *banque d'émission*, and he brushed aside Klotz's recommendation that the government seek Allied support for its economic policies in southern Russia. As the foreign minister put it, the Quai d'Orsay intended to inform neither its allies, nor the local anti-Bolsheviks of its plans until they were well underway.[68] This avowal again confirmed the trend in French policy toward dispensing with the co-operation of the other Allies. The Quai d'Orsay did not wish to solicit Allied support, as Klotz had recommended, because it intended to present them with a *fait accompli* reciprocating British action in northern Russia and excluding them from participation in the French bank.

After considerable prodding by the government, the Paribas, in mid-February, presented to the ministry of finance a formal proposal for the creation of a *banque d'émission* in southern Russia. This plan provided for the creation of a French bank with its main offices in Paris and under exclusive French control. The unit of currency to be circulated would be termed a *franc russe* and the issuing institution the Banque de l'Ukraine. The government was asked to support the currency in a manner similar to that requested by the Banque de l'Indochine. Unlike the BI project, however, the Paribas proposal called for the creation of a subsidiary organization termed the Société commerciale française de l'Ukraine which would control all trade in the region under French occupation.[69]

The letter from the Paribas did not enlarge upon the range of activities which the Société commerciale might have. However, a similar pro-

posal submitted in late November by A.I. Putilov, president of the
Russo-Asiatique, did discuss the possible objectives of such an enterprise.[70] Like the bank, the trading company envisaged by Putilov would
be French controlled. Apart from simple commercial exchanges, it
would have authority to allocate shipping tonnage and issue import and
export licences. It might also act as an intermediary for other countries
wanting to trade in Russia. Such an organization could thus assure the
provisioning of France in raw materials while at the same time establishing a market for French exports under conditions where competition
could be controlled.[71]

ANTI-BOLSHEVIK OPPOSITION TO
THE BANQUE D'ÉMISSION

This is where the negotiations stood when the military situation in the
Ukraine began to deteriorate in early March. The Paribas project, had it
been instituted, would have represented a far-reaching trespass on the
fiscal sovereignty of the Russian state. Even France's anti-Bolshevik
allies were none too pleased with what little they knew of French intentions in this regard. During the autumn of 1918 rumours began to circulate in Paris about Allied plans to impose controls over the Russian
economy. In October Arthur Raffalovich, former counsellor of the Russian ministry of finance and soon to be associated with the Russian Political Conference in Paris headed by Prince G.E. Lvov, complained in a
letter to Sergent of certain articles in Le Temps calling for an international commission of control for the Russian debt.[72] Raffalovich protested that this action would represent interference in Russian domestic
affairs and would alienate Russian sympathies. Joseph Louis de Fabry, an
official of the ministry of finance assigned to matters concerning Russia,
commented that Raffalovich's views were unfortunate since the Allies
could scarcely do otherwise than institute "financial control[s]" in this
sense.[73] In early December Raffalovich complained again in an interview with Sergent about the currency project for Siberia, indicating that
Paris would have to get approval for it from the Omsk government.
Sergent noted that he had taken a non-committal attitude during the
interview.[74]

The Quai d'Orsay also began to receive criticism about the BI project
from its own agents. Regnault reported in January 1919 that, if the government went ahead with its plans, France's example would soon be
followed by the other Allies, thus aggravating the monetary situation in
Siberia. Moreover, it was certain that the currencies of the other Allies
would be preferred to that of the Banque de l'Indochine because of the
insignificant level of French trade in Siberia. The BI notes would rapidly
depreciate, opening the Siberian market to the Japanese. This would

permit Japan to establish an economic position in Siberia from which it could not be dislodged. Regnault urged the government not to go through with the BI project which would only exacerbate the suspicions of the Russian population, already "more or less impregnated with Bolshevik ideas," and who tended to see everywhere "the exploitation of the proletariat by bourgeois, capitalist imperialism." Even Russians sympathetic to the Entente would regard such a project as an usurpation of Russian sovereign rights. In effect, it was not in Russia, but rather in China, that private banking establishments circulated paper money. To issue a BI currency in Siberia would wound Russian national sentiments, appear to treat Russia as a colony, and demonstrate that France no longer believed in the vitality of the Russian government or in the reconstitution of a great Russian state.[75] The Quai d'Orsay, however, would not listen to these objections, and instructed Regnault to disclaim the validity of such "unfounded appreciations."[76]

Raffalovich, for his part, continued to protest against an Allied currency issue, in either Siberia or southern Russia, as a violation of Russian sovereignty.[77] On 18 May Raffalovich sent a sharply worded letter to Sergent complaining about the BI project. He protested that Omsk had received no information directly from the Quai d'Orsay concerning the projected currency issue and that his government was completely opposed to the plan which could only affect adversely the value of the rouble. Raffalovich warned that the Omsk regime was strongly placed, and that consequently it would be "in the common interest to avoid any friction."[78] The ministry of finance was quite alarmed by the Raffalovich note and dissatisfied with the Quai d'Orsay's handling of the BI project. An unidentified marginal note made by someone in the ministry of finance noted that "I have asked at least ten times that the question of our incoherent attitude towards the Omsk government be taken up with the foreign ministry; unless we do that, we are in the midst of total confusion."[79] The incoherence of French policy rested on the assumption that France could pursue acquisitive economic objectives in Russia opposed by the anti-Bolshevik Russians, and yet hope to maintain a conservative great Russian state as a French ally. The protests of Raffalovich clearly indicated, at least to the ministry of finance, that the French government could not pursue such a policy.

As it turned out, there was never a direct confrontation between the French and anti-Bolshevik Russians over this issue because the French government abandoned its plans for a *banque d'émission* in the face of continued opposition from Omsk. In any case, by the summer of 1919 the French had little further interest in Siberia except to assure the safe withdrawal of the Janin mission and the Czech Legion. Hence, the Quai d'Orsay, though annoyed by the opposition of the Omsk government, quietly dropped the BI project.[80] As for the proposed Paribas bank in the Ukraine, it was abandoned at the time of the evacuation from Odessa in April 1919.[81]

The BI and Paribas banks of issue remain, nevertheless, an important indication of what the French government would have done to protect its interests, had it possessed the power to act. Cetainly, the Paribas *banque d'émission* represented the principal instrument by which the French government hoped to protect and expand its economic position in Russia. The bank of issue and trading company would have exercised far-reaching financial and commercial controls in the French-occupied Ukraine and would have served as an agency for funnelling grain and natural resources to France – resources any Russian government might reasonably have wanted to commit to the reconstruction of its own shattered economy. Indeed, according to Putilov's proposals, the Société commerciale associated with the *banque d'émission* would have had exclusive control over all commercial activities in the Ukraine as well as the power to regulate prices, presumably to make expensive French consumer goods more competitive. In short, the French government appears to have envisaged the setting up of a controlled market in the Ukraine for French traders and a privileged reservoir of grain and raw materials for export to France.[82]

## TRADING CONSORTIA, CONCESSIONS, AND INDEMNITIES

The French government also sought to obtain concessions, either through the *banque d'émission* or some other organ of Allied control, in order to indemnify French investors. The Quai d'Orsay pursued this objective with bulldog-like tenacity. In consultation with the Commission générale, it drew up formal proposals during 1919 and 1920 which were to be submitted to the Russian government and were designed to assure the indemnification and safeguarding of French investments in Russia. The Quai d'Orsay envisaged the creation of an international commission to supervise the refinancing and amortization of the Russian state debt and the indemnification of damages to the property of Allied nationals during the revolution.[83] According to the Quai d'Orsay, such an arrangement was necessary to avoid the indefinite prolongation of the Russian government's bankruptcy and the complete loss of French investments.[84] As in all the French government's plans for recovering its economic privileges, concessions for the indemnification of French investors were closely associated with the Quai d'Orsay's desire to obtain Russian grain and raw materials. On the one hand, the French government would acquire the foodstuffs and natural resources necessary for post-war reconstruction while, on the other, French investors could be compensated from the profits generated by the sale of these commodities in France.

Interestingly enough, this was not the first time that the French had tried to put a hand on Ukrainian resources. After the 1905 Russian Revolution private French economic groups sought to take advantage of the weakness of the tsarist government to negotiate far-reaching railway and industrial concessions for a French-organized consortium. These concessions would have given this French syndicate first option on the development of new railway lines, urban electrification projects, mines, and industries. Involved in the negotiations were among others the Banque de Paris et des Pays-Bas, the Banque de l'Union Parisienne (BUP), the Société Générale, as well as Maurice de Verneuil, the future president of the Commission générale. Although private economic groups took the initiative in these talks, the then French minister of finance, Joseph Caillaux, apparently supported their efforts. In the end, these agreements were not implemented, but their intent, according to one French historian, was clearly to "obtain the upper hand in the future development of the Russian economy."[85]

In 1918 and 1919 the circumstances were somewhat different. The disorder of the second Russian Revolution far surpassed that of the first. Moreover, after the Bolshevik seizure of power French businessmen were reluctant to make new financial commitments in Russia and wanted the government to take the initiative. The French government, of course, was hobbled by a lack of resources. Nevertheless, it can be presumed that if the Bolshevik regime had been overthrown, and if the necessary conditions of order had been re-established, French businessmen would have tried to recover and expand their positions in the Russian economy.

This presumption is reinforced by the fact that Maurice de Verneuil, who had been involved in the attempt to form a French consortium in Russia after 1905, made a similar proposal to the French government in the late spring of 1919. Certain unnamed Russian anti-Bolshevik elements had approached Verneuil with the idea of forming a "powerful financial and industrial group" which could participate in the reconstruction of the Russian economy after the destruction of the Bolsheviks. Verneuil favoured the creation of such an organization which he believed could protect and expand French economic influence in Russia. He therefore sought government approval for his plans, offering to allow an informal state control over the new organization.[86]

Although the ministry of finance favoured the Verneuil proposal, the Quai d'Orsay regarded it as premature in view of the continuing instability in anti-Bolshevik Russia.[87] For this reason the proposal did not elicit much interest, but similar plans were discussed by the government during the summer of 1919 and one such plan was later implemented. In August 1919, for example, the secretariat of the CIAF circulated a plan approved by the ministry of war and other government agencies which envisaged the creation in southern Russia of a network of "committees of resupply," together with an export-import company, similar to the one outlined in the earlier Paribas plan for the Ukraine. These organizations would be charged with the importation and distribution of Allied manufactured goods in exchange for Russian agricultural products and natural resources. The inter-Allied committees would also fix the quantities of Russian grain and raw materials which could be exported as well as setting customs duties and prices for both imported and exported commodities.[88]

Although this particular project does not appear to have gone beyond the planning stage, a consortium of French industrial, banking, and commercial groups was actually organized in December 1919. Planning for the consortium, which was called the Société commerciale, industrielle et financière pour la Russie et les pays limitrophes, appears to have begun in the late summer of 1919, no doubt as a result of the military victories won by the anti-Bolshevik armies of Denikin. This syndicate was organized by the Banque de Paris et des Pays-Bas and the Banque de l'Union parisienne. Both these banks had been involved in Verneuil's first attempt to organize a French consortium. Among the other participants in the old consortium who were also involved in the Société commerciale, were the influential Banque française pour le commerce et l'industrie, the Société Générale, and J. Gunzburg et Compagnie.[89] The new grouping, which was closely linked to the Commission générale, was to include French and Russian financial and industrial elements, but was to be controlled by its French members.[90] The BUP and the Paribas submitted their plans to the government for approval, and received authorization to organize the consortium.[91] Joseph Noulens, who had become Clemenceau's minister of agriculture in July 1919, was named president of the new organization.[92]

The consortium was intended to have the widest possible range of commercial, industrial, and financial activities in Russia. Among other objectives, it would set up a trading network to encourage the exchange of manufactured commodities for Russian natural resources.[93] It would provide financing for the reorganization and expansion of French industrial enterprises and could exploit concessions granted by the Russian government.[94] In short, the Société commerciale represented a potentially powerful instrument for the maintenance of the French economic presence in Russia. The affiliations of its members and member organizations show a remarkable criss-crossing of industrial and financial connections which could have speeded the mobilization of new capital for investment in Russia.

The Quai d'Orsay would naturally have tried to take advantage of any new French business or financial activity in the Ukraine. Indeed, its persistent interest in finding a way to acquire Ukrainian resources sprang from the same considerations that had prompted the French government to try to extract the fullest measure of reparations from Germany. The French treasury was running a large deficit, it had incurred a staggering war debt, and it was faced with the very considerable costs of economic reconstruction. These financial burdens might have been more easily borne had the French government been fully able to tax its citizens. But the conservative French parliament would not approve substantial direct income or surplus profit taxes. The Clemenceau government wished to avoid a confrontation on this issue, and therefore sought to meet its budgetary needs by extracting all it could in reparations from Germany.[95] The government also hoped to find in Russia some of the resources it needed to pursue post-war reconstruction at home. L'Allemagne payera was a popular slogan of the day in Paris, but so perhaps was the idea that Russia would pay as well.

There are, of course, flaws in this scenario for the French economic penetration of Russia after the destruction of the Bolshevik regime. The very lack of financial means which compelled the French government to look to Germany and to Russia for the wherewithal to pursue economic reconstruction impeded the French effort to draw upon Russian natural resources. New capital would be needed to restart French industrial production in Russia, yet the government assumed that reconstruction at home would absorb most surplus French savings. Hence, new capital for investment abroad would be strictly limited and would have to be directed, in the view of the Quai d'Orsay, to those areas where it could best serve the French national interest.[96] No doubt new investments for the maintenance and expansion of French industry in an anti-Bolshevik Russian state would have come under this rubric, but the days of unlimited capital for foreign investment had passed in France. This lack of resources would also have made it more difficult for the French government to maintain its pre-war position in Russia against the competitive economic activities of its allies. In fact, the Quai d'Orsay feared that French influence in Russia might be supplanted by that of the United States and Britain.[97]

Finally, the scope of French economic objectives in Russia depended on the strength or weakness of the anti-Bolshevik government or governments which might emerge from the revolution. If the anti-Bolsheviks had been strong, the French would probably have dropped their aggressive policies as they had after the first Russian revolution when the tsarist regime temporarily regained its vigour.[98] On the other hand, had the anti-Bolsheviks been weak and divided, it can be assumed that the French government would have taken advantage of these circumstances to seize collateral for previous, defaulted investments and to compete for economic advantage with its Allied rivals. Later on, in October 1919 when the anti-Bolsheviks seemed momentarily to have taken the upper hand in the civil war, the Quai d'Orsay noted that it would be better to recognize a weak Russian government dependent on France rather than a strong regime capable of standing on its own.[99] A weak government reliant on France would be compelled to accept its terms for support. One may safely assume that the French would have loaded aid negotiations with the Russians with all the conditions the traffic would bear.

In the end, of course, the Bolsheviks won the civil war and all the French government's projects for the protection of its economic interests in Russia came to nothing. Paradoxically, these abortive plans succeeded only in entangling the government in a veritable conundrum of contradictions concerning the aims of French policy in Russia. The Quai d'Orsay declared that it wanted to see the regeneration of a strong anti-Bolshevik Russian state, yet it planned to cut out for itself what amounted to an economic protectorate in the Ukraine. Had it been able, Paris would have saddled an anti-Bolshevik government with the heavy financial burden of indemnifying French investors ruined by the revolution. The imposition of such burdens would certainly have slowed Russian economic and military recovery.

The French attitude toward its allies was equally inconsistent. On the one hand, the Quai d'Orsay clamoured for unity against Bolshevism; on the other, it attempted to pursue an independent policy designed to protect its vested economic interests in Russia. Finally, as on the military side of the intervention, the Quai d'Orsay sought to undertake ambitious economic projects which it did not have the means to carry out. The subterfuge of going through the Banque de l'Indochine and the Paribas was necessitated by the government's inability to put its plans before parliament. And even when the Quai d'Orsay turned to the Parisian banks, it was unable to promise full support and expected them to bear the financial risks of the *banque d'émission*. In short, it was as though the French government, unable to reconcile itself to the continued existence of Bolshevism, would not face up to the weaknesses and inconsistencies of its policies in Russia. Only the near disaster of the military intervention in the Ukraine would lead to a reassessment and gradual reorientation of French policy.

## CHAPTER NINE

# *"Denikin or Petliura?"* *The French Search for Allies in the Ukraine*

## JANUARY-FEBRUARY 1919

When the French government intervened in southern Russia, it was with the expectation of co-operating with local anti-Bolsheviks who, it was hoped, would bear the main burden of fighting the Red Army. The anti-Bolsheviks, however, both the Ukrainian Directorate and the Volunteer Army in Odessa, were not capable of filling the role envisaged by the French. The Volunteers had won a not undeserved reputation as tsarists and reactionaries, while the Ukrainian nationalists were rapidly losing ground to the Bolsheviks. Neither proved capable of organizing large military forces, which left the French command to face a growing Bolshevik threat with only the bare bones of three French divisions. To cope with this dangerous situation, the French tried themselves to organize local armed forces and to encourage the Ukrainians and Volunteers to unite against Moscow. But the anti-Bolshevik factions hated one another and hated the French for trying to compel them to work together.

To make matters worse, economic conditions in the French zone of occupation were very bad. Basic necessities were in short supply or not available. Unemployment and wild inflation resulted, making life impossible for all but the privileged and wealthy. Odessa began to fall prey to Bolshevik propagandists as well as to speculators and hooligans of every description. It was dangerous to walk the streets during the day and impossible at night since armed bands prowled the city looking for prey and clashing with Volunteer patrols. The French command viewed this scene with increasing alarm, but could only sit by helplessly. Promised reinforcements were slow to arrive, and demobilization and Bolshevik propaganda ate away at what forces were already on hand. The situation boded ill for, if the French command had few troops, it had fewer still who would obey orders or fight the Bolsheviks.

## DEMORALIZATION AND MUTINY IN
## THE FRENCH ARMY OF OCCUPATION

In early February 1919 mutiny broke out among French military units located along the Bessarabian border. On 4 February French troops crossing the River Dniester from the town of Bendery, attacked the Russian city of Tiraspol, which was occupied by Bolshevik partisans. The assault was badly executed and not successful.[1] Although French troops suffered insignificant losses, they were not prepared to return to the attack. On 6 February when orders arrived for a renewed assault on Tiraspol, officers of the 58th Infantry Regiment began to fear that a majority of their men would not march. The following day, 7 February, the 19th Battery of the 2nd Regiment of Light Artillery refused to obey orders to move out and was loudly cheered by mutinous soldiers of the 58th Infantry.[2] During the evening disturbances broke out when officers tried to move their men to the front. Angry soldiers responded with curses and threats of violence. Mutiny sputtered and flared throughout the night with trouble being quelled in one unit only to break out in another.[3]

Although the artillerymen finally moved to the front, the 58th Infantry refused *en bloc* to prepare for the attack. French officers pleaded with their men, but to no avail. The morning of the attack 467 men of the 1st and 2nd Battalions of the 58th Infantry Regiment still refused to march.[4] Some of the mutinous soldiers told their officers that after four years of war, they had had enough and did not wish to be killed fighting "Russian socialists." Others declared that the Armistice had been signed and that the Entente was not at war with the Bolsheviks. Only volunteers, they said, were supposed to be sent to Russia.[5]

As a result of the mutiny, the local French command was forced to call off its attack. Tiraspol was taken by other Allied units moving up from Odessa.[6] Although discipline was re-established in the 58th Infantry, the significance of this "collective refusal of obedience" was not lost on the French command. General Antoine Eugène Nerel, commander of the 30th Infantry Division, reported that the mutiny in the 58th had not been precipitated by agitators, but rather by "an entente between the men" who had had enough of war and wanted only to return to their homes. General Berthelot indicated that the mutiny was due to a state of mind present in "practically all the regiments and units of the army." Most of the men were eligible for repatriation and did not wish to risk their lives when the war had ended and they could return home. The troops had heard it said too many times that the war was over. In addition the letters they received from home gave them the impression that the Allies were not in agreement about the intervention in Russia and that the action they were asked to undertake was not approved by the great majority of the nation. Newspapers from France confirmed this idea, especially those dating from the end of December 1918 which contained reports of the debates in the Chamber of Deputies concerning Russia.[7] Since there was no declaration of war, the troops did not want to consider the Bolsheviks as enemies.[8]

The war-weariness of French troops was ably exploited by the Bolsheviks. Even before the first landing in the Ukraine, Bolshevik tracts were passed among French troops in Bucharest and among sailors of the first French warships to reach Odessa.[9] The reports of the 156th Infantry Division indicate that Bolshevik propagandists were at work among French troops within days of their arrival in Russia.[10] General Berthelot commented in February that Bolshevik propaganda was "admirably organized" and showed up in every possible form in spite of stringent controls.[11] The French intelligence service at Odessa also indicated that Bolshevik agitators were making progress among the troops and that it was "absolutely certain" that soldiers in small numbers were frequenting secret Bolshevik meetings and circles. The great majority of French troops remained disciplined, but "the danger of contamination [was] always to be feared."[12]

The arguments of Bolshevik propaganda, according to one anti-Bolshevik observer, were "simple and convincing." The war was over and Germany had been defeated. Why then were the soldiers and sailors of France being sent to fight in Russia when they should logically be able to go home? The French government claimed that Bolshevik "criminals" and "bandits" had usurped power and were terrorizing the people. But these so-called brigands, said Soviet propaganda, aspired only to free the oppressed masses of Russia from tsarism: to defend the poor against the rich, the workers against the bosses, and the peasants against the landed aristocracy. In short, the Bolsheviks were no more "criminals" than those Frenchmen who fought in the "great French revolution." Clemenceau had ordered troops to Russia in order to strangle the Soviets because the French government feared the contagion of the Russian Revolution and wanted to recover its billions loaned to the tsar. Bolshevik tracts implored French soldiers and sailors not to be duped into serving interests which were not their own. The lost billions of the French bourgeoisie, it was said, were not worth the life of a single French soldier. Some tracts, therefore, exhorted French troops to turn their arms on their real enemies – capitalism and the bourgeoisie. Other tracts simply encouraged French troops to fraternize with Bolshevik partisans, to refuse to march against the Red Army, and to insist on repatriation.[13]

This propaganda was left in barracks or passed to soldiers and sailors in the streets of Odessa, Sevastopol, and elsewhere. The Bolshevik agitators even operated in the brothels of Odessa, which were, according to General Berthelot, the "most dangerous" centres of revolutionary propaganda in the French zone of occupation. Apparently Russian women offered themselves to French troops to bring them over to the revolution. Propaganda tracts were also thrown into cafes and bars where off-duty French soldiers gathered. There are even accounts of a French-speaking Bolshevik propagandist being spirited aboard ships of the French fleet to speak to groups of sailors.[14] The same questions were asked repeatedly: Why are you here? Against whom do you fight? Remember your own revolution and let us make ours.

The propaganda had its results. French soldiers in the streets of Odessa were often heard to express their bitter opposition to the intervention. "To hell with this," they said. "What the devil have we got against the Bolsheviks? In fact, the sooner they get to Odessa, the sooner we clear out of here!" "*Vive les Bolchéviks!*"[15]

Even in December 1918 such views were not uncommon. M.S. Margulies, a prominent member of anti-Bolshevik circles in Odessa, recounted how he had engaged a French sailor in a conversation about the intervention. He told him that the war could not end until the Bolsheviks, who had supported the Germans, were defeated. When the sailor proved unresponsive to this line of argument, Margulies held up to him the "17 billions" repudiated by the Soviet regime. The sailor replied with a shrug that of the 17 billion only a small sum belonged to him, and that he would gladly leave this to the Bolsheviks.[16] As another sailor put it, if French capitalists wanted to recover their investments in Russia, they could come themselves to fight the Bolsheviks.[17]

## DEVELOPMENT OF FRENCH RELATIONS
## WITH UKRAINIAN DIRECTORATE

The unreliability of French troops had much to do with the decision of the French government to move away from a large-scale military intervention in Russia to a more defensive strategy based on giving the anti-Bolsheviks the major role in overthrowing the Soviet regime. However, the success of such a strategy depended on strong anti-Bolshevik allies. This fact was never more apparent than at Odessa where local French commanders were in real need of indigenous support.

It will be remembered that the Ukrainian Directorate, whose military forces had occupied most of Odessa in early December, was anxious to enter into relations with the Entente. But General Berthelot, who was not sympathetic to the separatist aspirations of the Directorate, had given orders to the local French commander, General Borius, forbidding him to negotiate with Ukrainian representatives.[18] As a result, skirmishes broke out on the day of the landing between the Ukrainians and French and Volunteer forces. In the aftermath of these incidents, Ukrainian troops withdrew from Odessa but only to the outskirts of the city where they set up a blockade cutting off the flow of provisions from the countryside into the small French zone of occupation. General Borius did not attempt to break the blockade, and by the middle of January 1919 Odessa, which could not be supplied by sea because of a lack of shipping tonnage, had been reduced to a three-day stock of supplies. Even the municipal waterworks remained in Ukrainian hands.[19] Under these conditions, anti-Bolshevik representatives in Odessa urged Borius to expand the zone of occupation.[20]

The French command proved unresponsive to such plans because it did not have sufficient troops to force the Ukrainian blockade. Greek and colonial units, which were to reinforce skeletal French divisions, would only begin to arrive in strength during February and March. Nor did the French command have much confidence in the Volunteers. To be sure, the French general staff took a relatively favourable view of the Volunteer Army in October 1918 when planning began for a military occupation in southern Russia. In November Franchet d'Esperey even sent 30,000 rifles and 42 million rounds of rifle ammunition to Denikin in the Kuban.[21] But this auspicious beginning was soon undermined by the poor impression which the Volunteers in Odessa made on the local French command. It will be remembered that when Ukrainian troops first approached Odessa in the second week of December, French officers reported that Russian authorities had "disappeared" from the city.[22] Moreover, the French command soon discovered, to its dismay, that the Volunteers in Odessa were hated by the local population which regarded them as tsarists bent upon the re-establishment of the old order. The fact that Volunteer forces consisted almost entirely of officers seemed evidence to the French of this unpopularity. From the beginning of the occupation, therefore, Borius attempted to keep the Volunteers out of the working-class quarters of the city and away from Ukrainian outposts in order to avoid any clash of arms.[23]

It was the weakness of the Volunteers which led Borius to reject their requests for permission to move beyond Odessa. With only a small force of French troops, Borius could not expand the zone of occupation himself, nor could he risk the consequences of a major battle with the Ukrainians provoked by Volunteer efforts to move inland. But the French command had to raise the blockade of Odessa immediately if the city were to stay in French hands. Under the circumstances General Berthelot abandoned his opposition to negotiations with the Directorate.[24]

The actual initiative for the change in attitude toward the Directorate came from General Berthelot, not Paris. In early January he gave General d'Anselme, who was preparing to leave for southern Russia to take command of French and Allied forces there, verbal instructions to talk with the Ukrainian minister of war, M. Grekov, in order to secure the lifting of the blockade under Odessa.[25] D'Anselme arrived in the city on 14 January, and the following day met with Grekov for the first time. During this meeting Grekov told d'Anselme that the Ukrainians wanted French support to resist the Bolsheviks and that, as a *quid pro quo*, the Directorate was prepared to put its military forces under French command. But Grekov indicated that the Ukrainian army was disintegrating and that perhaps only a quarter of its troops were reliable. He therefore requested French assistance in organizing new military forces around reliable western Ukrainian troops in Galicia who had joined Petliura to gain an ally against a hostile Poland. D'Anselme responded that before being able to consider Grekov's proposal, he would need some signal proof of Ukrainian good intentions. He asked that the blockade of Odessa be lifted, that Ukrainian troops turn over strategic rail lines to French forces, and that Ukrainian military posts be maintained until Allied troops arrived to replace them. Grekov agreed to these terms, and a Ukrainian withdrawal from Odessa began immediately. French troops spread out along the rail lines toward Bendery and Nikolaev, and on 28 January the port city of Kherson, to the east of Odessa, was occupied.[26]

This disengagement of Odessa and the expansion of the French zone of occupation was due entirely to the co-operation of the Directorate. On both sides, the accommodation was motivated by military weakness. The Ukrainians were in serious danger because the Red Army was advancing on Kiev and because western Ukrainian troops were engaged against the Poles who had territorial designs on Lvov and eastern Galicia. The Directorate's military resources were badly strained and could not have withstood a third front against the French. D'Anselme concluded quite correctly that the Ukrainians were in trouble and that they would "do anything" to gain French support.[27] The French position, however, was scarcely better. The Ukrainians were acting as a shield against the Bolsheviks but, if they gave way, the French command would have to send its own unwilling soldiers against the Red Army.

The French command's attitude toward the Directorate as well as toward the Volunteers was largely the responsibility of Colonel Henri Freydenberg, d'Anselme's chief of staff. Freydenberg was a career soldier who had served in French Indochina. Like most French officers in Russia, he was thought to be cold and aloof, which did not help smooth the way with France's local allies. Indeed, to the Volunteers, Freydenberg was a *bête noire* who treated them as colonial subjects and manipulated d'Anselme into adopting a treacherous Ukrainian policy. At the end, Volunteer officers even accused him of taking bribes from the Bolsheviks to evacuate Odessa.[28] The Ukrainians, for their part, liked the French colonel little more than the Volunteers. The Ukrainian government considered Freydenberg to be an opponent of an independent Ukraine who demanded everything and conceded nothing in negotiations for French aid.[29] Freydenberg was thus hated by both the Ukrainians and Volunteers since each saw him to be the partisan of the other.

In fact, Freydenberg cared little for either side or their politics, but sought to enlist them both to strengthen the French position at Odessa. As he explained to M.S. Margulies, the French command would negotiate with the Ukrainians "if only to avoid sacrificing the lives of [French] soldiers." Later on, he said, the Directorate could always be abandoned. Margulies subsequently observed that French policy was based entirely on the formula that "not one drop of French blood" should be shed in Russia.[30] As he put it, since the Volunteer Army in Odessa consisted of only a few hundred undisciplined officers, and since the French would not commit their own men to battle, they would look for local allies where they could.[31] The shift in orientation toward the Ukrainians was symbolized by the disappearance of "Consul" Henno as an influence on the formulation of local French policy. A few days after the arrival of d'Anselme, Margulies recorded that Henno's once busy office was deserted. Henceforth, this broker for Volunteer interests would simply be ignored by the French command.[32]

From the French point of view the Ukrainians, if weak, at least were co-operative. D'Anselme was completely satisfied with the results of his talks with Grekov. For their part, the Ukrainians, having met d'Anselme's initial conditions, renewed their requests for French support. Serhi Ostapenko, then Ukrainian minister of commerce, came to Odessa in the last days of January to ask for Allied recognition of Ukrainian independence, war supplies and instructors, and the dispatch of French troops to help stop the Bolshevik advance on Kiev. As with Grekov, d'Anselme was cool to this new Ukrainian initiative, and responded with additional conditions for French aid. These terms included French supreme command of the Ukrainian army; French administration of the Ukrainian rail network and of Ukrainian finances; French approval for new members of the Ukrainian government; and the immediate resignation of Vinnichenko, "a notorious Bolshevik," of V.M. Chekhovskii, premier and foreign minister, and the departure of Petliura soon thereafter.[33] These were far-reaching demands, but d'Anselme knew that the Ukrainians were in desperate straits. Admiral Gustave Lejay, the deputy commander of the French Black Sea fleet, put it succinctly when he observed that d'Anselme had Petliura entirely in the palm of his hand.[34]

Freydenberg responded to the Ostapenko initiative by sending Captain L. Joseph Langeron, a French intelligence officer, back to Kiev with the Ukrainian delegation to communicate French conditions to Grekov and ask for a written statement of the Directorate's political proposals. Langeron left Odessa with Ostapenko on 29 January, but had been in Kiev only a few days when the capital fell to the Red Army on 5 February. He then followed the Ukrainian government south to Vinnitsa where discussions regarding French conditions were resumed. At this time Ostapenko, who would soon succeed Vinnichenko as head of the Ukrainian government, requested a meeting with d'Anselme in order to pursue negotiations.[35]

D'Anselme, who involved himself as little as possible in these political negotiations, sent Freydenberg to the town of Birzula, northwest of Odessa, where he met on 5 February with Ostapenko, Grekov, and others, along with Langeron. A list of French conditions prepared by Freydenberg was discussed, but no formal agreement was reached.[36] The French delegation refused to make any political or military commitments. Freydenberg, however, advised the Ukrainians to draw up a manifesto requesting Allied aid. In reply, Ostapenko indicated that he was prepared to turn over ultimate military and civilian control of his government to the French command. He also indicated in a secret meeting with Freydenberg that he intended to modify the composition of the Ukrainian government and that he was prepared to submit unofficially to the French command the names of all future appointments to the Directorate. In return, the Ukrainians renewed their requests for French military aid.[37]

Although no formal agreement was reached at Birzula, the Ukrainian delegation apparently yielded to the French demand for the resignations of Vinnichenko and Chekhovskii. On 6 February both men quit their posts. Ostapenko, as a sign of good will, also released a dozen Volunteer officers held by the Ukrainian government. At the end of the Birzula conference, Langeron accompanied the Ukrainian delegation back to Vinnitsa "to hasten discussions and to bring back [to Odessa] a response" to French terms.[38]

The French interest in haste was motivated by the need for troops. Reinforcements were proving difficult to find. The French attempt to organize volunteer brigades had failed, and there was serious opposition in Paris to the dispatch of conscripts. In early February General Berthelot told D.F. Andro, an anti-Bolshevik protégé of the French command in Odessa, that he was compelled to act with extreme caution in southern Russia since the least setback or even minimal casualties would set off "a storm of indignation in Paris" and could lead to the withdrawal of French troops. Under the circumstances, he said, the French command would continue to talk with the Ukrainians although not about "questions of general politics."[39]

As it happened, General Berthelot had received government sanction for the talks shortly before the conference at Birzula. In late January the ministry of war informed the French command at Bucharest that new intelligence reports concerning Petliura indicated that he was not a Bolshevik after all and that skirmishes with French troops in December had been a mistake. In view of these circumstances and because of Ukrainian resistance to the Red Army, the ministry of war directed General Berthelot to extend French assistance to Petliura. "The common enemy," said Clemenceau, "is Bolshevism and in order to resist it more effectively, we must establish a Ukrainian barrier."[40] Although the government knew little about the preliminary talks between the French command and Ukrainian agents in Odessa, Clemenceau's cable represented a strong endorsement of these negotiations. It appears to have been the last directive General Berthelot ever received concerning his conduct toward the Ukrainian government.

In response to Clemenceau's new instructions, General Berthelot informed Paris that he had already taken steps to reorient his policy toward Petliura. But Berthelot warned against putting too much confidence in the Ukrainian army, which appeared to be disintegrating.[41] As Berthelot would advise a few days later, "we should make use [of the Directorate] without giving it too much support."[42]

In spite of General Berthelot's pessimistic appraisal of the Ukrainians, the negotiations continued. But Langeron did not succeed in hurrying the acceptance of French conditions – apparently because of opposition within the Ukrainian government. As a result, the French command issued an ultimatum to the Directorate giving it twenty-four hours to come to terms.[43] Langeron was directed to return immediately to Odessa with or without the required response after the time limit expired.

The Directorate responded by giving Langeron a letter accepting "in principle the conditions posed by the French command." Langeron arrived in Odessa with this document on 14 February.[44] Shortly thereafter, Grekov and a Ukrainian delegation came down to continue negotiations. During these conversations Freydenberg himself dictated to the Ukrainians the text of a declaration which invited the French government to establish what amounted to a French protectorate over the Ukraine.[45] The Ukrainian government in Vinnitsa approved this document and submitted to the French command the draft of "an accord with the Entente." The accord apparently consisted of twelve points, including recognition of the Directorate, French approval for changes in the personnel of the Ukrainian government, and the subordination of

Ukrainian armed forces to French command.[46] D'Anselme responded verbally to Ukrainian representatives in Odessa apparently through Freydenberg that the draft treaty was unacceptable.[47] D'Anselme further stated that he had no authority to sign such a document, and that in any case changes would have to be made before it would be "presentable" in Paris. As a result of d'Anselme's objections, the Directorate submitted a new twelve-point accord on 1 March which dropped the demand for recognition and resembled closely the Freydenberg draft discussed at Birzula.[48]

This was essentially where negotiations stood when the military situation in the Ukraine began to deteriorate. In the five weeks before the evacuation of Odessa Ukrainian delegates often visited the city to talk with the French command. When the advance of Bolshevik forces cut the Ukrainian army in two, the French command took the isolated group under its orders. Langeron was sent to Birzula in late March with an armoured train carrying infantry munitions, and wounded Ukrainian soldiers were brought to hospitals in Odessa. This co-operation was cut short by the order from Paris to evacuate Odessa. The day of the evacuation Ostapenko and several ministers came to the city but Freydenberg told them that "it was too late to do anything."[49]

The negotiations between the Directorate and the French command are an important aspect of the intervention in the Ukraine – both as an indication of its shortcomings and of its methods and objectives. The French command turned to the Ukrainians out of weakness, but, once having done so, Freydenberg tried to obtain the co-operation of the Directorate entirely on his own terms. Contrary to what the Ukrainian diplomat, Arnold Margolin, wrote in his memoirs, the French command did not propose to extend recognition to the Ukrainian government.[50] In fact, the text of the draft accord containing a clause for recognition, which Margolin claimed the French presented to the Ukrainian delegation at Odessa, was, according to d'Anselme, submitted to the French command by the Directorate of 18 February. If anything, Freydenberg seems constantly to have tried to lead the Ukrainians toward acceptance of some kind of union with greater Russia so as to facilitate the broadest possible military front against the Bolsheviks.[51] He did this with a ruthless single-mindedness that made Ukrainian representatives look like cringing minions of the French.

## DRIFT IN FRENCH AND ALLIED POLICY IN PARIS

The determination of the local French command to bring the Ukrainians to heel was not matched in Paris by any close control over the direction of events in southern Russia. Indeed, Freydenberg complained that there was almost no guidance either from Paris or from General Berthelot concerning French relations with the Directorate.[52] As one French officer put it to Margulies, the French command in Odessa felt "ignored by Berthelot, abandoned by Franchet d'Esperey, and deserted by Paris."[53] This isolation of the Odessa command appears, to some degree, to have been due to poor communications. It normally took between five and seven days for a cable to reach Paris from Bucharest. Communications between Odessa and Bucharest were scarcely better.[54] Moreover, because the ministry of war had control over operations in the Ukraine, the Quai d'Orsay could not influence policy there. A "mission of information" under Erik Labonne sent to southern Russia by the Quai d'Orsay, was shipwrecked on the passenger liner *Chaouia* in January and did not reach Odessa.[55] As a result, the foreign ministry never had any independent sources of information in southern Russia, nor any local means of influencing policy there.

It should also be remembered that for much of January and February 1919, Allied policy-makers were deeply involved in discussions of the "Russian question" at the Paris Peace Conference. Clemenceau, Lloyd George, and Wilson argued for several weeks about how the Allies should deal with this most difficult problem. Clemenceau and the French government, of course, wanted a hostile Allied stance maintained toward the Soviet regime. But Lloyd George and Wilson vacillated and appeared to continue to favour coming to terms with the Bolsheviks. The result of these early discussions was the Prinkipo proposal, issued on 23 January, which called for a cessation of hostilities and invited all parties to the Russian civil war to a peace conference to be held on the Princes Islands near Constantinople in the Sea of Marmora. Clemenceau had vigorously opposed any talks with the Bolsheviks, especially when it seemed they might be invited to Paris to carry on negotiations. Their presence, Clemenceau told Balfour, could provoke violent street demonstrations and would certainly arouse the strong opposition of the French right. The old premier warned that if the other Allies tried to force such a policy on him, he would resign.[56] This was probably no more than a ruse since Clemenceau trusted no one else to run the government during the critical peace negotiations concerning Germany. More likely, he tried to bluff the British in hopes of blocking the talks with the Bolsheviks or at least in getting the negotiations moved away from Paris. In this, Clemenceau was partially successful; although he reluctantly agreed to the Prinkipo initiative, the talks were intended to take place far from the French capital on a Turkish island which during Byzantine times had served as a place of banishment.

In any case, French consent was one of pure form since the Quai d'Orsay apparently worked behind the scenes to sabotage the conference. Urgent cables arrived from French representatives in Omsk saying that any armistice in Siberia would result in a definitive end to hostilities. Janin warned that the inevitable influx of Bolshevik propaganda after fighting stopped would lead to the dissolution of the Siberian army.[57] Kolchak conveyed the same message to Regnault, acknowledging that the Siberian government could not survive an armistice with the Bolsheviks.[58] Indeed Martel, who succeeded Regnault as French high commissioner in Siberia, reiterated a short time later that the Kolchak regime would collapse without Allied support.[59]

These messages were clearly understood in Paris and explain why French representatives sought to discourage the anti-Bolshevik factions from attending the Prinkipo talks. Moreover, the Quai d'Orsay advised Omsk on 3 February that it did not favour any let-up in military operations against the Bolsheviks and would not slacken its support of the Kolchak government.[60] Nor were the French alone in opposing the intentions of Lloyd George and Wilson. Winston Churchill, who had recently become secretary of state for war, was a staunch anti-Bolshevik and informed Omsk that he would continue to provide war supplies until he received categorical orders not to do so. Churchill was determined to undermine Lloyd George's policies, but the prime minister could do little to discipline his troublesome colleague because of strong Conservative resistance to any negotiations with the Bolsheviks.[61]

As a result of this formidable opposition in both Paris and London, the Prinkipo conference was stillborn. Although the Bolsheviks agreed in principle to send delegates, representatives of the anti-Bolshevik governments of Siberia, southern Russia, and Arkhangelsk all refused to participate. They circulated a note to this effect on 16 February and a week later Pichon informed Clemenceau that the Prinkipo initiative was dead.[62]

These Allied wrangles in Paris most certainly contributed to the paralysis of French policy in the Ukraine. The French government seemed to get bogged down in issues of principle which diverted its attention from the military and political action it had undertaken in southern Russia. French ability to fashion policy was also impeded for a time in late February when Clemenceau was shot and wounded by a French anarchist.[63] Weakness, however, was the main cause of the drift in French policy. Indeed, there may have been some awareness in Paris that virtually all the government's options in the Ukraine except withdrawal were blocked by domestic opposition to the intervention or by a lack of military resources. In these circumstances, it could well have been easier for French policy-makers to let things drift rather than to face up to the insoluble problem of finding the means to continue the intervention.

Whatever the reasons for it, the lack of direction in French policy forced the local command to fend largely for itself. D'Anselme, on the basis of a verbal order from General Berthelot, began negotiations with the Ukrainians. The French command was able to obtain freedom to manœuvre around Odessa and brought to an end all hostilities with the military forces of the Directorate. In so doing, Freydenberg drove a hard bargain, one which really was not inconsistent with basic French policy. In the first place, the submission of the Directorate to the French command would have served the economic objectives of the Quai d'Orsay well in regard to both the *banque d'émission* and the acquisition of concessions for the indemnification of French investors. The Directorate had been so emasculated by Freydenberg that it could scarcely have resisted French economic pretensions in the Ukraine. In the second place, the French command's determination to align with any anti-Bolshevik factions showing signs of real power was also entirely consistent with the Quai d'Orsay's policy. If anything, the French command was less forthcoming on the question of Ukrainian independence than the Quai d'Orsay had been in the past or would be in the future.

### FRENCH DISSATISFACTION WITH
### THE VOLUNTEERS

The French command's interest in an arrangement with the Ukrainians was only intensified by its growing unhappiness with the Volunteers. This discontent stemmed from the continued weakness of the Volunteer Army in Odessa and by Denikin's insistence on centralizing all Russian civilian and military authority in the occupied zone in his own hands. The French made it clear to Denikin that they would not allow such an arrangement. In fact, d'Anselme considered the question "absurd" since the Volunteers had no real power base in the Ukraine.[64] But Denikin feared that Volunteer authority in Odessa might be undermined by the French command, and he therefore resisted any attempt to create a local administration not directly under his own control.[65] The French viewed Denikin as a nuisance and an obstacle to the establishment of a viable civilian administration in the occupied zone. Not only were the Volunteers unpopular around Odessa, but they were also too weak to compel the obedience of the local population. To make matters worse, the working classes of Odessa were proving responsive to Bolshevik propaganda which accused the Allies and the Volunteer Army of preparing a monarchist reaction in Russia.[66]

The French command also resented a commonly held view in anti-Bolshevik circles that the Allies would bear the brunt of combat against the Soviet regime. Admiral Amet complained about this attitude to S.D.

Sazonov, the former tsarist foreign minister, observing that France could not do all that was expected of it by the anti-Bolsheviks. But Sazonov replied that the expectations of Russian opinion only reflected the promises made by French agents concerning a large-scale intervention.[67]

There was some truth in Sazonov's observation. Certain French representatives like the consul Henno had made exaggerated and unauthorized promises of military support to the Volunteers. But the real cause of the growing estrangement between the French and Volunteer commands lay in their mutual impotence. This weakness compelled the French to turn to the Ukrainians. Since the Volunteers could not offer better, French commanders expected Denikin to co-operate. Denikin refused, however, because he regarded the Ukrainians as traitors and feared that they might eventually succeed in establishing an independent Ukraine.

To prevent this eventuality and to strengthen his own authority in Odessa, Denikin sent General A.S. Sannikov to replace Grishin-Almazov as military governor. Sannikov tried to work for an understanding with the French command, but by the middle of February both d'Anselme and Denikin were losing patience. D'Anselme, who had served in the Balkans campaign, was worn out by the war and not at all disposed to tolerate Denikin's intractability. Moreover, he had opposed the intervention at the outset and now saw his earlier misgivings fully justified by events. At times, he seemed disgusted by his mission and ready to wash his hands of it at the first opportunity. This French officer was certainly not the one to negotiate with Denikin and his agents in Odessa.

Relations between the two sides were only exacerbated by a French plan for mixed Franco-Russian brigades. As with General Berthelot's earlier proposal for Franco-Rumanian divisions, this scheme was intended to make up for shortages in manpower. It was also hoped that by putting these new formations under French command, recruits could be attracted who refused to serve directly under the Volunteers.[68] But Denikin would not tolerate any foreign interference in the Russian army and opposed the proposal. The French were equally unprepared to brook interference in the occupied zone. General Berthelot, while in Odessa on a tour of inspection, bluntly told Sannikov that he was expected to subordinate himself entirely to the French command. When Denikin heard of this turn of events, he forbade Sannikov to follow anyone's orders but his own. Although Denikin was still conciliatory at this point, his attitude hardened when Sannikov informed him that the French command intended to go ahead with plans for mixed Franco-Russian brigades. At the end of February he threatened to court-martial any Russian officer who served in these units.[69]

D'Anselme and Freydenberg were predictably infuriated by Denikin's refractory attitude. Even in early February French patience with the Volunteers had worn thin. Freydenberg minuted on a telegram from Denikin to General Berthelot complaining of the presence of Ukrainian troops in the French zone of occupation, "Denikin is an idiot. He does not know what is going on and his Volunteers are acting as badly and with the same procedures as the Bolsheviks."[70] D'Anselme also complained angrily to General Berthelot that Sannikov, while appearing to co-operate, sought to sabotage the policies of the French command.[71] Completely exasperated, d'Anselme made no secret of his anger with Denikin and his belief that working with him was impossible.[72]

French anger was fuelled by the continued inability of the anti-Bolshevik factions in Odessa to organize any substantial military forces. Amet complained in early February that Volunteer recruiting efforts had been unproductive, and that the anti-Bolsheviks continued to count heavily on Allied intervention.[73] Freydenberg rather brutally raised this same question with Margulies. The anti-Bolsheviks, he said, reproached the French because they did not want to die in Russia. But in Odessa, a city of nearly a million people, there were at least 100,000 men capable of military service. "Where are they?" asked Freydenberg. French soldiers, who had by some miracle survived the Marne or Verdun, were not eager to sacrifice themselves in an unpopular expedition in Russia when men capable of bearing arms idled in the streets of Odessa.[74]

Freydenberg's uncharitable and rather scornful attitude toward the Volunteers began to be criticized by British diplomats in Odessa. Consuls John Picton Bagge and Henry Cooke accused Freydenberg of being tactless and hostile to the Volunteers.[75] Both men recommended to the Foreign Office that it seek the recall of Freydenberg, who, aside from being exceedingly rude, was also Jewish, a trait which offended many of the anti-semitic Volunteers.[76]

British diplomats were scarcely less critical of the French command in general. As Picton Bagge commented, they did not seem to know "how to handle the Russian[s]." The French were too quick to get angry, he said, and "either ask too politely or demand too roughly...."[77] But quite apart from the question of friction between French and Russian officers, Picton Bagge was highly critical of the French command's policy toward the Directorate. In his view, French negotiations with the Ukrainians would only further strain relations with the Volunteer command. In any event, the Directorate was falling apart, and negotiating with it was like trying to strike "an agreement with a corpse." The French policy of seeking to unite all the anti-Bolshevik factions was understandable, he conceded, but was destined to fail because of the irreconcilability of the

Volunteers and Ukrainians.[78] It could only succeed in "alienat[ing] everybody's sympathies," and would eventually lead to "a disaster."[79]

ECONOMIC AND SOCIAL CONDITIONS IN
THE FRENCH ZONE OF OCCUPATION

Picton Bagge's comments, though salted with a good deal of smug self-righteousness, were not out of line with the French command's own views of the Directorate. Hence, when d'Anselme and Freydenberg could control their anger with Denikin, they still searched for the basis of an accommodation and the speedy formation of an anti-Bolshevik government subordinated to the French command.[80] This desire to form a Russian government in the occupied zone was motivated by the rapid deterioration of the military situation in southern Russia during February. Kiev had fallen to the Red Army early in the month and Vinnitsa, the new capital of the Directorate, was also menaced. The situation in the occupied zone was hardly better. Odessa was without electricity because of an acute shortage of coal, and wood for heat was so scarce that telegraph and telephone poles and trees along the streets of the city gradually disappeared.[81] Nor did the situation improve significantly after the lifting of the Ukrainian blockade. Foodstuffs and other necessities were still hard to obtain, especially in a city where much of the working-class population was unemployed.[82]

Yet not all of Odessa was poor. Anyone who could speculated in foodstuffs or foreign currencies. Fortunes were quickly made and wildly spent. The boulevards, cafes, and restaurants were crowded with dandies and hangers-on of every description. Champagne flowed like water in tawdry spectacles of *gourmandise* at the posh London Hotel, the main gathering place of the chic and wealthy. "Gambling saloons sprang up on all sides like mushrooms," thriving on a clientele of speculators, blackmarketeers, and the rich of the old order, who profited from the French occupation. Fabulous sums were wagered at roulette tables where bemedalled Russian officers, impoverished by the revolution, served as croupiers and where once-rich ladies of society, turned saloon girls, sought clients for the house.[83] This conspicuous display of wealth flaunted among so many who lacked basic necessities must have played into the hands of Bolshevik propagandists. D'Anselme also took in this grim spectacle and began to fear that growing popular unrest might lead to riot and insurrection.[84]

In these conditions, public safety was practically non-existent. Hold-ups and shootings were common. At night marauding bands of hungry men or simple hoodlums raided the homes of the rich and sometimes skirmished with patrols of police and Volunteer officers. But even during the day there was no security. Armed men, with increasing brazenness, held up people in the streets and looted shops and stores. In fact, local papers were full of stories of robberies and killings which the badly organized police proved incapable of stopping.[85]

The ineptitude of the police was not due to a lack of numbers. Indeed, there were so many police and counter-intelligence organs, both French and Russian, operating in Odessa that it was impossible to control them all.[86] As a result, they sometimes ran amok, summarily executing suspected Bolshevik sympathizers. In one such instance, a French communist, Jeanne Labourbe, who had come to Odessa from Moscow to help spread propaganda among French troops was, along with several comrades, tortured and shot by Volunteer officers.[87]

Life in Odessa was thus wretched beyond measure for much of the city's population. General Berthelot, after a tour of inspection in the city, sent a worried report to Paris. The situation in Odessa, he said, was "very grave." Basic necessities could only be obtained at ten times their normal value. The anti-Bolsheviks were divided and unpopular. In fact, the Volunteer Army was so disliked that its presence provoked rebellion behind French lines. The situation was all the more dangerous as French forces were melting away because of demobilization, while the morale of remaining troops was poor and continually subjected to Bolshevik propaganda.[88]

General Berthelot's despair about the shortage of troops in southern Russia emerged in a conversation he had with Baron V.V. Meller Zakomelskii while in Odessa. The baron, who headed the monarchist Council for State Unity, complained of French military inaction and the failure to expand the zone of occupation. Berthelot began to reply that the French command had been flooded with requests to move forward. Then, suddenly losing patience, he put his hands to his head and screamed, "I have nothing, nothing," There were no troops with which to move forward. All the French could do, he said, was stall for time until the arrival of colonial troops allowed a more aggressive policy.[89]

Time, however, would not wait for the French command. The Bolsheviks' military forces were moving steadily south against crumbling Ukrainian resistance. French defences were in a parlous state with mutinous troops and a restless, discontented population. D'Anselme tried to strengthen his position by negotiating with the Ukrainians, but in so doing, he provoked the fury of the Volunteers. In the end, the French command failed to find the strong local allies essential to the success of the intervention. The government in Paris should have been alarmed by these developments but instead seemed strangely unconcerned. French commanders, shaken by the lack of response from Paris and fed up with Denikin, began to despair. Their anxiety soon alerted the government to the looming military disaster which threatened it in the Ukraine.

## CHAPTER TEN

# The French Withdrawal from Southern Russia

## MARCH–APRIL 1919

In March 1919 French and Allied forces in the Ukraine suffered a series of defeats at the hands of Bolshevik irregulars. The lost battles were scarcely more than skirmishes, but they led to a contraction of the French zone of occupation, cutting off Odessa from its hinterland and making the city increasingly difficult to feed. These setbacks unnerved French commanders who doubted whether they could hold Odessa with mutinous troops and a potentially rebellious civilian population at their backs. In Paris, the government finally took note of the danger to its forces, and at the end of March Clemenceau ordered an evacuation of Odessa. Three weeks later French forces at Sevastopol in the Crimea were also withdrawn. The evacuation did not take place, however, before a widespread mutiny crippled the French Black Sea fleet.

The French government was thus compelled to give up its military efforts to overthrow the Soviets. But Bolshevism remained a potent force and threatened to spill over into Europe as indeed the establishment of a communist government in Hungary in March seemed to demonstrate. In these circumstances the French government could not sit idly by and so it fell back on the policy of containment that came to be known as the cordon sanitaire. A wall of client states and armies stretching from the Baltic to the Black Seas was erected to dam up the revolutionary tide of Bolshevism. Soviet Russia could "stew in its own juices" until the Russian people had seen the error of their ways and overthrown the Bolsheviks.

Events did not turn out in this way and French hopes were dashed, but the government did succeed in escaping from what very nearly was a military débâcle in southern Russia. The warnings of a potential disaster began to accumulate in early March. One indication of danger was the poor morale of French officers who no longer believed in the possibility of an Allied victory over the Bolsheviks. Everyone, recorded Margulies, thought only of returning to Paris.[1] This mood was reflected up the chain of command. In early March Franchet d'Esperey complained bitterly that the other Allies were pursuing without restraint their own particular political and economic ambitions in the east, while leaving to France the thankless role of *gendarme*. He warned that the French army was not capable by itself of undertaking this role and that circumstances might arise in which it could not act "without risking a disgrace to [the] flag."[2]

## THE BATTLE OF KHERSON
## AND ITS AFTERMATH

Franchet d'Esperey's premonitions of danger were soon justified by events. In early March the 1,000-man French and Greek garrison at Kherson came under attack from Bolshevik irregulars led by Ataman G. Grigoriev, a local freebooter who had temporarily thrown in with the Soviet regime. Gregoriev summoned the French in Kherson to evacuate the city. When the French command refused to comply, Grigoriev ordered an attack.

At first, French and Greek troops were able to hold their own, but after a few days Bolshevik forces began to gain the upper hand. The French position was weakened on 8 March when two companies of French reinforcements consisting of 150 men from the 176th Infantry Regiment refused to fight. Early the following morning, Grigoriev launched a general attack on French positions. By afternoon the entire Franco-Greek detachment was encircled in the city's old Turkish citadel and deprived of direct communications with French naval units on the River Dnieper. Reinforcements were held up by bad weather in spite of a wireless message from Kherson stating that the situation was "desperate" and that the detachment was "clinging to the ramparts." The French commander, Colonel Antoine Camille de Clavières, reported back that the entire city had risen against Allied forces. Civilians, armed with rifles and grenades, had joined Grigoriev's troops. Clavières believed that the situation had become impossible and during the afternoon of 9 March he ordered an evacuation of the city. Contact was re-established with the encircled citadel and the garrison withdrew, apparently inflicting heavy civilian casualties, in the early hours of 10 March.[3]

The fall of Kherson had a tremendous impact on the French command both in Odessa and Bucharest. In the first place, d'Anselme immediately ordered the evacuation of Greek troops at Nikolaev since he regarded this city as a trap with Kherson in enemy hands. The abandonment of Nikolaev precipitated a general contraction of the French

zone of occupation, and d'Anselme began to consider the establishment
of an entrenched camp around Odessa. He also warned General Berthelot that a continued deterioration of the military situation in southern
Russia would warrant a French evacuation of the entire area.[4] D'Anselme was particularly alarmed by the dwindling number of French
troops. "The supreme command," he warned, "does not seem to understand the situation. It appears that I have two French divisions; in reality
because of repatriations ... and because of the absence of any reinforcements whatever, I am left with 30 rifles per company, 15 by the end of
the month; that is [in all], 2,000 and soon only 1,200 rifles.[5]

The constant diminution of troops only added to the corrosive effects
of Bolshevik propaganda in destroying what remained of French morale.
D'Anselme noted in a March report that he had received a letter from a
German officer warning of the menace of Bolshevik propaganda. "You
cannot know," this officer wrote, "how powerful and how dangerous
Bolshevism is for the [army]." "It is true," commented d'Anselme, "and
if our men are not yet Bolshevik, it is because they are almost all repatri-
able. I am convinced now that I have seen the sickness from up close,
that the intervention with or without volunteers is the best way to
spread Bolshevism in France. Our men will all return affected by it."[6]
D'Anselme's views were shared by General Berthelot, who minuted at
the bottom of this report, "there is a real danger in contact with Bolshevism and the actual state of our troops shows the least perceptive
observer that the propaganda is obtaining results." As if this were not
sufficient warning, d'Anselme cabled Franchet d'Esperey three days
later,

You should know that French troops have become unemployable. Entire companies refuse to march even under fire and even to support their comrades. I
have [had] today for the fourth time a refusal of this sort. Sanctions or reasoning
[with the men are] impossible at this time. They all say they refuse to fight
against the Bolsheviks. The situation cannot long last like this. I must have
[colonial units] immediately in order to relieve French troops.[7]

The alarming state of morale among French forces was made all the
more critical by the growing hostility of the indigenous population.
D'Anselme warned General Berthelot that "the entire country" had
risen against the intervention and that a general insurrection could soon
be anticipated in spite of the arrival of reinforcements.[8] The area around
Odessa, reported d'Anselme, had still not suffered from Bolshevism.
There were a hundred thousand workers without jobs, without victuals,
and without coal, whose living conditions would worsen as the French
zone of occupation contracted. In short, Odessa was "Bolshevik, and the

least incident already sets off partial risings." General Berthelot endorsed d'Anselme's conclusions, warning of a "Sicilian vespers" if the Allies could not resupply Odessa.[9] He informed Paris on 17 March that there was no coal or wood in the city and only limited supplies of flour and meat. Continuing shortages, he said, "would lead rapidly to an uprising of a completely hostile population."[10]

## WORSENING FRENCH RELATIONS
## WITH THE VOLUNTEERS

As conditions in the zone of occupation deteriorated, so did relations between the French and Volunteer commands. Denikin was embittered by the French government's failure to come to his aid when the Red Army was pushing him out of the important Don valley.[11] The French command, however, viewed Denikin's recriminations in a different light. General Berthelot was angered by anti-Bolshevik reproaches that the Allies had not, as he put it, sent sufficient divisions to Russia to accomplish what the Volunteers could not do for themselves. Berthelot complained about Volunteer obstruction of French authority in Odessa and asked for help from Paris in dealing with Denikin.[12]

General Berthelot's calls of distress finally drew the attention of the government. The ministry of war directed the Quai d'Orsay to protest Denikin's behavior to Russian representatives in Paris. The Quai d'Orsay was also instructed to ask that Russian units in the zone of occupation be put under French orders, and that Denikin refrain from interfering with French efforts to organize those Russian troops who for political reasons would not serve under Volunteer command.[13]

Pichon forwarded these conditions to the Russian ambassador Maklakov, on 8 March, but the anti-Bolsheviks in Paris could not restrain Denikin's anger against the French command.[14] Moreover, with the rapid deterioration of the military situation around Odessa, the French themselves showed no further willingness to tolerate what they regarded as Denikin's obstructionist behaviour. On 15 March, shortly after the fall of Kherson, d'Anselme declared a state of siege in Odessa. At the same time the French sought to establish a local Russian government under its own authority to replace the administration headed by Denikin's representatives, Sannikov and Grishin-Almazov. D.F. Andro and General A.V. Shvarts were persuaded to co-operate in setting up this new regime. Andro, a conservative landowner who had served under Skoropadskii, was to head the civilian administration while Shvarts, a career officer, was named governor general and given responsibility for organizing a new Russian army.[15] The Volunteers considered the creation of this new administration a virtual *coup d'état* in spite of French

explanations that it was only to be temporary. Denikin ordered Sannikov not to submit to the French-sponsored regime.[16] But d'Anselme
apparently retaliated by ordering Sannikov and Grishin-Almazov out of
Odessa on 22 March.

Just as the French command's efforts to organize a new governmental
authority in Odessa were reaching their final stages, Generals Franchet
d'Esperey and Berthelot arrived for a tour of inspection. Berthelot, however, was no longer responsible for operations in Russia. He had asked to
be relieved of his command, and on 14 March the government had
complied, appointing Franchet d'Esperey to replace him.[17] The commander of the Armée d'Orient was infuriated by this turn of events,
believing that Berthelot had requested recall to escape responsibility for
the disaster that appeared to threaten French and Allied troops in southern Russia.[18] Franchet d'Esperey's anger was further heightened by a
personal dislike of Berthelot, whom he considered to be a pretentious,
impractical general officer.[19]

In fact, Berthelot was a vain and somewhat frustrated man who, having missed a chance for glory on the Western Front, had perhaps hoped
to find it in Russia at the head of a crusade against the Bolsheviks.[20]
When the crusade threatened to become a débâcle, tarnishing his reputation, he seemed to lose his nerve and to want to foist responsibility for
Russia onto Franchet d'Esperey.[21] The latter, of course, looked upon this
assignment with fastidious disgust, not caring to take on Berthelot's
unenviable command.

It is little wonder that Franchet d'Esperey was in an angry mood when
he arrived in Odessa on 20 March. What he saw there only reinforced
his earlier views. Nor was his temper improved by a growing disdain for
the Volunteer Army. Although previously well-disposed toward Denikin, Franchet d'Esperey had by then begun to echo criticisms of the
Volunteers made by Generals d'Anselme and Berthelot.[22] Franchet
d'Esperey, in any case, was a haughty, intolerant soldier, who, being
victorious in war, had little patience with the slough and corruption he
saw in southern Russia. According to Denikin, the commander of the
Armée d'Orient was offhand and even rude with Volunteer representatives and "did not conceal his contempt for the [anti-Bolshevik] Russians in conversation with members of the French command."[23] As
Franchet d'Esperey told his officers,

the Russians are barbarians and villains. Through them we were drawn into this
war and through their treachery were compelled to fight an extra year, bearing
the whole of the German pressure and suffering innumerable losses ... and now
these same traitors expect, even demand our help. I, as a soldier, obey the commands of my Government. But my heart is not in the enterprise. You must not

stand on ceremony with these people. Shoot them without further ado if any-thing occurs, commencing with the moujiks and ending with their highest representatives. I take the responsibility.[24]

In somewhat more subdued terms, Franchet d'Esperey cabled Paris that the Volunteer Army in Odessa was not making "a serious contribu-tion" to the defence of the French zone of occupation. Unlike the Red Army, discipline among the Volunteers was poor. "The officer corps was composed for the most part of listless men, without conviction, [and] ... little desirous of fighting...."[25] Given the minimal value of Volunteer support at Odessa, Franchet d'Esperey viewed Denikin's continued obstruction of French authority in southern Russia as "intolerable" and, like Berthelot, he asked the government to bring the Volunteers to heel.[26] But Denikin did not feel any more kindly toward the French command. Colonel Émile Auguste Corbel, the chief of the small French military mission at Ekaterinodar, informed d'Anselme that Denikin and his staff had adopted an intransigent attitude. They preferred, he said, a rupture with the French command to relations based on the anti-Volunteer policy of Freydenberg.[27]

THE BEGINNINGS OF
THE CORDON SANITAIRE

If Clemenceau was under pressure from his military commanders to get tough with Denikin, he was also receiving complaints from London about the estrangement between the French command in Odessa and the Volunteer Army. During March the British government delivered a series of notes to the Quai d'Orsay which protested the French com-mand's treatment of the Volunteers and its too intimate relations with the Ukrainians. In the latter regard, the British Foreign Office, echoing the views of consuls Picton Bagge and Cooke, opposed any contacts with the disintegrating Ukrainian Directorate.[28]

These British notes appear to have shaken up the Quai d'Orsay which knew virtually nothing about the contacts between the French com-mand and the Ukrainians. Nevertheless, Pichon hastened to assure the British ambassador that rumours, then circulating, of the French com-mand's recognition of Ukrainian sovereignty were completely false. He added that the French government opposed Ukrainian separatism, which it regarded as nothing more than "an Austro-German invention" intended to upset the security of western Europe.[29] The Quai d'Orsay also sought to reassure anti-Bolshevik representatives in Paris that the French government had no intention of taking sides "concerning the separatist aspirations of any part whatever of Russia," but sought only to enlist the support of those groups willing to fight the Bolsheviks.[30]

Although the Quai d'Orsay does not appear to have deliberately misinformed the British or anti-Bolshevik Russians about the conversations which had taken place between the French command and the Directorate, it was something less than candid about its policies toward the non-Russian nationalities. In the first place, Ukrainian separatism was not exactly "invented" by the Austro-Germans. On the contrary, the French were the first great power to extend *de facto* recognition to the Ukraine in January 1918.[31] This action represented an important indication that the French government was not as committed to the reconstruction of a great Russian state as its notes to Derby and Maklakov might imply.[32] Indeed, because of the failing intervention in the Ukraine and in view of the consistently unfavourable military reports on the Volunteers, a general reorientation in French policy toward Russia began to take place.

This shift in policy was marked by greater support of the new or expanding states situated along the Russian western frontier. The first sign of this change occurred in late February when Foch put before the Allied Council of Ten a plan calling for the organization of "a chain of independent states" capable of fighting the Bolsheviks.[33] Although Foch's plan does not appear to have gained the approval of the French government, it was a portent of things to come.

After the fall of Kherson, General Berthelot recommended to Paris that the entire question of the government's objectives in Russia be re-examined. "I can see no other solution," said Berthelot, "than the complete abandonment of the Russians to themselves and the organization of a defensive front from the Baltic to the Black Seas, [the manning of which] should be confided to the two most directly interested powers, Poland and Rumania.... [This] military barrage should be complemented by a complete economic and financial barrier around Bolshevism."[34] The ministry of war was quick to respond to General Berthelot's recommendations. While still ordering Odessa to be held, it indicated on 17 March that the government was in fact proceeding with the organization of a defensive front against the western expansion of Bolshevism.[35]

Similarly, the ministry of war began to examine the question of what material assistance should be given to the various anti-Bolshevik governments along the Russian border. The Quai d'Orsay favoured backing these states, but recognized that France by itself could not meet all their requests for aid. Priorities would therefore have to be established immediately, taking into account "present military necessities which," in the mind of the Quai d'Orsay, "could be summed up in one alone: the struggle against Bolshevism." In this order of priorities, the Quai d'Orsay believed that France's first efforts should be made in favour of Poland and Czechoslovakia. "In each of these countries a solid nucleus of forces should be constituted as rapidly as possible in order to ward off any blow from the [Red Army]. The use of these forces should be controlled by French military missions so as to guarantee that they will be used above all in the struggle against Bolshevism and all its manifestations...."[36] Clemenceau rapidly accepted these priorities, informing Foch a short time later that he envisaged the extension of military aid sufficient to arm ten Polish and five Czech divisions.[37]

The French shift toward the Poles had been in the making for some time. By September 1918 Paris favoured the creation of the "strongest possible" Polish state. A greater Poland in the view of the Quai d'Orsay would contribute to the strengthening of French defences against Germany and would facilitate French "action in Russia." Because of this growing Polish orientation, the Quai d'Orsay became increasingly willing to sanction the transfer of certain Russian territories to Poland.[38] Nevertheless, French policy remained intentionally ambiguous because of uncertainty as to whether a great Russian state would re-emerge after the revolution, or whether the border nationalities would succeed in establishing their independence or territorial claims. Consequently, the Quai d'Orsay preferred to avoid any irrevocable commitments to either side until one had prevailed over the other. As Kammerer put it in a note to Jules Laroche,

I do not share your view that Russia no longer exists and that there will only be many Russias in the future. In any case, as that has not yet been proven, we cannot without serious danger ... fail to take into account the factor of Russia itself in the attribution of former Russian provinces. No one can ask the Allies to pass out [territories which] they do not possess, except when it is a question of defeated enemies.[39]

The Quai d'Orsay's attitude is well illustrated by its reaction to reports of a popular insurrection in Bessarabia against Rumanian authority during February 1919. The Quai d'Orsay hastened to block the use of French troops in the suppression of this rising. Pichon observed to Clemenceau that although the French government could not oppose Rumanian territorial aspirations "without risking the ruin of [its] influence" in that country, neither did it want to alienate Russian elements sympathetic to France who opposed the cession of Bessarabia to Rumania. "Our situation in this regard," commented Pichon, "is particularly delicate in view of our long alliance with Russia."[40]

As Pichon's remarks suggests, French policy toward the nationalities and the great Russian factions was based on the simple criteria of expediency and real power. For example, in October 1918 when the anti-Bolshevik government of Siberia asked for Allied recognition, the Quai d'Orsay refused because the Siberian regime was not strong enough to merit such treatment. It was only "by acts," said the Quai d'Orsay, that the anti-Bolsheviks could demonstrate that they represented "a real government enjoying the necessary stability" to justify recognition.[41] French policy on this question, as well as its chief architect, emerge quite clearly from an entry in Lord Derby's diary. Derby noted that he had been to see Clemenceau concerning the question of recognition of the Siberian government.

[Clemenceau] knew nothing whatever about it, but he talked to Pichon on the telephone and told Pichon he would like him to see me at once and that he authorized him to speak in the name of the government, which for Pichon must be an entirely new experience. I went on to see Pichon who evidently knew nothing whatever about the subject but he got Berthelot and I must say I admire the clear way in which the latter put the whole position, declining on behalf of the French government to recognize the Omsk government for the very simple reason that they are not satisfied that it was ... sufficiently stable ... and that by recognizing it they might be prevented later from recognizing another government which would be formed in the south when our troops got up through the Caucasus....[42]

This wait-and-see attitude toward the anti-Bolshevik Russians applied as well to Poland and the other states along the Russian frontier. It was a passive policy based completely on the outcome of the struggle for power in Russia and its borderlands.[43] Had the anti-Bolshevik Russians won the civil war and snuffed out the independence of the nationalities, Paris would probably have reacted with no more than pious murmurings of regret. As long as the Bolsheviks maintained power, however, the French government would attempt to strip as much territory as possible from the Russian state. With the anti-Bolshevik Russians showing little combativeness in southern Russia, the French government began to shift its interest to Poland and the other states in eastern Europe capable of forming a barrier against Bolshevism.[44]

THE EVACUATION OF ODESSA
AND SEVASTOPOL

Although Paris began to reorient its eastern policy, it had still not abandoned the intervention in southern Russia, and Clemenceau ordered Odessa to be held. D'Anselme was not eager to do so, however, and after the fall of Kherson he had recommended the evacuation of the French zone of occupation before it was imposed by the enemy. General Berthelot supported d'Anselme's views but would not allow an evacuation except on explicit orders from Paris.[45] Besides, he said, the situation was still not critical since Odessa could only be attacked by regular troops through Berezovka, a town north of Odessa in French hands.[46] This proved to be cold comfort to d'Anselme whose troops were soon driven out of Berezovka in headlong disorder. Tanks were abandoned and artillery blown up as French and Greek troops retreated south.[47]

The road to Odessa lay open, and thoughts of evacuation began to grow ever larger in the minds of jittery French commanders. Franchet d'Esperey cabled Paris on 24 March that, without making it public, he had ordered preparations made for a withdrawal from Russia to the River Dniester and the establishment of new defensive positions along this line. He added that conditions in Odessa were very bad and that its population was largely hostile to the French presence. Moreover, he warned, in what by then had become a familiar refrain, that French soldiers were completely unreliable and should be kept away from newly arrived reinforcements to prevent the spread of demoralization.[48]

Franchet d'Esperey tried to save the French position at Odessa, but there was little he could do. The city was slowly starving. On 31 March stocks of flour ran out. He warned Paris that the supply of the occupied zone was "intimately linked" to the question of military operations. "We will have to evacuate Odessa," he said, "if this city cannot be revictualled at once...."[49]

Unbeknownst to the French command, the decision to evacuate had already been made in Paris. On 25 March the Council of Four, consisting only of the Allied leaders, Clemenceau, Lloyd George, Wilson, and V.E. Orlando of Italy, discussed the problems of supplying Odessa and, more generally, of resisting the westward spread of Bolshevism. A proposal was advanced to strengthen Rumania in view of the Bolshevik revolution in Hungary and the deteriorating military situation in southern Russia. Given limited Allied resources and the hostile attitude of the population around Odessa, Lloyd George and Wilson favoured the evacuation of the area and the reinforcement of Rumania. Neither Clemenceau nor Foch, who was brought into this discussion, voiced any particular objection. Foch preferred to hold on to Odessa as long as possible, but when asked pointblank by Lloyd George whether it was essential to send grain and coal to southern Russia, if Rumania was in need at the same time, the Allied generalissimo responded in the negative. He added that southern Russia had already been lost and could not be lost a second time by giving up Odessa. Foch also commented, no doubt reflecting the views of the French eastern command, that any supply effort made on Denikin's behalf would be a waste of time.[50]

On 27 March the Council of Four again discussed the situation in southern Russia. Foch presented the council with a plan, solicited by Lloyd George at the previous meeting, for military action in the east.

This plan, which recommended the formation of two large inter-Allied armies in Rumania for use against Hungary and Russia, was strongly opposed by Wilson as going too far beyond the scope of earlier discussions. Although Foch stressed that his proposals were defensive in nature, not even Clemenceau was prepared to support him. Wilson's view therefore prevailed and the council instructed Foch "to limit his recommendations to measures necessary for the reinforcement of the Rumanian army ... [and] the evacuation of Odessa...."[51]

While these discussions were going on within the Council of Four, domestic pressure in France was building against the intervention. The Socialist press had maintained a drumfire attack on the government's Russian policy since December. Although news of events in southern Russia was difficult to obtain, the Socialist press, despite continuing censorship, made it clear that all was not well with the French army of occupation. Rumours and bits of information were published which indicated that Allied forces had suffered reverses, that troop morale was poor, and that the evacuation of Odessa was being contemplated.[52]

The Socialists also provoked another lengthy debate in the Chamber of Deputies on government policy toward Russia. On 24 March Marcel Cachin rose to condemn the government, questioning the legality of the French military presence in Russia. France, he declared, was actually in a state of war with the Soviet republic without having consulted parliament and in spite of the certain opposition of public opinion. Since the government had not formally declared war, the intervention was illegal and should be ended immediately. French troops in the Ukraine, said Cachin, could scarcely be blamed for disobeying illegal orders and indeed would have his full support if they refused to fight the Bolsheviks.[53]

Cachin was loudly jeered by the right, but the four-day debate grew even more tumultuous as the long interpellations continued. Socialists Ernest Lafont and Barthélemy Mayéras rose to support Cachin's position. And Mayéras provoked further outbursts of rightist indignation when, to justify resistance to the "illegal" war against the Bolsheviks, he invoked the 1793 declaration of the rights of man which legitimized rebellion against injustice.[54]

On 26 March Pichon spoke in defence of the government's policy. France, he said, intended to remain loyal to those groups that continued to resist Bolshevik oppression. Moreover, the Allies had no choice but to maintain a cordon sanitaire around Russia to stop the spread of Bolshevism which threatened all the civilized world. Pichon's speech was frequently interrupted. Kienthalian Socialist Jean Raffin-Dugens broke in to compare Pichon's declaration with those of the monarchs of Europe in 1793, who were hell-bent on the destruction of the French

Revolution. Pichon tried to silence these interruptions by accusing the Socialists of being partisans of the Bolsheviks. But the Socialists were not intimidated and shouted back that they needed no lessons in socialism from blackleg reactionaries like Pichon.[55]

As the debate continued, non-Socialists also spoke out against the intervention. France, said one deputy, had suffered enough and could not afford further losses in blood and treasure. Reading a dispatch from d'Anselme, he noted that the French command could no longer count on its men, who were nearly all eligible for demobilization and who had no wish to serve in Russia. In mock distress, Socialist deputies broke in to suggest that, in view of the shortage of troops, Pichon and Clemenceau be rushed to the Ukraine to fill the gap in the struggle against the Bolsheviks.[56] Even Pierre Renaudel, who had previously supported the intervention, rose on the last day of the debate, 29 March, to condemn the government's policy.[57]

Nevertheless, in the vote after the debate, the government still obtained an impressive majority. Indeed, if Clemenceau had only to reckon with opposition in the Chamber to the intervention, he would not have been overly hindered in pursuing his policies toward Russia. But the debates took place before a backdrop of growing popular unrest. Membership in the French Socialist party and in the trade unions grew dramatically as inflation galloped out of control and the necessities of life became increasingly difficult to obtain. Juxtaposed to the ills of their own society, French workers could see Soviet Russia, striving to eradicate the injustices of capitalism and inflicting heavy defeats on the reactionary French and Allied governments.[58] As a result, working-class admiration for the Russian Revolution, which was already considerable, grew stronger. The intervention thus represented an additional provocation to an already highly discontented working class. And while increasing popular unrest did not threaten revolution, it made the intervention in southern Russia a costly liability which might provide the Socialists with an issue to rally opponents of the government.

In view of both domestic and Allied opposition to the French occupation of Odessa, Clemenceau ordered its evacuation on 29 March.[59] His directive reached Odessa only on 2 April, but d'Anselme, who was anxious to pull out of Russia, hastened to comply with these new orders.[60] He decided to carry out the evacuation in just five days beginning on 3 April. In this short period some 12,000 Allied and 50,000 Russian civilians as well as 30,000 French and Allied troops had to be evacuated.[61] D'Anselme planned to take the civilians out by sea and to march his troops overland to Bessarabia. Therefore, despite previous public assurances that the city would be held, on 3 April the French command made public its intention to abandon Odessa, giving what amounted to a forty-eight-hour deadline for civilians to leave. Panic ensued. Rumours spread wildly that the Chamber of Deputies had voted no confidence in the Clemenceau government and expressed itself in favour of a total French withdrawal from southern Russia. People mobbed the banks to withdraw their savings and flocked to the French passport office in search of visas and passage to Constantinople.[62]

D'Anselme was extremely uneasy during the final days of the occupation, because he feared the evacuation might become a "catastrophe," should an attack on the city coincide with an internal uprising. His apprehensions were not unjustified. As soon as it became known that Odessa would be abandoned, Russian seamen and railway workers went on strike to impede the evacuation. On the evening of 3 April the executive committee of the local Soviet warned d'Anselme that, although prepared to let Allied troops leave Odessa without difficulty, it was not disposed to permit the departure of the Russian bourgeoisie and the Volunteer Army. It threatened to unleash an immediate insurrection if the French command persisted in evacuating the anti-Bolshevik Russians. D'Anselme refused to yield, warning that he would repress any insurrection with the guns of the French fleet. During the night of 3–4 April the workers' committee capitulated and agreed not to hinder the Allied withdrawal or to oppose the evacuation of Russian nationals.

The capitulation of the workers' committee did not end d'Anselme's problems. On 4 April public order in Odessa began to break down completely. The police disappeared and looting broke out almost everywhere. Moreover, d'Anselme continued to be plagued by indiscipline among French soldiers. That day a section of artillery refused to fire on Bolshevik troops, and the following day yet another French company mutinied.[63] To make matters worse, barricades began to be erected in the streets while Volunteer and Polish troops ran amok, shooting up the city. The growing chaos led d'Anselme to hasten still more the evacuation. Even so, the French command could not fully control its own men, many of whom were reported to be in a drunken, hostile frame of mind.[64] In spite of these formidable difficulties d'Anselme succeeded in getting his forces out of Odessa by the evening of 6 April. The withdrawal to Bessarabia finished on 15 April without notable incident.[65]

Clemenceau's directive of 29 March ordering the evacuation did not cover Sevastopol in the Crimea, which had been occupied at the end of December 1918 by a regiment of French troops. From that time until the middle of March, Sevastopol had been an isolated backwater in the French zone of occupation. In fact, the commander of French forces there had no contact whatever with either Generals Berthelot or d'Anselme until units of the Red Army began to approach the Crimea. The nearness of Bolshevik troops emboldened the workers of Sevastopol who proclaimed a general strike on 15 March to force a transfer of power to the local Soviet. In response, the French command declared martial law and broke the strike. Relative peace was re-established but, with elements of the Red Army preparing to attack the Crimea, the calm was not expected to last.[66]

To meet a Bolshevik offensive, the French command had scarcely more than two thousand troops.[67] This was hardly sufficient strength to defend Sevastopol, and the ministry of war therefore prepared to evacuate French and Greek units from the city. The general staff reasoned that the city was expendable in view of the reduction of French military forces in the east and the need to concentrate what remained of them in the Balkans to defend against the spread of Bolshevism.[68] But the ministry of the navy objected to the surrender, wanting to retain Sevastopol as a naval base in the Black Sea. Consequently, Clemenceau ordered Franchet d'Esperey to try to hold the French position there.[69]

Conditions in Sevastopol, however, were not favourable to a long-term occupation by the French. Colonel Eugène Gervais Trousson, commander of French and Allied troops in the Crimea, reported in early April that the situation in the city was extremely grave. Like other French commanders, he complained bitterly of the anti-Bolshevik Russians. The Volunteer Army, he said, was "hated by all." With few exceptions, Volunteer officers did little but malinger in the local cafes and hotels. At the front, they amused themselves drinking and carousing. But if the Bolsheviks were signalled to be close by, "everything collapse[d], at the first shot, *sauve qui peut général*.... Nothing can be done with these people," wrote Trousson, "I do not even have enough men to shoot them." The situation had deteriorated to such an extent that even in Sevastopol one could not venture out without an armed escort. Moreover, Trousson complained that he was completely without the means to defend himself. "If I am attacked at all vigorously in the next three or four days, I will immediately be thrown into the sea." Trousson remained combative, but he told a friend that he was not sleeping too well – with a revolver on one side and a carbine at the other![70]

Such was Trousson's image of the war in the Crimea. To the French command, conditions in the Balkans seemed little better. The eruption of a communist revolution in Hungary led by Bela Kun was particularly alarming to Franchet d'Esperey because of the weakness of the French and Allied military presence in the east.[71] He warned Paris that the Hungarian revolution had taken on an "internationalist character" and was seeking support from Bolshevik Russia. If the preliminary decisions of the peace conference imposed heavy territorial sacrifices on Bulgaria, an explosion similar to the one in Budapest could be expected there.

Since the Allies could do no more, he said, it was essential to build up the armies of the east European states. "Any Serbian or Rumanian you arm saves a French soldier." The situation was too grave to hesitate, he warned; "the Entente needs strong armies to stop the revolutionary thrust coming from the east...."[72]

In spite of the weakness of French forces, Franchet d'Esperey wanted to launch an immediate invasion of Hungary to overthrow the revolutionary government in Budapest. He made such a proposal on 26 March, but Clemenceau rejected it.[73] Although Franchet d'Esperey continued to favour a Hungary offensive, Clemenceau remained skeptical of its advantages in view of inadequate Allied military strength.[74] In fact, the French premier chastised Franchet d'Esperey for his panicky warnings of "catastrophe" in the east.[75]

These blandishments not withstanding, Clemenceau did indeed seem to underestimate the dangers raised by his eastern commander. But ensconced in Paris, a victor in the war against Germany, the "Tiger" was little disposed to believe that ragtag revolutionary mobs could threaten the power of France. Yet the danger was real enough, especially in Bessarabia where an anticipated Bolshevik offensive against shaky French troops could have led to troublesome consequences.[76] Although Clemenceau continued to brush these dangers aside, he tended, because of limited French resources, to let his eastern commanders shift for themselves in trying to hold back the Bolshevik tide.

Franchet d'Esperey's aggressiveness with regard to Hungary was indicative of his sense of priorities in dealing with the spread of Bolshevik revolution. Although prepared to strike at Bolshevism behind the barrage being erected against Soviet Russia, he did not favour holding French positions in the Crimea and he advised on 13 April that Sevastopol should be evacuated.[77] Clemenceau, anticipating this advice, had ordered a withdrawal the previous day. The ministry of the navy objected, but Clemenceau responded that the government had no choice but to withdraw.[78]

In spite of the perilous situation at Sevastopol, Trousson succeeded in improving security around the city for a few days. Bolshevik military units made contact with French outposts before Sevastopol on 15 April, and fighting broke out soon thereafter. The outcome was determined by the guns of the French fleet in the harbour of Sevastopol which halted the Bolshevik advance. Negotiations between the two commands then led to an armistice. It was agreed that a week-long cessation of hostilities would be observed, and that a local Soviet administration of Sevastopol would be installed on 19 April. This armistice could be prolonged by common agreement or rejected by either side on twenty-four hours' notice.[79]

The favourable outcome of the initial fighting with Bolshevik forces persuaded Trousson that a withdrawal from Sevastopol was premature. With the support of Admiral Amet, Trousson asked for authorization to delay the evacuation.[80] Franchet d'Esperey agreed, although he would not countermand previous orders to withdraw. He continued to think in terms of a strategic conception based on safeguarding eastern Europe against Bolshevism and abandoning Russia.[81] Nevertheless, if Trousson had been able to maintain the upper hand at Sevastopol, he might eventually have asked for and received authorization to suspend the evacuation altogether. The Quai d'Orsay, which appears to have viewed the situation in southern Russia with less pessimism than the French command, could well have supported such a request.[82] As it was, the ministry of the navy, upon learning of the successful outcome of fighting before Sevastopol, recommended that the city be held "long enough to safeguard Allied interests and to assure the complete liberty of our movements in the Black Sea."[83]

### THE MUTINY OF THE FRENCH BLACK SEA FLEET

Unfortunately for Paris, the military situation which Trousson had considered so favourable on 17 April suddenly deteriorated two days later when mutiny broke out in the French fleet. The first signs of trouble came on 16 April when an engineering officer, André Marty, and another sailor aboard the destroyer *Protet*, Louis Badina, were arrested for plotting to seize control of the ship and take it over to the Bolsheviks.[84] On the evening of 19 April disturbances broke out on the battleship *France* and then spread to the flagship of the fleet, *Jean Bart*. On the *France*, members of the crew gathered on the foredeck to demand an end to the war in Russia, a return to the *métropole*, and better material conditions on board ship.[85] The next day protests spread rapidly from the *France* and *Jean Bart* to the battleships *Justice*, *Mirabeau*, *Vergniaud*, and other ships of the fleet.[86] The Red flag was hoisted for a few hours on the bowsprit of the *France* and the *Jean Bart*. Amet had to inform Paris in utmost secrecy that he lacked trustworthy elements for repression and that his words to rebellious sailors had remained "fruitless."[87] The men were exasperated with conditions on ship, he said, and after hearing of the debates at the end of March in the Chamber of Deputies, they "no longer want[ed] to fight the Red Army."[88]

The French command tried to undercut the mutiny by granting shore leave in Sevastopol. But this measure backfired when crew members became involved in a pro-Bolshevik rally on shore. The demonstration was fired on by a Franco-Greek patrol, and some twenty French sailors and Russian civilians were killed or wounded. Sailors returned to their ships swearing vengeance against the Greek soldiers and French marines who had fired on the demonstration.[89]

On 21 April the mood of the crews became more dangerous. The "gravity of the situation," Amet warned, could no longer be hidden. "Various indications" revealed the existence of Soviets among "unruly elements" of the fleet which were linked with Bolshevik organizations ashore. These groups, "followed like sheep" by the rest of the crews, were "fixed in their ideas of returning home and of no longer fighting the Soviets." Amet concluded that "Bolshevik propaganda aided by elements of [the French] press had manifestly succeeded" in subverting the loyalty of his men.[90]

The French command regarded the *France* as the principal generating force of the revolt and treated it like a plague ship to be separated from the rest of the fleet as quickly as possible. Some sailors aboard the *France*, apparently encouraged by Bolshevik elements ashore, wanted all the ships of the fleet to leave Sevastopol together. The French command, recognizing the dangers of such a move, tried to thwart this plan, but Amet signalled Paris that he still did not have sufficient authority to order the *France* to weigh anchor. "Orders to obey," he said, would be inefficacious and would unleash a revolt which I still hope to avoid." Amet also requested support from the British fleet since French commanders doubted whether their men would obey orders to fire on the Bolsheviks in the event of another attack on Sevastopol. Under the circumstances, Amet informed Paris that he was working "to hasten the evacuation, while trying to save as much face as possible."[91]

On 22 April French commanders began to regain control of their ships. Amet reported that mutineers aboard the *France* were losing their influence over the rest of the fleet. The large majority of the crews, he said, were prepared to follow orders except against the Bolsheviks or against protesting crew members.[92] On 23 April the *France* left Sevastopol, its crew having played into the hands of the French command by agreeing to weigh anchor without the rest of the fleet. Amet breathed a noticeable sigh of relief as he informed Paris that conditions were returning to near normal. He advised, however, that unrest would not completely disappear until the fleet had been pulled out of Russian waters and crews replaced.[93]

The effect of the mutinies at Sevastopol on the intervention was decisive. Trousson indicated that the revolt of the fleet caused him to abandon any idea of dragging out the evacuation.[94] Similarly, Amet recommended a disengagement from the Black Sea since "the struggle against [the] Soviet Republic [was] unpopular and destined to failure."[95] Franchet d'Esperey, upon learning of the mutiny, cabled Trousson to hasten the evacuation.[96] Foot-dragging ceased immediately, and on 28 April some six thousand men were pulled out of Sevastopol, bringing to a close the French military intervention in southern Russia.

## "THE COMPLETE FAILURE OF A RIDICULOUS ADVENTURE"

The events of the last two months of the French military occupation in Russia had a profound effect on the thinking of members of the French eastern command. D'Anselme complained bitterly to General Berthelot of the outcome of the intervention and of the unruliness and demoralization of his forces in Bessarabia. While French troops would no longer fight, the Greeks and Poles pillaged and "spread terror everywhere.... All that," said d'Anselme, "leaves me with an army of brigands like the bands of the Middle Ages." As for the evacuation from Odessa, it had been long and difficult. There were not enough rations and equipment was abandoned along the way. At least, however, they had not been pursued. Fortunately, the order to evacuate arrived in time because the situation in Odessa was rapidly becoming untenable. What had happened, concluded d'Anselme, was "the complete failure of a ridiculous adventure."[97]

Freydenberg asserted that the collapse of the intervention was the result of having put too much confidence in the Volunteer Army which was believed to be a national army liked and supported by the population. In fact, wrote Freydenberg, the Volunteer Army had no popular base of support and was incapable of bearing the main burden of combat against the Soviet government. Fearing a restoration of the *ancien régime* by the Volunteers, the people turned to the Bolsheviks. Similarly, the French association with the Volunteer Army, skilfully exploited by Bolshevik propaganda, had turned the Russian population against the Allied cause.[98]

Trousson drew similar conclusions in his final report on the evacuation of the Crimea. He noted that scarcely a third of the Volunteer Army, "already derisively weak," was of any value. Among this third, he said, "there [were] brave men.... Unfortunately, the greatest number, the other two thirds at least, include[d] only shirkers of all sorts, debauchees, thieves ... and even assassins.... One understands," wrote Trousson, "why such a band has incurred the hatred ... and disesteem of all who have seen it at work." Like Freydenberg, Trousson concluded that the failure of the intervention was the result of having accorded too much credit to the Volunteers.

To hear them, it sufficed to show a single French uniform in order to see everyone flock to their colours. It was far from being so. From the moment this fact was perceived ... a decision should have been taken either to withdraw or to remain by taking over the war ourselves with the necessary means. Instead, [the government] contented itself with half-way measures ... which were destined to fail.

The enormous fault committed [by us] was to want to tie our interests to the Volunteer Army which merits a thousand times the scorn that all have heaped upon it.[99]

The bitterness of French commanders toward the Volunteer Army was no doubt a reflection of their own sense of impotence. It was also reinforced by their perception of the Red Army as a disciplined fighting force committed to its cause and supported by the Russian population.[100] Moreover, as British accounts indicate, the French command, and d'Anselme in particular, suffered from "overwrought nerves" and a "tiredness of war."[101] As a result, French commanders were not really committed to the campaign in Russia and were unprepared to turn a blind eye to the shortcomings of their anti-Bolshevik allies. Of course, the failings of the Volunteers in the Ukraine and Crimea would not automatically have doomed the intervention to defeat if the French had been able to fill the gap. But domestic opposition and the general war-weariness of the French army prevented the government from doing so. Clemenceau himself acknowledged that "Parliament and public opinion in France ... [were] resolutely opposed to any expedition in Russia...."[102]

Bolshevik propaganda also contributed in an important way to depriving the French government of troops to fight the revolution. Generals Berthelot and d'Anselme and Admiral Amet all testified to its success among their men. In retrospect, it seems implausible that Bolshevik tracts printed on poor quality paper and often in ungrammatical French could have had such a powerful impact on French soldiers and sailors. But these men were sick of war and quite disposed to believe the claims of Bolshevik propaganda, the more so because they repeated what the French Socialist press had been saying since the Armistice.

To counter the effects of propaganda against the intervention, the French general staff tried to find soldiers to fight in southern Russia who would be impervious to Bolshevism. Volunteers and colonial troops were intended to replace unwilling conscripts. But the volunteers never materialized and colonial units came too late to save the intervention. Moreover, even some of the latter proved unwilling to march against the Bolsheviks.[103]

The inability of the government to provide adequate forces for the intervention made it impossible to occupy a large enough zone to provision Odessa in foodstuffs. This in turn brought on the danger of famine which eventually compelled an evacuation of French and Allied forces. Franchet d'Esperey later tried to explain to Denikin that the abandonment of Odessa and Sevastopol was forced solely by the inability to provision these cities and by the consequent danger of internal disorders. "From a military point of view," said Franchet d'Esperey, "we did not suffer any sort of defeat and if there had been no fear of dooming the populations of these two cities to starvation, we would have remained in position."[104] But this assertion has a spurious ring in view of Franchet d'Esperey's own previous avowal to Clemenceau that the supply of Odessa was "intimately linked" to the question of military operations.[105] Moreover, d'Anselme doubted whether his troops could cope with an external attack from advancing Bolshevik irregulars and a simultaneous internal rebellion precipitated by the absence of food supplies and other necessities. As for Sevastopol, its evacuation was ultimately hastened by the mutiny of the French fleet.

In the final analysis, however, the intervention in southern Russia failed because of its lack of popularity with the Russian population and because of the war-weariness of French troops. The latter refused to march against the Soviet regime, and the former rose up with Bolshevik partisans and the Red Army to oppose the intervention. To be sure, the problem of supply was an important factor in contributing to the evacuation, but this question was directly related to the popular dislike of the French military presence in Russia. If French soldiers had been ready to fight, and if the Russian population had been prepared to support the intervention, the zone of occupation would have expanded rapidly enough to provide for the revictualling of Odessa and Sevastopol.

The failing intervention in southern Russia strongly contributed to the gradual reorientation of French policy toward the cordon sanitaire. But this was not the only option open to the government in Paris. The French command's rather favourable impressions of the Red Army led some French officers to recommend an accommodation with the Bolsheviks. During the last two weeks of February, a French mission was in Ekaterinodar, at Denikin's headquarters, to evaluate the general military situation of the Volunteer Army. The report this mission issued was quite like other French intelligence estimates of the Volunteers at this time. It concluded, however, that in view of the weakness of the Denikin government, the Allies should either organize a military expedition capable of achieving its ends, or enter into relations with the Soviet regime – the sole viable governmental authority in Russia.[107] Although this was only a low-level intelligence mission, other higher ranking officers in the French army and navy drew similar conclusions. Admiral Louis Antoine Exelmans, commander of the French cruiser *Bruix* serving in the Black Sea, noted that the Soviet government was likely "to put a great deal of water in its revolutionary and communist wine" to gain recognition. The French government should encourage this development and withdraw from southern Russia. Not to do so, would risk alienating Russian nationalism which was forming under the aegis of Bolshevism, and would chance throwing Russia into the arms of Germany.[108]

The March intelligence bulletin of the Armée d'Orient gave an extremely favourable appraisal of the Bolsheviks. "It is not necessary to delude ourselves," said the report, "the troops opposing us in southern Russia give the impression of a national army, comparable to the one which served France in 1793." The constant increase in the strength of these forces "confirms the view that the army of the Soviets enjoys the support of the people and that it now represents the Russian nation in arms fighting against the [foreign] invader.... This impression which might not apply to northern Russia and Siberia," said the report, "certainly corresponds to the reality of the situation in the Ukraine and in southern Russia."[109]

Although the French eastern command would not venture an opinion about Bolshevik strength in Siberia or northern Russia, other French agents in these regions were drawing conclusions similar to those expressed by the Armée d'Orient. The weakness of the anti-Bolsheviks in Siberia was strikingly illustrated by the reports of French representatives in Omsk that the Kolchak government would collapse without Allied support.[110] Similar assessments also came from northern Russia. By the summer of 1919 the Quai d'Orsay frankly acknowledged that the majority of the population of Arkhangelsk was Bolshevik and that in all probability an Allied withdrawal from the area would lead to an immediate Bolshevik takeover.[111]

All of these analyses were, of course, consistent with earlier views of the French government that the Bolsheviks could not be overthrown by their internal enemies alone. In February and March 1918 this analysis had led to a *rapprochement* with the Soviet regime. In March and April 1919 the French eastern command seemed on the verge of moving in a similar direction. Amet informed Paris at the end of April in the aftermath of the mutinies at Sevastopol that he saw no other option for French policy than to avoid "irritating" the Bolsheviks by "an absolutely intransigent attitude."[112] Consequently, Amet concluded a draft convention with Bolshevik representatives in the Crimea whereby Soviet authorities would agree to abstain from hostile acts at sea against the Allies if they in turn would permit ships under Bolshevik flag carrying passengers or food supplies to ply between Russian ports.[113]

Unlike the period of February-March 1918, however, there was no sentiment in Paris during the spring of the following year favourable to a *modus vivendi* with the Bolsheviks. In spite of the devastating criticisms levelled at the Volunteer Army by the French command and in spite of the near-unanimous opinion of French agents that the people of Russia supported the Bolsheviks, Clemenceau indicated to Franchet d'Esperey that good relations would have to be maintained with the Volunteers. Whatever the "regrettable" and unpopular political tendencies of Denikin and his entourage, whatever "the mediocrity" of his army, he represented the sole organized and "clearly anti-Bolshevik force in southern Russia." The Allies, concluded Clemenceau, would therefore have to continue to support him.[114]

The French desire to maintain good relations with the Volunteers was motivated in part by pressure from London. Although Lloyd George apparently preferred to come to terms with the Bolsheviks, the Conservative members of his coalition government did not, and pressured him into taking a more hostile stance against the Soviet regime. Winston Churchill led these hard-liners and eventually succeeded in obtaining government approval for the extension of large-scale material support to Denikin.[115] As a result, the British government pressed the Quai d'Orsay to take a more positive attitude toward the Volunteers and to stop Amet's talks with Soviet representatives.[116] The French government, of course, needed little prodding and Clemenceau ordered an end to French contacts with Soviet officials in the Crimea. They were inappropriate, he said, since France was in a state of *de facto* hostilities with the Soviet regime.[117]

In short, circumstances in the spring of 1919 were not conducive to an accommodation with the Bolsheviks. In the first place, the Quai d'Orsay, at least, had still not abandoned hope of recovering its political and economic influence in Russia. More importantly, the barely organized cordon sanitaire had been breached by the revolution in Hungary. Even Franchet d'Esperey, although impressed by the military achievements and popular support of the Red Army, was extremely alarmed by the Hungarian revolution and the prospect of a further advance of Bolshevism into Europe. One might safely come to terms with the Soviet government in Russia as long as the rest of Europe was secure from its reach. But no accommodation was possible when popular unrest afflicted all the states of the continent and where Bolshevism seemed ready to spread like the red poppies in the churned fields of Flanders. In these circumstances, the French government had no desire to impede the efforts of the Volunteers and their British sutlers to overthrow the Bolsheviks.

But while peace with the Soviets was an impossible option for the French government, so also was a continuation of armed intervention. D'Anselme's forces in the Ukraine had narrowly escaped disaster, and mutinies in the fleet at Sevastopol had badly frightened the French command. Even before the evacuation, a reassessment of French policy was commenced in Paris. In view of the weakness of the anti-Bolshevik Russians, the French government began to concentrate its attention on building up the military strength of the Poles, Czechs, and Rumanians. If the armies of Kolchak and Denikin unexpectedly won the civil war, the French government could try to make its peace with the Volunteers and to re-establish or expand its pre-war influence in Russia. But the first concern in Paris was to contain the spread of Bolshevism through the creation of the cordon sanitaire. The French government was prepared to leave the more active role in the struggle against Moscow to its stronger British allies.

## CHAPTER ELEVEN

# The French Government and the End of the Russian Civil War

Although the civil war in Russia continued until the end of 1920, direct French military intervention came to a close with the evacuation of Sevastopol in April 1919. A small contingent of French troops remained for a time at Arkhangelsk and the Janin mission and Czech Legion were still in Siberia, but this military presence represented a vestige of previous French policy rather than evidence of a continuing commitment to direct intervention in Russia.[1] The French government had not become indifferent to the outcome of the anti-Bolshevik struggle, but limited resources forced it to play a less active role. To be sure, the Quai d'Orsay's interest in Russia was occasionally aroused when military fortune briefly favoured the anti-Bolsheviks or when it saw an advantage to be drawn from unfolding events. But essentially French eastern policy had become focused on Poland, Czechoslovakia, and the other states along the Russian frontier which could block the advance of Bolshevism and eventually form a counterweight to Germany.

The reorientation of French eastern policy was hastened in the spring of 1919 by the danger of a Bolshevik offensive through Bessarabia and across the Carpathian mountains to link up with revolutionary forces in Hungary. It was for this reason that in April 1919 the Polish Haller Army (between 70 and 80,000 men) which had been organized and equipped by the French government to fight on the Western Front, was started on its way to Poland. Later in the month, Paris consented to an initial credit of 100 million francs for the strengthening of the Polish army.[2] In May the French government approved a Czech and Rumanian occupation of the Carpatho-Ukraine in order to plug a weak point in the cordon sanitaire.[3] Similarly, when a Polish offensive into Galicia provoked the anger of Lloyd George and Wilson, Paris dragged its feet before protesting to Warsaw, apparently because it hoped to see a link-up of the Polish and Rumanian armies.[4] This junction, which took place on 27 May in the region between Stanislavov and Kolomea, led to the establishment of a continuous front against the Bolsheviks and lessened the danger of a link-up of Soviet and Hungarian military forces.

Events in Russia seemed to favour these French efforts to block the spread of Bolshevism in Europe. In early May the Soviet government ordered Grigoriev, the conqueror of Odessa, to march on Rumania. But Grigoriev refused to obey and raised a revolt against Soviet authority in the Ukraine. Although loyal Bolshevik troops put down the mutiny, plans for an offensive against the Rumanians had to be abandoned. To make matters worse, the rear of the Red Armies fighting Denikin was noticeably weakened just at the moment Volunteer forces went on the offensive. The Volunteers, who had been powerfully reinforced by large quantities of British military supplies, began an advance which was not halted until the following autumn a scant 400 kilometres from Moscow.[5]

This change in the military fortunes of the anti-Bolshevik Russians led Franchet d'Esperey and the Quai d'Orsay to press for an increase in aid to the Volunteer Army, intended to soften Denikin's hostility toward France and thus to afford some protection to French interests in the Ukraine.[6] The general staff, however, refused to consider any change in the distribution of French assistance. As Clemenceau observed, the Rumanians and Serbs were "more direct clients [of France] than Denikin," and were for the moment in greater need than the Volunteers who were being fully supplied by the British.[7] The Quai d'Orsay still urged greater support for the Volunteer Army, but the general staff would not make a change in policy.[8]

While the French government was unprepared to render material or financial assistance to the Volunteers, it still kept a hand in Russian affairs. In the spring of 1919 the Quai d'Orsay became involved in a rather squalid affair to buy the Russian gold reserve which the Kolchak government had captured from the Bolsheviks at Kazan in 1918. The Omsk regime offered to sell the gold to France in order to buy badly needed supplies which it could not acquire with its own depreciated roubles.[9] In Paris the French government considered the offer, but dallied in its response, scrupling briefly about the moral implications of buying gold it had previously insisted should continue to back the Russian rouble.[10] By the time the Quai d'Orsay put its misgivings aside and made an offer for the gold, it was too late.[11] The Omsk regime concluded a £10 million "short term loan" with an Anglo-American consortium headed by the Baring bank of London. To avoid wounding French *amour propre*, the Baring group invited the Crédit Lyonnais and the Paribas to join the consortium as minority participants.[12]

The Quai d'Orsay and ministry of finance were outraged by this turn of events and not at all placated by the offer made to the French banks, a concession regarded as totally inadequate and "humiliating" for France.[13] The Quai d'Orsay conveyed its displeasure to the Siberian government, and the latter, apparently to appease the French, offered them in August 12,000 kilograms of gold. This sale was eventually completed in November 1919 a few weeks after the fall of Omsk.[14]

The image the French government projected as it negotiated for Kolchak's gold was not a pretty one. The French seemed to be scavenging among the ruins of the Russian empire, and they were highly vexed to be chased away by the dying government of the old political order. This displeasure was only aggravated by the continued refusal of Omsk to permit the establishment of the BI *banque d'émission*.[15] These developments occurred at the precise moment the French government was reviewing its program of expenditures in Russia and left the Quai d'Orsay little disposed to continue aid to the Siberian government.

Because Paris had left to the British the responsibility of supplying the Volunteer Army, most French expenditures were incurred in Siberia. These were the result of the French agreement in July 1918 to maintain the Czech Legion in Russia and of a decision in early 1919 to provide a monthly credit of 18 million francs to the government of Kolchak. These expenditures amounted to an annual cost of some 700 million francs. The interministerial commission on Russian financial affairs (CIAF) regarded such expenses as a vestige of previous French policy, burdensome, and unproductive. In view of this assessment and the various complaints of the French government against Omsk, it decided to evacuate the Czechs and to end the credits to Kolchak.[16]

The decision of the French government to liquidate its financial commitments in Siberia represented a further step along the path to an eastern policy based solely on the cordon sanitaire. To be sure, in early September the general staff, perhaps as a concession to the Quai d'Orsay, approved the dispatch to Denikin's headquarters of a small eleven-man mission headed by General Charles Mangin. The French government also agreed to send some 30 million francs worth of supplies to the Volunteers.[17] But these were rather paltry efforts compared to the 375 millions in credits extended to the Poles between April and October 1919 and to the 600-man French military mission in Poland.[18] These belated efforts were also meagre by comparison with the £55 million in supplies and the 2,000 man British military mission operating in southern Russia.[19] In short, French resources remained committed to the cordon sanitaire in spite of Denikin's victories over the Red Army.[20]

Soon after the decision was made to send the Mangin mission to Russia, the military successes of the anti-Bolshevik Russian armies came to a sudden end. In October 1919 the Red Army successfully held off an attack on Petrograd by the anti-Bolshevik forces of General N.N. Iudenich and at the same threw back Denikin's offensive on Moscow. Iudenich's small army was rapidly pushed into Estonia where it was disarmed and interned. Denikin's forces were also decisively defeated and in March 1920 the debris of his army was thrown into the sea at Novorossiisk in the Kuban. Remnants of the Volunteer Army still held out in the Crimea, but it seemed just a matter of time before they too were swept away.

In Siberia where Janin and a French military mission had been stationed since the autumn of 1918, the Kolchak regime was also in a state of collapse. Although the French government decided to halt its financial aid to Omsk, Janin had still to supervise the repatriation of the Czech Legion and other smaller detachments of Poles, Rumanians, and Serbs. This was no mean task because of the growing disorder in what remained of anti-Bolshevik Siberia. Since May the armies of Kolchak had been reeling back to the east. First, the Urals were lost, then Cheliabinsk fell in July, and Omsk in early November.[21]

As these defeats mounted, the authority of Kolchak's government crumbled. Disorder and lawlessness spread quickly along the Trans-Siberian Railway where the scattered echelons of the Czech Legion sought to force their way east. Because the Czechs guarded and controlled the railway from Taiga, near Tomsk, all the way to Irkutsk, they were able to move first, shunting aside trains of Russian evacuees. Their bullying, heavy-handed practices angered Kolchak, and in late December he ordered the halting of Czech trains, if necessary by blowing up the tunnels along the southern shore of Lake Baikal. Kolchak, however, had no authority to enforce such an order which, when the Czechs learned of it, increased the bad blood between the two sides.[22]

This incident had fateful consequences because Kolchak was still on the Trans-Siberian Railway, at the mercy of the Czechs and far west of the relative safety of Irkutsk. The Czechs themselves were in considerable danger, being pressed on both sides of the railroad by partisans and from behind by the Red Army. In front of them, to the east, revolts broke out in the towns along the rail line, which threatened to block the evacuation.[23] Insurgent workers and townspeople wanted Kolchak turned over to them for quick, revolutionary justice. Ultimately, the humbled "Supreme Ruler" of Siberia had to seek Czech protection from the angry mobs.[24]

Janin gave instructions for the deposed dictator to be brought to safety, but the disorders grew more dangerous and the Czechs decided to turn over their charge to revolutionary authorities in exchange for safe passage to Vladivostok. To improve the offer, the Czechs also threw in the Siberian gold reserve which Kolchak had tried to take with him from Omsk.[25] Janin acquiesed, informing Paris that he had no other choice without risking the security of Czech forces. There were, he reported, more than a hundred echelons of the legion scattered over a thousand kilometres between Kansk and Irkutsk and hemmed in on all sides by hostile forces.[26] These Czech units could not be concentrated or moved rapidly, and every day they ran the risk of being cut off by sabotage of the rail line to the east. Moreover, the discipline of Czech soldiers was poor and Janin feared mutiny if he gave orders for a fight to save Kolchak.[27] This was no idle apprehension; on 10 January ten thousand men of the Polish division that made up the rear-guard of Czech forces capitulated to advancing units of the Red Army. Janin felt disaster nipping at his heels and began to think only of getting the Czechs and his mission safely out of Siberia.[28] In this, Janin was successful – the last Czech echelons cleared Irkutsk in early March. Kolchak was not so lucky. After a lengthy interrogation by insurgent Bolshevik authorities in Irkutsk, he was shot on the morning of 7 February as remnants of his broken army approached the city to effect his release.

The collapse of the various anti-Bolshevik Russian armies left the French government with little alternative but to rely completely on the east European states, and especially Poland, to contain the spread of Bolshevism. In early December 1919 Clemenceau told Lloyd George at an Allied conference in London that he "had come to think that the Powers had made a great mistake in interfering in the Russian civil war." They had wasted large sums of money without positive result. Clemenceau therefore opposed a continuation of previous Allied policy. Indeed, he told Lloyd George that he "was much more concerned about the future danger from Germany than he was about the spread of Bolshevism, either by force or subversion from Russia."[29] The French premier recommended that the Entente strengthen Poland in order to erect "a barbed wire entanglement" around Russia to prevent the Bolsheviks "from creating trouble outside, and to stop Germany from entering into relations with Russia, whether of a political or military character."[30]

Lloyd George, who had finally taken the upper hand over the interventionist Churchill, was pleased by the new French attitude. He hoped to reach an accommodation and re-establish trade relations with Moscow. These developments seemed to portend a rapid end to the Russian civil war. But Clemenceau resigned in January 1920 and was succeeded by Alexandre Millerand, who became premier and foreign minister. Millerand preferred to maintain an intransigent attitude toward the Bolsheviks. The Quai d'Orsay for a third time disregarded intelligence assessments from the French general staff, indicating that the Soviets were successfully building a Russian state capable of re-establishing a European balance of power. The general staff did not openly advocate a *modus vivendi* with Moscow, but its assessment of Bolshevik strength closely resembled similar intelligence estimates made during the brief Franco-Soviet *rapprochement* of 1918 and again during April 1919.

With the civil war coming to an end, the general staff's appraisal of the Bolsheviks could at least have served as the basis for improved relations with the Soviet state along the lines envisaged by Lloyd George. The Hungarian revolution had been strangled by the Allies in August 1919, alleviating the danger of a Bolshevik offensive into Europe. But the French government could still not reconcile its lost political and economic interests in Russia to even a limited accommodation with the Soviets. As a result, the Quai d'Orsay ignored numerous and urgent warnings from its agents abroad indicating that the Polish government was preparing an offensive against the Red Army to carry its frontiers eastward into the Ukraine. By abstaining from any action to discourage this Polish attack, the Quai d'Orsay seemed to give an offensive dimension, not intended by Clemenceau, to the concept of the cordon sanitaire.[31]

Without opposition from the French, the Polish army launched its offensive in late April 1920. The attack was initially successful and the Poles occupied Kiev at the beginning of May. But the Red Army counter-attacked, breaking through the Polish front in early June. The Soviet counter-offensive, striking first in the north and then in the south, rolled up the Polish army. In forty days, Soviet troops advanced some 600 kilometres to the west, reaching the outskirts of Warsaw in the middle of August. Here regrouped Polish forces stopped and drove back the Bolshevik onslaught. The Quai d'Orsay, encouraged by this turn in the tide of battle, tried to organize a union of Polish and Rumanian forces with the remnants of the Volunteer Army, then under the command of General Baron P.N. Wrangel, for a general offensive against the Bolsheviks. Because the Poles and Rumanians would not go along, this plan was abandoned in September, and the French government shifted back to Clemenceau's defensive conception of the cordon sanitaire.[32] In October an armistice was concluded between the Soviet and Polish governments, and the following month remnant Volunteer forces, which had been holding out in the Crimea, were evacuated.

These events represented the last acts of the intervention and civil war. The French government would not again make any serious commitments, either directly or through its east European allies, to the intervention against the Bolsheviks. But this evolution in policy was a long time in coming. For more than three years Paris had maintained an intransigent attitude toward the Bolsheviks. What accounted for this hostility? Why had the French government sought to overthrow the Soviet regime?

In early 1918 the priorities of French policy toward Russia were illustrated by the discussion within the government of whether to collaborate, on a limited basis, with the Bolsheviks against the Central Powers. The pros and cons of this question were discussed not only in Paris, but also within the French diplomatic and business communities in Russia. The French general staff, and paradoxically Foch, who would become a hard-line anti-Bolshevik after the war, were the strongest proponents of a limited *rapprochement* with the Soviet regime. They viewed the Bolsheviks as the only Russian political elements capable of organizing further resistance to the Central Powers. Since the general staff was primarily concerned with waging war against Germany, they argued that the Bolsheviks should be supported.

The Quai d'Orsay took a different view. Philippe Berthelot, the *éminence grise* of the French foreign ministry, held that even if the Bolsheviks could pose some minimal threat to Germany, their resistance would be too insignificant to be of real value to the Entente. Moreover, collaboration with the Soviet regime threatened to alienate the sympathies of the anti-Bolshevik parties whose continued goodwill was believed to be crucial to the maintenance of French political and economic interests in Russia. Essentially, the Quai d'Orsay argued that the war in Russia was finished, and that therefore the government should look to the protection of its post-war interests. To be sure, the Quai d'Orsay condemned the Soviet government for having signed the treaty of Brest-Litovsk. But condemning the Bolsheviks as traitors to the Allied cause, helped the Quai d'Orsay out of an awkward position *vis-à-vis* the French general staff.

Berthelot and his colleagues could not state plainly that French political and economic interests took precedence over military considerations because that would have appeared perverse, and would not have been convincing to the general staff. This was especially true in the early spring of 1918 when the German army threatened to break through the Western Front, and when any kind of military diversion in the east seemed worthy of support. For the Quai d'Orsay to gain its point, it had to tailor its arguments to win over or at least to neutralize the general staff. Thus the Bolsheviks were condemned as traitors and as revolutionary fanatics, who, because of their ill-considered, too advanced social ideas, would be incapable of organizing further resistance against Germany.

By using such arguments, the Quai d'Orsay could also urge the British and Americans to take action against the Soviet regime without offending too much Wilson's apparent "moral qualms" regarding intervention.

Perhaps, if the Quai d'Orsay had known of the Department of State's strong opposition to the Bolsheviks, it might have been more direct. On the other hand, domestic considerations dictated against an overly candid hostility to the Soviet government. With French working-class dissidence on the rise, it was more expedient for Paris to denounce the Bolsheviks for having signed a German peace than to cast them as dangerous social revolutionaries who threatened the vital interests of the French government. The former approach avoided any needless provocation of the left and stifled socialist criticism of the government's policy toward Russia.

In any event, the Quai d'Orsay's anxieties concerning British and American attitudes toward the Bolsheviks were soon quieted, first, by the British decision to abandon Lockhart's conciliatory policy, and then, by the uprising of the Czech Legion in May 1918. The Czech revolt overcame Wilson's hesitation to intervene and embroiled the Allies in a military conflict with the Soviet regime. For a short time the Bolsheviks stumbled on the brink of collapse. But the Czechs and anti-Bolshevik parties were too weak to overthrow the Soviets, while the Allies, preoccupied on the Western Front, could not intervene in sufficient force to put the anti-Bolsheviks into power.

During the early autumn the tide of battle began to turn in favour of the Bolsheviks. In Siberia the Red Army won important victories against the Czechs, and in the Ukraine the withdrawal of the Austro-German army of occupation threatened to open the way to a rapid expansion of Bolshevism into all of southwestern Russia. This explosion in the growth of Soviet power seriously alarmed the French government and led it to intervene militarily in the Ukraine and Crimea. The high command of the Armée d'Orient expressed serious misgivings about undertaking military operations in Russia, but neither Clemenceau nor the Quai d'Orsay were prepared to heed such pessimism. The Red Army was winning victories and growing more powerful. It threatened to advance into Europe carrying with it the "bacillus of Bolshevism" and doing incalculable harm to French strategic interests. The Soviet government, of course, offered to negotiate, hoping to divide its enemies and gain a further breathing space to consolidate its strength. The Quai d'Orsay, however, scorned this Red chicanery, thinking it pointless and dangerous to negotiate with the Bolsheviks.

An economic factor also influenced French policy. The Ukraine was the centre of French economic activity in Russia and the dispatch of troops there would not only strike a blow at the Red Army, but would also serve to protect important French-owned industries. The contemplation of such an operation seemed all the more feasible because the Black Sea and its ports were within the operational range of the powerful French Mediterranean fleet. To be sure, the desire to put down the revolutionary threat of Bolshevism remained paramount, but the protection of French economic interests was also an important preoccupation of French policy-makers.

Governmental discussions to this end came to focus on the creation of *banques d'émission* in the Ukraine and Siberia. The proposed banks were intended not only to provide an acceptable currency for an Allied army of occupation, but were also meant to protect and promote French economic interests in Russia. The Paribas proposal for a Ukrainian *banque d'émission* and subsidiary trading company was the more ambitious of the projects. Had this bank been formed, it would have represented a far-reaching usurpation of Russian sovereign rights. Indeed, if the French had been strong enough to maintain their military presence in southern Russia, they would no doubt have prevented the Volunteers from entering the French zone of occupation and would have sought to establish a Ukrainian protectorate, a sort of demi-colony, serving the various economic needs of the war-torn *métropole*.

These rather extensive economic pretensions were in fundamental contradiction with France's stated political objectives in Russia. The Quai d'Orsay appeared drawn between two opposing impulses: to treat Russia as an equal and an ally, or to deal with the Russian empire as a field for economic expansion. But the latter impulse tended to overcome the former since it was difficult to regard the weak and disorganized anti-Bolshevik opposition as an equal, or to abstain from action intended to protect endangered French investments. Certainly, if the anti-Bolshevik opposition had shown greater strength, the French government would not have acted as it did. But the anti-Bolsheviks were weak, and the actions of the other Allies, especially the British, frightened the Quai d'Orsay into taking independent action to protect its own menaced interests.

In the determination of this policy, the influence of outside economic pressure groups was not decisive. Of course, at the outset, the ministry of finance and Quai d'Orsay were concerned that public opinion might compel the government to pay the interest on the Russian bonds. This remained an important consideration of policy until September 1918 when the Chamber of Deputies approved the redemption of many of the defaulted coupons. The government's action appeased public opinion and took the ground from underneath the fractious group of industrialists and bankers who made up the Commission générale. Henceforth, the government formulated its policy toward Russia without undue interference from the French business and financial groups dispossessed by the revolution. This is not to say, however, that the government felt no sense of obligation to these groups. On the contrary, it sought within the measure of its means and on its own terms to recover French investments in Russia – not only to indemnify its citizens, but also to supply France with grain and natural resources.

In 1919 the latter objective had a high priority. Germany was defeated, but France was in deep financial straits. Its economy was shaken by inflation and shortages of every kind. These conditions bore most heavily on the French working class which became restive and all the more disposed to admire the Russian Revolution. The French government desperately needed access to Russian grain and natural resources both to speed economic recovery and to quiet working-class discontent. Of course, squeezing the Russians to aid French recovery worked at cross purposes with the other French objective of rebuilding a Russian counterweight to Germany. But this contradiction could be worked out later when the tranquillity of more prosperous times would allow the government the luxury of pursuing a less hand-to-mouth policy toward Russia.

In the interim, however, the acquisition of Russian raw materials remained an important objective, and, although very much weakened by the war, Paris meant to establish access to these resources by whatever means it could. In so doing, the Quai d'Orsay tended to see the bogey of competitive Allied activities almost everywhere. In Siberia, where there were no spheres of influence, Allied rivalries were particularly intense. Janin reported to Paris in March 1919 that he and the British General Knox were both desirous of providing war supplies to the Omsk regime in order to win favour for their respective governments. Because Knox was having the better of this rivalry, Janin feared that the British would squeeze the French out of a position of influence in Siberia.[33]

Japan and the United States were also involved in the rivalry among the Allied powers in Siberia: the former trying to establish its economic influence in the maritime province and in northern Manchuria, and the latter seeking to resist the Japanese while developing its own interests in these areas.[34] According to Janin, American policy was to sit back and wait for complete anarchy in Siberia in order "to buy the ruins at a bargain price."[35] Naturally, he said, each of the Allies claimed to be acting "for the good of Russia," while accusing its partners of endeavouring only to serve their own selfish interests. In fact, observed Janin, "*c'est de bonne guerre*." All the Allies, but especially the Americans and Japanese, saw Russia as "an immense field of exploitation," and each sought to avoid being squeezed out by the other.[36] It was also *de bonne guerre* as each of the Allies sought to support or bring to power its own reliable Russians. The latter naturally tried to defend themselves by playing off one ally against the other and by threatening to turn to the Germans in order to quiet Allied ambitions.[37]

Janin's interpretation of Allied aims in Siberia was not generous and may have been motivated, in part, by the bitter realization that France was being edged out of a position of influence. Yet, paradoxically, Janin's analysis accords in some respects with the Bolsheviks' own view of the relationship existing between the governments of the Entente. Lenin often held that Allied rivalries were a major reason for the failure of the intervention. He observed that there were "inherent contradictions" among the great powers where the tendency to unite against Bolshevism clashed with the tendency of each of the powers to go its own way or to form with others into rival groups.[38] In a sense, this assessment is appropriate to the French who, on the one hand, called for unity against the Bolsheviks and, on the other hand, were ready to plunge into rivalries with the other Allies for economic and political advantages in Russia. The latter tendency began to dominate French policy when the Quai d'Orsay could not reach agreement with Britain and the United States on an orderly penetration of Russia. At this point the Quai d'Orsay began to treat its allies as interlopers seeking to raid what had previously been a privileged French sphere of influence.

In effect, the French *Weltanschauung* remained essentially that of the late nineteenth and early twentieth centuries when the great imperialist powers swallowed up most of Africa and southeast Asia and jostled one another to prey upon the declining empires of Turkey and China. The World War did not change the French outlook. Even the institutions and paraphernalia that the Quai d'Orsay tried to employ in Russia - the Banque de l'Indochine, the Russo-Asiatique, the Chinese Eastern Railway, as well as the Boxer indemnity - all were the instruments of French or western imperialism in China and southeast Asia. In fact, the French tended to regard the Bolsheviks rather as Boxer rebels to be hunted down and punished. A new Boxer indemnity was envisaged in the form of concessions and international but preferably French controls to exact reparations and compensation for French investors. The Bolsheviks, however, proved to be a more formidable foe than the Chinese Boxers and they drove the French and other Allies out of Russia. Much like the rise of Kemal Ataturk in Turkey, the Soviet victory probably spared Russia the fate of China, which remained for more than a century the victim of western and later Japanese imperialism.

The French government made a poor adjustment to the revolution in Russia. But the loss of the relative security of the Franco-Russian alliance and the loss of valuable foreign investments to a regime that openly called for world revolution made adjustment difficult. A response to the

Bolshevik rise to power was complicated by divisions within the French government concerning the question of whether to overthrow the Soviet regime or to help it resist the German army. French policy-makers were pulled by opposing priorities and interests. Outside observers trying to analyse French or Allied policy saw confusion and contradiction.[39] But what these contemporary observers really saw was the effort to work out consistent policies by men of differing views. What added to the difficulties of the French government was its own weakness due to the great losses of the World War. This weakness caused the French to become more grasping in their efforts to protect menaced political and economic interests in Russia, especially after the British and American governments began to threaten French positions. Such inter-Allied rivalries were real, of course, and made it easier for the Bolsheviks to triumph in the civil war.

In the end, the French and Allied governments could no more halt the revolution in Russia than the Bolsheviks could spread it to the rest of Europe. After 1920 the two sides broke off the struggle to observe an uneasy truce. The unrepentant adversaries, eyeing each other warily, began to turn to the task of rebuilding on the ruins of their many unfulfilled ambitions.

# *Appendix*

FREYDENBERG'S THIRTEEN-POINT DRAFT AGREEMENT WITH
THE UKRAINIAN DIRECTORATE

1  ... le général [des] troupes alliées en Russie méridionale entre en accord
   avec le Directoire de la zone ukrainienne dans les questions de [la]
   lutte contre [le] bolchevisme.
2  En cas de changement dans le personnel du Directoire durant la
   période de lutte contre le bolchevisme, l'entrée de nouveaux membres
   se fait d'après l'assentiment du commandant en chef des forces alliées
   du sud de la Russie.
3  (Toutes) les troupes de la zone ukrainienne seront placées sous (un
   commandement unique, c'est à dire, sous les ordres et le contrôle du
   commandeur allié).[1] Le commandant allié a la haute direction et le
   contrôle des chemins de fer. Il détache, s'il le juge à propos, des com-
   missaires de gares et des officiers dans les gares et services de gares qui,
   ayant une plus grande importance, devraient être dirigés de plus près.
4  Le commandement allié prêtera son concours pour le rétablissement
   des finances de l'Ukraine. Dans ce but des représentants de la France
   sont délégués avec pleins pouvoirs.

---

This draft bears almost exact resemblance to the Ukrainian "project de convention" of 1 March. The major changes were as follows: point 5 of the
Freydenberg draft was dropped, and point 1 begins, "Ayant reçu la déclaration du Directoire d'Ukraine en date du 17 février 1919, le général
d'Anselme, commandant les troupes alliées en Russie méridionale, entre en
accord avec le Directoire pour les diverses questions indiquées dans cette
déclaration et notamment la lutte contre le Bolchevisme."

1 The words in parentheses were added by d'Anselme.

5 Le commandement allié n'opposera pas d'obstacles à la résolution de la question des colonies ukrainiennes en Sibérie et Asie Centrale. La question de la flotte de la mer noire est réservée.

6 Le commandement allié aidera les missions ukrainiennes à se rendre au congrès de la paix.

7 L'armée ukrainienne au point de vue de son organisation intérieure forme une unité indépendente.

8 Une commission mixte sera chargée de rechercher et d'inscrire les pertes de toutes sortes pendant la guerre ainsi que pendant la lutte contre les bolcheviks.

9 Le commandement allié ne s'opposera pas aux réformes d'ordre économique et social qui ne seraient pas de nature à troubler l'ordre.

10 Le stationnement du Directoire sera fait d'accord avec le commandement allié en tenant compte de nécessités de liaison.

11 Le matériel de toute sorte qui risquerait tomber entre les mains de l'ennemi sera évacué suivant un plan d'urgence établi par le commandement français et prévoyant éventuellement le transfert par la Roumanie.

12 Le commandement allié fera cesser les hostilités entre la Pologne et le Directoire ukrainien – une commission décidera des conditions de la suspension des hostilités, ligne d'armistice, question de Lemberg [i.e., Lvov]. De même il s'entremettra pour obtenir des termes de bon voisinage avec la Roumanie.

13 Les prisonniers politiques seront échangés.

# *Notes*

The following abbreviations have been used in the notes.

| | |
|---|---|
| AN | Archives nationales, Paris |
| ANPFVM | Association nationale des porteurs français de valeurs mobilières, Paris |
| BDIC | Bibliothèque de Documentation internationale contemporaine, Nanterre |
| BI | Banque de l'Indochine |
| BUP | Banque de l'Union parisienne |
| 3e Bureau A | 3e Bureau, Groupe de l'Avant |
| CAA | Commandement des armées alliées |
| CG | Commission générale de protection des intérêts français en Russie |
| CIAF | Commission interministérielle des affaires financières russes et roumaines |
| DI | Division d'Infantérie |
| FO | Foreign Office |
| MAÉ | Ministère des Affaires Étrangères |
| MM | Ministère de la Marine |
| Paribas | Banque de Paris et des Pays-Bas |
| SAR | Service des Affaires russes |
| SHA | Service historique de l'armée, Vincennes (Ministère de la Guerre) |

## PREFACE

1 See the statistics of the ANPFVM, Paris; and René Girault, "Problèmes de l'impérialisme économique à la veille de la première guerre mondiale," *Revue du Nord* (avril–juin 1975), 127.

2 From the journal of General Henri Albert Niessel, chief of the French military mission in Russia, notes of 23 January 1918, SHA, Fonds privés, carton 132, Don Niessel.

## CHAPTER ONE

1 R.H. Ullman, *Anglo-Soviet Relations, 1917-1921: Intervention and War*, vol. 1 (Princeton 1961), 4.
2 See, for example, M.T. Florinsky, *The Fall of the Russian Empire* (New York 1961).
3 Ullman, *Anglo-Soviet Relations* 1: 9.
4 Paléologue, no. 40, 9 January 1917, MAÉ, Guerre, 1914-1918 (hereafter referred to as Guerre), vol. 646. In these notes references to incoming cables to Paris cite only the sender, since his civilian or military status indicates the recipient ministry.
5 William H. Chamberlin, *The Russian Revolution*, vol. 1 (New York 1965), 70.
6 Paléologue, no. 358, 18 March 1917, 16N 3179 (All "N" numbers are from the SHA).
7 Paléologue, no. 316, 16 March 1917, ibid.
8 See n.6 above.
9 Lavergne, no. 1291, "Suite des événements et situation morale de l'armée russe du 10 au 16 avril 1917," 29 April 1917, 16N 3180.
10 Maurice Paléologue, *An Ambassador's Memoirs*, vol. 3 (New York 1972), 304-5; see also General Maurice Janin, chief of the French military mission in Russia, nos. 1358-67, 1 April 1917, 16N 3179; and Lavergne, no. 1685, "Suite des événements," 24 May 1917, 16N 3180.
11 "Rapport d'ensemble," no. 4, signed General Henri Albert Niessel, Janin's successor as chief of the French military mission, 7 November 1917, 16N 3181.
12 Paléologue, no. 546, 24 April 1917, 16N 3180; and "Rapport du colonel [Marie Gaston] Perchenet ...," no. 2151, 18 June 1917, 16N 3180.
13 Janin, nos. 1301-11, 24 March 1917, 16N 3179.
14 Paléologue, no. 487, 8 April 1917, MAÉ, Guerre, vol. 649.
15 Paléologue, no. 333, 15 March 1917, and Janin, nos. 1252-5, 17 March 1917, 16N 3179.
16 Paléologue, no. 323, 14 March 1917, MAÉ, Guerre, vol. 647.
17 A.J. Mayer, *Lenin vs. Wilson: The Political Origins of the New Diplomacy, 1917-1918* (Cleveland 1964), 85.
18 Alexandre Ribot, premier and minister of foreign affairs, to Paléologue, no. 684, 10 April 1917, MAÉ, Guerre, vol. 666.
19 Ribot to Paléologue, 13 April 1917, MAÉ, Papiers Jean Doulcet, dossier 20.

20  Ribot to Paléologue, nos. 557-9; and elsewhere, 24 March 1917, MAÉ Guerre, vol. 666. The slowness of the French response may also have been caused by a cabinet crisis which developed on 17 March when Aristide Briand, the premier, resigned. Ribot took office on 20 March.

21  See Margerie's minute on a dispatch from the French ambassador in Washington, J.J. Jusserand, no. 169, 20 March 1917, MAÉ, Guerre, vol. 648, and also Sir George Grahame, a member of the British embassy in Paris, to Sir Eric Drummond, private secretary to A.J. Balfour, British foreign secretary, 28 March 1917, PRO, Bertie Papers, FO 800, vol. 169, p. 59.

22  Nivelle to Janin, nos. 564-74, 14 March 1917, 16N 3018.

23  Janin, nos. 1272-6, 20 March 1917, 16N 3179.

24  Paléologue, nos. 525-6, 17 April 1917; no. 577, 27 April 1917, MAÉ, Guerre, vol. 650; and Paléologue, 18 April 1918, AN, Papiers Thomas, 94 AP 179.

25  "[Rapport] du général Janin," 10 May 1917, Papiers Thomas, 94 AP 179.

26  Journal, entry of 3 May 1917, ibid., 94 AP 176.

27  Thomas to Ribot, no. 91 AT/M, 6 May 1917; and no. 93 AT/M, 7 May 1917, ibid. 94 AP 179.

28  Louis de Robien, Journal d'un diplomate en Russie, 1917-1918 (Paris 1967), 46.

29  Thomas, nos. 580-2, 27 April 1917, MAÉ, Guerre, vol. 650.

30  Paléologue, no. 618, 4 May 1917, MAÉ, Guerre, vol. 651.

31  Thomas, no. 91 AT/M, 6 May 1917, Papiers Thomas, 94 AP 179.

32  Ribot to Thomas, no. 863, 6 May 1917; and Ribot to Thomas, 5 May 1917, ibid., 94 AP 178.

33  Thomas, no. 93 AT/M, 7 May 1917, ibid., 94 AP 179.

34  Ribot to Thomas, nos. 811-15, 30 April 1917, MAÉ, Guerre, vol. 650, and Ribot to Thomas, no. 823, 2 May 1917, MAÉ, Guerre, vol. 651.

35  Ribot to Thomas, no. 1027, 2 June 1917, Papiers Thomas, 94 AP 178.

36  Ribot to Jean Doulcet, French chargé d'affaires in Petrograd, nos. 1092-3, 9 June 1917, 16N 3064.

37  Paléologue to Doulcet, 28 June 1917, MAÉ, Papiers Doulcet, dossier 20; see also A. Ribot, Journal ... (Paris 1936), entry of 17 May, p. 102.

38  Ribot, Journal, entry of 13 May, p. 99; R. Poincaré, Au service de la France, vol. 9 (Paris 1932), 129; and Ribot to Thomas, no. 930, 14 May 1917, MAÉ, Guerre, vol. 673.

39  Paul Morand, Journal d'un attaché d'ambassade (Paris 1963), 239. The Quai d'Orsay finally prevailed upon the Radical politician and former government minister, Joseph Noulens, to accept the position, but he did so with little enthusiasm. See M. Roques, Thomas's deputy chef du cabinet, to Thomas, nos. 183-93, 31 May 1917, Papiers Thomas, 94 AP 178.

40  Ribot to Thomas, no. 1059, 6 June 1917, ibid., 94 AP 180.

41  Thomas, no. 424 AT/M, 14 June 1917, ibid., 94 AP 179.

42   Ibid.

43   Konstantin Paustovsky, *Story of a Life*, vol. 3 (London 1967), 12-13; R.H.B. Lockhart, *British Agent* (London 1933), 181-2; and A. Saint-Aulaire, *Confession d'un vieux diplomate* (Paris 1953), 388.

44   Janin, nos. 1835-6, 7 July 1917, and nos. 1846-8, 10 July 1917, 16N 3180.

45   Janin, nos. 1744-6, 15 June 1917, and nos. 1760-3, 17 June 1917, ibid.

46   Lavergne, no. 1576, "Suite des événements," 18 May 1917, ibid.

47   Janin, nos. 1734-42, 14 June 1917; and Perchenet to Janin, no. 3, 14 June 1917, ibid.

48   Janin, nos. 1744-6, 15 June 1917, ibid.

49   "Résumé des rapports du capitaine [Mathieu] de Maleissye de la mission Janin," 3e Bureau A, 11 July 1917, ibid.

50   Janin, nos. 1949-51, 24 July 1917, 16N 3181.

51   Janin, nos. 2112-13, 17 August 1917, ibid.

52   Colonel Eugène Rampont, member of the French military mission in Russia, to Janin, no. 157/R, "Conclusions nécessaires," 31 July 1917, 16N 3180.

53   Janin, nos. 1923-32, 22 July 1917, and nos. 2001-2, 30 July 1917, 16N 3181.

54   Janin, nos. 1923-32, 22 July 1917, ibid.

55   Ribot to Noulens, 3 August 1917; and Jules Cambon, secretary general of the Quai d'Orsay, to Noulens, no. 1582, 6 August 1917, MAÉ, Guerre, vol. 655.

56   Paul Painlevé, minister of war, to Janin, no. 4996BS, 2 August 1917, 16N 3019.

57   See, for example, Paul Cambon, *Correspondance, 1870-1924*, vol. 3 (Paris 1946), 260-1.

58   See, for example, "Note lue par le général Foch au Comité de Guerre," 13 August 1917, 16N 3020.

59   Paléologue to Doulcet, 21 July 1917, MAÉ, Papiers Doulcet, dossier 20; and Sir Francis Bertie, British ambassador in Paris, to Drummond, 2 July 1917, Bertie Papers, FO 800 191, p. 180.

60   Jean Delmas, "L'état-major français et le front oriental après la révolution bolchévique, novembre 1917-11 novembre 1918" (doctorat du troisième cycle, Université de Paris 1965), 33-5, 38.

61   "Conduite à tenir au cas où la Russie ferait défection," no. 6, 3e Bureau A, 21 July 1917, 16N 3019.

62   The earliest French reports of such talk came in June. See, for example, "Rapport du colonel Perchenet ... sur le front de l'armée de Dvinsk," no. 2151, 18 June 1917; and "Notes du capitaine de Maleissye ...," 8 June 1917, 16N 3180.

63   Gabriel Bertrand, French consul general in Moscow, nos. 70-1, 23 August 1917, MAÉ, Guerre, vol. 655; and Janin, nos. 2137-40, 23 August 1917, MAÉ, Guerre, vol. 755.

64  L.D. Trotsky, *My Life* (New York 1960), 316.

65  Noulens, no. 1307, 5 September 1917, 94 AP 186; Bertrand, no. 95, 12 September 1917, MAÉ, Guerre, vol. 656; Janin, nos. 2292-5, 15 September 1917, 16N 3181; see also L.D. Trotsky, *Histoire de la révolution russe*, vol. 2 (Paris 1950), 201-38; and A. Rabinowitch, *The Bolsheviks Come to Power* (New York 1976), 94-128.

66  Ullman, *Anglo-Soviet Relations* 1: 12-13.

67  Noulens, 10 September 1917, 16N 3181.

68  Margerie to Doulcet, 11 September 1917, MAÉ, *Papiers Doulcet*, dossier 21.

69  Noulens, no. 1363, 14 September 1917, and nos. 1432-3, 26 September 1917, MAÉ, Guerre, vol. 656.

70  The Groupe de l'Avant was the état-major of the French chief of staff and was responsible for the formulation of Russian policy in the ministry of war during Georges Clemenceau's tenure as premier.

71  On 3 September Pétain told the French Comité de Guerre that there was no hope of a military recovery for the Russian army which was in a state of complete decomposition. See Poincaré, *Au Service* 9: 267.

72  "Note au sujet de l'attitude qu'il convient d'adopter à l'égard de la Russie," 3ᵉ Bureau A, 11 October 1917, 16N 3021.

73  See F. Fischer, *Germany's Aims in the First World War* (New York 1967).

74  Paléologue to Doulcet, 28 June 1917, MAÉ, Papiers Doulcet, dossier 20.

75  Poincaré, *Au Service* 9: 177.

76  See chapter 2 above.

77  Poincaré, *Au service* 9: 293.

78  A.M. Gollin, *Proconsul in Politics: A Study of Lord Milner in Opposition and in Power* (New York 1969), 522-77.

79  See also Delmas, "L'état-major français," 33, 36.

## CHAPTER TWO

1  Jacques Sadoul, *Notes sur la révolution bolchévique*, réédition (Paris 1971), 46.

2  Noulens, no. 1602, 25 October 1917, MAÉ, Guerre, vol. 656.

3  Delmas, "L'état-major français," 40.

4  Sadoul, *Notes*, 94.

5  Noulens, nos. 1669-70, 8 November 1917, 16N 3182.

6  Major Robert Buchsenchutz, French deputy military representative at Russian general headquarters, nos. 2346-51, 8 November 1917, and nos. 2353-63, 8 November 1917, MAÉ, Guerre, vol. 755.

7  Joseph Noulens, *Mon ambassade en Russie soviétique, 1917-1919*, vol. 1 (Paris 1933), 123-7.

8  Trotsky, *Histoire* 2: 611-12.

9  Noulens, no. 1680, 10 November 1917, MAÉ, Guerre, vol. 666. Clemenceau rejected Noulens's recommendation because of the shortage of

troops; *Clemenceau* to Pichon, no. 11281 BS/3, 21 November 1917, 16N 3021. For outgoing directives, each cable carried the name of the minister from whose department it was sent. This did not mean, of course, that the policy represented in the dispatch was formulated by the minister himself. For this early period there appear to have been three sources of policy making concerning Russia in the ministry of war: Clemenceau, Foch, and the 3ᵉ Bureau of the Groupe de l'Avant. Because there are no cabinet minutes and practically no handwritten drafts of directives and memoranda in the archives of the SHA, it was impossible to determine who actually was responsible for any given policy. In so far as the French government's policy in Russia is concerned, Clemenceau's interaction with Foch and the 3ᵉ Bureau is largely unknown, though it is likely that the general staff had a greater influence than is now believed. This problem does not arise so much with material from the archives of the Quai d'Orsay where many of the original drafts of policy directives and memoranda have been preserved. To avoid confusion, outgoing cables will always be cited by the minister's name. Names following in parenthesis in war directives are those actually appearing at the bottom of the dispatch and will be cited where deemed important. If Clemenceau signed the directive, his name is in italics.

10  Notes from Niessel's daily journal for 13 November, SHA, Don Niessel.

11  Buchsenchutz, nos. 2376-85, 13 November 1917, and nos. 2391-5, 16 November 1917, MAÉ, Guerre, vol. 755.

12  Noulens, nos. 1710, 18 November 1917, and no. 1731, 21 November 1917, MAÉ, Guerre, vol. 666.

13  Noulens, nos. 1809-11, 6 December 1917, MAÉ, Guerre, vol. 667.

14  Robien, *Journal d'un diplomate*, 97, 101, 147.

15  Noulens had been minister of war in the Doumergue government of December 1913-June 1914 and minister of finance in the Viviani government of June-August 1914.

16  Sadoul, *Notes*, 233-4.

17  Cambon, *Correspondance* 3: 180.

18  Ibid., 177.

19  Sadoul, *Notes*, 234.

20  Pierre Pascal, *Journal de Russie* (Lausanne 1975), 287.

21  Noulens was a lawyer for this conglomerate. *Le Progrès civique* (Paris), 16 August 1919.

22  Noulens, nos. 1920-1, 23 December 1917, MAÉ, Guerre, vol. 667.

23  Noulens, no. 1963, 30 December 1917, MAÉ, Guerre, vol. 357.

24  Ullman, *Anglo-Soviet Relations* 1: 21.

25  *Clemenceau* to Niessel, no. 11355 BS/3, 22 November 1917, 16N 3021.

26  George Kennan, *Soviet-American Relations, 1917-1921: Russia Leaves the War*, vol. 1 (Princeton 1956), 89-93.

27  Clemenceau to Pichon, no. 11879 BS/3, 1 December 1917, MAÉ, Guerre, vol. 356; and *Clemenceau* to Berthelot, no. 11415 BS/3, 23 November 1917, 16N 3021.

28  Clemenceau (Foch) to Niessel, no. 11528 BS/3, 25 November 1917, 16N 3021; and "Note secrète …," no. 11783 BS/3, signed Foch, 29 November 1917, MAÉ, Guerre, vol. 356.

29 Noulens, no. 1765, 29 November 1917, MAÉ, Guerre, vol. 694.

30  Delmas, "L'état-major français," 52–4.

31  Niessel, no. 6397, 5 December 1917, and no. 6583, 9 December 1917, 4N 40, dossier 1.

32  Niessel, no. 6963, 18 December 1917, and no. 7013, 19 December 1917, ibid.

33  "Note pour M. le Président du Conseil, Ministre de Guerre," no. 11249 BS/3, signed Gramat, 21 November 1917, 16N 3021; see also "Note sur la situation générale," 3e Bureau A, 6 December 1917; and "Note sur la situation en Russie," 3e Bureau A, 20 December 1917, with Gramat's minute, 16N 3060.

34  Clemenceau to Niessel, no. 13442 BS/3, 24 December 1917, MAÉ, Guerre, vol. 667.

35  Georges Suarez, *Briand*, vol. 4 (Paris 1940), 326.

36  Pichon to Saint-Aulaire, no. 488, 4 December 1917, MAÉ Guerre, vol. 356. In January Pichon specified that unlimited credits had been opened to General Berthelot for the supply of the Rumanian army and to Saint-Aulaire for "political action." These credits, he said, were not to be confused with others, notably the 100 million francs allowed for the Russian General M.V. Alekseev in the Don region and the 20 million roubles extended to Colonel Pierre Auguste Chardigny for French action in the Caucasus. See Pichon to Saint-Aulaire, nos. 17–18, 4 January 1918, MAÉ, Guerre, vol. 358. Ten million roubles were also put at the disposal of Niessel for the organization of a Polish legion, made up essentially of former troops from the Russian army. Clemenceau (Foch) to Niessel, no. 13123 BS/3, 20 December 1917, MAÉ, série Z, Europe, 1918–1929, vol. 447 (hereafter cited as Z, followed by geographical subheading). Most of these credits were never used.

37  Pichon to Cambon, nos. 5258–9; and elsewhere, 18 December 1917, MAÉ, Guerre, vol. 357; and Pichon to Saint-Aulaire, nos. 502–4, 12 December 1917, MAÉ, Guerre, vol. 356.

38  Clemenceau (Foch) to Pichon, no. 12831 BS/3, 16 December 1917, MAÉ, Guerre, vol. 357.

39  Clemenceau to Niessel, no. 13529 BS/3, 25 December 1917, 7N 921, dossier 1.

40  See, for example, Pichon to Barrère, no. 2824, 6 December 1917, MAÉ, Guerre, vol. 667.

41 Pichon to Barrère, *non-envoyé*, 28 December 1917, ibid.

42 Ullman, *Anglo-Soviet Relations* 1: 54

43 The 23 December convention, which came to light during the early twenties, has been interpreted variously as an expression of the economic, imperialistic, or military designs of the French and British governments. Both Bolshevik and anti-Bolshevik opinion has condemned the convention as "a program for the exploitation of Russia." Ullman, *Anglo-Soviet Relations* 1: 55. The respected historian of the Russian Revolution, W.H. Chamberlin, noted that the territorial arrangements of the agreement coincided with British and French pre-war investments in southern Russia and the Caucasus. Chamberlin, *Russian Revolution* 2: 153–4. More recently, R.H. Ullman has asserted that the convention was "simply a strategic document intended to set forth spheres for military action" (*Anglo-Soviet Relations* 1: 55).

44 See n.23 above.

45 Berthelot, nos. 48–52, 30 December 1917, 7N 921, dossier 1.

46 Clemenceau (Foch) to Berthelot, no. 147 BS/3, 3 January 1918, 4N 42, dossier 3.

47 "Note de M. Kammerer," 19 December 1917, MAÉ, Guerre, vol. 683.

48 Noulens, no. 1830, 10 December 1917, MAÉ, Guerre, vol. 694.

49 Pichon to Noulens, no. 2348, 13 December 1917, ibid.

50 Berthelot, nos. 30–35, 16 December 1917, 4N 40, dossier 3.

51 See, for example, Saint-Aulaire, *Confession*, 367–8.

52 Berthelot, no. 1768, 1 February 1918, 4N 40, dossier 3.

53 Clemenceau to Pichon, no. 13008 BS/3, 18 December 1917, 4N 41, dossier 1.

54 Berthelot, nos. 36–7, 21 December 1917, MAÉ, Guerre, vol. 694.

55 Niessel, no. 7521, 2 January 1918, 4N 40, dossier 1.

56 Noulens, no. 1910, 21 December 1917, MAÉ, Guerre, vol. 694.

57 Clemenceau to Berthelot, no. 13625 BS/3, 26 December 1917, MAÉ, Guerre, vol. 695.

58 Pichon to Noulens, no. 27; and elsewhere, 5 January 1918, draft by Margerie, ibid; and "La France, a-t-elle reconnu le gouvernement ukrainien? Note de Clément-Simon," 20 February 1918, MAÉ, Guerre, vol. 697. Following the French lead, the British government also "officially" recognized the Ukrainian regime. See Foreign Office to Sir Francis Bertie, British ambassador in Paris, no. 37, 5 January 1918, FO 371 3283, p. 31; and FO to Sir John Picton Bagge, British consul general in Odessa, no. 10, 8 January 1918, ibid., p. 84.

59 Pichon to Paul Beau, French minister in Berne, no. 34, 8 January 1918, MAÉ, Guerre, vol. 695; see also Pichon to Noulens, nos. 35–7; Saint-Aulaire, nos. 25–7, 5 January 1918, MAÉ, Guerre, vol. 358.

60 Pichon to Barrère, nos. 58–61, 6 January 1918, draft by Margerie, MAÉ, Guerre, vol. 710; and Pichon to Jusserand, nos. 32–3; and elsewhere, 4 January 1918, MAÉ, Guerre, vol. 358.

61 See n.48 above.

62 Saint-Aulaire, nos. 79–90, received 10 January 1918, MAÉ, Guerre, vol. 358.

63 Clemenceau (Gramat) to Berthelot, no. 202 BS/3, 4 January 1918, 16N 3022; and Cambon, *Correspondance* 3: 216–17.

64 Saint-Aulaire, nos. 102–20, received 12 January 1918, MAÉ, Guerre, vol. 695.

65 Berthelot, no. 1648, 17 January 1918, 4N 40, dossier 3.

66 Saint-Aulaire, nos. 139–49, 18 January 1918, MAÉ, Guerre, vol. 358.

67 Ibid.; also Niessel, no. 8582, 30 January 1918, 4N 40, dossier 2; Noulens, no. 286, 31 January 1918, MAÉ, Guerre, vol. 696; and Sir George Barclay, British minister in Jassy to FO, no. 58, 19 January 1918, FO 371 3283, p. 278.

68 The money spent by the Berthelot mission went to a number of different sources – to Russian officers, contingents of non-Russian troops, and for propaganda and newspaper subsidies. French financial records indicate that French agents in Russia disbursed funds rather unsystematically, at their own initiative, and not in very large sums. Moreover, accounts are disorganized and incomplete, and were often destroyed to keep them out of the wrong hands. See 8N 15–16.

69 "La situation en Ukraine," no. 1874 BS/3, 3ᵉ Bureau A, 29 January 1918, 4N 41, dossier 1.

70 See n.59 above.

CHAPTER THREE

1 See, for example, R.H. Ullman, *Anglo-Soviet Relations: Anglo-Soviet Accord*, vol. 3 (Princeton 1972), 455; G. Kennan, *Soviet-American Relations: Decision to Intervene*, vol. 2 (Princeton 1956), 438; Kennan, *Russia and the West under Lenin and Stalin* (New York 1962), 79–80, 99, 113, 115; and George I. Brinkley, *The Volunteer Army and Allied Intervention in South Russia, 1917–1921* (Notre Dame 1966), 276–7. Ullman maintains that the intervention developed as "part of the grand strategy of the war against the Central Powers. Involvement of Allied forces," he states, "came about almost imperceptibly, by small increments, often from the execution of particular tasks assigned through military channels by officers acting with only the vaguest sort of political guidance" (3: 455). Kennan writes that, in spite of the Allied and especially French dislike of Bolshevism, the intervention against the Soviet government developed as a product of circum-

stances strained by "the climate of confusion and suspicion that prevailed at this culminating moment of war and revolution" and inflamed beyond control by the uprising of the pro-Allied Czech Legion in May 1918 (2: 164–5); see also Ullman, *Anglo-Soviet Relations* 1: 185–6. Some American historians have either wholly or partially challenged Kennan's interpretation of the origins of the U.S. intervention in Russia. See, for example, N. Gordon Levin, *Woodrow Wilson and World Politics: America's Response to War and Revolution* (New York 1968); and William A. Williams, "American Intervention in Russia, 1917–1920," (pt 1), *Studies on the Left*, III (fall, 1963), 24–48; pt 2, IV (winter, 1964), 39–57.

2 See, for example, A.I. Gukovskii, *Frantsuzskaia interventsiia na iuge Rossii, 1918–1919* (Moscow 1928), 8–9; and M.N. Pokrovskii, *Vneshniaia politika Rossii v XX veke* (Moscow 1926), 79–86.

3 M.I. Levidov, *K istorii soiuznoi interventsii v Rossii*, vol. 1 (Leningrad 1925), 173–81; and S.F. Naida and V.P. Naumov, *Sovetskaia istoriografiia grazhdanskoi voiny i inostrannoi voennoi interventsii v SSSR* (Moscow 1966), 86.

4 See, for example, J.M. Thompson, "Allied Intervention in Russia, 1918–1921," in C.E. Black, ed., *Rewriting Russian History: Soviet Interpretations of Russia's Past* (London 1957).

5 Delmas, "L'état-major français," 169.

6 Pichon to Cambon, no. 191; and elsewhere, 11 January 1918, MAÉ, Guerre, vol. 668.

7 Clemenceau (Gramat) to Pichon, no. 748 BS/3, 13 January 1918, ibid.

8 "Note sur la conduite à tenir en Russie," no. 1665 BS/3, 3e Bureau A, 25 January 1918, 16N 3023.

9 *Clemenceau* to Pichon, no. 76/HR, 27 January 1918, MAÉ, Guerre, vol. 358.

10 Pichon to Saint-Aulaire, nos. 136–7, 22 January 1918, ibid.

11 Clemenceau (Foch) to Niessel, no. 1744 BS/3, 27 January 1918, MAÉ, Guerre, vol. 696.

12 Noulens, no. 303, 1 February 1918, MAÉ, Guerre, vol. 669.

13 Clemenceau (Foch) to Berthelot, no. 2171 BS/3, 3 February 1918, ibid. These instructions were repeated again on 11 and 15 February. See cable nos. 2764 BS/3 and 2992 BS/3, 16N 3023.

14 Clemenceau (Foch) to Niessel, no. 3066 BS/3, 17 February 1918, 16N 3023.

15 Pichon to Noulens, no. 285, 17 February 1918, MAÉ, Guerre, vol. 669.

16 V.I. Lenin, *The Revolutionary Phrase* (Moscow 1968), 19.

17 R.K. Debo, *Revolution and Survival: The Foreign Policy of Soviet Russia, 1917–1918* (Toronto 1979), 136–47; and S.P. Mel'gunov, *Tragediia admirila Kolchaka*, pt. 1 (Belgrade 1930), 11.

18 Clemenceau (Foch) to Pichon, no. 3238 BS/3, 20 February 1918; Clemenceau (Foch) to Niessel, no. 3239 BS/3, 20 February 1918; and Clemenceau (Foch) to General Pierre Henri Lafont, French military attaché at Jassy,

no. 4569 BS/3, 18 March 1918, 16N 3023. The question of the Central Powers being able to break the Allied maritime blockade by drawing foodstuffs from southern Russia was discussed at an 3 April meeting of the high level Commission interministérielle des affaires financières russes et roumaines. Attention was drawn to the reports of General Tabouis, the former French high commissioner in Kiev, which indicated that unless Germany wanted to occupy the country, "village by village," the chaos of the revolution would prevent it from getting significant quantities of grain out of the Ukraine. The commission concluded that the Allied blockade retained its efficacy. See the session of 3 April 1918, F30 1083 (all carton numbers beginning F30 are from the archives of the ministry of finance). For more information on the Commission interministérielle, see chapter 6.

19 Clemenceau (Gramat) to various military attachés, no. 3192 BS/3, 19 February 1918, 16N 3023.

20 Clemenceau (Gramat) to Niessel, no. 4042 BS/3, 8 March 1918; and Clemenceau (Foch) to Niessel, no. 4194 BS/3, 11 March 1918, ibid.

21 Fernand Grenard, French consul general in Moscow, no. 135, 22 March 1918, MAÉ, Guerre, vol. 669; Noulens, no. 100, 12 April 1918, MAÉ, Guerre, vol. 760; and Delmas, "L'état-major français," 165.

22 Clemenceau (Foch) to Lavergne, no. 4863 BS/3, 24 March 1918, 16N 3023.

23 Clemenceau (Alby) to Lavergne, Niessel, no. 5090 BS/3, 29 March 1918, ibid.

24 Lavergne went so far as to say that it would not be in French interests to see the Bolsheviks overthrown since any government likely to replace them would be pro-German. Lavergne, no. 1, 29 March 1918, 6N 220.

25 "Note au sujet de la conduite à tenir dans l'Orient russe et asiatique," no. 5516 BS/3, signed Gramat, 5 April 1918, 4N 41, dossier 2.

26 Noulens, nos. 20-2, 9 March 1918, 4N 40, dossier 2; Noulens, nos. 25-6, 13 March 1918, 16N 3185; and Noulens, no. 28, 16 March 1918, MAÉ, Guerre, vol. 669.

27 Noulens, nos. 31-3, 19 March 1918, 4N 41, dossier 2; and Noulens, no. 35, 20 March 1918, MAÉ, Guerre, vol. 760.

28 Note by Joseph Louis de Fabry, inspecteur des finances, 3 March 1919, F30 1111; also Noulens, no. 1122, 12 December 1918, Z – Russie, vol. 494.

29 Chevilly to Albert Thomas, 19 February 1918; and Chevilly to Thomas, 5 March 1918, Papiers Thomas, 94 AP 201. Chevilly sent numerous letters to associates in Paris, condemning the détente with the Bolsheviks, which ended up in the dossiers of the Quai d'Orsay and ministry of war. See for example 5N 280, dossiers 2-4; and MAÉ, Guerre, vol. 684.

30 Pichon to Cambon, 8 March 1918, draft by Berthelot, MAÉ, Guerre, vol. 751.

31  Pichon to Noulens, nos. 18–24, 30 March 1918, MAÉ, Guerre, vol. 669.

32  Pichon to Noulens, no. 31, 1 April 1918, draft in Pichon's hand, MAÉ, Guerre, vol. 760. On the 3ᵉ Bureau's copy of this cable in reference to Pichon's observation that a Red Army could be used against those "elements of action" (i.e., the anti-Bolsheviks) which France might employ to throw back the German invasion, is written the sarcastic marginal comment "which ones?" See 16N 3066.

33  Pichon to Auguste Boppe, French minister in Peking, no. 169, 1 April 1918, MAÉ, Guerre, vol. 670.

34  Clemenceau (Foch) to Pichon, no. 3850 BS/3, 4 March 1918, 16N 3023.

35  Niessel, nos. 67–9, 26 March 1918, 4N 48, dossier 1.

36  Lavergne, nos. 73–6, 9 April 1918, 5N 179.

37  Clemenceau (Alby) to Lavergne, no. 5497 BS/3, 5 April 1918, 4N 42, dossier 1.

38  Cf., Delmas, "L'état-major français," 175.

39  Clemenceau (Alby) to Pichon, no. 5502 BS/3, 5 April 1918, 16N 3024.

40  Noulens, no. 89, 9 April, received 15 April 1918, 16N 3066.

41  Pichon to Clemenceau, no. 1567, 16 April 1918, ibid.

42  Clemenceau (Gramat) to Lavergne, no. 6097 BS/3, 16 April 1918, 16N 3024.

43  See Delmas, "L'état-major français," 44, 149, 297.

44  See his marginal notes on the memorandum "La Russie au lendemain de la paix," written by Colonel Jacques Langlois, Niessel's chief of staff, 30 March 1918, 16N 3185.

45  For more information on this subject, see chapter 6.

46  See the statistics of the ANPFVM and Girault, "Problèmes de l'impérialisme," 127.

47  Pichon to Cambon, nos. 5072–3, 9 December 1917, F30 1092/93.

48  Consignes of 19 January, of the night of 27–8 January 1918, and passim, BDIC, Censure économique et financière, F 270 réserve, CEF, 1917–1918.

49  La Cote de la bourse et de la banque [Cote Vidal], articles by Emmanuel Vidal, 16, 24, and 28 January, 30 April, 14 May 1918; see also La Revue économique et financière, articles by Charles Thollet, 2, 23 March, 6 April 1918; and L'Agence économique et financière, articles by Yves-Guyot, 4 February, 29 April, 6 May 1918.

50  La Cote Vidal, articles by E. Vidal, 19 March and 14 and 15 May 1918.

51  Various entries between January and May 1918, BDIC, Censure économique et financière.

52  Ibid.; see also Le Journal du peuple, a paper of the Socialist minoritaires, 4 February, 25, 28, and 29 May, 18 June 1918.

53  See the commentaries in La Revue économique et financière, 2 February 1918; L'Agence économique et financière, 1 February 1918; and La Cote Vidal, 1 February 1918.

54 "Note pour le ministre," 26 November 1917, MAÉ, Guerre, vol. 1427.

55 See, for example, *La Vague*, 12 January 1918 (Pierre Brizon); and *Le Populaire*, 26 January 1918 (Paul Mistral).

56 Robert Wohl, *French Communism in the Making, 1914-1924* (Stanford 1966), 104-5.

57 Entries for the period November 1917 to May 1918, Censure, consignes, F 270 réserve C. See especially cahier no. 7 (8 October 1917-12 February 1918), the consigne of 28 November 1917 and Georges Mandel's order of 3 February 1918.

58 "Note sur la réorganisation d'une Armée Rouge," no. 6503 BS/3, 25 April 1918, 4N 42, dossier 1.

59 British embassy to Pichon, 4 May 1918, MAÉ, Guerre, vol. 671.

60 Cambon, nos. 589-90, 7 May 1918, ibid.

61 Noulens, no. 145, 5 May 1918, ibid.

62 Noulens, nos. 63-6, 7 April 1918; and no. 85, 12 April 1918, MAÉ, Guerre, vol. 670.

63 Noulens, nos. 239-40, 9 May 1918; no. 255, 11 May 1918, MAÉ, Guerre, vol. 671; and Grenard, nos. 204-6, 9 April 1918, MAÉ, Guerre, vol. 670.

64 Noulens, no. 248, 9 May 1918, MAÉ, Guerre vol. 671.

65 Pichon to Clemenceau, no. 251, 24 January 1918, MAÉ, Guerre, vol. 746.

66 Kennan, *Soviet-American Relations* 1: 475.

67 Regnault, no. 66, 23 February 1918, MAÉ, Guerre, vol. 750.

68 Pichon to Jusserand, no. 510, 26 February 1918, draft by Berthelot, ibid.

69 Regnault, nos. 74-6, 1 March 1918, 4N 47, dossier 1.

70 Pichon to Jusserand, nos. 629-33; and elsewhere, 9 March 1918, MAÉ, Guerre, vol. 751.

71 Ullman, *Anglo-Soviet Relations* 1: 128-30. For a somewhat different view of the British attitude towards the Japanese intervention, see David R. Woodward, "The British Government and Japanese Intervention in Russia during World War I," *Journal of Modern History* 46, no. 4 (1974): 663-85.

72 "Note sur l'action des Alliés en Extrême Orient," no. 7975 BS/3, 3e Bureau A, 20 May 1918, MAÉ, Guerre, vol. 753.

73 See n.30 above; also Pichon to Cambon, no. 1529, 16 April 1918, draft by Berthelot, MAÉ, Guerre, vol. 752, and numerous other directives in this volume, most of which were prepared by Berthelot and signed without alteration by Pichon.

74 Regnault, nos. 151-2, 17 April 1918, MAÉ, Guerre, vol. 752.

75 Pichon to Cambon, no. 1816, 8 May 1918, draft by Margerie, MAÉ Guerre, vol. 671.

76 Noulens, nos. 138-40, received 24 April 1918; and nos. 177-8, 28 April 1918, MAÉ, Guerre, vol. 752.

77 "Intervention japonaise," in Berthelot's hand, April 1918, ibid. As Jean Gout, chief of the Asia sub-division of the Quai d'Orsay, put it, the pro-

visional Siberian government would be a "useful screen" behind which to launch the Japanese intervention, and it would be unfortunate not to make use of it. Unlabelled note, n.d., signed Jean Gout, ibid.

78 Pichon to Cambon, nos. 1765-7 and elsewhere, 4 May 1918, draft by Berthelot, MAÉ, Guerre, vol. 753.

79 There are at least three other memoranda and one lengthy draft cable concerning the Siberian intervention written by Berthelot between February and August 1918, all of which are entirely consistent with outgoing Quai d'Orsay directives on this question. "Le problème russe et l'intervention japonaise, 1er note Berthelot," n.d. (probably February 1918), MAÉ, Papiers Pichon, vol. 5; "Intervention japonaise ...," 31 May 1918, in Berthelot's hand, MAÉ, Guerre, vol. 753; "Politique en Sibérie, Note de M. Berthelot," 26 June 1918, MAÉ, série E, Asie, 1918-1929, Sibérie, vol. 2 (hereafter cited as E, followed by geographical subheading); and Berthelot to Jusserand, *non-envoyé*, 3 August 1918, Z - Russie, vol. 217.

80 See for example R.D. Challener, "The French Foreign Office: The Era of Philippe Berthelot," in *The Diplomats, 1919-1939*, ed. G.A. Craig and F. Gilbert, vol. 1 (New York 1965), 49-85.

81 Entry from the diary of the British ambassador in Paris, Lord Derby, Sunday, 18 August 1918, British Museum, Balfour Papers, dossier no. 49743; see also Cambon, *Correspondance* 3: 203-4.

82 Derby to Balfour, 20 November 1918, Balfour Papers, no. 49743; see also Cambon to Barrère, 3 October 1918, and 26 March 1919, MAÉ, Papiers Barrère, vol. 1.

83 Morand, *Journal*, 190; and also Pichon to Margerie, 29 November 1918, MAÉ, Papiers Margerie, Lettres particulières de diplomates.

84 Derby to Balfour, n.d., F/52/2/38; Derby to Balfour, 14 December 1917, F52/2/52; and Bertie to Balfour, 11 December 1917, F/51/4/66, Beaverbrook Library (now the library of the House of Lords), Lloyd George Papers.

85 Morand, *Journal*, 13, 17, 130, 163; and Suarez, *Briand* 5: 125-9.

86 Margerie to Pichon, 4 December 1918, Papiers Margerie; and n. 85 above.

87 Cambon, *Correspondance* 3: 260-1: and Morand, *Journal*, 120.

88 Levidov, *K istorii*, 116.

89 Cambon, *Correspondance* 3: 260-1. Most of these cables can be found in MAÉ, Guerre, vol. 752.

90 Niessel, nos. 3653-7, 16 March 1918, 16N 3185.

91 Noulens, nos. 177-8, 28 April 1918, MAÉ, Guerre, vol. 752; and Grenard, nos. 202-3, 8 April 1918, 16N 3185.

92 Pichon to Jacques de Fontenay, French minister to the Serbian government in exile on Corfu, no. 27, 13 April 1918, draft by Margerie, MAÉ, Guerre, vol. 670; Pichon to Alexandre Conty, French minister in Copenhagen, nos. 99-100, 4 May 1918, MAÉ, Guerre, vol. 671.

93  "Situation en Russie et la ligne de conduite à adopter par l'Entente dans ce pays," no. 7609 BS/3, 3e Bureau A, 13 May 1918, MAÉ, Guerre, vol. 671. The conclusions of this note were approved by Clemenceau. See "Urgence de régler la question des tchèques de Russie," no. 8278 BS/3, signed Alby, 26 May 1918, 4N 42, dossier 3. It is interesting to note the differences of emphasis between this general staff note and Pichon's 30 March directive to Noulens (see pp. 40–1 above).

94  Kennan, *Soviet-American Relations* 2: 108–9; see also Ullman, *Anglo-Soviet Relations* 1: 136; and Delmas, "L'état-major français," 152–3.

95  Kennan, *Soviet-American Relations* 2: 129.

96  Ibid., 122.

97  Kennan, *Soviet-American Relations* 1: 471; and Ullman, *Anglo-Soviet Relations* 1: 136–7.

98  Delmas, "L'état-major français," 169

## CHAPTER FOUR

1  Pichon to Grenard, no. 134, 5 April 1918, draft by Margerie; and also Pichon to Grenard, no. 139, 6 April 1918, Guerre, vol. 670.

2  James Bunyan, *Intervention, Civil War, and Communism in Russia, April–December 1918* (Baltimore 1936), 175–84.

3  Grenard, nos. 178–9, 2 April 1918; and nos. 222–6, 13 April 1918, MAÉ, Guerre, vol. 670.

4  Grenard, nos. 204–6, 9 April 1918, ibid.

5  Grenard, no. 215, 11 April 1918, ibid.; and no. 228, 13 April 1918, MAÉ, Guerre, vol. 749.

6  Grenard, nos. 235–6, 16 April 1918, MAÉ, Guerre, vol. 670.

7  Ibid.; cf., Lockhart, *British Agent*, 210–11.

8  Noulens, nos. 124–5, 15 April 1918, MAÉ, Guerre, vol. 670; and also nos. 270–1, 14 May 1918, 4N 40 dossier 2.

9  Grenard, no. 253, 20 April 1918, MAÉ, Guerre, vol. 670.

10  Grenard, no. 257, 21 April 1918, ibid.

11  Grenard, nos. 260–2, 22 April 1918, ibid.

12  Noulens, no. 219, 5 May 1918, MAÉ, Guerre, vol. 671. Testimony by Savinkov to a Soviet court in 1924 suggests that the 500,000 roubles were in fact received in the manner directed by Noulens. See E. Iaroslavskii et al., *Delo Borisa Savinkova* (Moscow n.d.), 38.

13  Noulens, *Mon ambassade* 2: 110.

14  Grenard to Pichon, 2 December 1918, Z – Russie, vol. 210.

15  Grenard, no. 304, 4 May 1918, Z – Russie, vol. 414.

16  Pichon to Grenard, no. 206, 6 May 1918, draft by Berthelot, MAÉ, Guerre, vol. 1432.

17  Pichon to Noulens, no. 130, 7 May 1918, MAÉ, Guerre, vol. 1425.

18 Noulens, no. 196, received 14 May 1918; and no. 269, 14 May 1918, MAÉ, Guerre, vol. 671.

19 Noulens, nos. 270-1, 14 May 1918, 4N 40, dossier 2.

20 Noulens, no. 248, 9 May 1918, MAÉ, Guerre, vol. 671.

21 Noulens, no. 318, 24 May 1918, ibid.

22 Pichon's minute on Barrère's no. 199, 30 April 1918, MAÉ, Guerre, vol. 670; and Pichon to Barrère, no. 470, 7 May 1918, MAÉ, Guerre, vol. 671.

23 See chapter 5 above.

24 Ullman, *Anglo-Soviet Relations* 1: 163-6.

25 Debo, *Revolution*, 255-9.

26 Clemenceau (Foch) to Lavergne, no. 4722 BS/3, 21 March 1918, 7N 627; and Clemenceau (Foch) to Lavergne, no. 4863 BS/3, 24 March 1918, 16N 3023.

27 "Note pour M. le général Spiers," no. 5176 BS/3, 30 March 1918; Janin to Clemenceau, no. 538, 2 April 1918, 7N 627; and Clemenceau (Alby) to General Arthur Louis de La Panouse, chief of the French military mission in London, no. 5620 BS/3, 7 April 1918, 16N 3023.

28 John Bradley, *La légion tchécoslovaque en Russie, 1914-1920* (Paris 1965), 73-4; and Bunyan, *Intervention*, 75-81.

29 Ullman, *Anglo-Soviet Relations* 1: 153.

30 "Note pour le général Spiers," no. 6285 BS/3, signed Gramat, 20 April 1918, 16N 3024.

31 Clemenceau to Lavergne, no. 7134 BS/3, 4 May 1918; no. 7367 BS/3, 9 May 1918, Z - Russie, vol. 217.

32 See n.31; also Clemenceau to General Sir Henry Wilson, chief of the Imperial General Staff, no. 7755 BS/3, 16 May 1918, 4N 42, dossier 3.

33 Grenard, from Noulens, nos. 442-3, 14 June 1918, Z - Russie, vol. 217.

34 J. Bradley, *Allied Intervention in Russia, 1917-1920* (London 1968), 85.

35 Ibid., 88; and Ullman, *Anglo-Soviet Relations* 1: 153.

36 Ullman, *Anglo-Soviet Relations* 1: 171-2; and Kennan, *Soviet-American Relations* 2: 150-3.

37 Thomas R. Peake, "The Impact of the Russian Revolutions upon French Attitudes and Policies toward Russia, 1917-1918" (PHD diss., University of North Carolina 1974), 185, citing a Noulens letter in the Loucheur Papers at the Hoover Institute.

38 Noulens, no. 195, 1 May 1918, 7N 627; cf., Kennan, *Soviet-American Relations* 2: 160-3.

39 Noulens, no. 251, 10 May 1918, 4N 40, dossier 2.

40 Noulens, no. 277, 16 May 1918, 4N 49, dossier 2.

41 Noulens, nos. 301-3, 20 May 1918, 4N 42, dossier 3.

42 Clemenceau to Lavergne, no. 8034 BS/3, 22 May 1918, Z - Russie, vol. 217.

43 Lavergne, nos. 390-3, 397-402, 1 June 1918, Z - Tchécoslovaquie, vol. 13.

44 Noulens, no. 360, 31 May 1918, ibid.; and Noulens to Grenard, no. 131, 1 June 1918, MAÉ, Russie, Petrograd, Mesures de défense contre les Bolcheviques.

45 Noulens to Grenard, for Lavergne, no. 136, 3 June 1918, MAÉ, Mesures de défense.

46 Noulens to Grenard, for Lavergne, no. 141, 8 June 1918, ibid.

47 Noulens, nos. 417-19, 12 June 1918, Z - Tchécoslovaquie, vol. 13. On Noulens and the origins of the Czech uprising, see also O.F. Solov'ev, *Velikii Oktiabr' i ego protivniki* (Moscow 1968), 230-2.

48 Kennan, *Soviet-American Relations* 2: 282-92.

49 Berthelot's minute on Clemenceau's no. 8419 BS/3, 29 May 1918, Z - Russie, vol. 217.

50 What may also have strengthened Noulens's hand were the subsidies French agents gave to the Czechs. Between 7 March and 13 May the French consulate general in Moscow paid out approximately 15 million roubles to Czech agents. See Lavergne, no. 1343, 21 June 1918, 16N 3185; and the accounting sheet in 8N 17.

51 Delmas, "L'état-major français," 201.

52 Ibid., 205.

53 See n.43 above.

54 Lavergne, nos. 434-40, 10 June 1918, 16N 3185.

55 Noulens, no. 410, 11 June 1918, 4N 42, dossier 3.

56 See n.47 above.

57 Pichon to Noulens, nos. 236-7, 10 June 1918, Z - Russie, vol. 217; and Clemenceau (Alby) to Lavergne, no. 9176 BS/3, 14 June 1918, 4N 42, dossier 3.

58 See n.30 above.

59 Lavergne, nos. 464-9, 14 June 1918, 4N 42, dossier 3.

60 Clemenceau to Lavergne, no. 9446 BS/3, 20 June 1918; and no. 9859 BS/3, 30 June 1918, ibid.

61 Clemenceau (Alby) to Lavergne, no. 9994 BS/3, 5 July 1918, ibid.; and *Clemenceau* to Major Henri Robert de Lapomarède, French military attaché in Tokyo, no. 10051 BS/3, 7 July 1918, ibid., dossier 4.

62 Clemenceau (Alby) to Pichon, no. 10168 BS/3, 12 July 1918, ibid., dossier 4.

63 On this latter point, see chapter 5.

64 As one note from the Groupe de l'Avant observed, the anti-Bolsheviks had finally begun "to emerge from their [state of] torpor." "La situation des tchéques en Russie et en Sibérie," no. 9394 BS/3, 19 June 1918, 4N 42, dossier 3.

65 Ibid.

66 Delmas, "L'état-major français," 266.

67  See, for example, Clemenceau (Alby) to Pichon, no. 10168 BS/3, 12 July 1918, 4N 42, dossier 4.

68  Louis Fischer, *The Soviets in World Affairs*, vol. 1 (London 1930), 117–18.

69  Lavergne, nos. 531-3, 29 June 1918, 4N 48, dossier 1.

70  Noulens, nos. 506–10, 6 July 1918, received October 1918 by courier, Z – Russie, vol. 217.

71  Pichon to Grenard, no. 324, 1 July 1918, Z – Russie, vol. 206.

72  "Action de Grenard sur les partis russes," written by F.A. Kammerer, chief of the Service financier and soon also of the Service des Affaires russes of the Quai d'Orsay, 2 July 1918, ibid.

73  Pichon to Grenard, from Kerensky, 1 July 1918, ibid.

74  G. Eybert, French agent in Arkhangelsk, from Grenard, no. 36, 14 July 1918, ibid.

75  This information may never be known since the French consulate general either disguised or burned its records to keep them out of Bolshevik hands. See Grenard to Pichon, 23 December 1918, 8N 16; Lavergne, nos. 635-7, 8 August 1918, 5N 180; and the accounting sheets in 8N 20.

76  Lavergne, no. 676, 31 August 1918, 16N 3185; and Lavergne, no. 699, 15 August 1918, 16N 3186.

77  Interview with Pierre Pascal, a former lieutenant in the French military mission in Russia during the revolution, Neuilly, 8 March 1974; see also R. Marchand, *Why I Support Bolshevism* (London 1919), 46-7; and Iaroslavskii, *Delo Borisa Savinkova*, 39–40. Savinkov claimed in 1924 that Grenard had told him that French agents had been involved in some way in the Left SR assassination of Mirbach (Iaroslavskii, *Delo Borisa Savinkova*, 40). This is also the view of Pascal, who stated that Iakov Bliumkin, the assassin of Mirbach, was in "very close relations" with the French consulate general in Moscow, and especially with Captain P.T. Laurent, who headed French espionage efforts against the Bolsheviks.

78  Ullman, *Anglo-Soviet Relations* 1: 231-2; and Iaroslavskii, *Delo Borisa Savinkova*, 39.

79  Fischer, *Soviets* 1: 119; and Iaroslavskii, *Delo Borisa Savinkova*, 38.

80  Iaroslavskii, *Delo Borisa Savinkova*, 37-9; see also Fischer, *Soviets* 1: 118-19.

81  Fischer, *Soviets* 1: 119-20; and Marchand, *Bolshevism*, 28, 35.

82  Iaroslavskii, *Delo Borisa Savinkova*, 38.

83  See n.70 above; and Ullman, *Anglo-Soviet Relations* 1: 234.

84  Lavergne, nos. 640-50, 8 August 1918, 4N 41, dossier 3.

85  F. Grenard, *La révolution russe* (Paris 1933), 322.

86  Iaroslavskii, *Delo Borisa Savinkova*, 40.

87  See n.70 above. On this point, see also Solov'ev, *Veliki Oktiabr'*, 223.

88  Noulens, no. 411, 11 June 1918, Z – Russie, vol. 205.

89  For example, see n.8 above.

90 This was also the view of the general staff. See "Note sur la situation en Russie ...," no. 8593 BS/3, 2 June 1918, 16N 3024.

CHAPTER FIVE

1 Regnault, from Brylinski, no. 217, 26 May 1918, 4N 63, dossier 3.
2 Jusserand, no. 669, received 31 May 1918, ibid.
3 Jusserand, no. 738, received 13 June 1918, E - Japon, vol. 18.
4 Pichon to Jusserand, no. 1269, 14 June 1918, Z - Russie, vol. 205.
5 Pichon to Clemenceau, no. 2243, 3 June 1918, 4N 47, dossier 2, file II.
6 Ullman, *Anglo-Soviet Relations* 1: 196.
7 Jusserand, nos. 437–41, received 11 April 1918, 4N 46, dossier 1.
8 Ullman, *Anglo-Soviet Relations* 1: 199.
9 Ibid., 200; Kennan, *Soviet-American Relations* 2: 58–71; and "Note au sujet de l'action entreprise par le capitaine Semenoff en Sibérie-Orientale," no. 7726 BS/3, 3e Bureau A, 15 May 1918, 16N 3024. Initially, both the French and British governments supported Semenov financially. The French had at first been reluctant, but on British insistence Paris agreed to pay half of a monthly subsidy of £10,000. Shortly thereafter, the French government sent a liaison officer, Captain Paul Eugène Pelliot, to report on Semenov's activities. Pelliot recommended continued support for him, and in May Paris responded to a British request to stop aid to Semenov by according him a credit of 4 million roubles. See the 3e Bureau's note cited above; and Clemenceau to Pichon, no. 3090 BS/3, 17 February 1918, 16N 3023.
10 Ullman, *Anglo-Soviet Relations* 1: 200–1.
11 Ibid., 204.
12 Pichon to Jusserand, no. 1239, 9 June 1918, draft by Pichon, E - Japon, vol. 18.
13 Untitled note in Berthelot's hand, 7 June 1918, Z - Russie, vol. 205. This project was sent out as official policy in late June. See Pichon to Cambon, nos. 2392–5; Jusserand, nos. 1343–6; and elsewhere, 26 June 1918, E - Japon, vol. 18.
14 Eugene P. Trani, "Woodrow Wilson and the Decision to Intervene in Russia: A Reconsideration," *Journal of Modern History* 48, no. 3 (Sept. 1976): 458–9; and Williams, "American Intervention in Russia," pts 1 and 2.
15 Levin, *Wilson*, 67.
16 Ibid., 59, 72; and Robert J. Maddox, *The Unknown War with Russia: Wilson's Siberian Intervention* (San Rafael, Calif. 1977), 33, 77.
17 This was Lansing's view in February 1918. See Levin, *Wilson*, 72.
18 Levin, *Wilson*, 80, 89–90.
19 Ibid., 80.
20 Maddox, *Unknown War*, 28, 33, 35, 84.

21  Ibid., 38-9, 41.

22  Ibid., 48.

23  Ullman, *Anglo-Soviet Relations* 1: 212.

24  The local armistice at Irkutsk held until 21 June when Czech troops attacked the city, which fell on 11 July. Kennan, *Soviet-American Relations* 2: 292.

25  Kennan, *Soviet-American Relations* 2: 393-5; and Ullman, *Anglo-Soviet Relations* 1: 213.

26  Kennan, *Soviet-American Relations* 2: 396-7.

27  Ibid., 398.

28  Pichon to Cambon, nos. 2759-61; Jusserand, nos. 1547-9; and elsewhere, 21 July 1918, draft by Berthelot, E - Japon, vol. 19.

29  Clemenceau to Lapomarède, no. 10695 BS/3, 1 August 1918, 16N 3025.

30  Maddox, *Unknown War*, 49-50; and Levin, *Wilson*, 108-9.

31  See, for example, *Clemenceau* to Janin, no. 11933 BS/3, 9 September 1918, 16N 3025.

32  Pichon to Jusserand, *non-envoyé*, 3 August 1918, draft by Berthelot, Z - Russie, vol. 217.

33  Pichon to Clemenceau, no. 2849, 18 July 1918, 16N 3066.

34  Pichon to Cambon, nos. 2801-2, 23 July 1918, draft by Berthelot, Z - Tchécoslovaquie, vol. 14.

35  Pichon to Clemenceau, no. 2938, 26 July 1918, draft by Berthelot, ibid.

36  Pichon to Cambon, nos. 2983-4; Jusserand, nos. 1679-80; and elsewhere, 7 August 1918, 16N 3067.

37  Kennan, *Soviet-American Relations* 2: 408.

38  Jusserand, no. 1090, received 13 August 1918, E - Sibérie, vol. 31.

39  Ullman, *Anglo-Soviet Relations* 1: 227-8; Kennan, *Soviet-American Relations* 2: 411-12.

40  Ullman, *Anglo-Soviet Relations* 1: 229.

41  Kennan, *Soviet-American Relations* 2: 413.

42  Jusserand, nos. 1129-32, received 23 August 1918, E - Sibérie, vol. 18.

43  Pichon to Jusserand, no. 1813, 24 August 1918, draft by Pichon, E - Sibérie, vol. 31.

44  Pichon to Regnault, no. 463, 29 August 1918, draft by Berthelot, E - Sibérie, vol. 18.

45  Ibid.; and Pichon to Regnault, no. 474; Cambon, no. 3436; and elsewhere, 7 September 1918, draft by Berthelot, E - Sibérie, vol. 31.

46  See n.32 and 36 above.

47  See Kennan, *Soviet-American Relations* 2: 409.

48  Unsigned note in Gout's hand, n.d. (end of April), MAÉ, Guerre, vol. 752. Margerie's minute is added to the note. See also Pichon to Cambon, nos. 1772-3, 4 May 1918, MAÉ, Guerre, vol. 753 (this cable reflected Gout's views of Horvat).

49 L.H. Grondijs, *Le cas-Koltchak* (Leiden 1939), 31; see also James W. Morley, *The Japanese Thrust in Siberia, 1918* (New York 1957), 94.

50 Pichon to Jusserand, no. 1637; Cambon, no. 2917; and elsewhere, 1 August 1918, draft by Berthelot, E - Sibérie, vol. 3.

51 Pichon to Jusserand, nos. 1734-6, 15 August 1918, ibid.

52 General Paris (Vladivostok), nos. 62-3, 2 August 1918, 16N 3190.

53 Pichon to Noulens, no. 177, 25 May 1918, MAÉ, Guerre, vol. 753.

54 Boppe, no. 382, 8 July 1918, E - Sibérie, vol. 2.

55 Boppe, nos. 386-7, 10 July 1918, ibid.

56 Pichon to Boppe, no. 293, 12 July 1918, draft by Berthelot, ibid.

57 Pichon to Cambon, nos. 2656-9, 12 July 1918, Z - Tchécoslovaquie, vol. 14; Pichon to Jusserand, nos. 1545-6, 20 July 1918; and Pichon to Cambon, no. 2859; and elsewhere, 28 July 1918, draft by Berthelot, E - Sibérie, vol. 2.

58 Pichon to Regnault, no. 348, 12 July 1918, draft by Berthelot; and Pichon to Boppe, no. 294, 12 July 1918, draft by Berthelot, E - Sibérie, vol. 2.

59 See n.57 above.

60 "Note pour le ministre," signed Berthelot, 11 August 1918, E - Sibérie, vol. 3.

61 Levin, *Wilson*, 110.

62 Ibid., 67; and Maddox, *Unknown War*, 41.

63 Clemenceau (Alby) to Foch, no. 11324 BS/3, 21 August 1918, 16N 3025.

64 Ullman, *Anglo-Soviet Relations* 1: 155.

65 "Procès-verbal de la conférence réunie le mardi 2 juillet 1918 à la présidence du conseil," Z - Russie, vol. 446.

66 Grahame to Pichon, 16 July 1918, ibid.

67 Pichon to Derby, 15 August 1918, ibid.

68 Derby to Pichon, 7 October 1918, Z - Russie, vol. 208. The Quai d'Orsay apparently never replied to this note.

69 "Note au sujet du réglement interallié des dépenses en Russie-Sibérie," no. 4720 BS/1, 30 September 1919, Z - Russie, vol. 447.

70 See, for example, "Dépenses pour les troupes russes de Sibérie," 25 September 1918, ibid.

71 Pichon to Klotz, no. 1419, 24 July 1918, Z - Russie, vol. 446.

72 See chapter 2 above on the convention; Ullman, *Anglo-Soviet Relations* 1: 55.

73 Clemenceau to Pichon, no. 1073 BS/3, 1 February 1919, 16N 3027.

74 Pichon to Derby, 14 February 1919; and also 22 March 1919, Z - Russie, vol. 271.

75 Clemenceau (Alby) to Pichon, no. 1455 BS/1, 1 May 1919, Z - Russie, vol. 271; and Clemenceau to Pichon, no. 1927 BS/1, 27 May 1919, Z - Pologne, vol. 22.

76 See, for example, Pichon to Derby, 14 February 1919, z - Russie, vol. 271; and Clemenceau (Alby) to Pichon, no. 672 bs/3, 21 January 1919, z - Russie, vol. 226.
77 Pichon to Regnault, no. 449, 18 August 1918, draft by Pichon, e - Sibérie, vol. 3.
78 Pichon to Noulens, nos. 568–70, 8 September 1918, e - Sibérie, vol. 31.
79 Pichon to Derby, 11 September 1918, e - Sibérie, vol. 4; see also Pichon to Jusserand, no. 1926; Cambon, no. 3487; and elsewhere, 9 September 1918, draft by Berthelot, e - Japon, vol. 21.
80 Ullman, *Anglo-Soviet Relations, 1917–1921: Britain and the Russian Civil War*, vol. 2 (Princeton, 1968), 32.
81 Clemenceau (Alby) to Pichon, no. 12237 bs/3, 18 September 1918, 16N 3025.
82 Pichon to Klotz, 26 September 1918, 7N 628; and Pichon to Clemenceau, no. 3898, 4 October 1918, z - Russie, vol. 447.
83 Klotz to Pichon, no. 9080, 7 October 1918, F30 1071, dossier 1; and Pichon to Cambon, nos. 4185–90; Jusserand, nos. 2324–9; and elsewhere, 11 October 1918, e - Sibérie, vol. 18.
84 Unlabelled note initialled J.G. (Jean Gout), n.d. (November 1918), e - Japon, vol. 21.
85 V.I. Lenin, *Collected Works*, vol. 27 (Moscow 1965), 367–70.
86 See, for example, Ullman, *Anglo-Soviet Relations* 1: 55; Brinkley, *Volunteer Army*, 277; and Kennan, *Russia and the West*, 49–50, 66–7.

CHAPTER SIX

1 Girault, "Problèmes de l'impérialisme," 127; and A.G. Shlikhter, ed., *Chernaia kniga: sbornik statei i materialov ob interventsii antanty* (Ekaterinoslav-Kharkov 1925), 19–21. French capital amounted to 32.6 per cent of total foreign investment in Russia; British, 22.6 per cent; German, 19.7 per cent; and Belgian, 14.3 per cent. See René Girault, *Emprunts russes et investissements français en Russie, 1887–1914* (Paris 1973), 135, n.129.
2 Girault, *Emprunts russes*, 511–14; P.V. Ol', *Inostrannye kapitaly v Rossii* (Petrograd 1922), 29–30; and N. Vanag, *Finansovyi kapital v Rossii* (Moscow 1925), 42–50.
3 Darcy was president of the Société métallurgique de l'Oural-Volga and of the Société métallurgique de Donetz-Yourieffka. See Annuaire Chaix, *Les principales sociétés par action ...* (Paris 1919); and Compagnie des agents de change, Chambre syndicale, *Annuaire des valeurs admises à la cote officielle* (Paris), 1918–21. All information listed below on the affiliations of French capitalists is drawn from these annuals. A Quai d'Orsay note written in the summer of 1918 described Darcy as "one of the most important Frenchmen in Russia." See "Note pour le cabinet du ministre," n.d. [August 1918], z - Russie, vol. 575.

4 Darcy to Édouard Gruner, director general of the Société des minerais de fer de Krivoi-Rog, letters of 12 April and 19 June 1917, ANPFVM, dossier no. 34. Gruner was also a member of the boards of directors of the Aciéries de Paris et de d'Outreau and the Société des sels gemmes et houilles de la Russie méridionale, and was secretary general and vice president of the Comité des houillères, the French coal owners' association, linked to the influential Comité des forges.

5 Gruner to Darcy, 8 May 1918, ANPFVM, dossier no. 34. The enterprises making up the Groupe industriel included the Société Berestow-Krinka, Société des ciments de Guelendjik, Société cotonnière russo-française, Société d'Ekaterinowka, Société des forges et aciéries du Donetz, Société franco-russe de produits chimiques et d'explosifs, Société anonyme des usines franco-russes, Société de Huta-Bankowa, Société industrielle du Platine, Société de la Kama, Société de Krivoi-Rog, Société métallurgique du Caucase, Société de l'Oural-Volga, Société de la providence russe, Société des sels gemmes, MM. Schneider, Union minière et métallurgique en Russie, Compagnie des houillères de Dombrowa, Société de Czélatz. Gruner to Maurice de Verneuil, former head of the Paris stockbrokers, 31 July 1918, ANPFVM, dossier no. 33. A history of many of the above enterprises, some of them quite important, can be found in Girault, *Emprunts russes*, and in John P. McKay, *Foreign Entrepreneurship and Russian Industrialization, 1885–1913* (Chicago 1970).

6 "Note sur la création d'un comité de protection des intérêts français engagés en Russie," Office national, 9 January 1918, MAÉ, Guerre, vol. 1430. See Kammerer's minute on this document.

7 CIAF, session of 7 March 1918, F30 1083.

8 "Note confidentielle, remise à titre personnel et confidentiel à François-Marsal, le 21 février 1918," draft by Kammerer, MAÉ, Guerre, vol. 1430.

9 Girault, *Emprunts russes*, 130.

10 "M. Chevalier téléphone ...," 22 February 1918, MAÉ, Guerre, vol. 1430; Procès verbaux de la Commission générale de protection des intérêts français en Russie (CG), session of 18 February 1918, ANPFVM, dossier no. 33.

11 Machart to Pichon, 5 February 1918; to Klotz, no. 870, 20 February 1918, ANPFVM, dossier no. 33.

12 Chanove also sat on the boards of directors of the Forges et aciéries de Huta-Bankowa and the Compagnie industrielle du Platine.

13 Gruner to Verneuil, 31 July 1918, ANPFVM, dossier no. 33.

14 *Documents politiques, diplomatiques et financiers* (Paris), 1ère année, no. 1 (janvier 1920), 6; and chapter 2, n.21 above.

15 The groupe financier also included the Crédit mobilier, MM. Hottinquer et Compagnie, the Banque Française pour le Commerce et l'industrie, the Société Centrale des Banques de province, and the Banque Privée. Bénac to Verneuil, 21 August 1918, ANPFVM, dossier no. 33.

16 Girault, *Emprunts russes*, 363.

17 For information on Bénac's activities and connections before the war, see M.J. Rust, "Business and Politics in the Third Republic: The Comité des Forges and the French Steel Industry, 1896–1914" (PHD diss., Princeton University 1973).

18 Lion was also a member of the boards of directors of numerous other French industrial enterprises such as the Société métallurgique Donetz-Yourieffka and the Société d'outillage mécanique et d'usinage d'artillerie.

19 Pichon to the Crédit Lyonnais, 15 January 1918, draft by Kammerer, MAÉ, Guerre vol. 1427; and Gruner to Darcy, 8 January 1918, ANPFVM, dossier no. 34.

20 CG, session of 24 April 1918, ANPFVM, dossier no. 33.

21 CG, session of 2 May 1918, ibid.

22 Ibid.

23 CG, session of 10 May 1918, ibid.

24 CG, session of 15 May 1918, ibid.

25 *La Cote Vidal*, Vidal's articles of 18, 19 March 1918.

26 Ibid., 19, 20 March 1918; see also Vidal's article on 28 January 1918. Verneuil, as head of the Paris Bourse, had carried on numerous negotiations with the tsarist government before the war, occasionally on behalf of the Quai d'Orsay or ministry of finance. See Girault, *Emprunts russes*. These activities may explain Vidal's suspicion of Verneuil as well as the ministry of finance's desire to place him at the head of the Commission générale. The government may have thought Verneuil would be co-operative.

27 CIAF, session of 19 June 1918, F30 1083.

28 Gruner to Pichon, 22 June 1918, Z – Russie, vol. 467.

29 "Demande d'une allocation en faveur du bureau industriel français de Petrograd, remise par M. Gruner," 31 July 1918, Z – Russie, vol. 575.

30 Verneuil to F. Des Closières, secretary general of the Office national, 22 June 1918, ANPFVM, dossier no. 33; and CG, session of 4 July 1918, ibid.

31 Ibid.

32 Chevalier to Verneuil, 13 July 1918, ANPFVM, dossier no. 50.

33 Sergent and Celier saw advanced copies of the Comité de défense statutes and statement of principles. Chevalier to Verneuil, 13 July 1918, ANPFVM, dossier 50; and "Note de Fabry," 31 August 1918, F30 1094. The Comité de défense des porteurs français de fonds d'état russe was officially formed in September 1918.

34 Darcy to Gruner, 12 June, received 16 July 1918, ANPFVM, dossier no. 34.

35 Verneuil to Darcy, no. 220, 19 July 1918, ibid.

36 Darcy to Verneuil, July 1918, received October 1918, ibid.

37 "Plan d'action pour la défense des intérêts français en Russie et la reprise des affaires," 13 August 1918, draft by Kammerer, Z – Russie, vol. 472.

38  Verneuil to Darcy, no. 595, 30 October 1918, ANPFVM, dossier no. 34; and CG, session of 17 October 1918, ibid., dossier no. 33.

39  See, for example, CIAF, session of 19 June 1918, ibid.

40  CIAF, sessions of 7 March and 1 May 1918, F30 1083.

41  "Note pour le cabinet du ministre," n.d., z - Russie, vol. 575; and also CIAF, session of 31 July 1918, F30 1083.

42  See n.37 above.

43  Auguste Bréal, *Philippe Berthelot* (Paris 1937), 76.

44  See n.37 above.

45  See, for example, z - Russie, vol. 472, passim. In October Noulens went so far as to suggest the division of Russia into Allied "spheres of influence" to facilitate the re-establishment of order and to protect preponderant French interests. Noulens, no. 863, 14 October 1918, z - Russie, vol. 208.

46  Pichon to Klotz, no. 1358, 15 July 1918, F30 1065.

47  "Note pour le conseil des ministres du 6 août," 6 August 1918, draft by Berthelot, minute by Pichon, z - Russie, vol. 472; and Pichon to Jusserand, nos. 1741-2; Cambon, no. 3129, 15 August 1918, ibid.

48  Étienne Clémentel, minister of commerce, to Pichon, for Noulens, no. 556, 6 September 1918, z - Russie, vol. 575. It should be remembered that Noulens was linked to Loucheur and Giros et Compagnie (i.e., the Société générale d'entreprises).

49  CIAF, session of 28 November 1918, F30 1083.

50  "Note au ministre," Service financier, n.d.; "Note," 8 August 1918, draft by Kammerer, z - Russie, vol. 472.

51  Girault, *Emprunts russes*, 58, 305-8; see also Olga Crisp, "The Russo-Chinese Bank: an Episode in Franco-Russian Relations," *Slavonic and East European Review* 52, no. 127 (April 1974): 197-212.

52  Girault, *Emprunts russes*, 501-3; Olga Crisp, "French Investment in Russian Joint-Stock Companies, 1894-1914," *Business History* (Liverpool), vol. 2 (1960), 89; and Vanag, *Finansovyi kapital*, 43-4.

53  Bénac to Gout, 8 January 1918, 5N 280.

54  "Remis par M. Bénac," 5 January 1918, plus enclosures, E - Chine, vol. 111. The Boxer indemnity was the reparations exacted by the great powers after the abortive Boxer rebellion in 1900.

55  "Note," 8 January 1918, "vu de Margerie," E - Chine, vol. 111.

56  Pichon to Charles Martel, French chargé d'affaires in Peking, no. 94, 21 February 1918, E - Chine, vol. 108.

57  Martel, no. 75, 11 February 1918; and nos. 106-7, 27 February 1918, ibid.

58  Ibid.

59  Pichon to Martel, nos. 118-19, 1 March 1918, draft by Kammerer and Berthelot, ibid.

60  Auguste Wilden, French consul general in Shanghai, no. 16, 19 March 1918; and Wilden, 10 March 1918, ibid.

61  Pichon to Martel, nos. 138–41, 14 March 1918, draft by Kammerer and Berthelot; nos. 145-6, 16 March 1918, ibid.; and "Note remise par M. Berthelot à M. [Nicholas] Raffalovich," 14 March 1918, E – Chine, vol. 105.

62  Pichon to Jusserand, nos. 980-2, 29 April 1918, draft by Kammerer, E – Chine, vol. 105.

63  M. Verstraete to his brother Georges in Paris, 13 February 1918, Papiers Thomas, 94 AP 191. Verstraete wrote a series of letters to his brother between December 1917 and April 1918 which indicate that the debate over the pros and cons of co-operation with the Bolsheviks also percolated through the French business community in Petrograd. See the series of nine letters in 94 AP 191.

64  CIAF, session of 19 June 1918, F30 1083; and Pichon to Klotz, 25 August 1918, draft by Kammerer, E – Chine, vol. 106.

65  Ibid.

66  Pichon to Noulens, nos. 284-6, 23 June 1918, draft by Kammerer and Berthelot, Z – Russie, vol. 414. Verstraete and Boutry were eventually stripped of their authority in the bank. Pichon to Noulens, no. 595; Boppe, no. 441, 14 September 1918, E – Chine, vol. 106.

67  CIAF, session of 17 July 1918; and also sessions of 6 and 13 August 1918, F30 1083.

68  CIAF, session of 31 July 1918, ibid.

69  CIAF, sessions of 14 and 28 August 1918, ibid.

70  CIAF, session of 14 August 1918, ibid.

71  "Note de la Banque Russo-Asiatique, remise par M.N. Raffalovich le 26 août 1918," E – Chine, vol. 111.

72  Pichon to Jusserand, nos. 1898-1900, 5 September 1918; and Pichon to Boppe, no. 455, 23 September 1918, ibid.

73  Pichon to Cambon, no. 1788; and elsewhere, 5 September 1918, draft by Kammerer, Z – Russie, vol. 478.

74  Klotz to Pichon, no. 7836, 28 August 1918; and Pichon to Klotz, no. 1554, 12 August 1918, ibid.

75  Kammerer commented in another context that such an inter-Allied organization would be useful in preventing "competition between allies in search of compensation" for their nationals in occupied Russia. See n.37 above.

76  CIAF, session of 6 August 1918, F 30 1083.

77  See n.74 above.

78  This was the hope of the French government. See ibid.

79  Marchand, *Bolshevism*, 27; and Ia. Ioffe, *Organisatsiia interventsii i blokady Sovetskoi respubliki, 1918-1920* (Moscow 1930), 39.

CHAPTER SEVEN

1 Clemenceau to Chardigny, no. 13288 BS/3, 18 October 1918, 16N 3026.
2 "Note sur le plan d'action générale en Russie-Sibérie," no. 12817 BS/3, 4 October 1918, ibid.
3 "Instruction personnelle et secrète pour le général Franchet d'Esperey ... et le général Berthelot ...," no. 12913 BS/3, signed Clemenceau, 7 October 1918, ibid.
4 Lavergne, nos. 87580-89095, 10 October 1918, 4N 41, dossier 3.
5 Noulens, no. 877, 15 October 1918; and no. 886, 18 October 1918, z - Russie, vol. 208.
6 J.M. Thompson, *Russia, Bolshevism, and the Versailles Peace* (Princeton 1966), 25.
7 Pichon to Jusserand, nos. 2506-7; Cambon, nos. 4453-4; and elsewhere, 16 October 1918, z - Russie, vol. 208; and Pichon to Cambon, nos. 4505-7; and elsewhere, 16 October 1918, z - Russie, vol. 219.
8 Derby to Balfour, 18 October 1918, Balfour Papers, no. 49744.
9 Derby to Balfour, 15 November 1918, ibid.
10 Pichon to Jusserand (no cable number); and elsewhere, 14 November 1918, z - Russie, vol. 209.
11 "Note sur l'orientation de l'action des alliés en Russie," no. 13285 BS/3, signed Georges, 17 October 1918; and "Note pour le président du conseil sur l'orientation de l'action des alliés en Russie," no. 13372 BS/3, signed Georges, 19 October 1918, 16N 3026. In fact, the strength of the Red Army at this time was closer to half a million men. See P. Kenez, *Civil War in South Russia, 1918-1919* (Berkeley, 1977), 13.
12 *Clemenceau* to Pichon, no. 13530 BS/3, 23 October 1918, 16N 3026.
13 J.M. Thompson, "Lenin's Analysis of Intervention," *American Slavic and East European Review* 17, no. 2 (1958): 153; and Thompson, *Bolshevism*, 83-8.
14 Edmond Bapst, French minister in Christiana, no. 620, 5 November 1918, z - Russie, vol. 154.
15 Pichon to Bapst, no. 555, 10 November 1918, draft by Berthelot; see also Pichon to Cambon, no. 5619, 13 November 1918, ibid. According to a subsequent communication, the Bolsheviks were ready to halt the Red Terror, to agree to a large-scale amnesty, to abstain from all revolutionary propaganda in the Allied states, and "to satisfy Allied economic demands," though the Soviet government could not immediately resume servicing of the tsarist debt. See Louis Delavaud, French minister in Stockholm, no. 4, 2 January 1919; and Conty, no. 7, 2 January 1919, ibid.
16 Pichon to Cambon, no. 5588; and elsewhere, 12 November 1918, ibid. According to the Service des affaires russes, the French government rejected at least eight different attempts by the Soviets between October

1918 and March 1919 to begin talks with the Entente. See "Paix avec les Bolcheviks," SAR, 10 February 1920, z – Russie, vol. 156.

17 Pichon to Cambon, nos. 95-7; and elsewhere, 2 January 1919, z – Russie, vol. 154.

18 For differing views, see Thompson, *Bolshevism*, 53-60, Brinkley, *Volunteer Army*, 73, 76; Ullman, *Anglo-Soviet Relations* 2: 10-16; and Kennan, *Russia and the West*, 113.

19 Maddox, *Unknown War*, 80; Levin, *Wilson*, 187-8; and Thompson, *Bolshevism*, 13-16.

20 Thompson, *Bolshevism*, 14; and C.E. Callwell, *Field-Marshal Sir Henry Wilson: His Life and Diaries*, vol. 2 (London 1927), 148.

21 Thompson, *Bolshevism*, 24.

22 See n.12 above; see also Clemenceau's oft-cited 27 October directive outlining this strategy to Franchet d'Esperey in Jean Xydias, *L'intervention française en Russie, 1918-1919: souvenirs d'un témoin* (Paris 1927), 113-15; and A.J. Mayer, *Politics and Diplomacy of Peacemaking* (New York 1967), 296.

23 Denikin took over full control of the Volunteer Army in October after the death of Alekseev.

24 "Note sur le plan d'action militaire de l'Entente," no. 13844 BS/3, signed Alby, Georges, 2 November 1918, z – Russie, vol. 209; and *Clemenceau* to General Berthelot, no. 13862 BS/3, 2 November 1918, z – Russie, vol. 224.

25 "Note sur l'action des alliés en Russie," no. 14272 BS/3, 13 November 1918, 16N 3026.

26 *Clemenceau* to Franchet d'Esperey, no. 14476 BS/3, 21 November 1918, ibid.

27 "Étude du 3e Bureau au sujet des conditions d'un armistice," 3e Bureau A, no. 13119 BS/3, 12 October 1918, ibid.

28 Franchet d'Esperey, no. 5920/3, 15 November 1918, 20N 225.

29 Franchet d'Esperey, no. 6207/3, 6 December 1918, ibid.; and P. Azan, *Franchet d'Esperey* (Paris 1949), 242.

30 Xydias, *L'intervention française*, 345; and Michel Graillet, French consul in Salonika, no. 261, 5 December 1918, z – Russie, vol. 225.

31 "Lettre de Fleuriau," 16 October 1918, z – Russie, vol. 208.

32 Noulens, no. 886, 18 October 1918, ibid.

33 See various cables in z – Russie, vols. 224-5, 668; and 16N 3170.

34 Franchet d'Esperey, no. 5955/3, 18 November 1918, 16N 3147; and no. 5722/3, 3 November 1918, 20N 225.

35 Berthelot, no. 83/3, 4 December 1918, 16N 3172.

36 Berthelot, no. 139/3, 15 December 1918, ibid.

37 Franchet d'Esperey, no. 6119/3, 30 November 1918, 16N 3147.

38 "Rapport fait au ministre au sujet du recrutement de volontaires pour servir en Russie," no. 14862 BS/3, signed Alby, 3 December 1918, 16N 3026.

39 *Clemenceau* to Franchet d'Esperey, no. 15318 BS/3, 18 December 1918, ibid.
40 See n.38 above.
41 Saint-Aulaire, nos. 860-2, 15 December 1918; no. 867, 21 December 1918; and nos. 897-8, 26 December 1918, Z - Russie, vol. 225.
42 Pichon's minute on Franchet d'Esperey's no. 6165/3, 4 December 1918, ibid.
43 Pichon to Saint-Aulaire, no. 762, 9 December 1918, in Pichon's hand; and Pichon to Saint-Aulaire, nos. 805-7; and elsewhere, 19 December 1918, in Pichon's hand, ibid.
44 Guiard, nos. 1149-56, 27 December 1918, Z - Russie, vol. 210.
45 Pichon to Guiard, no. 1029; and elsewhere, 29 December 1918, draft by Berthelot, ibid. This cable is cited in Mayer, *Politics*, 302-3.
46 See various articles in *L'Humanité, Le Populaire, Le Journal du Peuple*, and *La Vérité*, June-September 1918.
47 See various articles in November-December 1918.
48 *L'Humanité*, 17 December 1918.
49 *Le Populaire*, 22 December 1918.
50 The French bureau of the censor tried to prevent the publication of numerous Socialist appeals to the French working class against the intervention. See the notebooks entitled "Consignes des périodiques" and "Avis" for November-December 1918, BDIC, Censure, Consignes, F 270 C réserve.
51 Wohl, *French Communism*, 114-18.
52 France, *Débats parlementaires*, sessions of 27 and 29 December 1918, 3631-4, 3720-5.
53 Ibid., session of 29 December 1918, 3720-34.
54 Maddox, *Unknown War*, 85; and Mayer, *Politics*, 331-3.
55 Thompson, *Bolshevism*, 13; and Mayer, *Politics*, 325-8.
56 Thompson, *Bolshevism*, 51-4, 90-2.
57 Clemenceau to Janin, no. 15176 BS/3, 13 December 1918, Z - Russie, vol. 225.
58 See n.34 above.
59 *Clemenceau* to Georges Leygues, minister of the navy, no. 14925 BS/3, 5 December 1918, Z - Russie, vol. 225.
60 Pichon to Saint-Aulaire, no. 42, 13 January 1919, Z - Russie, vol. 226.
61 Saint-Aulaire, no. 857, 18 December 1918, Z - Russie, vol. 225; and Xydias, *L'intervention française*, 123-4, 126-7.
62 The above account of the political situation in southern Russia at the end of 1918 is based on Brinkley, *Volunteer Army*, 80-8, unless otherwise noted.
63 Amet to Admiral Ferdinand Jean Jacques de Bon, c. en c. 1ère Armée Navale, no. 200B, 10 December 1918, MM, U - 8; see also the December reports from the captain of the battleship *Mirabeau*, Abel Jules Revault, in MM, A - 172.
64 Pichon to Saint-Aulaire, no. 762, 9 December 1918, Z - Russie, vol. 225.

65 Amet to Leygues, no. 2118, received 12 December 1918, ibid.; see also M.S. Margulies, *God interventsii*, vol. 1 (Berlin 1923), 89-90.

66 Franchet d'Esperey, no. 6276/3, 14 December 1918, z - Russie, vol. 225.

67 "Note au sujet de la situation en Russie mériodionale," n.d. signed Lt. Colonel Joanny Marcel Garchery (hereafter referred to as Rapport Garchery), 16N 3188; "Rapport du Lt. colonel [Henri] Freydenberg," 22 April 1919 (hereafter Rapport Freydenberg), 7N 803, dossier 6; and d'Anselme to Franchet d'Esperey, no. 1723/3, "Rapport sur les relations du commandement militaire français à Odessa avec les gouvernments locaux du 14 janvier 1919 au 6 avril 1919," 20 May 1919 (hereafter Rapport d'Anselme), 16N 3149. The French estimate of the number of Ukrainian troops in Odessa was initially put at 12,000, but later was adjusted downward to about 3,000. See Rapport Amet, 23 December 1918, z - Russie, vol. 225.

68 Amet to de Bon, 14 December 1918, MM, U - 8.

69 Amet to de Bon, 12 December 1918, ibid.

70 Rapport Amet, 23 December 1918, z - Russie, vol. 225; and Rapport Garchery.

71 Franchet d'Esperey to Berthelot, no. 6297/3, 15 December 1918, 20N 225.

72 Berthelot to Borius, nos. 276-7, 16 December 1918, 20N 729.

73 The deletion of this sentence from the final draft of the dispatch did not make it any less an appropriate indication of the Quai d'Orsay's attitude toward the Ukraine and indeed toward the other nationalities of Russia. See Pichon to Paul Dutasta, French minister in Berne, no. 2057, 7 November 1918, z - Russie, vol. 668.

74 Pichon to Clemenceau, no. 4930, 11 December 1918, 16N 3067.

75 Clemenceau (Alby) to Franchet d'Esperey, no. 15277 BS/3, 16 December 1918, 16N 3026.

76 Rapport Garchery.

77 Ibid. Volunteer losses for the day were approximately 40 killed and 60 wounded. The French suffered 2 wounded (see Rapport d'Anselme; and Rapport Amet, z - Russie, vol. 225).

78 Compte Rendu, no. 4207/3, 156ᵉ DI, 20 December 1918, 20N 763, dossier 6; Rapport Garchery; and Rapport Amet, z - Russie, vol. 225.

79 Rapport d'Anselme.

80 Rapport Garchery.

81 Rapport Amet, z - Russie, vol. 225.

82 Mayer, *Politics*, 647-8; and Wohl, *French Communism*, 114.

## CHAPTER EIGHT

1 *Clemenceau* to Pichon, no. 13530 BS/3, 23 October 1918, 16N 3026.

2 These delegates were Charles Sergent, Alexandre Celier, F.A. Kammerer, F. François-Marsal, and Paul Tirard, future French high commissioner in the Rhineland.

3   CG, session of 12 September 1918, ANPFVM, dossier no. 33.
4   Klotz to Chevalier, no. 2511, 1 March 1919, ANPFVM, dossier no. 46 bis and
    *Débats parlementaires*, 19 September 1918, 2426-7, 2430, 2432-3, 2436-9.
5   "Problème financier franco-russe," F/M (François-Marsal), 24 January 1918;
    and "La speculation sur les fonds russes," F/M, 2 August 1918, 5N 280.
6   CIAF, "Note: L'état français doit-il continuer à payer le coupon russe?
    annexe à la séance du 29 mai 1918," by Claude Aulagnon, counsellor for
    foreign commerce, a sometime member of the CIAF, and an administrator
    of the Union métallurgique de Russie, F30 1083.
7   "Problème financier franco-russe," F/M, 24 January 1918, 5N 280.
8   CIAF, session of 29 May 1918, "Discussion sur l'exposé de M. Aulagnon,"
    F30 1083.
9   Pichon to Machart, 23 October 1918, ANPFVM, dossier no. 46 bis.
10  Verneuil to des Closières, 5 November 1918, ANPFVM, dossier no. 50.
11  François-Marsal anticipated that even after the Russian government re-
    sumed payment of the coupon, the arrears of the revolutionary period
    might never be recovered. See n.7 above.
12  See n.9 above.
13  Darcy to Gruner, 19 June 1917, ANPFVM, dossier no. 34.
14  Klotz to Pichon, no. 10527, 17 December 1917, MAÉ, Guerre, vol. 1430.
15  See various documents in Z - Russie, vol. 576.
16  CIAF, sessions of 10 April and 29 May 1918 (annexe), F30 1083.
17  Pichon to Klotz, no. 1126, 8 June 1918, and enclosure "M. Klotz estime ...,"
    13 June 1918, F30 1092/93.
18  Machart to Pichon, no. 4662, 15 November 1918, ANPFVM, dossier no. 46
    bis.
19  Pichon to Cambon, nos. 3235-6; and elsewhere, 23 August 1918, Z -
    Russie, vol. 413.
20  Pichon to Klotz, no. 1726, 9 September 1918, and enclosed instructions
    for Noulens, F30 1069.
21  Ibid.
22  Pichon to Noulens, no. 781; and elsewhere, 22 October 1918, Z - Russie,
    vol. 478.
23  Pichon to Noulens, no. 590, 13 September 1918, Z - Russie, vol. 413.
24  Pichon to Cambon, nos. 2282-3; and elsewhere, 31 March 1919; Z -
    Russie, vol. 532, see also several other directives in this file, pp. 82, 97, 123,
    162. Cf., Ioffe, *Organisatsiia interventsii*, 121, 125-7.
25  CG, sessions of 21 November, 19 and 26 December 1918, ANPFVM, dossier
    no. 33.
26  Verneuil to Clemenceau, 6 January 1919, Z - Russie, vol. 576.
27  Ibid.
28  Pichon to Regnault, nos. 18-19, 11 January 1919, draft by Kammerer,
    E - Sibérie, vol. 24.
29  Cf., Thompson, *Bolshevism*, 27.

30  See n.26 above.

31  CG, session of 15 January 1919, ANPFVM, dossier no. 33.

32  See chapter 6 above.

33  Jusserand, no. 470, 12 October 1918, z - Russie, vol. 473.

34  Ullman, *Anglo-Soviet Relations* 2: 24-6.

35  Pichon to Jusserand, nos. 2018-22, 22 September 1918, draft by Kammerer, z - Russie, vol. 478.

36  See n.20 above.

37  See chapter 6; and "Note pour le ministre," signed Sergent, 3 January 1919, F30 1068.

38  Klotz to Pichon, no. 11234, 11 December 1918, F30 1072.

39  Pichon to Noulens, no. 878, 21 November 1918, z - Russie, vol. 474.

40  Kammerer to Paul Gerard West, financial attaché in Arkhangelsk, 9 November 1918, z - Russie, vol. 478.

41  Klotz to Pichon, no. 10301, 15 November 1918; and no. 11041, 6 December 1918, z - Russie, vol. 474.

42  Klotz to Pichon, no. 11041, 6 December 1918, z - Russie, vol. 474.

43  Pichon to Noulens, no. 933, 1 December 1918, z - Russie, vol. 474.

44  See n.40 above.

45  Klotz to Pichon, no. 9080, 7 October 1918, F30 1071, dossier 1.

46  "Note de la Société Générale sur la Banque Russo-Asiatique," November 1918, E - Chine, vol. 111.

47  Henri Simon, minister of colonies, to Klotz, 6 August 1918, F30 1071.

48  "Note pour le ministre," signed Celier, Sergent, 28 November 1918, F30 1072.

49  Unlabelled note from the ministry of finance, appears to be Fabry's hand, 22 December 1918, E - Sibérie, vol. 24.

50  Klotz to the Banque de l'Indochine, no. 10862, 1 December 1918, F30 1072.

51  Banque de l'Indochine to Klotz, 19 December 1918, plus enclosure, z - Russie, vol. 486.

52  Klotz to Pichon, no. 742, 17 January 1919, E - Sibérie, vol. 24; and also Pichon to Klotz, no. 306, 5 February 1919, F30 1072.

53  See n.35 above.

54  Klotz to the Banque de l'Indochine, no. 1099, 28 January 1919, F30 1072.

55  Banque de l'Indochine to Klotz, 4 February 1919, ibid.

56  This committee appears to have represented the same banks as the Groupe financier of the Commission générale.

57  Conseil d'administration de la Banque de Paris et des Pays-Bas, session of 29 October 1918 (the author had only very limited access to this source); and also "Procès-verbal de la conférence tenue le 25 octobre chez M. Kammerer au sujet de la création d'une monnaie pour la Russie du sud," z - Russie, vol. 224.

58  Pichon to Klotz, no. 2270, 7 November 1918, F30 1068.
59  Ibid.; see also Pichon to Klotz, no. 2430, 6 December 1918, F30 1068; and Pichon to Clémentel, no. 2704, 11 December 1918, z – Russie, vol. 509.
60  See, for example, n.1 above; *Clemenceau* to Franchet d'Esperey, no. 14476 BS/3, 21 November 1918, 16N 3026; and "Note sur le plan d'action militaire de l'Entente," no. 13844 BS/3, signed Alby, Georges, 2 November 1918, z – Russie, vol. 209.
61  Cf., A.I. Gukovskii, *Frantsuzskaia interventsiia na iuge Rossii, 1918–1919* (Moscow 1927), 31–2.
62  Pichon to Klotz, no. 2430, 6 December 1918, F30 1068.
63  "Projet et note remis par M. Turrettini," 5 December 1918, F30 1068.
64  "Note pour le ministre," signed Sergent, 3 January 1919, ibid.; and Klotz to Pichon, 13 January 1919, z – Russie, vol. 247.
65  "Note au ministre," Direction des Affaires politiques, 23 November 1918, E – Sibérie, vol. 24; and CIAF, session of 29 January 1919, F30 1083.
66  "Création d'une banque pour la Russie du sud," n.d. (February 1919), F30 1068; and also an untitled note by Fabry, 11 February 1919, ibid.
67  Klotz to Pichon, 13 January 1919, z – Russie, vol. 247.
68  Pichon to Klotz, no. 204, 23 January 1919, ibid.
69  Paribas to Klotz, 19 February 1919, and enclosures, F30 1068.
70  Putilov was involved in the negotiations for the *banque d'émission* (see n.57 above).
71  See the memorandum submitted under cover of a note from Putilov to Sergent, 30 November 1918, F30 1068. This proposal resembled Verneuil's submitted in January 1919; see n.26 above.
72  See *Le Temps*, "Semaine financière," 15 September, 14 and 28 October 1918.
73  A. Raffalovich to Sergent, 14 October 1918; and Fabry to Sergent, 21 October 1918, F30 1065. Arthur Raffalovich, who was a principal figure involved in the payment of bribes by the tsarist government to the French press during the Revolution of 1905, should not be confused with Nicholas Raffalovich, an executive officer of the Russo-Asiatique.
74  Note by Sergent, 4 December 1918, F30 1072.
75  Regnault, no. 200, 5 January 1919; and also Martel (Vladivostok), no. 92, 23 December 1918, F30 1072.
76  Pichon to Regnault, no. 17, 13 January 1919, E – Sibérie, vol. 24.
77  Raffalovich to Sergent, 5 January 1919, F30 1071, dossier 1; and also CIAF, session of 19 February 1919, F30 1083.
78  Raffalovich to Sergent, 18 May 1919, F30 1072, dossier 3.
79  "Roubles en Sibérie," n.d. (response to the Raffalovich letter), ibid.
80  Klotz to the Banque de l'Indochine, no. 17533, 21 November 1919; and Banque de l'Indochine to François-Marsal, then minister of finance, 1 June 1920, ibid.

81  CIAF, session of 9 April 1919, F30 1083.

82  In the short run, the Société commerciale could have bought up foreign and especially American manufactured goods and then sold them in the Ukraine.

83  Alexandre Millerand, premier and foreign minister, to Martel, then French high commissioner to the south Russian government of General P.N. Wrangel, "Instructions concernant le réglement de la dette russe et dommages subis par les français," 6 September 1920, ANPFVM, dossier no. 25; see also Millerand to François-Marsal, no. 796, 15 April 1920, F30 1092/93; and Des Closières to Klotz, 29 July 1919, plus enclosure, F30 1094.

84  Millerand to Martel, 6 September 1920, ANPFVM, dossier no. 25.

85  Girault, *Emprunts russes*, 468-78; and Olga Crisp, "Some Problems of French Investment in Russian Joint-Stock Companies," *Slavonic and East European Review*, 35, no. 84 (Dec. 1956): 237-8.

86  Klotz to Pichon, 29 May 1919; and Verneuil to Klotz, 14 June 1919, Z - Russie, vol. 479.

87  Pichon to Klotz, 10 July 1919, ibid.

88  G. Eybert, chief of the CIAF secretariat, to Verneuil, 19 August 1919, and enclosure, ANPFVM, dossier no. 25.

89  Among the other stockholders in the Société commerciale were the Banque Russo-Asiatique, the Crédit mobilier, Schneider et Compagnie, the Société d'entreprises, the Banque Privée, the Compagnie des forges de Chatillon, Commentry et Neuves-Maisons, the Compagnie des forges et Aciéries de la Marine et d'Homécourt, the Compagnie des messageries maritimes, and la Société métallurgique de Montbard-Aulnoye. "Société Commerciale ... Liste des principaux souscripteurs," n.d., Paribas.

90  "Société Commerciale ... Exposé" (circulated by the Paribas and BUP), 29 September 1919, Paribas.

91  Pichon to Klotz, 5 December 1919, Z - Russie, vol. 475.

92  Three members of the Commission générale, Bénac, Gruner, and Louis Lion, were on the board of directors of the Société commerciale. Also on the board were Armand de Saint-Sauveur of Schneider et Compagnie, N. Raffalovich and A.I. Putilov of the Russo-Asiatique, and Claude Aulagnon, who had semi-official government status. See "Société Commerciale ... Conseil d'administration," n.d., Z - Russie, vol. 495. For a complete list of the members of the board of directors and a copy of the consortium's statutes, see F30 1114.

93  In this regard, see also "Procès-verbal de la réunion tenue le 27 novembre 1919 au ministère de la reconstitution industrielle," F30 1068; Pichon to Pascalis, president of the Paris Chamber of Commerce, 20 October 1919, Z - Russie, vol. 640; and Henry Bérenger, commissioner-general for petroleum and fuels, to Klotz, no. 1149c, 10 December 1919, F30 1112.

94 See n.90 above; and Paribas/BUP to Pichon, 20 November 1919, Z - Russie, vol. 475.

95 Mayer, *Politics*, 647-54.

96 Pichon to Klotz, 4 November 1918, F30 1092/93; and Pichon to Klotz, no. 1812, 30 July 1919, Z - Russie, vol. 578.

97 Pichon to Clemenceau, no. 4191, 4 August 1919, 7N 802, dossier "A.E."

98 Girault, *Emprunts russes*, 479-91.

99 "Note au ministre," Direction politique, 24 October 1919, E - Sibérie, vol. 21.

## CHAPTER NINE

1 "Rapport du chef de bataillon François ..." (hereafter Rapport François), 10 February 1919, 16N 3172.

2 Ibid.

3 "Rapports sur les incidents survenus ... le 7 et le 8 février à Bender, chef d'escadron Dewulf ...," 10 February 1919, ibid.

4 Rapport François, ibid.

5 Colonel Edmond Lejay to General Berthelot, *confirmation*, 10 February 1919; see also Rapport François and "Rapport au sujet des incidents qui se sont produits au 58e R.I. et au 7e groupe du 2e R.A.M. ...," signed General Antoine Eugène Nerel, 12 February 1919, ibid.

6 "Rapport au sujet des faits graves d'indiscipline collective qui s'est produit dans le détachment de Bender ...," signed Colonel Lejay, 11 February 1919, ibid.

7 See chapter 7 above.

8 "Rapport du général Nerel," no. 2502/1, 18 May 1919; and Berthelot, no. 405/3, 22 February 1919, 16N 3172.

9 Propaganda tracts collected in carton 20N 763 are labelled as coming from Bucharest in early December. See also Margulies, *God interventsii* 1: 66. Margulies was a representative of the monarchist Council for State Unity in Odessa. The first volume of his journal is a valuable source concerning French activities in the Ukraine during most of the occupation.

10 Comptes rendus, 21, 22, and 24 December 1918, signed Borius, 26N 448.

11 Berthelot to Clemenceau, no. 385/3, "Rapport sur la situation en Russie méridionale," 17 February 1919, 20N 273.

12 Captain L. Joseph Langeron, French intelligence officer at Odessa, to d'Anselme, 21 February 1919, 20N 763, dossier 1.

13 See Margulies, *God interventsii* 1: 66; and various pamphlets, tracts, etc., in 16N 763.

14 See n.11 above; César Fauxbras, *Mer Noire: les mutineries racontées par un mutin* (Paris 1935), 158-60; V. Elin, "Kak my rabotali v okkupatsionnykh voiskakh," in *Chernaia kniga*, ed. Shlikhter, 407-8; E.N. Trubetskoi, "Iz

putevykh zametok bezhentsa," *Arkhiv Russkoi Revoliutsii* 18 (1926): 163-4; and V.G. Konovalov, *Inostrannia kollegiia* (Odessa 1958).

15 Trubetskoi, "Iz putevykh zametok," 172.

16 Margulies, *God interventsii* 1: 66-7.

17 Fauxbras, *Mer Noire*, 93-4.

18 See chapter 7 above.

19 Margulies, *God interventsii* 1: 163; and A.I. Denikin, *Ocherki russkoi smuty*, vol. 5 (Berlin 1926), 32.

20 Denikin, *Ocherki* 5: 32-3; and Gukovskii, *Frantsuzskaia interventsiia*, 119-20.

21 Franchet d'Esperey, no. 5797/3, 6 November 1918; no. 12564/2ch, 6 November 1918, 20N 225; and Foch to Leygues, then premier, no. 193/MT, 13 October 1920, Z – Russie, vol. 644. This direct French aid to Denikin did not continue because the French government considered his army to be operating in the British "zone of influence." For this reason, no French troops were sent to the Kuban and only a small military mission of three officers was established at Denikin's headquarters. Clemenceau (Alby) to Franchet d'Esperey, no. 95 BS/3, 3 January 1919; and no. 727 BS/3, 28 January 1919, 16N 3027.

22 Amet to Leygues, no. 2118, 12 December 1918, Z – Russie, vol. 225.

23 Rapport Garchery and Rapport d'Anselme. D'Anselme put the strength of the Volunteer Army in Odessa at 2,000 men (1,900 officers and 100 other ranks).

24 Cf., Gukovskii, *Frantsuzskaia interventsiia*, 133.

25 Berthelot to Franchet d'Esperey, no. 240/3, 10 January 1919, 20N 729; and also Rapport d'Anselme.

26 Nikolaev was occupied by a German division of some 12,000 men which for want of Allied troops was forced to co-operate with the French command. Only on 2 March did two Greek battalions take up positions there. See Rapport d'Anselme.

27 "Extraits des rapports d'ensemble," from d'Anselme, 16 January 1919, 16N 3149.

28 Trubetskoi, "Iz putevykh zametok," 173; and A.I. Gukovskii, ed., "Iz istorii frantsuzskoi interventsii v Odesse," *Krasnyi Arkhiv* 45 (1931), 60.

29 See, for example, Margulies, *God interventsii* 1: 190, 267.

30 Ibid., 163, 234; and Denikin, *Ocherki* 5: 34.

31 Margulies, *God interventsii* 1: 190-1.

32 Ibid., 169, 187, 192; and Trubetskoi, "Iz putevykh zametok," 173.

33 Rapport Freydenberg; Rapport d'Anselme; "Rapport du capitaine Langeron," 11 May 1919 (hereafter referred to as Rapport Langeron), 16N 3149; also S. Ostapenko, "Direktoriia i okkupatsiia Ukrainy," in *Chernaia kniga*, ed. Shlikhter, 262.

34 "Rapport mensuel sur la situation à Odessa," no. 228, signed Admiral Lejay, 5 February 1919, MM, U-7.

35 Rapport Freydenberg.
36 Unlabelled note listing 13 conditions in Freydenberg's hand with minor corrections by d'Anselme, n.d., 20N 765, dossier 2 (see appendix for text); see also Ostapenko, "Direktoriia," 266; and Margulies, *God interventsii* 1: 219.
37 Rapport d'Anselme; Rapport Langeron; and Langeron to Freydenberg, 6 February 1919, 20N 765.
38 Rapport Freydenberg; and Rapport Langeron.
39 Margulies, *God interventsii* 1: 193; and Trubetskoi, "Iz putevykh zametok," 173-5.
40 *Clemenceau* to Franchet d'Esperey, Berthelot, no. 902 BS/3, 29 January 1919, 16N 3027.
41 Berthelot, no. 353/3, 12 February 1919, 16N 3172.
42 See n.11 above.
43 Cf., Gukovskii, *Frantsuzskaia interventsiia*, 151.
44 Rapport Langeron; and Margulies, *God interventsii* 1: 225.
45 Rapport Langeron; and Rapport d'Anselme, *annexe* 12.
46 Rapport d'Anselme, *annexe* 13, "1er projet d'accord avec l'Entente présenté par le Directoire, le 18 février 1919." This version has only ten points, but it would appear that the last two conditions were inadvertently omitted since the projected accord is almost identical to the 12-point draft treaty found in A. Margolin, *From a Political Diary....* (New York 1946), 189-90.
47 Rapport d'Anselme.
48 Ibid., *annexe* 14. D'Anselme forwarded this draft to General Berthelot, but then heard no more about it.
49 Rapport Freydenberg.
50 Margolin, *Diary*, 37.
51 See, for example, "Rapport d'ensemble," signed d'Anselme, 20 February 1919, 20N 763; and Margulies, 1: 189-90, 251-2, and passim.
52 Rapport Freydenberg.
53 Margulies, *God interventsii*, 1: 299.
54 See, for example, Berthelot, no. 164/3, 21 December 1918, 16N 3172.
55 Labonne to Pichon, 31 January 1919, Z - Russie, vol. 226.
56 David S. Payne, "The Foreign Policy of Georges Clemenceau, 1917-1920" (PHD diss., Duke University, 1970), 306-8, citing a Balfour letter to Lloyd George, 19 January 1919. Interestingly enough, the Soviet government sent a Red Cross mission to France under D.Z. Manuilskii in February 1919, ostensibly to supervise a prisoner exchange but really to try to negotiate an end to the French involvement in the intervention. The Manuilskii mission landed in France, but was shut up in Malo-les-Bains near Dunkirk and never had any direct contact with the French government. It returned to Russia in April. See R.K. Debo, "The Manouilsky Mission," unpublished manuscript.

57  Janin, nos. 480-2, 25 January 1919, 16N 3191.

58  Regnault, nos. 41-2, 27 January 1919; and Janin, nos. 489-91, 27 January 1919, ibid.

59  Martel, no. 63, 8 February 1919, ibid. For similar conclusions, see Clemenceau (Alby) to Foch, no. 3117 BS/3 26 March 1919, 16N 3028.

60  Pichon to Martel, no. 66, 16 February 1919, E - Sibérie, vol. 7.

61  Thompson, *Bolshevism*, 119-23; Ullman, *Anglo-Soviet Relations* 2: 105-6; and Mayer, *Politics*, 419, 442-4.

62  Pichon to Clemenceau, no. 1150, 24 February 1919, 16N 3069. A few months later Pichon claimed that the French government had been principally responsible for stopping the Prinkipo initiative. Pichon to Barrere, nos. 2234-6; and elsewhere, 16 July 1919, z - Russie, vol. 212. For a more detailed account of the Prinkipo negotiations, see Thompson, *Bolshevism*, 82-130; and Mayer, *Politics*, 410-49. The question of the Prinkipo proposal is not examined further in the present study since the French documents concerning it were apparently destroyed during World War II. Under the circumstances there is no point in repeating what has been discussed at length in Mayer and Thompson.

63  Thompson, *Bolshevism*, 147-8.

64  Margulies, *God interventsii*, 1, 266; and Trubetskoi, "Iz putevykh zametok," 173.

65  Brinkley, *Volunteer Army*, 119.

66  Amet, no. 973, 5 February 1919, z - Russie, vol. 226.

67  Amet to Leygues and to de Bon, no. 67D, 9 January 1919, MM, U - 9; and also Admiral Jules Théophile Docteur, *Carnet de bord, 1914-1919* (Paris 1932), 211-30.

68  Berthelot, no. 809/2, 2 March 1919, 16N 3172; and Trubetskoi, "Iz putevykh zametok," 195.

69  Brinkley, *Volunteer Army*, 121-2; and Denikin, *Ocherki* 5: 39-40.

70  Denikin to General Berthelot, 11 February 1919, 20N 778, dossier 18.

71  "Rapports d'ensemble," signed d'Anselme, 20 February, 4 March 1919, 20N 763.

72  Margulies, *God interventsii* 1: 250, 259, 263-4.

73  Amet, no. 973, 5 February 1919, z - Russie, vol. 226.

74  Margulies, *God interventsii* 1: 258; and Ostapenko, "Direktoriia," 267.

75  Picton Bagge to FO, no. 90, 22 February 1919, FO 371 3963, p. 517.

76  Memorandum, Picton Bagge, 20 March 1919, ibid., pp. 525-30; and Cooke to FO, no. 144, 4 March 1919, FO 371 3978, p. 200.

77  Picton Bagge, to FO, no. 40964, 4 February 1919, FO 371 3963, p. 57.

78  Picton Bagge to FO, no. 134, 3 March 1919, FO 371 3978, p. 193.

79  Cooke, Picton Bagge to FO, no. 162, 6 March 1919, ibid., p. 216

80  Margulies, *God interventsii* 1: 279.

81  See n.77 above.

82  Margulies, *God interventsii* 1: 217-18, also 192, 200, and passim; and Gukovskii, *Frantsuzskaia interventsiia*, 77-8.

83  Cooke to FO, 14 April 1919, FO 371 3964, p. 342; V.I. Gurko, "Iz Petrograda cherez Moskvu, Parizh i London v Odessu," *Arkhiv Russkoi Revoliutsii*, vol. 15 (1924), 76; and Trubetskoi, "Iz putevykh zametok," 163-5.

84  Margulies, *God interventsii* 1: 260; and "Rapport d'ensemble," d'Anselme, 4 March 1919, 20N 763.

85  See n.77 above; Gukovskii, *Frantsuzskaia interventsiia*, 79-80; and Trubetskoi, "Iz putevykh zametok," 164.

86  Gukovskii, *Frantsuzskaia interventsiia*, 79.

87  For a collection of documents on the shooting of Labourbe, see 7N 800, dossier 8. See also L. Zak, *Des français dans la révolution d'octobre* (Paris 1976), 134-5, and passim; and A. Marty, *La révolte de la mer Noire*, vol. 1, réédition (Paris 1970), 102-6.

88  Berthelot to Clemenceau, no. 385/3, "Rapport sur la situation en Russie méridionale," 17 February 1919, 20N 273.

89  Margulies, *God interventsii* 1: 220; and Trubetskoi, "Iz putevykh zametok," 174.

## CHAPTER TEN

1  Margulies, *God interventsii* 1: 287, 299; see also Trubetskoi, "Iz putevykh zametok," 172.

2  Franchet d'Esperey, no. 7012/3, 3 March 1919, 20N 226.

3  General Berthelot to Franchet d'Esperey, *bordereau d'envoi*, no. 574/3, 27 March 1919, 20N 273; "Opérations de Kherson et de Nicolaief," signed d'Anselme, March 1919, 20N 780; and the various reports from the captains of the French warships at Kherson in MM, Bj-8. Allied losses at Kherson were 4 French killed, 22 wounded, 1 missing, and 61 Greek killed, 131 wounded, and 51 missing, out of a contingent of 700 Greek and 300 French troops. Reinforcements brought Allied troop strength at Kherson to 2,010 men, though not all were committed to the battle. Berthelot, no. 508/3, 15 March 1919, 16N 3172 and "Rapport sur les opérations à Kherson," no. 260, signed Lejay, 12 March 1919, Bj-8. On the question of civilian casualties, there are many sources, but see *Chernaia kniga*, ed. Shlikhter, 151-2 and passim; and Marty, *Révolte* 1: 124-8.

4  Rapport d'Anselme, *annexe* 2; and also Margulies, *God interventsii* 1: 300.

5  "Note secrète du 5 mars du général d'Anselme au général Berthelot et au Franchet d'Esperey," in "Opérations de Kherson et de Nicolaief," 20N 780, dossier 4.

6  "Rapport sur la situation au 13 mars 1919," signed d'Anselme, 16N 3172.

7  D'Anselme to Franchet d'Esperey, no. 7284/3, 16 March 1919, 20N 770.

8 See n.4 above; Berthelot, no. 505/3, 12 March 1919; and nos. 396–7, 12 March 1919, 7N 802.

9 See n.6 above. General Berthelot was making reference to a massacre of French troops by inhabitants of the town of Palermo in Sicily on 30 March 1282.

10 Berthelot, no. 1240/4, 17 March 1919, 16N 3172. French intelligence estimated that there were from 40 to 80,000 armed workers in Odessa, "ready to revolt." "Note pour le ministre," SAR, 19 March 1919, Z – Russie, vol. 228; and Margulies, *God interventsii* 1: 260. Both estimates were exaggerated. See F. Bolkun, "Moi vstrechu s d'Anselmom," in *Chernaia kniga*, ed. Shlikhter, 397.

11 Colonel Émile Auguste Corbel, chief of the French military mission at Denikin's GHQ, to Franchet d'Esperey, nos. 211–13, 27 February 1919, 7N 802.

12 Berthelot, no. 808/2, 1 March 1919; no. 809/2, 2 March 1919; and no. 832/2, 4 March 1919, 16N 3172.

13 Clemenceau to Pichon, no. 2235 BS/3, 4 March 1919, 7N 800, dossier 2. Nevertheless, the government did not approve the proposal for mixed Franco-Russian brigades. Berthelot to d'Anselme, no. 569/3, 20 March 1919, 20N 770.

14 Pichon to Maklakov, 8 March 1919, Z – Russie, vol. 227.

15 Ordre, no. 7349/3, 21 March 1919, 20N 770; Brinkley, *Volunteer Army*, 127–9; and Denikin, *Ocherki*, 5: 45–6.

16 Brinkley, *Volunteer Army*, 129–31; and Denikin, *Ocherki* 5: 46.

17 *Clemenceau* to Berthelot, Franchet d'Esperey, no. 2649 BS/3, 14 March 1919, 16N 3028.

18 Franchet d'Esperey, no. 4728, 11 March 1919, 16N 3148; and also Azan, *Franchet d'Esperey*, 247.

19 Azan, *Franchet d'Esperey*, 241, 247.

20 In 1917 Berthelot had pressed impatiently for a transfer from Rumania to the Western Front. See Lavergne, nos. 1959–61, 7 June 1917, 16N 3180.

21 Franchet d'Esperey, no. 7160/3, 16 March 1919, 16N 3148; and Azan, *Franchet d'Esperey*, 247.

22 Franchet d'Esperey, no. 7107/3, 12 March 1919, ibid.

23 Denikin, *Ocherki* 5: 49; see also D Kin, ed., "K istorii frantsuzskoi interventsii na iuge Rossii," *Krasnyi Arkhiv* 19 (1927): 32–3; and Gurko, "Iz Petrograda," 57.

24 "Review of the Political Situation in South Russia," 23 March 1919, FO 371 3979, pp. 14–15.

25 Franchet d'Esperey, no. 7262/3, 26 March 1919, 20N 226.

26 Franchet d'Esperey's minute on d'Anselme's no. 62, 26 March 1919, which reported Denikin's orders to Sannikov not to co-operate with Andro, 20N 273.

27  Corbel to d'Anselme, nos. 64–6, 2 April 1919, 20N 762, dossier 7.

28  Derby to Pichon, 1 March 1919 (two notes), Z – Russie, vol. 227; Cambon, no. 160, 21 March 1919, with enclosure; and Derby to Pichon, 23 March 1919, Z – Russie, vol. 228.

29  Pichon to Derby, 25 March 1919, Z – Russie, vol. 228; and also Pichon to Clemenceau, no. 1446, 6 March 1919, 16N 3069.

30  Pichon to Maklakov, 21 March 1919, 16N 3069; and Pichon to Derby, 11 March 1919, Z – Russie, vol. 227.

31  See chapter 2 above.

32  Prevailing interpretation holds that the French government supported the ideal of a united and indivisible Russia. See P.S. Wandycz, *France and her Eastern Allies, 1919–1925* (Minneapolis 1962), 118–19; and also Ullman, *Anglo-Soviet Relations* 3: 28, n.37.

33  U.S. Dept. of State, *Papers Relating to the Foreign Relations of the United States, Paris Peace Conference* (Washington, D.C. 1942–7), 4: 120–3.

34  Berthelot, nos. 398–9, 12 March 1919, 7N 802; and nos. 400–2, 12 March 1919, 16N 3172.

35  Clemenceau to Franchet d'Esperey, Berthelot, no. 2741 BS/3, 17 March 1919; and also no. 2626 BS/3, 13 March 1919, 16N 3028.

36  Pichon to Clemenceau, no. 1705, 17 March 1919, 16N 3069. The Finnish historian, Kalervo Hovi, holds that the French government's interest in Poland and the other east European states was due primarily to its desire to build up a *barrière de l'est* against Germany. The anti-Bolshevik dimension of this policy (i.e., the cordon sanitaire) was only of secondary importance. See Kalervo Hovi, *Cordon Sanitaire or Barrière de l'Est? ...* (Turku, Finland 1975), 196, 216–17, and passim. In fact, the French preoccupation in the one or the other concern depended on the circumstances. When the Bolsheviks were most threatening between October 1918 and May 1919, the Quai d'Orsay at least was primarily interested in stopping the Red Army. Germany was beaten, as Kammerer put it, and posed no immediate threat. The anti-Bolshevik element in French policy also seemed to dominate for a time in 1920. See Carley, "The Politics of Anti-Bolshevism: the French Government and the Russo-Polish War, December 1919–May 1920," *Historical Journal* 19, no. 1 (March 1976): 163–89; and "Anti-Bolshevism in French Foreign Policy: the Crisis in Poland in 1920," *International History Review* 2, no. 3 (July 1980): 410–31.

37  *Clemenceau* to Foch, no. 932 BS/1, 29 March 1919, 16N 3102.

38  "Note pour le ministre," 19 September 1918; Pichon to Paul Dutasta, French minister in Berne, 25 September 1918, Z – Lituanie, vol. 1; and Pichon to Beau, nos. 167–8, 5 February 1918, MAÉ, Guerre, vol. 731.

39  "Note pour M. [Jules] Laroche," written by Kammerer, 4 March 1919, Z – Russie, vol. 619. Laroche was in the European bureau or sub-division of the Quai d'Orsay.

40 Pichon to Clemenceau, no. 1000, 18 February 1919, 16N 3069.
41 Pichon to Cambon, nos. 4305-7; and elsewhere, 13 October 1918, E - Sibérie, vol. 18; cf., Gukovskii, *Frantsuzskaia interventsiia*, 152; and Brinkley, *Volunteer Army*, 343-4, n.54.
42 Diary entry, Friday, 15 November 1918, Balfour Papers, dossier no. 49744.
43 Cf., Margolin, *Diary*, 45, or Margolin, *Ukraina i politika antanty* (Berlin 1921), 150-2.
44 Cf., Gukovskii, *Frantsuzskaia interventsiia*, 11-14. Margulies, who went to Paris in March, also took note of this shift in French policy. See Margulies, *God interventsii* 1: 321, 324, 328, 330, 349; 2: 11-12, 19.
45 Berthelot, no. 505/3, 12 March 1919, 7N 802.
46 Berthelot to d'Anselme, no. 506/3, 12 March 1919, 20N 772.
47 Berthelot, nos. 439-42, 20 March 1919, 16N 3172.
48 Franchet d'Esperey, nos. 7245/3-7246/3, 24 March 1919, 16N 3148.
49 Franchet d'Esperey, no. 7311/3, 31 March 1919, ibid.
50 Paul Mantoux, *Les délibérations du Conseil des Quatre*, vol. 1 (Paris 1955), 18-25; see also Mayer, *Politics* 597-600; and Thompson, *Bolshevism*, 200-2.
51 Mantoux, *Délibérations* 1: 49-57; Mayer, *Politics*, 600-2; and Thompson, *Bolshevism*, 202-6.
52 See *L'Humanité*, *Le Populaire*, *La Vérité*, and *Le Journal du Peuple* for the months January-March 1919.
53 *Débats parlementaires*, 24 March 1919, 1406-10, 1412-13.
54 Ibid., 25 March 1919, 1446-8.
55 Ibid., 26 March 1919, 1476-9.
56 Ibid., 1471-3.
57 Ibid., 29 March 1919, 1617-24.
58 Wohl, *French Communism*, 120-1.
59 *Clemenceau* to Franchet d'Esperey, no. 3216 BS/3, 29 March 1919, 16N 3028.
60 "Rapport sur l'évacuation d'Odessa du général d'Anselme," 4 May 1919 (hereafter referred to as Rapport sur l'évacuation), 16N 3149.
61 This force consisted of 1,800 French troops; 5 battalions of Algerians, the avant-garde of a force of 31,000 colonial troops intended as reinforcements for Odessa; upwards of 15,000 Greek troops (as of the middle of March) of an intended force of 30,000 men; between 2,000 and 4,000 Volunteers; and a small force of Poles. These figures are based on incomplete data and should be regarded only as approximations. See the various sheets of cable analyses in 7N 800, dossier 6.
62 "Statement of the Circumstances Leading to and Accompanying the Abandonment of Odessa ...," H. Cooke, 12 April 1919, FO 371 3964, pp. 347-61; V. Margulies, *Ognennye gody: Materialy i dokumenty po istorii grazhdanskoi voiny na iuge Rossii* (Berlin 1923), 50; and Xydias, *L'intervention française*, 315-19.

63 Berthelot to Franchet d'Esperey, no. 705/3, 19 April 1919, 20N 262.

64 Franchet d'Esperey, no. 7358/3, 5 April 1919, 16N 3148; and "Memorandum on the Evacuation of Odessa," Picton Bagge, 8 May 1919, FO 371 3964, pp. 372–80.

65 Unless otherwise noted the above description of the evacuation is taken from d'Anselme's Rapport sur l'évacuation.

66 "Rapport du colonel [Eugène Gervais] Trousson sur l'occupation de Sevastopol," 8 May 1919, 20N 273; and daily journal of 156DI, 26N 447, dossier 3.

67 Ibid.

68 Clemenceau (Alby) to Leygues, no. 3398 BS/3, 3 April 1919, 16N 3028.

69 *Clemenceau* to Franchet d'Esperey, no. 3567 BS/3, 8 April 1919, ibid.

70 Trousson to Colonel Jean Louis Bouchez, then Franchet d'Esperey's chief of staff, 6 April 1919, 20N 273.

71 Franchet d'Esperey, no. 7275/3, 26 March 1919, 16N 3148.

72 Franchet d'Esperey, no. 37/H, 9 April 1919, ibid.

73 Clemenceau to Franchet d'Esperey, no. 3226 BS/3, 29 March 1919, 16N 3028.

74 Franchet d'Esperey, no. 7591/3, 2 May 1919, 20N 226; and *Clemenceau* to Franchet d'Esperey, no. 5175 BS/3, 30 May 1919, 16N 3029.

75 *Clemenceau* to Franchet d'Esperey, no. 3233 BS/3, 30 March 1919, 16N 3028.

76 Franchet d'Esperey to Berthelot, no. 7417/3, 12 April 1919, 20N 226.

77 Franchet d'Esperey, no. 7421/3, 13 April 1919, Z – Russie, vol. 229.

78 *Clemenceau* to Franchet d'Esperey, no. 3775 BS/3, 12 April 1919; and *Clemenceau* to Leygues, no. 3855 BS/3, 15 April 1919, 16N 3028.

79 Albert Jules de France, French high commissioner at Constantinople, no. 200, 12 May 1919, Z – Russie, vol. 230.

80 Trousson to Franchet d'Esperey, 18 April 1919; and Amet to Franchet d'Esperey, 18 April 1919, 20N 273.

81 Franchet d'Esperey to Trousson, no. 7489/3, 19 April 1919; and Franchet d'Esperey, no. 7495/3, 21 April 1919, 20N 226.

82 "Note pour le ministre," SAR, 19 March 1919, see Ph. Berthelot's minute, Z – Russie, vol. 228.

83 Leygues to Clemenceau, 20 April 1919, in Leygues to Pichon, bordereau récapitulatif, 4 June 1919, Z – Russie, vol. 231.

84 Léon Jules Welfelé, captain of the *Protet*, to Amet, no. 69 arrived 18 April 1919, MM, U-6, see also Marty, *Révolte* 2: 142–76.

85 Amet, no. 2963, 19 April 1919, U-6. There were some 20 ships of the French fleet in the harbour of Sevastopol with crews totalling approximately 10,000 men. See Jean Le Ramey and Pierre Vottero, *Mutins de la mer Noire* (Paris 1973), 137.

86 Amet, no. 2985, 20 April 1919, U-6.

87  Amet, no. 2967, 20 April 1919, ibid.
88  Amet, no. 2985, 20 April 1919, ibid.
89  Ibid.; Amet, no. 3072, 24 April 1919, U-6; "Note de renseignements," no. 309/3, Service de Renseignements (SR), Marine, signed Lt. de vaisseau Albert de Carsalade du Pond, 3 May 1919, Z - Russie, vol. 230; and Marty, *Révolte* 2: 226-7.
90  Amet, no. 3002, 21 April 1919, U-6; cf., Marty, *Révolte* 2: 234-5, 238.
91  Ibid.
92  Amet, nos. 3021-2, 22 April 1919, ibid.
93  Amet, no. 3060, 23 April 1919, ibid.
94  "Rapport du colonel Trousson sur l'occupation de Sebastopol," 8 May 1919, 20N 273.
95  Amet, nos. 3030-1, 22 April 1919, U-6.
96  Franchet d'Esperey, no. 7521/3, 23 April 1919, Z - Russie, vol. 229. Mutinies and unrest in the French navy persisted until the beginning of the summer. There were demonstrations of varying degrees of intensity among other ships in the Black and Mediterranean seas and at bases in Toulon, Bizerte, and elsewhere. But these events are not within the scope of this study. Moreover, the archives of the ministry of the navy in Paris were not open for study of the mutinies, and this author gained only the most limited access to these documents.
97  D'Anselme to Berthelot, personal letters of 13 and 15 April 1919, 20N 729.
98  Rapport Freydenberg.
99  See n.94 above. These views, as severe as they were, closely resembled those of British and Canadian officers attached to the Volunteer Army. See H.W.H. Williamson, *Farewell to the Don* (London 1970), 33, 41, 43, 70-1, 207, and passim; and R. MacLaren, *Canadians in Russia, 1918-1919* (Toronto 1976), 267-8.
100  See especially Franchet d'Esperey, no. 14598 2/ch, 18 March 1919, Z - Russie, vol. 228.
101  "Note on French Activities in South Russia," FO 371 3963, pp. 497ff.
102  *Clemenceau* to Winston Churchill, no. 3601 BS/3, 9 April 1919, 16N 3028.
103  Franchet d'Esperey, no. 7421/3, 13 April 1919, Z - Russie, vol. 229.
104  Brinkley, *Volunteer Army*, 138; and Denikin, *Ocherki* 5: 69.
105  Franchet d'Esperey, no. 7311/3, 31 March 1919, 16N 3148.
106  Rapport d'Anselme, 13 March 1919, 16N 3149.
107  "Analyse: Compte rendu d'une mission auprès du général Denikin," no. 2870 BS/3, 20 March 1919, 4N 42, dossier 1.
108  Exelmans to Amet, no. 131, 18 March 1919, MM, Bj-8.
109  "Compte rendu mensuel," March 1919, signed Franchet d'Esperey, 16N 3152; and Azan, *Franchet d'Esperey*, 246. The Bolsheviks did indeed enjoy popular support when they first marched into the Ukraine, but they lost

some of it in the ensuing months. See A.E. Adams, *Bolsheviks in the Ukraine* (New Haven 1963), 115–37.

110 See p. 153.
111 Pichon to Jusserand, nos. 772–3, 18 July 1919, Z – Russie, vol. 221.
112 Amet, nos. 3186–7, 28 April 1919, U–6.
113 Leygues to Pichon, bordereau récapitulatif, 4 June 1919, Z – Russie, vol. 231.
114 *Clemenceau* to Franchet d'Esperey, no. 3426 BS/3, 4 April 1919, 16N 3028.
115 Ullman, *Anglo-Soviet Relations* 2: 118–20, 134, 151–7.
116 Derby to Pichon, 25 April 1919, Z – Russie, vol. 229.
117 *Clemenceau* to Leygues, no. 4068 BS/3, 19 April 1919, 16N 3028.

CHAPTER ELEVEN

1 "Note pour le ministre, situation militaire," SAR, 24 May 1919; and "Situation de l'Armée d'Orient," 10 June 1919, Z – Russie, vol. 212.
2 "Pologne, convention financière," 23 April 1919, Z – Pologne, vol. 22.
3 Clemenceau to Pichon, no. 5178 BS/3, 20 May 1919, Z – Russie, vol. 670.
4 Eugène Pralon, French minister in Warsaw, nos. 59–66, 16 May 1919; Dutasta, then secretary general of the peace conference, to Pralon, no. 58, 21 May 1919; and Dutasta to Pralon, nos. 72–4, 27 May 1919, Z – Pologne, vol. 84.
5 Chamberlin, *Russian Revolution* 2: 171, 215–18.
6 Franchet d'Esperey, no. 7917/3, 6 June 1919; Pichon to Clemenceau, no. 3422, n.d. (19 or 20 June 1919), Z – Russie, vol. 231.
7 *Clemenceau* to Franchet d'Esperey, no. 6376 BS/3, 27 June 1919, 16N 3029.
8 Clemenceau (Alby) to Franchet d'Esperey, no. 7166 BS/3, 26 July 1919, 4N 49, dossier 4.
9 Martel, nos. 240–1, 22 April 1919; Pichon to Klotz, no. 1144, 9 May 1919, F30 1071, dossier 9; and Martel, nos. 337–8, 24 May 1919, Z – Russie, vol. 486.
10 Pichon to Klotz, no. 1144, 9 May 1919, F30 1071, dossier 9.
11 Pichon to Martel, nos. 223–4, 24 June 1919, E – Sibérie, vol. 26.
12 Klotz to Pichon, no. 9531, 11 July 1919, Z – Russie, vol. 486; and Martel, no. 465, 15 July 1919, E – Sibérie, vol. 26.
13 "Emprunt sur l'or sibérien," in Fabry's hand, n.d., F30 1071, dossier 9; and Pichon to Klotz, no. 1713, 17 July 1919, E – Sibérie, vol. 26.
14 Martel, no. 541, 14 August 1919; no. 547, 18 August 1919; and G. Maugras, who succeeded Martel as French high commissioner in Siberia, no. 666, 26 November 1919, Z – Russie, vol. 486.
15 See n.13 above.
16 "Note pour le ministre, extrait du procès-verbal de la 69ème séance tenue le 25 juin par la Commission interministérielle ..."; "Note sur les dépenses

de Sibérie," Service financier, 1 July 1919, Z – Russie, vol. 447; and Pichon to Martel, nos. 288-91, 4 August 1919, E – Sibérie, vol. 27.

17  "Liste de matériel ...," 16 October 1919, Z – Russie, vol. 250.

18  "Avenant entre les gouvernments français et polonais," 24 October 1919, Z – Pologne, vol. 239; and Wandycz, *France and her Eastern Allies*, 146, n.55. The French also spend some 350 million francs on the organization, equipping, and maintenance of the Haller army. At the end of 1920 the total amount of French assistance to the Poles, including costs for the Haller army, was put at 826 million francs. See "Note pour le directeur politique, dettes et créances de la Pologne vis-à-vis de la France," 9 December 1920, Z – Pologne, vol. 239.

19  See Ullman, *Anglo-Soviet Relations* 2: 211-12; 3: 60. Total costs for the maintenance of the Czechs and other smaller units of non-Russian nationalities amounted to 474 million francs and credits to the Omsk government, 170 million. Total costs for the intervention were put at 1.19 billion francs, but this figure did not include the costs of military operations in southern Russia or the credits to the Poles, Czechs, and Rumanians. See Le contrôleur, chef du service interministériel des dépenses à l'étranger to E. Labonne, no. 9353 A/9, 23 November 1921, Z – Russie, vol. 448. Judging from the available evidence, it does not appear that the French government ever determined the total cost of the intervention.

20  Clemenceau (Alby) to Pichon, no. 4183 BS/1, 3 September 1919, Z – Russie, vol. 282.

21  M. Janin, *Ma mission en Sibérie* (Paris 1933).

22  Janin, nos. 2257-81, 20 January 1920, 7N 810.

23  Janin, nos. 2939-52, 18 January 1920, 17N 620.

24  Janin, nos. 3008-20, 23 January 1920; and nos. 3065-94, 29 January 1920, 17N 606.

25  General Jan Syrovy, commander of Czech forces, to Janin, no. 247, 11 February 1920, E – Sibérie, vol. 14; and Janin, *Ma mission*, 260.

26  See n.23 above; Janin, nos. 2966-84, 27 January 1920, E – Sibérie, vol. 22; and Janin, nos. 3252-5, 19 March 1920, E – Sibérie, vol. 15.

27  "Note au sujet de l'amiral Koltchak," signed Buchsenchutz, 27 June 1920, E – Sibérie, vol. 22.

28  Janin, Rapport, 30 May 1920, 7N 810; Janin, nos. 2939-52, 18 January 1920, 17N 606; and Janin, nos. 3252-5, 19 March 1920, E – Sibérie, vol. 15.

29  Ullman, *Anglo-Soviet Relations* 2: 313-15.

30  Great Britain, Foreign Office, *British Documents on Foreign Policy*, 1st series, vol. 2 (London 1949), 744-6.

31  Carley, "Politics of Anti-Bolshevism."

32  Carley, "Anti-Bolshevism in French Foreign Policy."

33  Janin, nos. 2746-52, 21 March 1919; nos. 1051-4, 27 April 1919; Martel, nos. 267-8, 2 May 1919, 16N 3191; cf., Arno W.F. Kolz, "British Eco-

nomic Interests in Siberia during the Russian Civil War, 1918–1920," *Journal of Modern History* 48, no. 3 (Sept. 1976): 486 and passim.

34  Cf., B.M. Unterberger, *America's Siberian Expedition, 1918–1920* (Durham, N.C. 1956).

35  Janin, "Rapport no. 5," 5 April 1919, 7N 810.

36  Janin, "Rapport no. 7," signed Buchsenchutz, 24 June 1919; Janin, 23 November 1919, ibid.; and Janin, no. 146cl., 6 December 1919, 7N 809.

37  Janin, "Rapport no. 7," 24 June 1919, 7N 810.

38  Thompson, "Lenin's Analysis of Intervention," 153, 159 n.33.

39  Mel'gunov, *Tragediia admirala Kolchaka*, pt. 1, 7–19, 32–3, 43–4, 46.

# *Bibliography*

## MANUSCRIPT SOURCES

*France*

*Ministère des Affaires étrangères*
- *Série A, Guerre, 1914-1918*
  Balkans – Roumanie; Russie; Affaires financières, Russie
- *Série E, Asie, 1918-1929*
  Chine; Japon; Sibérie
- *Série Z, Europe, 1918-1929*
  Estonie; Grande Bretagne; Lettonie; Lituanie; Pologne; Roumanie; Russie; Tchécoslovaquie
- Papiers d'agents
  Camille Barrère; Jean Doulcet; Fernand Grenard; Pierre de Margerie; Stephen Pichon
- Papiers de l'ambassade de France à Petrograd
  Russie, Petrograd, Mesures de défense contre les Bolchéviques, 2 cartons

*Service historique de l'armée (Ministère de la Guerre), Vincennes*
- 4N, Conseil supérieur de la Guerre
- 5N, Cabinet du ministre
- 6N, Fonds Clemenceau
- 7N, État-major de l'armée
- 8N, Contrôle
- 16N, Grand quartier général, Groupe de l'Avant
- 17N, Missions militaires françaises
- 20N, Commandement des armées alliées (Armée d'Orient)

*Ministère des Finances, Mouvement des fonds*
- F30 1065, 1068-9, 1071-2, 1083, 1092-5, 1111-12, 1114

*Archives nationales*
- Papiers Albert Thomas, 94 AP 176, 178-9, 186, 191, 201-2

*Bibliothèque de Documentation internationale contemporaine, Nanterre*
- Consignes of the bureau of the censor, 1917-1919

*Association nationale des porteurs français de valeurs mobilières, Paris*
- Archives of the Commission générale de protection des intérêts français en Russie, 50 dossiers

*Great Britain*

*British Museum*
- Balfour Papers, Derby letters

*Beaverbrook Library, London*
- Lloyd George Papers, Bertie/Derby letters

*India Office, London*
- Curzon Papers, Derby letters

*Public Record Office*
- Foreign Office, Political Correspondence Relating to Russia
FO 371 3283, 3963-64, 3978-79; Bertie Papers

NEWSPAPERS

*L'Agence économique et financière, L'Action française, La Cote de la bourse et de la banque (Cote Vidal), La Croix, L'Écho de Paris, Le Figaro, L'Humanité, Le Journal des débats, Le Journal du peuple, Le Populaire, La Revue économique et financière, Le Temps, La Vague, La Vérité*

PUBLISHED DOCUMENTS, MEMOIRS,
DIARIES, AND LETTERS

Body, Marcel. "Les groupes communistes français de Russie (1918-1921)." In *Contributions à l'histoire du Comintern*, edited by Jacques Freymond. Geneva: Librairie Droz, 1965.

Bullitt, William C. *The Bullitt Mission to Russia*. New York: B.W. Huebsch, 1920.

Bunyan, James. *Intervention, Civil War, and Communism in Russia, April-December 1918: Documents and Materials*. Baltimore: Johns Hopkins Press, 1936.

Callwell, C.E. *Field-Marshal Sir Henry Wilson: His Life and Diaries*. 2 vols. London: Cassell, 1927.

Cambon, Paul. *Correspondance, 1970-1924*. Vol. 3. Paris: Éditions Bernard Grasset, 1946.

Churchill, Winston S. *The Aftermath*. New York: Charles Scribner's Sons, 1929.

Claudel, Paul. "Philippe Berthelot." In *Accompagnements*. Paris: Gallimard, 1949.

Denikin, A.I. *Ocherki russkoi smuty*. Vol. 5. Berlin: Russkoi Natsional'noe Knigoizdatel'stvo, 1926.

Docteur, Jules Théophile. *Carnet de bord, 1914-1919*. Paris: La Nouvelle Société d'Édition, 1932.

Fauxbras, César. *Mer Noire: Les mutineries racontées par un mutin*. Paris: Flammarion, 1935.

France, Journal officiel de la République française, Chambre des Députés. *Débats parlementaires*, session ordinaire, 1917-19.

Graves, William S. *Amerca's Siberian Adventure, 1918-1920*. New York: Peter Smith, 1941.

Great Britain, Foreign Office. *Documents on British Foreign Policy, 1919-1939*. 1st series. Vols. 2-3. Edited by E.L. Woodward and R. Butler. London: His Majesty's Stationery Office, 1949.

Grondijs, L.H. *Le cas-Koltchak*. Leiden: A.W. Sijthoff's, 1939.

Gukovskii, A.I., ed. "Iz istorii frantsuzskoi interventsii v Odesse." *Krasnyi Arkhiv* 14 (1931): 53-80.

Gurko, V.I. "Iz Petrograd cherez Moskvu, Parizh i London v Odessu, 1917-1918." *Arkhiv Russkoi Revoliutsii* 15 (1924): 5-84.

Iaroslavskii, E. et al. *Delo Borisa Savinkova*. Moscow: Gosizdat, n.d.

Janin, Maurice Pierre. *Ma mission en Sibérie*. Paris: Payot, 1933.

Kin, D., ed. "K istorii frantsuzskoi interventsii na iuge Rossii." *Krasnyi Arkhiv* 19 (1927): 3-38.

Labry, Raoul. "Notre politique en Russie, les méthodes, les hommes." *Mercure de France* 138 (1920): 5-24.

- "Comment nous avons été renseignés sur la Russie." *Mercure de France* 138 (1920): 653-80.

Laroche, Jules. *Au Quai d'Orsay avec Briand et Poincaré, 1913-1926*. Paris: Hachette, 1957.

Le Ramey, Jean, and Pierre Vottero. *Mutins de la mer Noire*. Paris: Éditions Sociales, 1973.

Lobanov-Rostovsky, A. *The Grinding Mill: Reminiscences of War and Revolution in Russia, 1913-1920*. New York: Macmillan, 1935.

Lockhart, R.H.B. *Memoirs of a British Agent*. London: Putnam, 1932.

Lukomskii, A.S. *Vospominaniia*. Vol. 2. Berlin: Otto Kirchner, 1922.

Mantoux, Paul. *Les délibérations du Conseil des Quatre, 24 mars-28 juin 1919*. 2 vols. Paris: Éditions du Centre national de la recherche scientifique, 1955.

Marchand, René. *Why I Support Bolshevism*. London: British Socialist Party, 1919.

Margolin, A.D. *Ukraina i politika antanty*. Berlin: Izdatel'stvo S. Efron, 1921.

- *From a Political Diary: The Ukraine and America, 1905-1945*. New York: Columbia University Press, 1946.

Margulies, M.S. *God interventsii*. Vols. 1-2. Berlin: Izdatel'stvo Z.I. Grzhebina, 1923.

Margulies, Vladimir. *Ognennye gody: Materialy i dokumenty po istorii grazhdanskoi voiny na iuge Rossii*. Berlin: Izd. "Manfred," 1923.

Marty, André. *La révolte de la mer Noire*. 2 vols. Re-edition. Paris: François Maspero, 1970.

Morand, Paul. *Journal d'un attaché d'ambassade, 1916-1917*. Paris: Gallimard, 1963.

Mordacq, J.J.H. *Le ministère Clemenceau, journal d'un témoin*. 4 vols. Paris: Plon, 1933.

Moulis, E., and E. Bergonier, eds. *En marge du conflit mondial: La guerre entre les alliés et la Russie*. Paris: Librairie Générale de Droit et de Jurisprudence, Imp. H. Jehan, 1937.

Niessel, Henri Albert. *Le triomphe des bolchéviques et la paix de Brest-Litovsk: souvenirs, 1917-1918*. Paris: Plon, 1940.

Noulens, Joseph. *Mon ambassade en Russie soviétique, 1917-1919*. 2 vols. Paris: Plon, 1933.

Pascal, Pierre, *Journal de Russie*. Lausanne: L'Age d'Homme, 1975.

Paustovsky, Konstantin, *Story of a Life*. Vols. 2-4. London: Harvill, 1965-8.

Poincaré, Raymond. *Au service de la France*. Vols. 9-10. Paris: Plon, 1932-3.

Ribot, Alexandre. *Journal et correspondances inédites, 1914-1922*. Paris: Plon, 1936.

Robien, Louis de. *Journal d'un diplomate en Russie, 1917-1918*. Paris: Éditions Albin Michel, 1967.

Sadoul, Jacques. *Notes sur la révolution bolchévique*. Re-edition. Paris: François Maspero, 1971.

Saint-Aulaire, Auguste de Beaupoil, comte de. *Confession d'un vieux diplomate*. Paris: Flammarion, 1953.

Savinkov, B.V. *Bor'ba s bolshevikami*. Warsaw: Izdanie Russkago Politicheskago Komiteta, 1920.

Shliapnikov, A.G., ed. *Les Alliés contre la Russie avant, pendant et après la guerre mondiale: faits et documents*. Paris: A. Delpeuch, 1926.

Shlikhter, A.G., ed. *Chernaia kniga: Sbornik statei i materialov ob interventsii antanty na Ukraine, 1918-1919*. Kharkov: Gosizdat Ukrainy, 1925.

Tabouis, Georges M. "Comment je devins commissaire de la république française en Ukraine." *Spohadi* (Warsaw) 8 (1932): 142-64.

Tillon, Charles. *La révolte vient de loin*. Paris: 10/18, 1972.

Trotsky, L.D. *My Life*. New York: Universal Library, 1960.

- *Histoire de la révolution russe*. 2 vols. Paris: Seuil, 1950.

Trubetskoi, E.N. "Is putevykh zametok bezhentsa," *Arkhiv Russkoi Revoliutsii* 18 (1926): 137-207.

U.S., State Department. *Papers Relating to the Foreign Relations of the United States, The Paris Peace Conference*. Vols. 3-9. Washington, D.C., 1942-7.

Williamson, H.W.H. *Farewell to the Don.* Edited by John Harris. London: Collins, 1970.

Xydias, Jean. *L'intervention française en Russie, 1918-1919.* Paris: Éditions de France, 1927.

## BOOKS, ARTICLES, AND DISSERTATIONS

Adams, Arthur E. *Bolsheviks in the Ukraine.* New Haven: Yale University Press, 1963.

Arslanian, Artin Hogop. "The British Military Involvement in Transcaucasia, 1917-1919." PHD diss., University of California, Los Angeles, 1974.

Auffray, Bernard. *Pierre de Margerie (1861-1942) et la vie diplomatique de son temps.* Paris: Librairie C. Klincksieck, 1976.

Azan, Paul. *Franchet d'Esperey.* Paris: Flammarion, 1949.

Babel, Isaac. *Cavalerie rouge.* Lausanne: Éditions l'Age d'Homme, 1972.

Baerlein, Henrÿ. *The March of the Seventy Thousand.* London: Leonard Parsons, 1926.

Belkin, I. "Vliianie velikoi oktiabr'skoi sotsialisticheskoi revoliutsii na revoliutsionnoe dvizhenie vo Frantsii v 1918-1919." *Voprosy Istorii* 6, no. 9 (Sept. 1949): 65-82.

Bernachot, Jean. *Les armées françaises en orient après la guerre de 1918.* Vol. 2. Paris: Imprimerie nationale, 1970.

Borschak, Élie. "L'Ukraine à la Conférence de la Paix." Parts I-III. *Le Monde Slave,* XIVe année, 1 (janvier 1937): 451-71; 2 (avril 1937): 397-418; 3 (juillet 1937): 58-85.

Bouvier, Jean. "Les traits majeurs de l'impérialisme français avant 1914." *Mouvement Social* 85 (1974): 3-24.

Bradley, J.F.N. *La légion tchécoslovaque en Russie, 1914-1920.* Paris: Centre national de la recherche scientifique, 1965.

- *Allied Intervention in Russia, 1917-1920.* London: Weidenfeld & Nicolson, 1968.

Bréal, Auguste. *Philippe Berthelot.* Paris: Gallimard, 1937.

Brinkley, George I. *The Volunteer Army and Allied Intervention in South Russia, 1917-1921.* Notre Dame: University of Notre Dame Press, 1966.

Carley, Michael Jabara. "Anti-Bolshevism in French Foreign Policy: The Crisis in Poland in 1920." *International History Review* 2 (1980): 410-31.

- "The Politics of Anti-Bolshevism: The French Government and the Russo-Polish War, December 1919-May 1920." *Historical Journal* 19, no. 1 (March 1976): 163-89.

Carroll, E. Malcolm. *Soviet Communism and Western Opinion, 1919-1921.* Chapel Hill, N.C.: University of North Carolina Press, 1965.

Chamberlin, William Henry. *The Russian Revolution.* 2 vols. New York: Universal Library, 1965.

Coates, W.P., and Zelda K. Coates. *Armed Intervention in Russia, 1918-1922*. London: Gollancz, 1935.

Crisp, Olga. "The Russo-Chinese Bank: An Episode in Franco-Russian Relations." *Slavonic and East European Review* 52, no. 127 (April 1974): 197-212.

- "French Investment in Russian Joint Stock Companies, 1894-1914." *Business History* (Liverpool) 2 (1960): 75-90.

- "Some Problems of French Investment in Russian Joint Stock Companies, 1894-1914." *Slavonic and East European Review* 35, no. 84 (1956): 223-40.

Crutwell, C.R.M.F. *A History of the Great War*. Oxford: Clarendon Press, 1934.

Debo, Richard K. *Revolution and Survival: The Foreign Policy of Soviet Russia, 1917-1918*. Toronto: University of Toronto Press, 1979.

- "Mésentente Glaciale: Great Britain, France, and the Question of Intervention in the Baltic, 1918." *Canadian Journal of History* 12, no. 1 (April 1977): 65-86.

- "Lockhart Plot or Dzerzhinskii Plot?" *Journal of Modern History* 43, no. 3 (Sept. 1971): 413-39.

Delmas, Jean. "Une mission militaire française à Petrograd après la révolution d'octobre (octobre 1917-mars 1918)." *Revue de la Défense Nationale* (1966): 1084-94.

- "L'état-major français et le front oriental après la révolution bolchévique, novembre 1917-11 novembre 1918." Doctorat du troisième cycle, Université de Paris, 1965.

Duclos, Jacques. *Octobre 17: vu de France*. Paris: Éditions Sociales, 1967.

Fischer, Fritz. *Germany's Aims in the First World War*. New York: Norton, 1967.

Fischer, Louis. *The Soviets in World Affairs*. 2 vols. London: Jonathan Cape, 1930.

- *Lenin*. New York: Harper & Row, 1964.

Fleming, Peter. *The Fate of Admiral Kolchak*. London: Rupert Hart-Davis, 1963.

Footman, David. *Civil War in Russia*. New York: Praeger, 1961.

Fowler, W.B. *British-American Relations, 1917-1918: The Role of Sir William Wiseman*. Princeton: Princeton University Press, 1969.

Gaworek, Norbert. "From Blockade to Trade: Allied Economic Warfare Against Soviet Russia, June 1919 to January 1920." *Jahrbücher für Geschichte Osteuropas* 23 (1975): 39-69.

- "Allied Economic Warfare against Soviet Russia, November 1917 to March 1921." PHD diss., University of Wisconsin, 1970.

Gilbert, Martin. *Winston S. Churchill*. Vol. 4. London: Heinemann, 1975.

Girault, René. "Problèmes de l'impérialisme économique français en Russie à la veille de la première guerre mondiale." *Revue du Nord*, avril-juin 1975, 123-31.

- *Emprunts russes et investissements français en Russie, 1887-1914*. Paris: Librairie Armand Colin, 1973.

Gordon, Alban. *Russian Civil War*. London: Cassell, 1937.

Grenard, Fernand. *La révolution russe*. Paris: A. Colin, 1933.

Gukovskii, A.I. *Frantsuzskaia interventsiia na iuge Rossii, 1918-1919*. Moscow: Gosizdat, 1928.

Hovi, Kalervo. *Cordon Sanitaire or Barrière de l'Est? The Emergence of the New French Eastern European Alliance Policy, 1917-1919*. Turku, Finland: Turun Yliopisto, 1975.

Iakushkin, E. *Frantsuzskaia interventsiia na iuge, 1918-1919*. Moscow: Gosizdat, n.d.

Institut d'Études slaves, *La guerre polono-soviètique de 1919-1920*. Paris, 1975.

Ioffe, Ia. *Organisatsiia interventsii i blokady sovetskoi respubliki, 1918-1920*. Moscow: Gosizdat, 1930.

Kenez, Peter. *Civil War in South Russia, 1919-1920: The Defeat of the Whites*. Berkeley: University of California Press, 1977.

Kennan, George F. *Russia and the West under Lenin and Stalin*. New York: Mentor, 1962.

– *Soviet-American Relations, 1917-1920*. Vol. 1, *Russia Leaves the War*; vol. 2, *The Decision to Intervene*. Princeton: Princeton University Press, 1956-8.

Kettle, Michael. *The Allies and the Russian Collapse, March 1917-March 1918*. Minneapolis: University of Minnesota Press, 1981.

Kolz, Arno W.F. "British Economic Interests in Siberia during the Russian Civil War," *Journal of Modern History* 48, no. 3 (Sept. 1976): 483-91.

Konovalov, V.G. *Inostrannaia kollegiia*. Odessa: Odesskoe Oblastnoe Izdatel'stvo, 1958.

Kuznetsova, N.V. "Bor'ba frantsuzkogo naroda protiv omkrytoi antisovetskoi interventsii antanty, vesnoi 1919," *Voprosy Istorii* 14, no. 11 (Nov. 1957): 111-26.

Levidov, M.I. *K istorii soiuznoi interventsii v Rossii*. Vol. 1. Leningrad: Rabochee Izdatel'stvo "Priboi," 1925.

Levin, N. Gordon. *Woodrow Wilson and World Politics: America's Response to War and Revolution*. New York: Oxford University Press, 1968.

Long, John Wendell. "Civil War and Intervention in North Russia, 1918-1920." PHD diss., Columbia University, 1972.

McKay, John P. *Foreign Entrepreneurship and Russian Industrialization, 1885-1913*. Chicago: University of Chicago Press, 1970.

MacLaren, R. *Canadians in Russia, 1918-1919*. Toronto: Macmillan, 1976.

Maddox, Robert J. *The Unknown War with Russia: Woodrow Wilson's Siberian Intervention*. San Rafael, Calif.: Presidio Press, 1977.

Mayer, Arno J. *Politics and Diplomacy of Peacemaking: Containment and Counter-Revolution at Versailles, 1918-1919*. New York: Knopf, 1967.

Mel'gunov, S.P. *Tragediia admirala Kolchaka*. Parts 1-2, 3, t. 1. Belgrade: Russkaia Biblioteka, 1930.

Morley, James W. *The Japanese Thrust in Siberia, 1918*. New York: Columbia University Press, 1957.

Morris, L.P. "The Russians, the Allies, and the War, February–July 1917." *Slavonic and East European Review* 50 (1972): 29–48.

Naida, S.F., and V.P. Naumov. *Sovetskaia istoriografiia grazhdanskoi voiny i inostrannoi voennoi interventsii v SSSR*. Moscow: Izdatel'stvo Moskovskogo Universiteta, 1966.

Noble, George B. *Policies and Opinions at Paris, 1919*. New York: H Fertig, 1968.

Ol', P.V. *Inostrannye kapitaly v Rossii*. Petrograd: Instityt Ekonomicheskikh Issledovanie, 1922.

Parfenov, P.S. *Grazhdanskaia voina v Sibiri, 1918-1920*. Moscow: Gosizdat, 1924.

Pastor, Peter. *Hungary between Wilson and Lenin: The Hungarian Revolution of 1918-1919 and the Big Three*. Boulder, Colo.: East European Quarterly, 1976.

Payne, David S. "The Foreign Policy of Georges Clemenceau, 1917-1920." PHD diss., Duke University, 1970.

Paz, Maurice. *Les révoltes de la mer Noire*. Paris: Librairie du Travail, 1922.

Thomas R. Peake. "The Impact of the Russian Revolutions upon French Attitudes and Policies toward Russia, 1917-1918." PHD diss., University of North Carolina, 1974.

Pierre, André. "L'intervention française en Russie méridionale, 1918-1919." *Le Monde Slave* 1 (janvier 1927): 143-60.

Pokrovskii, M.N. *Vneshniaia politika Rossii v XX veka*. Moscow: Gosizdat, 1926.

Rabinowitch, Alexander. *The Bolsheviks Come to Power: The Revolution of 1917*. New York: Norton, 1976.

Rakowsky, Jeremy. "Franco-British Policy toward the Ukrainian Revolution, March 1917 to February 1918." PHD diss., Case Western Reserve University, 1974.

Resheter, John S. *The Ukrainian Revolution, 1917-1920*. Princeton: Princeton University Press, 1952.

Rosenberg, William. *Liberals in the Russian Revolution*. Princeton: Princeton University Press, 1974.

Sakoian, Carol Knuth. "Jacques Sadoul and the Bolshevik Revolution." PHD diss., Boston University Graduate School, 1977.

Schillinger, Philippe. "Un projet français d'intervention économique en Russie." *Relations Internationales* 1, no. 1 (1974): 115-22.

Sholokhov, M. *Le Don paisible*. 4 vols. Paris: Livre de Poche, 1959.

Silverlight, John. *The Victors' Dilemma*. New York: Weybridge & Talley, 1970.

Sinanoglou, Ioannis. "France Looks Eastward: Perspectives and Policies in Russia, 1914-1918." PHD diss., Columbia University, 1974.

Slovès, H. *La France et l'Union soviètique*. Paris: Les Éditions Rieder, 1935.

Smirnov, A.P. *Soldaty i matrosy Frantsii otkasalis' streliat'*. Leningrad: Ogiz "Priboi," 1931.

Solov'ev, O.F. *Velikii Oktiabr' i ego protivniki*. Moscow: Izdatel'stvo "Mysl'," 1968.

Soutou, Georges. "L'impérialisme du pauvre: La politique économique du gouvernement français en Europe centrale et orientale de 1918 à 1929." *Relations Internationales* 7 (1976): 219–39.

Suarez, Georges. *Briand, sa vie - son œuvre*. Vols. 4–5. Paris: Plon, 1940–1.

Suprunenko, M.I. *Ocherki istorii grazhdanskoi voiny i inostrannoi voennoi interventsii na Ukraine, 1918-1920*. Moscow: Nauka, 1966.

Swettenham, John. *Allied Intervention in Russia, 1918-1919*. Toronto: Ryerson, 1967.

Thompson, John M. *Russia, Bolshevism, and the Versailles Peace*. Princeton: Princeton University Press, 1966.

- "Lenin's Analysis of Intervention." *American Slavic and East European Review* 17, no. 2 (April 1958): 151–60.

- "Allied and American Intervention in Russia, 1917-1921." In *Rewriting Russian History: Soviet Interpretations of Russia's Past*, edited by C.E. Black. London: Macmillan, 1957.

Trani, Eugene P. "Woodrow Wilson and the Decision to Intervene in Russia: A Reconsideration." *Journal of Modern History* 48, no. 3 (Sept. 1976): 440–61.

Ulam, A.B. *The Bolsheviks*. New York: Macmillan, 1965.

Ullman, R.H. *Anglo-Soviet Relations, 1917-1921*. Vol. 1, *Intervention and the War*; vol. 2, *Britain and the Russian Civil War*; vol. 3, *The Anglo-Soviet Accord*. Princeton: Princeton University Press, 1961–72.

Unterberger, Betty Miller. *America's Siberian Expedition, 1918-1920*. Durham, N.C.: Duke University Press, 1956.

Vanag, N. *Finansovyi kapital v Rossii nakanune mirovoi voiny*. Moscow: Izdanie Im. Sverdlova, 1925.

Vasiukov, V.S. *Predystoriia interventsii*. Moscow: Iz-vo Politicheskoi Literatury, 1968.

Völgyes, Ivan, ed. *Hungary in Revolution, 1918-1919*. Lincoln: University of Nebraska Press, 1971.

Wade, Rex. *The Russian Search for Peace, February-October 1917*. Stanford: Stanford University Press, 1969.

Wandycz, P.S. *France and Her Eastern Allies, 1919-1925*. Minneapolis: University of Minnesota Press, 1961.

Warth, Robert. *The Allies and the Russian Revolution*. Durham, N.C.: University of North Carolina Press, 1954.

Wheeler-Bennett, J.W. *Brest-Litovsk: The Forgotten Peace, March 1918*. London: Macmillan, 1963.

Williams, William A. "American Intervention in Russia, 1917-1920." Parts 1–2. *Studies on the Left* 3 (fall 1963): 24–48; 4 (winter 1964): 39–57.

Wohl, Robert. *French Communism in the Making, 1914-1924*. Stanford: Stanford University Press, 1966.

Woodward, D.R. "The British Government and Japanese Intervention in Russia during World War I." *Journal of Modern History* 46, no. 4 (Dec. 1974), 663–85.

Zak, Ludmilla. *Des français dans la révolution d'octobre*. Paris: Éditions Sociales, 1976.

# Index

## DATE DUE

| 14 Aug 86 | | | |
|-----------|---|---|---|
| | | | |
| | | | |
| | | | |
| | | | |
| | | | |
| | | | |
| | | | |
| | | | |
| | | | |
| | | | |
| | | | |
| | | | |
| | | | |

GAYLORD

PRINTED IN U.S.A.